21世纪专业英语系列丛书

城市规划与管理专业英语
（第2版）

English in City Planning and Management

主　编　周文博　李安娜
副主编　王　星　吴　迪
主　审　徐苏宁

哈尔滨工业大学出版社

内容提要

本书结合城市规划专业知识体系,精选其核心内容,题材广泛,涉及城市规划与管理专业领域知识、内容。本书由专业阅读、专业学术信息、专业词汇三部分组成。第一部分为主干内容,均在美、英等国出版的经典原版城市规划与设计教材、最新专著和近期刊物原文素材基础上编写,涉及城市规划理论、城市形态、城市模型与城市设计理论、城市风景、城市建筑、城市雨水处理系统、居住环境等内容。第二部分主要包括国内外期刊、网站、学术组织等学术信息。第三部分基本涵盖了本专业的专业词汇和术语。

本书可作为高等学校城市规划与管理、建筑学、市政工程、管理等学科的本科生、研究生专业英语教材,还可作为大学英语选修课教材或行业培训参考书。

图书在版编目(CIP)数据

城市规划与管理专业英语/周文博,李安娜主编. —2版. —哈尔滨:哈尔滨工业大学出版社,2016.7(2024.1重印)
21世纪专业英语系列丛书
ISBN 978 – 7 – 5603 – 5981 – 6

Ⅰ.①城… Ⅱ.①周… ②李… Ⅲ.①城市规划-英语-高等学校-教材 ②城市管理-英语-高等学校-教材
Ⅳ.①H31

中国版本图书馆CIP数据核字(2016)第088994号

责任编辑	田新华
封面设计	卞秉利
出版发行	哈尔滨工业大学出版社
社　　址	哈尔滨市南岗区复华四道街10号　邮编150006
传　　真	0451 – 86414749
网　　址	http://hitpress.hit.edu.cn
印　　刷	哈尔滨圣铂印刷有限公司
开　　本	880mm×1230mm　1/32　印张14　字数440千字
版　　次	2013年8月第1版　2016年7月第2版 2024年1月第3次印刷
书　　号	ISBN 978 – 7 – 5603 – 5981 – 6
定　　价	48.00元

(如因印装质量问题影响阅读,我社负责调换)

21世纪专业英语系列丛书

编委会

主　　任　赵毓琴
副主任　闫纪红
编　　委　（按姓氏笔画排序）
　　　　　　于云玲　马玉红　王　洋　王　旸
　　　　　　王　星　王倩玉　王艳薇　关　兵
　　　　　　任　丽　任　莉　任铭静　刘秀杰
　　　　　　李　莉　李安娜　李慧杰　陈晓宁
　　　　　　陈　楠　杨　皓　吴　迪　张凌岩
　　　　　　周文博　栾　岩　盖晓兰　葛乃晟
总策划　田新华
总主编　赵毓琴　李慧杰

前　言

为适应经济全球化的发展趋势,满足国内广大学生和读者了解、学习、借鉴国外先进理论,了解前沿动态的需求,使学生通过大量阅读英语文章来扩充词汇量,提高熟练获取信息和独立阅读原著的能力,我们编写了此书。

本书由专业阅读、专业学术信息、专业词汇三部分组成。第一部分为主干内容,精选城市规划类文章,主要选自美、英等国出版的城市规划与城市设计经典教材、最新专著和近期刊物原文,涉及城市规划、城市设计、城市建筑、城市雨水处理系统、居住环境等内容。本书设有每章导读,结合课文配有单词、词组(包括专有名词)解释。第二部分包括专业学术期刊、专业学术会议、专业网站、专业学会与组织等相关学术信息。第三部分按英文字母检索方式排出词汇供读者参考。

本书内容新颖,选材精当,编排合理,重点突出,具有实用性、知识性等特点,力求培养学生专业英语运用能力,提高学生阅读理解专业英语文章的水平,能有效促进学生提高专业水平并为其日后工作打下必要的语言基础。此外,注释合理,可读性强。选文中的难点和重点词汇、句子都配有相应的中文解释和实用例句,能够激发学生进一步学习的积极性。

本书适用范围较广,既可作为高等学校城市规划、建筑学、市政工程、管理等学科本科生、研究生专业英语教材,还可作为大学英语选修课教材或行业培训参考书。

本书由周文博、李安娜任主编；王星、吴迪任副主编。本书第一部分专业阅读共 10 章，具体分工如下：周文博负责统稿、定稿；周文博、李安娜负责专业文章挑选、分类及专业学术信息部分编写；第 1 章、第 2 章、第 3 章、第 4 章由李安娜编写；第 5 章由吴迪编写；第 6 章、第 7 章、第 8 章、第 10 章由周文博编写；第 9 章由王星编写。第二部分专业学术信息和第三部分专业词汇由各位作者共同编写，吴迪负责编辑。本书由哈尔滨工业大学博士生导师徐苏宁教授主审。

在编写过程中，我们参考了一些作者的成果，在此一并表示感谢。由于时间仓促，且编者水平及经验有限，书中不妥和疏漏之处在所难免，恳请广大读者批评指正。

编　者

2016 年 7 月

CONTENTS

PART ONE ACADEMIC READING
第一部分 专业阅读

1 Urban Design Education in Britain and America
英国和美国的城市设计教育 ·············· 3
◇ 本章导读 ·············· 3
  1.1 Educational Structure
      教育结构 ·············· 3
  1.2 Educational Program
      教育规划 ·············· 9
  1.3 Educational Method
      教育方法 ·············· 18

2 Urban Utopias in the Twentieth Century
20 世纪的城市乌托邦 ·············· 26
◇ 本章导读 ·············· 26
  2.1 Town-country Magnet
      城乡磁铁 ·············· 27
  2.2 Garden City
      花园城市 ·············· 34
  2.3 The Contemporary City
      现代城市 ·············· 42
  2.4 The Plan of the Contemporary City
      现代城市规划 ·············· 48

  2.5 Plan Voisin
    伏瓦生规划 ………………………………………………… 53
  2.6 The Radiant City
    光明城市 …………………………………………………… 61
  2.7 Broadacre City
    广亩城市 …………………………………………………… 68
  2.8 The Living City
    活着的城市 ………………………………………………… 73

3 Sustainable and Report of the Asia Pacific Urban Forum
可持续发展与亚太城市论坛报告 …………………………………… 80
◎ 本章导读 …………………………………………………………… 80
  3.1 Sustainable Design and Construction
    可持续发展设计和建设 …………………………………… 80
  3.2 Example
    实例 ………………………………………………………… 88
  3.3 Global Trade Agreements, Economic Reforms and Their
    Impact on Cities
    全球贸易协定和经济改革对城市的影响 ………………… 95
  3.4 Cities as the Engines of Economic Growth
    城市——经济发展的动力 ………………………………… 99
  3.5 Civic Engagement and the Role of Media
    市民的参与与媒体的作用 ………………………………… 104
  3.6 Urban Transport and Communications
    城市交通 …………………………………………………… 109
  3.7 Urban Physical and Social Space
    城市的物质空间与社会空间 ……………………………… 117
  3.8 Housing and Urban Indicators
    住房和城市的基本情况 …………………………………… 119

4 City for Human Development
适合人类发展的城市 ………………………………………………… 125

◎ 本章导读 ·· 125

4.1　Eighteen Hypotheses
　　　18 个假说 ·· 125

4.2　Great City versus Small City
　　　巨型城市 vs. 微型城市 ································ 142

4.3　Economics and Ecology of the City
　　　城市的经济与生态 ······································ 145

5　City Form
城市形态 ·· 151

◎ 本章导读 ·· 151

5.1　Imageable City Form
　　　可意象的城市形态 ······································ 151

5.2　Designing the Paths
　　　设计路径 ·· 158

5.3　Form Qualities
　　　形态特性 ·· 165

5.4　The Sense of the Whole
　　　整体的感知 ·· 172

5.5　Metropolitan Form
　　　大都市形态 ·· 178

5.6　The Process of Design
　　　设计过程 ·· 185

5.7　Specifying Form or Performance
　　　指定形态或性能 ·· 191

5.8　The Baroque Network Model
　　　巴洛克典型型制 ·· 196

5.9　An Imaginary Model
　　　一个虚构的模式 ·· 202

5.10　City Design
　　　 城市设计 ·· 208

6 Place

场所 ……………………………………………………… 213
◎ 本章导读 …………………………………………… 213

6.1 The Phenomenon of Place
场所现象 ……………………………………… 213

6.2 Space
空间 …………………………………………… 219

6.3 The Character of Place
场所的性格 …………………………………… 224

6.4 The Structure of Place
场所的结构 …………………………………… 229

6.5 The Spirit of Place
场所精神 ……………………………………… 236

6.6 Natural and Manmade Place
自然场所与人造场所 ………………………… 242

6.7 Meaning of Place
场所的意义 …………………………………… 248

6.8 Identity of Place
场所的特性 …………………………………… 254

6.9 History of Place
场所的历史 …………………………………… 261

7 Townscape

街道美学 ………………………………………………… 268
◎ 本章导读 …………………………………………… 268

7.1 Streets
街道形态 ……………………………………… 268

7.2 Buildings
建筑的布局 …………………………………… 273

7.3 The Type of Townscape
街道美学的类型 ……………………………… 277

8 The Architecture of the City
城市建筑学 ·················· 283
◎ 本章导读 ·················· 283

   8.1   Urban Artifacts
          城市建筑体 ·················· 283

   8.2   Urban Ecology and Psychology
          城市生态学和心理学 ·················· 289

   8.3   The Development of Industry
          工业的发展 ·················· 296

   8.4   Urban Scale
          城市规模 ·················· 301

   8.5   The Size of a City
          城市的尺度 ·················· 305

9 Urban Stormwater System Plan and Management
城市雨水处理系统设计规划与管理 ·················· 313
◎ 本章导读 ·················· 313

   9.1   Introduction to Urban Stormwater Management in Australia
          澳大利亚城市雨水管理概述 ·················· 314

   9.2   Water Sensitive Urban Design
          节水城市设计 ·················· 320

   9.3   Constructed Wetlands
          湿地建设 ·················· 327

10 Cities Designed for Winter
寒地城市设计 ·················· 336
◎ 本章导读 ·················· 336

   10.1   Common Problems and Five Emphases
           常见的问题以及5个要点 ·················· 336

   10.2   Lowertown—a Case Study
           个案研究——圣保罗"低城区"的改造 ·················· 345

   10.3   Vernacular Agricultural Townships/Villages in Harbin

Region: Conscious Response to Nature
哈尔滨本土的农业乡镇/乡村:依照自然条件而建 ⋯ 351

10.4 General Structure of Harbin: Compact Pattern and Multiple-function Divisions
哈尔滨总体构架:密集型结构与多功能分区 ⋯⋯⋯⋯ 356

10.5 Infrastructure Aspects of Harbin: a Few Highlights
哈尔滨基础设施的一些特点 ⋯⋯⋯⋯⋯⋯⋯⋯⋯⋯⋯ 359

10.6 Residential Environment of Harbin
哈尔滨的居住环境 ⋯⋯⋯⋯⋯⋯⋯⋯⋯⋯⋯⋯⋯⋯⋯ 363

10.7 Winter Image and Activities in Open Spaces: Match the Summer with Winter
开放空间的冬季景观和活动:冬夏交融 ⋯⋯⋯⋯⋯⋯ 370

PART TWO　ACADEMIC INFORMATION
第二部分　专业学术信息

1 Academic Journals
专业学术期刊 ⋯⋯⋯⋯⋯⋯⋯⋯⋯⋯⋯⋯⋯⋯⋯⋯⋯⋯ 377

2 Academic Conferences
专业学术会议 ⋯⋯⋯⋯⋯⋯⋯⋯⋯⋯⋯⋯⋯⋯⋯⋯⋯⋯ 382

3 Academic Websites
专业学术网站 ⋯⋯⋯⋯⋯⋯⋯⋯⋯⋯⋯⋯⋯⋯⋯⋯⋯⋯ 384

4 Academic Associations and Organizations
专业学会与组织 ⋯⋯⋯⋯⋯⋯⋯⋯⋯⋯⋯⋯⋯⋯⋯⋯⋯ 386

PART THREE　ACADEMIC GLOSSARY
第三部分　专业词汇

REFERENCES ⋯⋯⋯⋯⋯⋯⋯⋯⋯⋯⋯⋯⋯⋯⋯⋯⋯⋯⋯⋯ 435

PART ONE
ACADEMIC READING

第一部分 专业阅读

1

Urban Design Education in Britain and America
英国和美国的城市设计教育

【本章导读】 伦敦大学巴特利特建筑与规划学院的马丁·赛米斯(Martin Symes)教授在走访了10余所美国高校之后,对英、美在城市规划教育上的异同进行了比较,着重比较了专业结构、课程设置和时间安排三个方面;并且介绍了城市规划与建筑学之间的关系及两个专业的毕业去向,以及其与环境设计、工业设计之间的联系。

1.1 Educational Structure
教育结构

Overlap of Architecture and Planning

If it is taken that architecture is mostly concerned with understanding the built environment and town planning with the management of urban life, then an interdisciplinary study could be proposed which concerns itself with applying the techniques of planning to the production and use of the built environment[①]. Some American courses of urban design education do indeed use just such a definition, but others do not. Even those that do must take on board serious uncertainties about intellectual content and professional orientation—the scope of architecture has rarely been defined precisely and the theory and practice of planning probably never.

At one time in Britain, shortly after the 1947 Town and Country Planning Act, town planning may seem to have been firmly established as a sub-section of the architectural activity, but this was hardly the case in the United States (where cities such as Houston have no planning function at all), and the alignment has been seriously questioned in Britain itself for more than a decade.

The Structure of the Professions

In architecture, the British profession plays a more public role than the American one. Both central and local government employ architects in some quantity and a considerable proportion of the major construction effort, that in housing, remains under their control. In the United States I understand this to be less the case. In the latter country, moreover, planning is not normally established as a dominant power in local government, as it is in Britain. Nor does it embody British traditions of concern for the quality of what is built and of what is added to the street scene by development. Thus where graduates of either type of professional school in Britain may seek and, until recently, at least, were likely to find, employment within the public sector which allowed them to combine an interest in design with that in the social use of space, their American counterparts are faced with fewer opportunities and have to seek them on a wider range of fronts[②].

A few large cities, San Francisco, for example, have design control departments which guide developers｢ proposals: some public organizations may direct funds to groups, such as that at the Pratt Center in New York, which make design services available to community groups. The majority of U. S. graduates in this subject area, however, are probably constrained either to take positions with consulting firms serving the development industry or to practice overseas in whatever conditions prevail there.

Structure of the Schools

There is an enormous diversity of American college and university courses in architecture and in environmental design, planning and urban studies. This range is much greater than is to be found in Britain, where the R. I. B. A. and R. T. P. I. seem to have greater control or influence over the scope of courses offered than do their U. S. counterparts. This study is concerned only with those courses in urban design offered where architecture is also taught.

So far as I have been able to discover, almost all the urban design courses in the U. S. A. are offered at post-graduate level. What this classification means as a guide to academic achievement is, of course, another question, for some schools will be offering a one-or two-year course to students who have already completed five years of professional training, either at the same or at another school, while others will be offering a course up to four years in length for students who have previously majored in another, unrelated subject. There are other possibilities within this range, and some schools offer more than one of them.

Recent Institutional Changes

There is a great deal of interest in the United States at the present time in the question of urban design education. Much of this has been aroused by institutional developments in four of the leading universities where the conjuncture of architecture and planning departments was called into question. At Harvard, the new Kennedy School has been able to centralize the university's various interests in government and at Princeton the Woodrow Wilson School of Public Affairs has been reorganized to include parts of other departments. In both these cases the courses in city planning formerly taught in the school of architecture have been transferred to the policy studies area. At the University of Pennsylvania, a similar institutional upheaval was planned but failed to materialize and at the University of California at Berkeley a professorial vacancy caused the search committee, at least, to question the continuing association of city planning with the design professions.

If there have thus been internal reasons, in these places, for the structure and curricula of urban design courses to be reconsidered, and in at least one case reinvented, it would nonetheless be unwise to leave readers with the impression that these were the only reasons. There have also been changes in the number of overseas and American candidates coming forward to take the courses, and there has been a developing tendency among architects to treat the application of social sciences to their area with greater caution. Where these factors have coincided with institutional change, new courses are being created[③].

Words and Expressions

overlap ['əuvə'læp] v. (与……)交叠
interdisciplinary [ˌintə(ː)'disiplinəri] adj. 各学科间的
alignment [ə'lainmənt] n. 队列;结盟
counterpart ['kauntəpɑːt] n. 副本;极相似的人或物;配对物
conjuncture [kən'dʒʌŋktʃə] n. 事态;接合
upheaval [ʌp'hiːvəl] n. 剧变
urban design 城市设计
built environment 城市环境
town planning 城镇规划
take on board 考虑;接受
Town and Country Planning Act 城市和乡村规划(苏格兰)法令
street scene 街道
public sector 公共部门
control department 控制部;管理部门

Pratt Center 美国丹佛市的普拉特社区发展中心(在规划的广泛参与性、综合发展目标、规划的操作性及城市交通的综合设计等方面均有独到之处)
consulting firm 咨询公司
environmental design 环境设计
R. I. B. A. (Royal Institute of British Architects) 英国皇家建筑师学会
R. T. P. I. (Royal Town Planning Institute) 英国皇家城市规划学会
institutional change 机构改革
call into question 怀疑;对……表示异议
the Kennedy School 哈佛大学肯尼迪学院
the Woodrow Wilson School of Public Affairs 伍德罗·威尔逊公共和国际关系学院
the University of Pennsylvania 宾夕法尼亚大学
the University of California at Berkeley 加利福尼亚大学伯克利分校
search committee 遴选委员会

Difficult Sentences

① If it is taken that architecture is mostly concerned with understanding the built environment and town planning with the management of urban life, then an interdisciplinary study could be proposed which concerns itself with applying the techniques of planning to the production and use of the built environment.
如果有人认为建筑大多与理解城市环境、城镇规划及城市生活的管理密切相关,那么就应倡导跨学科的学习,以将规划技巧应用到生产及城市环境的建设中。

② Nor does it embody British traditions of concern for the quality of what is built and of what is added to the street scene by development. Thus where graduates of either type of professional school in Britain may seek and, until recently, at least, were likely to find, employment within the public sector which allowed them to combine an interest in design with that in the social use of space, their American counterparts are faced with fewer opportunities and have to seek them on a wider range of fronts.

（美国的城市规划）也不像英国那样既涵盖城市的建筑品质又关乎城镇开发式的街道建设。因此，毕业于英国城市规划专业学校的毕业生，至少到目前为止，大多就职于政府的公共部门，并有机会使他们将城市设计的特长与社会需要结合起来。相比之下，美国的同等专业的毕业生这样的就业机会却很少，只能涉足其他领域。

③ There have also been changes in the number of overseas and American candidates coming forward to take the courses, and there has been a developing tendency among architects to treat the application of social sciences to their area with greater caution. Where these factors have coincided with institutional change, new courses are being created.

海外以及美国本土的求学者的数量一直在不断刷新，而且建筑师中也有越来越多的人更加关注将社会科学应用到他们的专业领域。这些因素再加上教育的体制改革，使得全新的课程纷纷涌现。

Phrases and Patterns

1. It is taken that... 有人认为

   It is taken that Town and Country Planning is the land use planning system by which the British government seeks to maintain a balance between economic development and evironment quality in the United Kingdom.

   有人认为城市和乡村规划是英国政府试图保持经济发展和环境质量平衡的土地利用规划体系。

   It is taken that World Town Planning Day is a special day to recognize and promote the role of planning in creating livable communities.

   有人认为世界城市规划日是一个特别的日子，使人们认识并促进城市规划在营造适宜居住的社区中的作用。

2. in the question of... 关于……

There is a great deal of interest at the present time in the question of providing courses in the technical and design aspects of architecture, landscape architecture and urban planning.

目前,关于提供建筑、风景建筑和城市设计等技术和设计方面的训练课程已引起人们的诸多关注。

There is a great deal of interest at the present time in the question of a just and rational international economic order.

目前,关于建立公正合理的国际经济新秩序的问题已引起人们的诸多关注。

Questions

1. What is the difference between American and British classification of town planning?
2. What are the changes that urban design education is undergoing?

1.2　Educational Program
教育规划

University of London Program

The University of London has, as its only professional school concerned with the built environment, located in University College, a single-department Faculty of Environmental Studies. This includes the former Department of Town Planning, the former Bartlett School of Architecture, with its subdivisions of History of Architecture and Building and Environmental Design and Engineering, and the formerly independent Development Planning Unit. It maintains links with the Center for Environmental Studies and with Wye Agricultural College. At the same time the University of London has established a special committee, chaired by Sir Peter Swinnerton-Dyer, to report on the overall structure of the university. It is widely believed that this committee will make recommendations for economies in the running of the university.

The Bartlett's undergraduate degree in architecture, planning, building and environmental studies is currently oriented towards a continuing high-level of demand for professional education in architecture. Its post-graduate courses include a M. Phil. in Planning with professional options, M. Sc. courses in a variety of architectural studies, a professional diploma in architecture and a choice of courses in development planning. New courses in urban design, or further teaching in urban design within existing courses, could be developed within many of these frameworks and might take advantage of untapped student demand or unrealized teaching potential[①].

There seems to be in most of the American schools I visited, a sense that a new area of practice has developed outside their doors which is in need of explanation. Whether the intellectual tools are being developed with which this can be done is still an open question.

The Master Plan Approach

If the genesis of urban design is no longer necessarily sought by academics in the physical facts of the city, the popular importance of a plan or designed map on that scale has hardly disappeared. It remains enshrined in the town planning legislation in Britain, and in America appears familiar through the executed layout of cities such as Washington. D. C. The study of such city-forms is still for some schools of architecture a center in the teaching effort: in this tradition an inspired teacher may often help students develop a very wide understanding of the options available when they reorganize part of the urban fabric. He or she may also generate a deep sensitivity to the human issues which will arise.

These advantages of teaching through clear images are however sometimes paralleled by disadvantages: domination by preconceived solutions, the pursuit of an idée fixé, the development of a private language. This is a robust tradition, especially in schools of architecture where planning is not taught as a separate subject, but one which has been severely criticized by those who see in it not the essence of urban design but a series of utopian abstractions.

The Idea of Comprehensive Design

When the first course in urban design was established at Harvard, the influence of Walter Gropius and the theories of the Werkbund and the Bauhaus were clearly to the fore. As other courses were established, these definitions appear to have been employed by others. In 1966, a survey of courses was undertaken on behalf of the Ford Foundation: its authors had no doubt in their minds that " Urban design is . . . inter-professional collaboration in the execution of large and complicated building projects. It has been used for such undertakings as central city commercial area redevelopment and has contributed to the skills with which larger problems of environmental design are approached as in the design of waterfronts and urban open space. "

The authors referred to such larger-than-the-single-building types as the campus, medical center, airport, housing estate and shopping center. The ideal curriculum, in their view, for a postgraduate course was that it should grow out of a good course in architecture, and have " a strong input from landscape and from city planning on the one hand and from the social sciences on the other. "

They did note, however, various dilemmas this proposal engendered: namely the excessive length of course which could be required, a conflict between the ideals of producing talented designers and of producing well-rounded persons, and severe difficulties the schools were experiencing, even then, with interdisciplinary teaching.

Specialist Contributions

Partly in response to such difficulties in developing new course units in the related subjects, but partly also in response to problems within architectural education itself (such as those of selection and of assessment), a school of thought then developed which started from the educational needs of environmental design as a whole and attempted to divide the total academic problem into reasonably sized parts within it[2].

The AIA commissioned a report on this approach in which its authors attempted to lay once and for all the Jeffersonian ghost of a well-educated layman. The authors quoted the then recently-retired dean at Harvard, who had compiled a list of all the courses a well-rounded designer ought to take and had concluded that "the result was a 20-year-long program." The solution proposed was that new courses should be developed in various aspects of environmental design, one of which could no doubt be called urban design, if that fitted the pattern. The principal aims should be:

to introduce students to real-world constraints;

to help the students comprehend the forces which make for change and develop the capacity to adapt to them;

to encourage the formulation of ideas about a better environment.

The authors noted that these aims were incompatible with each other and presumably expected some schools to emphasize one and some schools another. This emphasis on educational aims in their own right has of course been maintained in the Bartlett School over the years. This experience will no doubt prove extremely valuable when taken together with whatever ideas are accepted about the ways a subject matter might be defined, but it does not solve that problem.

A Critical Approach

Moshe Safdie, the chairman of a recent conference on urban design, introduced Jane Jacobs by remarking that the basic ideas of urban design had been established by her in her first book. This may not be, strictly speaking, true, but it does summarize a certain point of view. Increasingly, it would seem from that conference, the practitioners of urban design in North America are concerned with local planning issues, to which they give a physical dimension, and with the process of implementation, in which they are often called upon to take an advocacy position. No longer do they look for the overall pattern, or attempt to present the public interest[3].

Physical Planning as the Model

All of the approaches so far described have depended on a definition of urban design as in some way, or at some scale, derived from architecture. A number of schools, however, report that students are coming forward at graduate level who have little or no experience in design and who do not wish to become architects, at least in the professionally accepted sense, but who are interested in the physical aspects of town planning. This is a new phenomenon and may not last: it could be a defensive reaction by students expecting congestion in the job market for policy planners. Nevertheless, these schools have little option but to take any kind of demand seriously at the present time and are attempting to create a package of courses to suit these needs. The typical package as it emerges will probably have three components:

a practice component drawing on the experience of both advocacy and public planning offices;

a set of theoretical courses drawn from fields beyond the range currently covered in urban design (the students already have a grounding in social science and are looking to, say, anthropology for more advanced studies);

a studio component which starts from day one of an architectural student's career but covers the field in a more generalized way.

Clearly the problem the design of these courses will have to face is that of time: the length of study needed to make them worthwhile educational experience at graduate level could be such that it more than outweighs the advantages of being able to include social science studies at a truly graduate level. Three- or four-year post-graduate courses may be possible for a few students in the American financial context, but it seems very doubtful that they could be successfully mounted on a large scale there, or at all in Britain.

Words and Expressions

untapped [ʌn'tæpt] adj. 未使用的
genesis ['dʒenisis] n. 起源
enshrine [in'ʃrain] v. 铭记
legislation [,ledʒis'leiʃən] n. 立法;法律的制定(或通过)
layout ['lei,aut] n. 规划;设计;布局图
sensitivity [,sensə'tiviti] n. 敏感;灵敏(度);灵敏性
preconceived ['pri:kən'si:vd] adj. 预想的
idée fixé [i:del'fi:ks] <法>固定观念;对一事的偏执
robust [rə'bʌst] adj. 精力充沛的
utopian [ju:'təupjən] adj. 乌托邦的;理想化的
abstraction [æb'strækʃən] n. 抽象化;空想;抽象派作品
waterfront ['wɔ:təfrʌnt] n. 水边地码头区;滨水地区
landscape ['lændskeip] n. 风景;山水画;地形
commission [kə'miʃən] v. 委任;任命;委托;委托制作
constraint [kən'streint] n. 约束;强制
incompatible [,inkəm'pætəbl] adj. 性质相反的;矛盾的;不调和的
practitioner [præk'tiʃənə] n. 从业者;开业者

advocacy ['ædvəkəsi] *n.* 拥护；鼓吹；辩护
congestion [kən'dʒestʃən] *n.* 拥塞；拥挤
anthropology [ˌænθrə'pɔlədʒi] *n.* 人类学
M. Phil. (Master of Philosophy) 哲学硕士学位
M. Sc. (Master of Science) 理学硕士学位
AIA (abbr. = American Institute of Architects) 美国建筑学会
master plan 总平面图；总体规划
urban fabric 城市建筑
comprehensive design 综合设计
to the fore 在近处；在手头；在前面
building project 建设项目
housing estate 居民区；居住区
overall pattern 总体图
physical planning 实体规划；形体规划
physical aspects 物理性质

Difficult Sentences

① Its post-graduate courses include a M. Phil. in Planning with professional options, M. Sc. courses in a variety of architectural studies, a professional diploma in architecture and a choice of courses in development planning. New courses in urban design, or further teaching in urban design within existing courses, could be developed within many of these frameworks and might take advantage of untapped student demand or unrealized teaching potential.
其研究生课程包括可自选专业的哲学硕士、多方向的建筑学的理学硕士、建筑领域的专业文凭、可选修的发展规划课程。城市设计专业的新课程或是现有课程的深度教学，能够在这些课程设置框架内不断推进，并可能会开发学生尚未得到兑现的需求或尚未充分挖掘的教学潜力。

② Partly in response to such difficulties in developing new course units in the related subjects, but partly also in response to problems within architectural education itself (such as those of selection and of assessment), a school of thought then developed which started from the educational needs of environmental design as a whole and attempted to divide the total academic problem into reasonably sized parts within it.

一半是为了应对在相关学科设置课程的过程中出现的难题,也有一半是为了针对建筑工程教育本身的问题(诸如选修课程、考试评估等),一种适应环境设计的教育需要,试图将庞大的学术问题分解为简单易行的分支的学派就应运而生了。

③ Increasingly, it would seem from that conference, the practitioners of urban design in North America are concerned with local planning issues, to which they give a physical dimension, and with the process of implementation, in which they are often called upon to take an advocacy position. No longer do they look for the overall pattern, or attempt to present the public interest.

此次大会越来越多地展示,在北美地区从事城市设计的从业者较为关注当地的规划事宜,他们会对此给予较为实际的考量,并且在此操作过程中摇旗呐喊、大力倡导这一做法。他们不再将目光聚焦于总体设计图,或是试图体现公众利益。

Phrases and Patterns

1. It is widely believed that... 人们普遍相信……

   It is widely believed that New York City is undergoing rapid transformation—a wave of real estate development is changing not only the shape of neighborhoods, but also who lives and works in them.

   人们普遍相信纽约市正在经历迅速转型———一波房地产开发热潮不仅正在改变全城的面貌,而且也改变着人们的生活和工作。

   It is widely believed that urban planning is a dynamic profession that works to improve the welfare of people and their communities by creating more convenient, equitable, healthful, efficient, and attractive places for present and future generations.

人们普遍相信城市规划是一个充满活力的专业工程,以改善人民的福利和社区的状况,为当代人和子孙后代创造更多的方便、公平、健康、高效和有吸引力的地方。

2. ... is oriented towards 旨在;面向

The course was orientated towards foreign students.

该课程是专为外国学生开设的。

The Pratt Center is currently oriented towards New York neighborhoods across the city to identify what New Yorkers need from the built environment and help them shape their communities through the city planning process.

普拉特中心目前面向纽约全城,以确定纽约市民所需要的建筑环境,并帮助他们通过城市规划过程形成自己的社区。

3. be paralleled by... 与……共存

Now, with the advent and popularity of the home computer, its advantages are however sometimes paralleled by disadvantages.

现在,随着家用电脑的出现和普及,它的好处与弊端也同时展现。

Currently, the advantages of Shanghai suburb's quick development are however paralleled by disadvantages like the increasing population and the over-exploitation of the construction land.

当前,上海郊区城乡进入了快速发展期,然而在看到诸多优势的同时也出现了很多弊端,诸如人口增速迅猛,建设用地增幅惊人。

Questions

1. Generalize the latest trend in architectural education in British universities.
2. What kind of ideal curriculum should be implemented in order to accomplish the idea of comprehensive design?

1.3 Educational Method
教育方法

Frameworks for Teaching Urban Design

The epistemological problem—what is the source of knowledge about urban design? —should help organize this discussion. Does appropriate knowledge lie in the matrix of forces which shape our towns and cities, and in their expression as the development, modification or preservation of their physical fabric? Or is it, on the other hand, to be found in a series of abstract intellectual models which allow us to visualize not only town maps and central places but also capital accumulation and rental functions[①].

This is a complex pair of questions to which it is difficult to find definitive answers. In developing the various aspects of a new course, the course designer must nevertheless come to some conclusion on these questions at each step in his or her progress. If what is important for a student is exposure to the facts, he or she will need to be taught in the field, using as data the surroundings and events which he or she can observe, be they physical or socioeconomic. Such a course must be designed around practice; entry qualifications will tend to include previous experience; recognition by the professions will rarely be problematic[②]. If, conversely, the course designer feels it is the students' powers of critical insight which should be developed, the outcome of all these issues will be reversed. The students' work should be personal, their subjects academic, previous scholastic achievement a major criterion for selection and professional recognition something which has to be argued very closely indeed[③].

Educational Methods

The courses at ten schools were studied in depth. The structure of a course seemed to be composed of up to five different types of educational experience:

Studios: Every course required studio work. In some cases there were introductory studios for those having little graphic experience. In many cases the studio was clearly the centerpiece of the course. It could include analytic as well as synthetic work, group work as well as individual exercises.

Workshop and seminars: Most courses included these. They are essentially practical studies in which the students' production is not primarily graphic but oral. Debate and discussion may also be developed in class situations where more abstract methods and techniques are covered.

Required lecture courses: Formal presentations of established subject-matter formed an important part of the requirements in about half the courses. Term papers were sometimes required but the primary testing method is a written examination.

Electives: To a greater or lesser degree almost every course considered a choice of special subjects in their own or related departments of educational value. In all cases, however, the electives only occupied time left over after other requirements had been met; a complete free-for-all is clearly out of fashion.

Thesis: An individual written and/or design dissertation was required in some cases. How to define its design component is clearly a difficult question for those courses with academic pretentions.

Subject Matter

Required subject matter, outside studio work which was universal (but undefined), covered a broad range of practical and theoretical areas. Whether this reflects a priori thinking about the needs of the subject or whether it reflects a diversity of staff abilities could not be discovered in a limited study such as this one.

Practice information: Design and development, law, transportation infrastructure, finance, programming and similar topics could be included under this heading.

Analytic methods: This could be mainly technical, for example in statistics, or more abstract, such as the philosophy of science.

Policy studies: Units were included in about half the courses to bring together the evaluation techniques which have been developed in town planning practice: zoning diagrams, building envelope studies, flow diagrams and impact analysis, to name but a few.

Social and economic studies: More of the latter than the former was evident in the American schools visited. Its most frequent appearance was social and economic geography or simply as location theory. Only two courses had the staff available to teach cognitive mapping.

History: Only two schools admitted this to their standard curriculum, and when they did so it was with a rather limited interest in certain periods of European city building activity.

Entry Qualifications

The majority of courses studied assume that new entrants to one-or two-year courses have previously completed a five-year professional course in architecture. Such a course is not strictly equivalent to the five-year course at R. I. B. A. Part II in Britain as it starts at a lower academic level, and it does not usually include as much technical information. It is thus a more general education than most British students would have had.

Some schools have taken the implication of this generality to be that urban design can also be offered as a two- or three-year masters' course, to students who have taken a four-year general B. A. degree in which they had only majored in a design discipline. There is no British equivalent to that kind of first degree, but some indication of its status may be given by the observation that Cambridge normally allows American B. A. graduates to complete their own B. A. course to Part I R. I. B. A. in two years.

Only in two instances were graduate courses discovered which would take entrants with any previous degree, but here other criteria for selection were stringently applied. In one case, the course was three and one half years in duration, in the other no finishing time was specified, with individual students' programs being worked out after they started the course. Despite the influence of students' previous attainment in studio work on course length, each type of course can still last a surprisingly different length of time. The variation in one group is more than 100 percent.

Professional Recognition

In most cases there was no accreditation for the special courses in urban design. In one case the course was accredited for planning but not for architecture; in another, the course was accredited for both professions. This latter was the longest course and the former the largest of its type. Whether or not the course required students to have or to obtain practical office experience (usually called an internship) seems not to correlate with professional recognition. Clearly the situation is not as simple in the U. S. A. as in Britain, where both institutes require a standard form of practical experience before students can take their final registration examination.

Length of Courses

Of the 10 schools visited, four ran courses in which the orientation is primarily towards urban design practice, three ran courses in which the orientation is towards academic studies which impinge on design, and three ran courses which offer a sampling of both approaches. This comprehensive curriculum may be the most robust and adaptable approach. The average length of the practical courses is three semesters, while that of the academic courses and the comprehensive courses is five semesters.

The prerequisite for shorter academic and comprehensive courses is, I would argue, a resolution of our continuing uncertainty about an appropriate basis for knowledge in design, and the condensing of both studio and lecture course teaching. Until such a resolution can be achieved, we shall be faced with a choice between practical short courses and academic or comprehensive long ones. Small (or impoverished) schools will no doubt be forced to make this choice and opt for one or the other approach, probably the practical one. Large (or wealthy) schools may be able to avoid premature judgment by mounting courses of both kinds.

Words and Expressions

epistemological [ˌepisti(ː)məˈlɔdʒikəl] adj. 认识论的
matrix [ˈmeitriks] n. 矩阵；发源地；策源地
modification [ˌmɔdifiˈkeiʃən] n. 更改；修改；修正
preservation [ˌprezə(ː)ˈveiʃən] n. 保存；保藏；保护
visualize [ˈvizjuəlaiz] v. 使看得见；使具体化；想象；显形
definitive [diˈfinitiv] adj. 最后的；确定的；权威性的
entry [ˈentri] n. 登录；进入；入口
problematic [ˌprɔbləˈmætik] adj. 问题的；有疑问的；或然性的
studio [ˈstjuːdiəu] n. 工作室；演播室；电影制片厂
graphic [ˈgræfik] adj. 绘画似的；图解的
centerpiece [ˈsentəpiːs] n. 中心件；中心装饰品
analytic [ˌænəˈlitik] adj. 分析的；解析的
synthetic [sinˈθetik] adj. 合成的；人造的；综合的
workshop [ˈwəːkʃɔp] n. 研讨会；专题研究组
seminar [ˈseminɑː] n. 研究班；专题讨论会
subject-matter [ˈsʌbdʒiktˈmætə] n. 主题；素材

elective [i'lektiv] *n.* 选修课程
thesis ['θi:sis] *n.* 论题;论文
dissertation [ˌdisə(:)'teiʃən] *n.* (学位)论文;专题;学术演讲
priori(a priori) [eiprai'ɔ:rai] *adj.* 〈拉〉先验(的)
infrastructure ['infrə'strʌktʃə] *n.* 基础结构;基础设施
zoning ['zəuniŋ] *n.* 分带;分区制
diagram ['daiəgræm] *n.* 图表;图解;框图;立体图
entrant ['entrənt] *n.* 新会员;新成员;进入者
generality [ˌdʒenə'ræliti] *n.* 一般性;概论;概说;大要
stringently ['strindʒəntli] *adv.* 严厉地;迫切地
accreditation [əˌkrediteiʃən] *n.* 委派;信赖;鉴定合格
internship ['intɛ:nʃip] *n.* 实习医师;实习期
prerequisite ['pri:'rekwizit] *n.* 先决条件;必备条件
physical fabric 相关组构,机能组构
town map 城镇图
capital accumulation [经] 资本积累
transportation infrastructure 运输基本设施
building envelope 建筑物外体
flow diagram 流程图;作业图;生产过程图解
impact analysis 冲击分析
social geography 社会地理学
economic geography 经济地理
location theory 企业选地理论
cognitive mapping 认知制图
technical information 技术情报
design discipline 设计原则;设计规程

Difficult Sentences

① Does appropriate knowledge lie in the matrix of forces which shape our towns and cities, and in their expression as the development, modification or preservation of their physical fabric? Or is it, on the other hand, to be found in a series of abstract intellectual models which allow us to visualize not only town maps and central places but also capital accumulation and rental functions.

（关于城市设计）相应的知识是取决于构筑我们的城镇、展现城镇发展、修饰或是维护相关组构的鳞次栉比的建筑？还是体现在不仅显现城镇地图和中心地带，也会展现资本积累和租赁业的一系列抽象的知识结构之中？

② If what is important for a student is exposure to the facts, he or she will need to be taught in the field, using as data the surroundings and events which he or she can observe, be they physical or socioeconomic. Such a course must be designed around practice; entry qualifications will tend to include previous experience; recognition by the professions will rarely be problematic.

如果说对学生来说重要的是要了解事实，那么在这一领域我们应该用学生能切身观察到的身边的环境和事件的资料来进行教学，无论它们是来自于自然科学的还是社会经济学的素材。这样的课程必须围绕实践操作进行设计，入学资格往往会考量该生先前的工作经验，一般而言也会获得同业人士的赞誉。

③ If, conversely, the course designer feels it is the students' powers of critical insight which should be developed, the outcome of all these issues will be reversed. The students' work should be personal, their subjects academic, previous scholastic achievement a major criterion for selection and professional recognition something which has to be argued very closely indeed.

相反，如果课程设计者认为学生的批判性思维能力亟需完善，那么所有这些问题的结果将逆转。学生的工作将会由本人独立完成，科目也将是理论型为主，以前的学业成绩将成为遴选的主要标准，专家的认可和表扬也将被仔细置评。

Phrases and Patterns

1. in depth 深入地

Following the handbook style this book is compiled to introduce methods of pattern drawing and exemplary drawings for various architectural components in depth.

本书以指南手册的方式编辑而成,旨在深入地介绍各种建筑元素的起模方法,并辅以示范图样。

The paper analyzes an example of Tonghe cultural square in Pingdu in depth and introduces the conception of chinese landscape paintings into cultural square design.

本论文深入分析了平度市同和文化广场的实例,借此将中国的山水画概念引入到广场设计之中。

2. ... covered a broad range of practical and theoretical areas……涵盖了实践和理论的广泛范畴

It is evident that many branches of applied science cover a broad range of practical and theoretical areas.

很显然,许多应用科学的分支涵盖了实践和理论的广泛范畴。

This thesis, which covers a broad range of practical and theoretical areas, inquires into the relationship of urban water system and urban characteristic and the countermeasure how to reserve urban water system and urban characteristic in southern areas.

此篇论文探讨了城市水系与城市特色的关系以及如何在城市水系方面传承江南地区城市特色的对策措施,涵盖了实践和理论的广泛范畴。

Questions

1. What should be the principles on which urban design teaching operates?
2. Give a brief list of prevailing subject matter taught in American schools. What other courses should be included in your opinion?

2

Urban Utopias in the Twentieth Century
20世纪的城市乌托邦

【本章导读】 进入20世纪,城市规划受到乌托邦主义的影响,产生了许多影响深远的规划思想。本章选取了三位大师的规划思想。

2.1、2.2介绍了英国社会活动家霍华德(Ebenezer Howard)提出的"田园城市"设想,他认为应该建设一种兼有城市和乡村优点的理想城市,城市四周被农地围绕以自给自足,严格控制城市规模,保证每户居民都能极为方便地接近乡村自然。

2.3~2.6都是柯布西耶(Le Corbusier)的规划设想,柯布西耶在1922年首先提出了300万人的理想城市规划,1925年在300万人城市的基础上提出了一个巴黎市中心部分地区的改建方案,就是有名的"伏瓦生规划"。1935年,柯布西耶又展出了他一项城市规划的研究方案"光明城市",用规则的、有机的发展模式取代传统的同心圆式的城市格局。

2.7、2.8介绍了赖特(Frank Lloyd Wright)的城市思想——"广亩城市"梦想,这个研究的最后成果写在了他的《活着的城市》一书中。"广亩城市"是一个人性占首要地位的自由城市,力求保护居民免受机器时代城市"机器怪物"的影响,力图使人从"群居"的状态中解脱出来。

2.1　Town-country Magnet
城乡磁铁

So presented, the problem may appear at first sight to be difficult, if not impossible, of solution. "What", some may <u>be disposed</u> to ask, "can possibly be done to make the country more attractive to a workaday people than the town—to make wages, or at least the standard of physical comfort, higher in the country than in the town; to secure in the country equal possibilities of social intercourse, and to make the prospects of advancement for the average man or woman equal, not to say superior, to those enjoyed in our large cities?" The issue one constantly finds presented in a form very similar to that. The subject is treated continually in the public press, and in all forms of discussion, as though men, or at least working men, had not now, and never could have, any choice or alternative, but either, on the one hand, to stifle their love for human society—at least in wider relations than can be found in a straggling village—or, on the other hand, to forgo almost entirely all the keen and pure delights of the country. The question is universally considered as though it were now, and for ever must remain, quite impossible for working people to live in the country and yet be engaged in pursuits other than agricultural; as though crowded, unhealthy cities were the last word of economic science; and as if our present form of industry, in which sharp lines divide agricultural from industrial pursuits, were necessarily an enduring one[①]. This fallacy is the very common one of ignoring altogether the possibility of alternatives other than those presented to the mind. There are in reality not only, as is so constantly assumed, two alternatives—town life and country life—but a third alternative, in which all the advantages of the most energetic and active town life, with all the beauty and delight of the country, may be secured in perfect combination; and the certainty of being able to live this life will be the magnet which will produce the effect for which we are all striving—the spontaneous movement of the people from our crowded cities to the bosom of our kindly mother earth, at once the source of life, of happiness, of wealth, and of power②. The town and the country may, therefore, be regarded as two magnets, each striving to draw the people to itself—a rivalry which a new form of life, partaking of the nature of both, comes to take part in. This may be illustrated by a figure of "The Three Magnets" (see Fig. 2.1), in which the chief advantages of the Town and of the Country are set forth with their corresponding drawbacks, while the advantages of the Town-Country are seen to be free from the disadvantages of either.

The Town magnet, it will be seen, offers, as compared with the Country magnet, the advantages of high wages, opportunities for employment, tempting prospects of advancement, but these <u>are</u> largely <u>counterbalanced by</u> high rents and prices. Its social opportunities and its places of amusement are very alluring, but excessive hours of toil, distance from work, and the "isolation of crowds" tend greatly to reduce the value of these good things. The well-lit streets are a great attraction, especially in winter, but the sunlight is being more and more shut out, while the air is so vitiated that the fine public buildings, like the sparrows, rapidly become covered with soot, and the very statues are in despair. Palatial edifices and fearful slums are the strange, complementary features of modern cities.

The Country magnet declares herself to be the source of all beauty and wealth; but the Town magnet mockingly reminds her that she is very dull for lack of society, and very sparing of her gifts for lack of capital. There are in the country beautiful vistas, lordly parks, violet-scented woods, fresh air, sounds of rippling water; but too often one sees those threatening words, "Trespassers will be prosecuted". Rents, if estimated by the acre, are certainly low, but such low rents are the natural fruit of low wages rather than a cause of substantial comfort; while long hours and lack of amusements forbid the bright sunshine and the pure air to gladden the hearts of the people. The one industry, agriculture, suffers frequently from excessive rainfalls; but this wondrous harvest of the clouds is seldom properly ingathered, so that, in times of drought, there is frequently, even for drinking purposes, a most

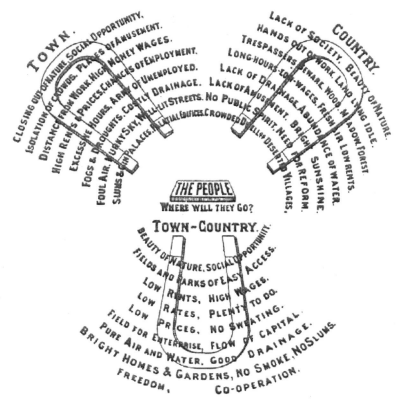

Fig. 2.1 The Three Magnets
图 2.1 三种磁力理论

insufficient supply. Even the natural healthfulness of the country is largely lost for lack of proper drainage and other sanitary conditions, while, in parts almost deserted by the people, the few who remain are yet frequently huddled together as if in rivalry with the slums of our cities.

But neither the Town magnet nor the Country magnet represents the full plan and purpose of nature. Human society and the beauty of nature are meant to be enjoyed together. The two magnets must be made one. As man and woman by their varied gifts and faculties supplement each other, so should town and country. The town is the symbol of society—of mutual help and friendly co-operation, of fatherhood, motherhood, brotherhood, sisterhood, of wide relations between man and man—of broad, expanding sympathies—of science, art, culture, religion. And the country! The country is the symbol of God's love and care for man. All that we are and all that we have comes from it. Our bodies are formed of it; to it they return. We are fed by it, clothed by it, and by it are we warmed and sheltered. On its bosom we rest. Its beauty is the inspiration of art, of music, of poetry. Its forces propel all the wheels of industry. It is the source of all health, all wealth, all knowledge. But its fullness of joy and wisdom has not revealed itself to man. Nor can it ever, so long as this unholy, unnatural separation of society and nature endures. Town and country must be married, and out of this joyous union will spring a new hope, a new life, a new civilization. It is the purpose of this work to show how a first step can be taken in this direction by the construction of a Town-country magnet; and I hope to convince the reader that this is practicable, here and now, and that on principles which are the very soundest, whether viewed from the ethical or the economic standpoint[3].

Words and Expressions

stifle ['staifl] v. 使窒息;抑制;扼杀
straggling ['strægliŋ] adj. 脱离队伍的;落后的
forgo [fɔː'gəu] v. 摒绝;放弃
partaking [pɑː'teikiŋ] n. 参与;分担;分享
counterbalance [ˌkɑuntə'bæləns] v. 使平均;使平衡;弥补
alluring [ə'ljuəriŋ] adj. 迷人的;吸引人的;诱惑的
vitiated ['viʃieitid] adj. 损坏的;污浊的;失效的
soot [sut] n. 煤烟;烟灰
palatial [pə'leiʃəl] adj. 富丽堂皇的;宏伟的;庄严的
edifice ['edifis] n. 大厦;大建筑物
sparing ['spεəriŋ] adj. 节俭的;保守的
vista ['vistə] n. 狭长的景色;街景
lordly ['lɔːdli] adj. 有威严的;贵族似的;高傲的
rippling ['ripliŋ] adj. 起涟漪的;潺潺流水般声音的
trespasser ['trespəsə] n. 侵害者;违反者;侵入者
wondrous ['wʌndrəs] adj. 令人惊奇的;非常的
ingather [in'gæðə] v. 收获;收入;收集
drainage ['dreinidʒ] n. 排水;排水装置
sanitary ['sænitəri] adj. (有关)卫生的;(保持)清洁的
propel [prə'pel] v. 推进;驱使
social intercourse 社交
the last word 定论;最新成就;最新品种
sharp line 尖锐谱线;清晰谱线
spontaneous movement 固有运动

Difficult Sentences

① The question is universally considered as though it were now, and for ever must remain, quite impossible for working people to live in the country and yet be engaged in pursuits other than agricultural; as though crowded, unhealthy cities were the last word of economic science; and as if our present form of industry, in which sharp lines divide agricultural from industrial pursuits, were necessarily an enduring one

人们普遍认为这是现有的而且会一直存续的问题,即劳动者是不可能一方面居住在郊区,另一方面又追求不同于乡土气息的生活;仿佛拥挤不堪、有害健康的大城市才是经济学发展的最终结局,仿佛在农业与工业之间划上巨大鸿沟的、我们现有的工业形式会必然持续到永久。

② There are in reality not only, as is so constantly assumed, two alternatives—town life and country life—but a third alternative, in which all the advantages of the most energetic and active town life, with all the beauty and delight of the country, may be secured in perfect combination; and the certainty of being able to live this life will be the magnet which will produce the effect for which we are all striving—the spontaneous movement of the people from our crowded cities to the bosom of our kindly mother earth, at once the source of life, of happiness, of wealth, and of power.

事实上,正如人们经常所希望的那样,我们不仅仅只有两种选择——城市生活和乡村生活——而是拥有第三种选择。这种选择将城市生活中最富活力和生机的优点同乡村生活的美丽和愉悦完美地结合起来,这种选择之下所确保的生活将形成一个磁极,它能使我们一直努力达成的效果成为现实——人们自发地从拥挤不堪的城市回归到大地母亲的怀抱——生命、快乐、财富和权势的起源地。

③ It is the purpose of this work to show how a first step can be taken in this direction by the construction of a Town-country magnet; and I hope to convince the reader that this is practicable, here and now, and that on principles which are the very soundest, whether viewed from the ethical or the economic standpoint.

本项研究的目的在于向大家展示如何迈出构建城乡结合体的第

一步,本人希望无论读者从何种角度去审视,伦理道德也好,经济发展也罢,都能够相信这是切实可行的,并且是基于非常充分的原则基础之上的。

Phrases and Patterns

1. be disposed to do 有意;愿意;倾向于

   It is clear that many theorists are disposed to observe the development law of urban planning theory on the basis of its historical development trend these days.

   很显然,近年来,很多理论家愿意从历史演进的态势去考察城市规划理论的发展规律。

   Our company is disposed to bring innovative, buildable, sustainable, marketable and ecologically responsible projects to clients across the globe.

   本公司乐意向全球的客户提供创新型的、可信赖的、可持续性的、有市场潜力的、绿色环保的服务工程。

2. be counterbalanced by... 被……所抵消(影响)

   This new urban waterfront offers advantages of connecting the city back to the water and creating distinctive public spaces, but these are largely counterbalanced by a fallacy in infrastructure.

   这个全新的城市海岸建筑有很多优点,诸如使城市回归到水乡风情、开辟了独特的公共空间等,但是由于基础设施的设计失误,使其光彩大打折扣。

   Urban design offers the advantages of the common essential property with design in general like the diversity of value property and the creativity in design, but these are largely counterbalanced by future uncertainty of the design product, and the utopian tendency.

   城市设计具有同一般意义上的设计一样的本质属性的诸多优点,体现在价值属性的多元化和设计的创作性,但是这些优点却被设计成果的未来不确定性及乌托邦定势所影响。

Questions

1. What characteristics does the city magnet or the town magnet respectively have?
2. How do you understand the expression that "town and country must be married"? And what will their offspring be like?

2.2 Garden City
花园城市

Garden City, which is to be built near the centre of the 6,000 acres, covers an area of 1,000 acres, or a sixth part of the 6,000 acres, and might be of circular form, 1,240 yards (or nearly three-quarters of a mile) from centre to circumference. (Fig. 2.2 is a ground plan of the

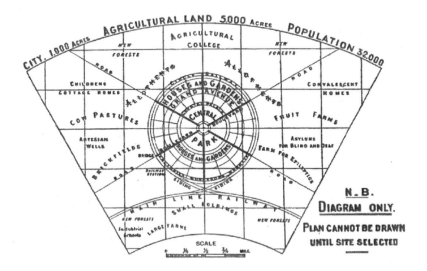

Fig. 2.2 Garden City and Rural Belt
图2.2 花园城市单元

whole municipal area, showing the town in the centre; and Fig. 2.3, which represents one section or ward of the town, will be useful in following the description of the town itself—a *description which is, however, merely suggestive, and will probably be much departed from.*)

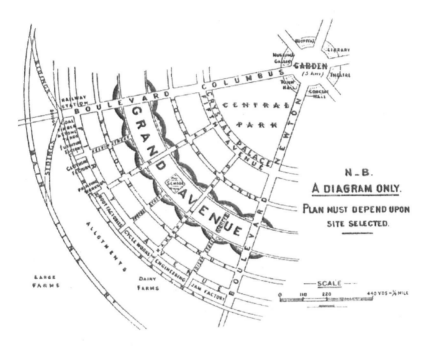

Fig. 2.3 Ward and Center of Garden city
图2.3 花园城市:各区与中心

Six magnificent boulevards—each 120 feet wide—traverse the city from centre to circumference, dividing it into six equal parts or wards. In the centre is a circular space containing about five and a half acres, laid out as a beautiful and well-watered garden; and, surrounding this garden, each standing in its own ample grounds, are the larger public buildings—town hall, principal concert and lecture hall, theatre, library, museum, picture-gallery, and hospital[①].

The rest of the large space encircled by the "Crystal Palace" is a public park, containing 145 acres, which includes ample recreation grounds within very easy access of all the people.

Running all round the Central Park (except where it is intersected by the boulevards) is a wide glass arcade called the "Crystal Palace", opening on to the park. This building is in wet weather one of the favourite resorts of the people, whilst the knowledge that its bright shelter is ever close at hand tempts people into Central Park, even in the most doubtful of weathers. Here manufactured goods are exposed for sale, and here most of that class of shopping which requires the joy of deliberation and selection is done. The space enclosed by the Crystal Palace is, however, a good deal larger than is required for these purposes, and a considerable part of it is used as a Winter Garden—the whole forming a permanent exhibition of a most attractive character, whilst its circular form brings it near to every dweller in the town—the furthest removed inhabitant being within 600 yards[2].

Passing out of the Crystal Palace on our way to the outer ring of the town, we cross Fifth Avenue—lined, as are all the roads of the town, with trees—fronting which, and looking on to the Crystal Palace, we find a ring of very excellently built houses, each standing in its own ample grounds; and, as we continue our walk, we observe that the houses are for the most part built either in concentric rings, facing the various avenues (as the circular roads are termed), or fronting the boulevards and roads which all converge to the centre of the town[3]. Asking the friend who accompanies us on our journey what the population of this little city may be, we are told about 30,000 in the city itself, and about 2,000 in the agricultural estate, and that there are in the town 5,500 building lots of an average size of 20 feet × 130 feet—the minimum space allotted for the purpose being 20 × 100. Noticing the very varied architecture and design which the houses and groups of houses display—some having common gardens and co-operative kitchens—we learn that general observance of street line or harmonious departure from it are the chief points as to house building, over which the municipal authorities exercise control, for, though proper sanitary arrangements are strictly enforced, the fullest measure of individual taste and preference is encouraged.

Walking still toward the outskirts of the town, we come upon "Grand Avenue". This avenue is fully entitled to the name it bears, for it is 420 feet wide, and, forming a belt of green upwards of three miles long, divides that part of the town which lies outside Central Park into two bells. It really constitutes an additional park of 115 acres—a park which is within 240 yards of the furthest removed inhabitant. In this splendid avenue six sites, each of four acres, are occupied by public schools and their surrounding playgrounds and gardens, while other sites are reserved for churches, of such denominations as the religious beliefs of the people may determine, to be erected and maintained out of the funds of the worshippers and their friends. We observe that the houses fronting on Grand Avenue have departed (at least in one of the wards—that of which Fig. 2. 3 is a representation)—from the general plan of concentric rings, and, in order to ensure a longer line of frontage on Grand Avenue, are arranged in crescents—thus also to the eye yet further enlarging the already splendid width of Grand Avenue.

On the outer ring of the town are factories, warehouses, dairies, markets, coal yards, timber yards, etc., all fronting on the circle railway, which encompasses the whole town, and which has sidings connecting it with a main line of railway which passes through the estate. This arrangement enables goods to be loaded direct into trucks from the warehouses and workshops, and so sent by railway to distant markets, or to be taken direct from the trucks into the warehouses or factories; thus not only effecting a very great saving in regard to packing and cartage, and reducing to a minimum loss from breakage, but also, by reducing the traffic on the roads of the town, lessening to a very marked extent the cost of their maintenance. The smoke fiend is kept well within bounds in Garden City; for all machinery is driven by electric energy, with the result that the cost of electricity for lighting and other purposes is greatly reduced.

The refuse of the town is utilized on the agricultural portions of the estate, which are held by various individuals in large farms, small holdings, allotments, cow pastures, etc.; the natural competition of these various methods of agriculture, tested by the willingness of occupiers to offer the highest rent to the municipality, tending to bring about the best system of husbandry, or, what is more probable, the best systems adapted for various purposes. Thus it is easily conceivable that it may prove advantageous to grow wheat in very large fields, involving united action under a capitalist farmer, or by a body of co-operators; while the cultivation of vegetables, fruits, and flowers, which requires closer and more personal care, and more of the artistic and inventive faculty, may possibly be best dealt with by individuals, or by small groups of individuals having a common belief in the efficacy and value of certain dressings, methods of culture, or artificial and natural surroundings.

Words and Expressions

circular ['sə:kjulə] *adj.* 圆形的;循环的
circumference [sə'kʌmfərəns] *n.* 圆周;周围
municipal [mju(:)'nisipəl] *adj.* 市政的;市的;自治区的;内政的
boulevard ['bu:livɑ:d] *n.* 林荫大道
traverse ['trævə(:)s] *v.* 横过;穿过;经过;在……来回移动
ample ['æmpl] *adj.* 大量的;充足的;丰富的
intersect [ˌintə'sekt] *v.* 相交;交叉
arcade [ɑ:'keid] *n.* 拱廊;有拱廊的街道

resort [ri'zɔːt] n. 常去之地；胜地
whilst [wɑilst] conj. 当……的时候；和……同时
deliberation [di͵libə'reiʃən] n. 熟思；从容；商议；考虑
avenue ['ævinjuː] n. 大街；途径；林荫路
converge [kən'vəːdʒ] v. 聚合；集中于一点
allot [ə'lɔt] v. (按份额)分配；分派
denomination [di͵nɔmi'neiʃən] n. 命名；票面金额
frontage ['frʌntidʒ] n. 房子的正面；前方；临街地
crescent ['kresnt] n. 新月；月牙
cartage ['kɑːtidʒ] n. 货车运输；货车运费
breakage ['breikidʒ] n. 破坏；破损；破损量
maintenance ['meintinəns] n. 维护；保持；生活费用
fiend [fiːnd] n. 魔鬼；邪；能手
refuse [ri'fjuːz] n. 废物；垃圾
holding ['həuldiŋ] n. 把握；支持；持有；所有物；财产
municipality [mjuː͵nisi'pæliti] n. 市政当局；自治市
husbandry ['hʌzbəndri] n. 管理；农事；饲养业
efficacy ['efikəsi] n. 功效；效验
dressing ['dresiŋ] n. 穿衣；装饰
ground plan 平面图
public building 公共建筑物；国家建筑物
town hall 市政厅
outer ring 外环
concentric ring 同心环
building lot 建筑房屋用地；建筑地基
street line 街道线
house building 住宅建筑物
sanitary arrangement 卫生设备
to the eye 从表面上看来；当面；公然

Difficult Sentences

① Six magnificent boulevards—each 120 feet wide—traverse the city from centre to circumference, dividing it into six equal parts or wards. In the centre is a circular space containing about five and a half acres, laid out as a beautiful and well-watered garden; and, surrounding this garden, each standing in its own ample grounds, are the larger public buildings—town hall, principal concert and lecture hall, theatre, library, museum, picture-gallery, and hospital.

六条宽阔宏伟的林荫大道——每条大道达到120英尺宽——从城市中心延展到圆形地带的周边,横跨整个城市并将其分割成六个面积相等的区域。卧居城市中心的是一片占地约5.5英亩的圆形的开阔空间,那是一个风景优美、碧波荡漾的花园,环绕花园耸立的是气势宏伟的公共建筑物——市政厅、市音乐厅、市礼堂、剧院、图书馆、博物馆、美术馆和医院。

② The space enclosed by the Crystal Palace is, however, a good deal larger than is required for these purposes, and a considerable part of it is used as a Winter Garden—the whole forming a permanent exhibition of a most attractive character, whilst its circular form brings it near to every dweller in the town—the furthest removed inhabitant being within 600 yards.

然而,被"水晶王宫"环绕的场地如此宽敞开阔,远远超出一个公园所需的面积,并且其中的一大片地被用来当作冬季园林。这一广袤的空间形成了一个展示当地最富魅力的特色景观的绝佳去处,它的圆形构造使城里的居民都能便利地就近去公园,住得最远的居民距公园也不会超过六百码。

③ Passing out of the Crystal Palace on our way to the outer ring of the town, we cross Fifth Avenue—lined, as are all the roads of the town, with trees—fronting which, and looking on to the Crystal Palace, we find a ring of very excellently built houses, each standing in its own ample grounds; and, as we continue our walk, we observe that the houses are for the most part built either in concentric rings, facing the various avenues (as the circular roads are termed), or fronting the boulevards and roads which all converge to the centre of the town.

在穿过"水晶王宫"去城市的外环地带的途中,我们会穿越第五大道,道路两旁绿树成荫,面朝大道并与"水晶王宫"相对的是一片环形的气势恢宏的建筑,每栋建筑都伫立在一片开阔的空地上;继续往前走,我们会发现这些建筑大多要么建在同心环的道路上,面向被称为环形路的道路而立,要么傲临着向市中心辐合汇聚的林荫大道和条条公路。

Phrases and Patterns

1. lay out 展开;设计;布置;划定

   In the heart of the city lays out a modern residential development which is a special tropical landscape design set amongst seven uniquely different swimming pools.
   在城市的中心地带展现的是一片有七处设计独特的泳池的现代住宅开发区的热带都市景观。
   Amongst exotic tropical gardens lays out a five star luxury accommodation center.
   在热带风情花园当中设计有一处五星级的豪华餐饮中心。

2. It is easily conceivable that... 可想而知……

   It is easily conceivable that garden city design is about modern living and has high recreational values that provide a strong compliment to the project investment.
   可想而知,花园城市设计不仅打造新的时尚生活,更能带动市场潜力与高经济休闲产业。
   It is easily conceivable that urban environmental design has become a major theme in city design.
   可想而知,城市环境设计已成为城市设计的一个主要议题。

Questions

1. Which part of the Garden City design most impresses you? Why?
2. Taking into account the Chinese characteristics and reality, talk about your own vision of a Garden City in China.

2.3　The Contemporary City
现代城市

LE CORBUSIER has recounted the origin of his first plan for an ideal city, the "Contemporary City for Three Million People". In 1922 he was asked by the organizers of the Salon d'Automne to prepare an exhibition on urbanism. "What do you mean by urbanism?" Le Corbusier asked the salon's director. "Well, it's a sort of street art," the man replied, "for stores, signs, and the like; it includes such things as the ornamental glass knobs on railings." "Fine", said Le Corbusier, "I shall design a great fountain and behind it place a city for three million people."

This "Just So" story contains at least one element of truth. The 100-square-meter diorama depicting the Contemporary City which he prepared for the salon reflected his own grand conception of urbanism. The Contemporary City was the answer to the social problems which he had raised in the Esprit nouveau articles. If, as he had argued, these problems require for their solution the rebuilding of industrial society, then the urbanist must forsake mere decoration and prepare to undertake "great works"①. His task was to create a complete environment in which man, nature, and the machine would be reconciled. The Contemporary City was Le Corbusier's first systematic attempt to envision such an environment and to put forward the general principles of its design.

The ideas for the Contemporary City can be traced back to sketches Le Corbusier made at La Chaux-de-Fonds in 1914 ~ 1915 while he was working on the Dom-Ino houses. He continued to develop the plans after he moved to Paris, but turned to the ideal city in earnest only after his brick factory had gone bankrupt in the recession of 1921, dragging down with it the Society for Industrial Enterprises. His architectural practice was meager; his small income came almost entirely from the sale of his paintings. Like Howard and Wright, he undertook to plan the society of the future at a time when he was isolated, unheeded, without influence, and certainly without power. Le Corbusier's position sharply contrasts with that of the Bauhaus theorists—Gropius, Mies, Hilberseimer—who shared many of his ideas. Their ties to the Socialist parties encouraged them to think in pragmatic terms. They produced many partial plans but no ideal cities. Le Corbusier, however, could rely only on the inherent persuasiveness of his vision. His plans therefore took the form of a complete alternative society which would take power first in the imagination and then in fact.

The title of this plan, "A Contemporary City for Three Million People", was a proclamation that this was not an exercise in science fiction but "the city for our times." It was, he wrote, "an act of faith in favor of the present." He believed the time had come for a series of "great works" which would sweep away the "leavings of a dead era" and inaugurate the age of "collective spirit" and "civic pride."[2] The decision to build the new city would mean that the "radiant hour of harmony, construction, and enthusiasm" had finally arrived. <u>It would be the crucial act</u> separating the past from the future; it would restore order to industrial society and make the world safe for beauty.

Although the city began in the struggle against the chaotic forces of nature, its highest aim is to reconcile man with these forces. Geometrical order, triumphant, no longer needs to exclude nature as an alien presence; rather, it seeks out the Green City as the necessary counterpart to itself. Similarly, the triumph of the world of administration means that it no longer need engross man's whole life. The triumph or administration is the liberation of man from its clutches, the liberation of man to live another life of individual creativity in the midst of his family.

The Contemporary City is thus a city of leisure as well as order, a city of meditation as well as production. To the man at work, the city is one great organization; after work he sees it from a very different perspective③. His family life exists outside the hierarchy of authority. Le Corbusier designed each apartment to be as private as a monk's cell at Ema. Each is an independent home, a site of abundance and love. Outside is the garden of delights, the Green City, the realm of art and play. The apartments and their surroundings form a coherent environment, a world of individual fulfillment and creation. Le Corbusier's two paths to the sublime meet at the Contemporary City.

Words and Expressions

recount [ri'kaunt] v. 叙述
urbanism ['ə:bə,nizəm] n. 城市规划；都市建筑规划；都市生活方式
ornamental [,ɔ:nə'mentl] adj. 装饰性的；装饰的；装饰用的
railing ['reiliŋ] n. 栏杆；扶手
fountain ['fauntin] n. 泉水；喷泉
diorama [,daiə'rɑ:mə] n. 透视画；西洋景；立体模型
forsake [fə'seik] v. 放弃；抛弃
reconcile ['rekənsail] v. 使和解；使和谐；使顺从
envision [in'viʒən] v. 想象；预想
sketch [sketʃ] n. 略图；草图；概略
meager ['mi:gə(r)] n. 兆
pragmatic [præg'mætik] adj. 实际的；注重实效的
proclamation [,prɔklə'meiʃn] n. 宣布；宣言
inaugurate [i'nɔ:gjureit] v. 举行开幕
civic ['sivik] adj. 市的；市民的；公民的
radiant ['reidjənt] adj. 发光的；辐射的；容光焕发的

harmony ['hɑːməni] n. 协调；融洽
enthusiasm [in'θjuːziæzəm] n. 狂热；热心；积极性；激发热情的事物
chaotic [kei'ɔtik] adj. 混乱的；无秩序的
geometrical [dʒiə'metrikəl] adj. 几何学的；几何的
triumphant [trai'ʌmfənt] adj. 胜利的；成功的；狂欢的
alien ['eiljən] adj. 外国的；相异的；不同的；背道而驰的
engross [in'grəus] v. 吸引；使全神贯注；独占
clutch [klʌtʃ] n. 抓住；攫住
perspective [pə'spektiv] n. 透视（画，画法）；远景；景色
hierarchy ['haiərɑːki] n. 体系［制］；系统；谱系
authority [ɔː'θɔriti] n. 权威；权力；权势
abundance [ə'bʌndəns] n. 丰富；充足；富裕
realm [relm] n. 王国；国土
coherent [kəu'hiərənt] adj. 黏着的；有凝聚力的；互相密合的
individual [ˌindi'vidjuəl] adj. 个人的；个体的；单独的；独特的
fulfillment [ful'filmənt] n. 履行；实行
sublime [sə'blaim] adj. 极度的；完全的；极端的；异常的
Le Corbusier 勒·柯布西耶(1887~1965) (20世纪最重要的建筑师之一)
Salon d'Automne 法国巴黎秋季沙龙
Esprit nouveau《新精神》杂志
La Chaux-de-Fonds 拉乔克斯·德·芳兹职业艺术学院
Dom-Ino house 多米诺住宅
the Society for Industrial Enterprises 军工企业协会
alternative society 替换社会(其文化价值标准完全不同于现存社会秩序的一种社会集团)
collective spirit 集体精神

Difficult Sentences

① This "Just So" story contains at least one element of truth. The 100-square-meter diorama depicting the Contemporary City which he prepared for the salon reflected his own grand conception of urbanism. The Contemporary City was the answer to the social problems which he had raised in the Esprit nouveau articles. If, as he had argued, these problems require for their solution the rebuilding of industrial society, then the urbanist must forsake mere decoration and prepare to undertake "great works."

这个"随口说说便成真"的轶事至少体现了一个事实。这个一百平方米的立体透视图描绘了他为秋季沙龙所准备的现代城市的构思,反映了他对于都市建筑规划的宏伟设想。现代城市理论回答了他在《新精神》杂志里提出的社会问题。如他所说,如果这些问题需要重建工业社会才能解决,那么都市建筑规划必须摆脱仅仅靠装饰取胜的老路,而要准备去承担"更伟大的工作"。

② The title of this plan, "A Contemporary City for Three Million People" was a proclamation that this was not an exercise in science fiction but "the city for our times." It was, he wrote, "an act of faith in favor of the present." He believed the time had come for a series of "great works" which would sweep away the "leavings of a dead era" and inaugurate the age of "collective spirit" and "civic pride."

他的设想方案题为"三百万人口的现代城市",向大家大声宣告这不是一个科幻小说里的故事,而是"我们时代的城市"。他写道:"这是面向现在的信念的体现"。他坚信诞生一系列"伟大的作品"的时代已经到来,旧有时期的建筑必须进行彻底的改造,我们必将迎来"集体精神"和"平民的骄傲"的新时代。

③ The Contemporary City is thus a city of leisure as well as order, a city of meditation as well as production. To the man at work, the city is one great organization; after work he sees it from a very different perspective.

因此,现代城市既是休闲之城又是秩序之城,既是沉思之所又是生产之地。对于劳动者来说城市就是一个庞大的组织,下班之后他就会从全然不同的角度对它加以审视。

Phrases and Patterns

1. be traced back to... 追溯至……
   The general outlook upon cities and the prospects for urban life can be traced back to the last quarter of the twentieth century.
   关于城市的规划和都市生活的发展前景的总体观点可以追溯至20世纪的70、80年代。
   Postmodern design and planning, traced back to the 1960s, incorportes the restoration and re-creation of traditional "classical" urban vlues, which includes the restoration of older urban fabric, the re-habilitation to new uses, and creation of new spaces that express traditional visions with modern technologies and materials.
   追溯至20世纪60年代的后现代主义的设计和规划,将恢复和再造传统的"经典"都市价值观结合起来,其中包括恢复旧有的城市结构,以新的用途创造新的空间,用现代的技术和材料表达传统的梦想。

2. It would be the crucial act doing/to do sth. ……将成为关键之举
   It would be the crucial act for urbanists to overcome the ills of industrialization itself, emphasizing construction and the natural antagonism and mutual accommodation as a building inhabited cultural arts of the U.S. total containers.
   对于都市建筑规划者来说,对工业化本身的弊病进行克服、强调建筑与自然对立中的相互包容和建筑作为人类居住文化总容器的艺术之美,将成为关键之举。
   It would be the crucial act for modern architects to design cities that would promote industrial efficiency and as well, in the face of massive housing shortages, standardize dwelling types capable of mass production.
   对于现代建筑师来说,关键的一步是要设计促进工业效率的城市,并且在面临大规模的住房短缺问题时,使具有大批量生产能力的住宅类型标准化。

Questions

1. In what aspects is Le Corbusier different from the Bauhaus designers?
2. Sum up Le Corbusier's general principles of his design embodied in the plan "A Contemporary City for Three Million People".
3. What are Le Corbusier's two paths?

2.4 The Plan of the Contemporary City
现代城市规划

The basic principles we must follow are these:
(1) We must de-congest the centers of our cities.
(2) We must augment their density.
(3) We must increase the means for getting about.
(4) We must increase parks and open spaces.

At the very centre we have the STATION with its landing stage for aero-taxis.

Running north and south, and east and west, we have the MAIN ARTERIES for fast traffic, forming elevated roadways 120 feet wide.

At the base of the sky-scrapers and all round them we have a great open space 2,400 yards by 1,500 yards, giving an area of 3,600,000 square yards, and occupied by gardens, parks and avenues. In these parks, at the foot of and round the skyscrapers, would be the restaurants and cafes, the luxury shops, housed in buildings with receding terraces: here too would be the theatres, halls and so on; and here the parking places or garage shelters[①].

The sky-scrapers are designed purely for business purposes.

On the left we have the great public buildings, the museums, the municipal and administrative offices. Still further on the left we have the "Park" (which is available for further logical development of the heart of the city).

On the right, and traversed by one of the arms of the main arterial roads, we have the warehouses, and the industrial quarters with their goods stations.

All round the city is the *protected zone* of woods and green fields.

Further beyond are the *garden cities*, forming a wide encircling band.

Then, right in the midst of all these, we have the *Central Station*, made up of the following elements:

(a) The landing-platform; forming an aerodrome of 200,000 square yards in area.

(b) The entresol or mezzanine; at this level are the raised tracks for fast motor traffic: the only crossing being gyratory.

(c) The ground floor where are the entrance halls and booking offices for the tubes, suburban, main line and air traffic.

(d) The "basement": here are the tubes which serve the city and the main arteries.

(e) The "sub-basement": here are the suburban lines running on a one-way loop.

(f) The "sub-sub-basement": here are the main lines (going north, south, east and west).

Here we have twenty-four sky-scrapers capable each of housing 10,000 to 50,000 employees; this is the business and hotel section, etc., and accounts for 400,000 to 600,000 inhabitants.

The residential blocks, of the two main types already mentioned, account for a further 600,000 inhabitants.

The garden cities give us a further 2,000,000 inhabitants, or more.

In the great central open space are the cafes, restaurants, luxury shops, halls of various kinds, a magnificent forum descending by stages down to the immense parks surrounding it, the whole arrangement providing a spectacle of order and vitality②.

Words and Expressions

augment [ɔːgˈment] v. 增大；增加
density [ˈdensiti] n. 浓度；密度
skyscraper [ˈskaiskreipə(r)] n. 摩天大楼
recede [riˈsiːd] v. 退回；后退；向后倾斜
terrace [ˈterəs] n. 柱廊；平屋顶
warehouse [ˈwɛəhaus] n. 仓库；货栈
aerodrome [ˈɛərədrəum] n. 飞机场；航空站
entresol [ˈɔntrəsɔl] n. 夹层；阁楼；半楼[层]
mezzanine [ˈmezəniːn] n. (尤指介于一层与二层之间的)中层楼
track [træk] n. 轨道；车辙
crossing [ˈkrɔsiŋ] n. 交叉点；十字路口；人行横道
gyratory [ˈdʒaiərətəri] adj. 旋转的
tube [ˈtjuːb] n. 隧道；地下铁道
suburban [səˈbəːbən] adj. 郊区的；在城郊的
basement [ˈbeismənt] n. 底；基层；地下室
sub-basement [ˈsʌbˌbeismənt] n. 地下室以下的地下室(建筑物的最底层)
loop [luːp] n. 让车道；环道
vitality [vaiˈtæliti] n. 生命力；活力；生气；生动性
get about 走动；旅行
open space 露天场所；空地(特指城市中没有建筑物的空地)
landing stage 栈桥
main artery 主要干线
fast traffic 快速运输
elevated roadway 高架车道
parking place 停车场
industrial quarter 工业区
goods station 货运站；货运码头
protected zone 防护带；被保护区域

green fields 绿色场;绿地
garden city 花园城市;田园城市
encircling band 环形带
landing platform 起降平台
ground floor 第一层
entrance hall 门廊
booking office 售票处
main line 干线;大静脉
air traffic 空中交通
suburban line 郊区线路
one-way 单行道的
business section 商业区
residential block 住宅区

Difficult Sentences

① In these parks, at the foot of and round the skyscrapers, would be the restaurants and cafes, the luxury shops, housed in buildings with receding terraces: here too would be the theatres, halls and so on; and here the parking places or garage shelters.
在摩天大楼的脚下及周边地带,在这些公园之中,将建造餐馆、咖啡屋、豪华的店铺、有梯形看台的室内剧院等,还会设有停车场或车库。

② In the great central open space are the cafes, restaurants, luxury shops, halls of various kinds, a magnificent forum descending by stages down to the immense parks surrounding it, the whole arrangement providing a spectacle of order and vitality.
位于开阔的中心绿地的是咖啡馆、餐馆、豪华的店铺,各种功能的厅堂,还有一个气势恢宏的报告礼堂,门前的台阶一直延伸到周围的公园,整体设计壮观有序,充满生机和活力。

Phrases and Patterns

1. The basic principles we must follow are these: 我们要遵循以下几种

基本原则：

For modern designers and planners, the basic principles we must follow are these: Technology Serves Humans; Design is not Art; The Experience Belongs to the User; Great Design is Invisible; Simplicity is the Ultimate Sophistication.

对于现代设计者和规划者来说,我们要遵循以下几种基本原则:技术为人民服务;设计非艺术;体验属于用户;伟大的设计是无形的;简洁是终极哲学。

As a concrete approach to create the urban shape and spatial environment, the basic principles we must follow in urban design are "top down" and "bottom up" approaches.

作为一种塑造城市形态和空间环境的具体方法,我们在城市设计中必须要遵循的原则应当是"自上而下"和"自下而上"的结合。

2. be designed purely for business purposes 专门设计用于商业用途

Such street features and street landscapes are designed purely for business purposes.

这样的街道特色和风貌的设计纯粹是出于商业角度的考虑。

Based on Australian tropical style, the garden, which compliments the sensational architecture of the new Haiwan Bridge, is designed not purely for business purposes.

以澳大利亚热带风貌为规划基调,此公园为新海滨大桥带来一气呵成的壮丽景色,在设计上并不单纯考虑商业目的。

Questions

1. How does these principles create a complete environment in which man, nature, and the machine would be reconciled?
2. Can you put the description in the reading passage into cartography?

2.5 Plan Voisin
伏瓦生规划

The Contemporary City had no history. It sprang full-grown from one man's imagination. In planning his ideal city, Le Corbusier had absolute freedom to create the rules of urban design and to apply them without exception. Within his realm he was, as he put it, an absolute sovereign who could "organize the world on his drawing board." No intractable subjects—not even time itself—disturbed his perfect symmetries.

When he attempted to move from theory to practice he was immediately dethroned. He was forced to confront the limitations which particular sites and particular societies imposed. Le Corbusier dealt effectively with nature's constraints; his most imaginative plans, e. g., those for Algiers and Rio de Janeiro, were brilliant applications of his principles to challenging terrains. His responses to social limitations were less serene. He became obsessed with the many obstacles to large-scale planning: the laws of property that divided the city into thousands of tiny independent holdings; the fragmentation of governmental authority; the forms that the city of the past had imposed on the present; the citizens who clung to their old cities and refused to make way for the "era of great works."

Although most of Le Corbusier's work from the 1920s has mellowed into respectability, the Plan Voisin still arouses the same horror it did at its original showing. It has to bear not only the burden of its own audacity but also its status as the archetype for so many disastrous plans that others subsequently carried out[①]. For better or worse, the concepts embodied in the Plan Voisin represent Le Corbusier's contribution to the practice of urban planning. It is important, therefore, to understand his reasons for prescribing such drastic change.

First, the plan addresses itself to the central city because Le Corbusier believed that the center was the heart of the problem. Undeveloped areas at the outskirts of old cities might seem more appropriate locales for the new order he wished to establish, but Le Corbusier was wary of creating regions that lacked a clear focus. He had great respect for the idea of the center, the one area consecrated by history and geography to be the capital of a region or nation. This center must be attacked head on, for victory there would decide the issue.

The great city commands everything: peace, war, work. The great cities are the spiritual workshops where the work of the world is turned out.

The solutions found in the great city are those which will be followed in the provinces: fashions, styles, intellectual movements, technology. This is why, once the urbanization of the great city has been achieved, the whole country will at once be won.

Le Corbusier was thus committed to transforming the area most resistant to change, the place where population was greatest, property values highest, and tradition most firmly entrenched. He was committed, moreover, not merely to modifying the center but to destroying its network of narrow streets, knocking down almost all the buildings that lined them, opening vast spaces crisscrossed by superhighways in the middle of Paris, and erecting freestanding skyscrapers on a scale that dwarfed all other structures in the city[②]. This dramatic rending of the older urban texture has convinced many critics that Le Corbusier was a misdirected formalist who understood nothing of the real sources of urban beauty and urban vitality. His attempt to "destroy" the street—and, consequently, urban streetlife—lies at the heart of the critics' case[③]. Here, however, it is important to distinguish between the Plan Voisin and subsequent projects which superficially resemble it. Le Corbusier, to be sure, wanted to destroy the street—but only to save it.

He was well aware of the value of what he called the "Balzacian drama" of urban life. "There is so much to enjoy in the street if we know how to see it; it is better than the theater, better than a novel: the faces and the emotions." Yet he believed that the traditional "corridor street" had become an impossible setting for the urban drama. These dark canyons clogged with heavy traffic (with was still an offensive novelty in the 1920s)—these "streets without Joy," as he called them— could neither "create in us the joy which is the effect of architecture, nor the pride which is the effect of order; nor the spirit of enterprise which is at home in large spaces... Only pity and commiseration at the shock of seeing other people's faces and the hard labor of the lives."

In the age of the automobile and the skyscraper, the corridor street had become a "dead organ" incapable of fulfilling its function. In the Plan Voisin, Le Corbusier analyzed this function into two parts, transportation and sociability, and created two new urban forms to deal with them. Transportation is provided by the superhighways, avenues of unobstructed motion. And, in the midst of the skyscrapers, rising from the parks, are elevated pedestrian malls, "streets of repose" wholly separate from automobile traffic, "tucked in among the foliage of the trees." These "streets of repose" have three levels. The first is a broad mall punctuated by fountains and sidewalk cafes; gently sloping ramps lead to two upper promenades which are lined with an array of shops, clubs, and restaurants. At the top level, as Le Corbusier enthusiastically pictured the scene, "one is almost on top of the greenery: one sees a sea of trees; and here and there are those majestic crystals, pure prisms, limpid and gigantic [the skyscrapers]. Majesty, serenity, joy." These "gardens of Semiramis" in the middle of Paris would become the most attractive district for shopping and strolling—the counterparts in the realm of leisure to the crystalline towers of administration[④].

Finally, to those who charged that he was a barbarian whose plan was a futurist assault on Paris and her heritage, Le Corbusier replied that his plan was "wholly in accord with tradition." The monuments of the past would be saved from destruction and preserved like museum pieces in the parks that surround the skyscrapers. More importantly, he could consider himself a "traditionalist" because tradition for him meant a series of revolutionary breaks with custom. The Gothic of Notre-Dame was a startling repudiation of Romanesque; the Pont Neuf discarded the Gothic. Consciousness unfolds in history; no one can stop it without exalting imitation and risking decay. For Le Corbusier, being true to the monuments of the past meant continuing in their revolutionary spirit. "At certain times man begins again to create; and those are the happy times." The Plan Voisin announced that a new era was at hand; only a sterile antiquarianism could deny it. "In the name of the past: the present."

He believed that the Plan Voisin was particularly appropriate to the urban planning traditions of Paris. The men he admired—Louis XIV and his Place Vendôme and Invalides, Napoleon and his rue de Rivoli, above all Baron Haussmann—were those who tried to bring a measure of geometrical order to Paris. The Plan Voisin would be the necessary sequel to this tradition, bringing the quest for order into the age of the automobile and the skyscraper.

Words and Expressions

full-grown ['fʊl'grəʊn] adj. 生长完全的；发育完全的
sovereign ['sɔvrin] n. 统治者；主权者
intractable [in'træktəbl] adj. 难驾驭的；难管理的；难处理的；难加工的
symmetry ['simitri] n. 对称；调和；匀称美
dethrone [di'θrəʊn] v. 撵走；推翻权力地位
Algiers [æl'dʒiəz] n. 阿尔及尔（阿尔及利亚首都）

Rio de Janeiro ['ri(ː)əudədʒə'niərəu] n. 里约热内卢(巴西港市, 州名)
terrain ['terein] n. 地域; 地带; 地势; 地形
serene [si'riːn] adj. 宁静的; 没有风波的
fragmentation [ˌfrægmen'teiʃən] n. 破碎; 分裂
mellow ['meləu] v. 软化
respectability [rispektə'biləti] n. 可尊敬之人或物; 值得尊敬之性质或状态
audacity [ɔː'dæsiti] n. 大胆; 胆识
archetype ['ɑːkitɑip] n. 原始模型; 典型
prescribe [pris'krɑib] v. 指示; 规定; 建议
drastic ['dræstik] adj. 激烈的; 猛烈的
outskirts ['ɑutskɛːts] n. 边界; (尤指)市郊
locale [ləu'kɑːl] n. (事故等发生的)现场; 地点; 场所
consecrate ['kɔnsikreit] v. 把……供祭祀用; 奉献, 使神圣
province ['prɔvins] n. [pl.] 地区, 乡间; (首都或大城市以外的)地方
urbanization ['əːbənɑizeiʃən] n. 使具有城市特点; 城市化
entrench [in'trentʃ] v. 使盘踞; 固守; 牢固树立; 使处于有利地位
crisscross ['kriskrɔs] v. 交错; 交叉
freestanding ['friːstændiŋ] adj. 独立式的; 不需依靠支撑物的
formalist ['fɔːməlist] n. 形式主义者
Balzacian [bæl'zeiʃən] adj. (法国小说家)巴尔扎克的; 巴尔扎克风格的
canyon ['kænjən] n. 峡(谷)
commiseration [kəˌmizə'reiʃən] n. 同情
sociability [ˌsəuʃə'biliti] n. 交际活动
unobstructed ['ʌnəb'strʌktid] adj. 无阻的; 不受阻拦的
repose [ri'pəuz] n. 休息; 睡眠; 静止
foliage ['fəuliidʒ] n. 树叶; 植物
punctuate ['pʌŋktjueit] v. 加标点于; 不时打断
sloping ['sləupiŋ] adj. 倾斜的; 有坡度的
ramp [ræmp] n. 坡道; 斜坡
promenade [ˌprɔmi'nɑːd] n. 散步的场所
greenery ['griːnəri] n. 温室; 草木
majestic [mə'dʒestik] adj. 宏伟的; 庄严的
crystal ['kristl] n. 水晶; 水晶饰品

prism ['prizəm] n. 棱镜；棱柱
limpid ['limpid] adj. 清澈的；透明的
gigantic [dʒai'gæntik] adj. 巨人般的；巨大的
Semiramis [se'mirəmis] n. 塞米勒米斯(古代传说中的亚述女王)
crystalline ['kristəlain] adj. 水晶的
barbarian [bɑː'bɛəriən] adj. 野蛮(人)的；未开化的；不文明的
Notre-Dame [ˌnəutrə'dɑːm] n. [法](巴黎)圣母院
repudiation [riˌpjuːdi'eiʃən] n. 批判
Romanesque [ˌrəumə'nesk] n. 罗马式
antiquarianism ['ænti'kwɛəriənizəm] n. 古物研究；好古癖
Vendôme ['vendəm] n. 巴黎的凡登广场
Invalides [in'vælidis] n. 巴黎荣军院；残老军人院
sequel ['siːkwəl] n. 继续；后续；续集[篇]；下篇
Plan Voisin "伏瓦生规划"方案(柯布西耶为巴黎市中心区改建提出的规划方案)
drawing board 制图板
large-scale 大规模的；大比例尺的；大范围的
the spirit of enterprise 进取精神
pedestrian mall 步行街；人行林荫路
an array of 一排；一群；一批
Pont Neuf 巴黎新桥(塞纳河上所有桥梁中最为古老、最长的桥)
rue de Rivoli 巴黎的里沃黎街
Baron Haussmann 豪斯曼男爵(拿破仑三世时期的法国城市设计师)

Difficult Sentences

① Although most of Le Corbusier's work from the 1920s has mellowed into respectability, the Plan Voisin still arouses the same horror it did at its original showing. It has to bear not only the burden of its own audacity but also its status as the archetype for so many disastrous plans that others subsequently carried out.
虽然柯布西耶20世纪20年代时期的大部分设计作品都沦为空想，只能供人们神而往之，但是他的"伏瓦生规划"方案一如当时

横空出世时所引起的石破天惊的效应,现在仍然会激起人们同样的惊骇。它不仅要承担大胆的想象的后果,而且由于成为人们标榜的模型而不得不为后来有些人将其付诸实践却又惨遭失败的教训买单。

② Le Corbusier was thus committed to transforming the area most resistant to change, the place where population was greatest, property values highest, and tradition most firmly entrenched. He was committed, moreover, not merely to modifying the center but to destroying its network of narrow streets, knocking down almost all the buildings that lined them, opening vast spaces crisscrossed by superhighways in the middle of Paris, and erecting freestanding skyscrapers on a scale that dwarfed all other structures in the city.

因此,柯布西耶致力于变革最不情愿改变的地域,也就是人口最为密集、财产价值最为高昂、传统思想最为根深蒂固的地方。此外,他还不满足于仅仅将市中心改建,而是一心彻底摧毁原有的狭窄的街道,拆除道路两旁的建筑,在巴黎的市中心扩大城市绿地,棋盘式高速公路穿越整个城市的中心,修建独立的"一览众山小"的摩天办公大楼。

③ This dramatic rending of the older urban texture has convinced many critics that Le Corbusier was a misdirected formalist who understood nothing of the real sources of urban beauty and urban vitality. His attempt to "destroy" the street—and, consequently, urban streetlife—lies at the heart of the critics' case.

对旧有城市结构的大刀阔斧的解体使很多评论界人士认为,柯布西耶是一个辨不清方向的形式主义者,根本不懂得什么是真正的城市之美,什么是城市的生命力所在。因此,他想摧毁街道即城市的生命线的举动成为众多批评者的众矢之的。

④ These "streets of repose" have three levels. The first is a broad mall punctuated by fountains and sidewalk cafes; gently sloping ramps lead to two upper promenades which are lined with an array of shops, clubs, and restaurants. At the top level, as Le Corbusier enthusiastically pictured the scene, "one is almost on top of the greenery: one sees a sea of trees; and here and there are those majestic crystals, pure prisms, limpid and gigantic [the skyscrapers] Majesty, serenity, joy." These "gardens of Semiramis" in the middle of Paris would become the most attractive district for shopping and strolling—the counterparts in the realm of leisure to the crystalline towers of administration.

这些"游憩街道"分为三层。第一层是有喷泉和人行便道的广阔的林荫路,其缓坡一直通往两个位于上层的公众散步场所,那里两边是一家家的店铺、俱乐部和餐馆。柯布西耶充满热情地描述到,位于顶层的是"几乎傍依于一片绿意之中,满眼尽是一排排青青的树篱,随处都是壮丽的晶体建筑、璀璨的玻璃柱体,透明的、宏大的摩天大厦张扬着辉煌、恬静与欢乐。"这些位于巴黎市中心的"塞米勒米斯花园"将会成为人们购物与散步的首选之所,与周围的玻璃行政办公大楼遥相呼应,形成一个休闲的好去处。

Phrases and Patterns

1. address to 着手;从事;对付

   Transformation of a 2,000 hec site into a complex of thirteen wetlands addresses itself to establish habitat for migrating birds.

   将广达2,000公顷的地域面积改造成13处湿地,目的是为迁移过境的鸟类提供栖息之地。

   Our extensive experience in locating, preparing and shipping plants in many sizes and volume and landscape materials addresses itself to meet exacting quarantine and quality requirements of the nation.

   我们能够提供相关指定的植物,安排运输及采购包含各型植物材积以及景观与土壤等要求,以符合并提供各国家检疫的要求。

2. be committed to 投入;专心致志于

   In the artistic theory, the Bauhaus School was committed to a new approach to architecture that incorporated artistic design, craftsmanship, and modern machine technology.

从艺术理论上来讲,包豪斯流派致力于一种建筑新方法,将艺术设计、工匠技能和现代的机械技术有效地结合起来。

To welcome the 29th Summer Olympics in 2008, to build the urban cultural landscape, Beijing Planning Committee, entrusted by Beijing People's Municipal Government, was committed to an overall plan of Beijing Olympic Park Environmental Facilities Designs Collection.

为了迎接2008年第29届奥运会,为了筹建富有文化气息的城市景观,在北京市人民政府的授权下,北京市规划委员会全力向全社会征集北京奥林匹克公园环境设施设计方案。

Questions

1. When Le Corbusier attempted to apply his "Plan Voisin" to practice, what challenges was he confronted with?
2. How was most of Le Corbusier's work from the 1920s accepted by the people at that time?
3. What are the contributions of Le Corbusier's "Plan Voisin"?
4. Why did Le Corbusier put stress on cities but not suburbs in his plan?

2.6 The Radiant City
光明城市

The Radiant City retained the most important principle of the Contemporary City: the juxtaposition of a collective realm of order and administration with an individualistic realm of family life and participation[①]. This juxtaposition became the key to Le Corbusier's attempt to resolve the syndicalist dilemma of authority and participation. Both elements of the doctrine receive intense expression in their respective spheres. Harmony is in the structure of the whole city and in the complete life of its citizens.

The Radiant City was a more daring and difficult synthesis than the Contemporary City. In his effort to realize the contradictory elements of syndicalism, Le Corbusier made the Radiant City at once more authoritarian and more libertarian than its predecessor②. Within the sphere of collective life, authority has become absolute. The Contemporary City had lacked any single power to regulate all the separate private corporations which accomplished the essential work of society; Le Corbusier had then believed that the invisible hand of free competition would create the most efficient coordination. The Great Depression robbed him of his faith. He now held that organization must extend beyond the large corporations. They had rationalized their own organizations, but the economy as a whole remained wasteful, anarchic, irrational. The planned allocation of manpower and resources which had taken place within each corporation must now be accomplished for society. In the Radiant City every aspect of productive life is administered from above according to one plan. This plan replaces the marketplace with total administration; experts match society's needs to its productive capacities.

The preordained harmony which Le Corbusier had called for in urban reconstruction would now be imposed on all productive life. The great works of construction would become only one element in the plan. This was a crucial extension of the concept of planning. Ebenezer Howard and Frank Lloyd Wright had believed that once the environment had been designed, the sources of disorder in society would be minimized and individuals could be left to pursue their own initiatives. This belief rested on a faith in a "natural economic order," a faith which Le Corbusier no longer shared. He confronted a world threatened by chaos and collapse. It seemed that only discipline could create the order he sought so ardently. Coordination must become conscious and total. Above all, society needed authority and a plan.

"Plans are not political," Le Corbusier wrote. The plan's complex provisions, covering every aspect of production, distribution, and construction, represent a necessary and objective ordering of society. The plan is necessary because the Machine Age requires conscious control. It is objective because the Machine Age imposes essentially the same discipline on all societies. Planning involves the rational mastery of industrial process and the application of that mastery to the specific conditions of each nation. The plan is a "rational and lyric monument" to man's capacity to organize.

The plan is formulated by an elite of experts detached from all social pressure. They work "outside the fevers of mayors' and prefects' offices," away from the "cries of electors and the cries of victims." Their plans are "established serenely, lucidly. They take account only of human truths." In the planner's formulations, "the motive forces of a civilization pass from the subjective realm of consciousness to the objective realm of facts." His plans are "just, long-term, established on the realities of the century, imagined by a creative passion."

This plan for Le Corbusier was more than a collection of statistics and instructions; it was a social work of art. <u>It brought to consciousness the complex yet satisfying harmonies of an orderly productive world.</u> It was the score for the great industrial orchestra. The plan summed up the unity that underlay the division of labor in society; it expressed the full range of exchange and cooperation which is necessary to an advanced economy[③].

The centers of life in the Radiant City are the great highrise apartment blocks, which Le Corbusier calls "Unites." These structures, each of which is a neighborhood with 2,700 residents, mark the culmination of the principles of housing that he had been expounding since the Dom-Inos of 1914. Like the Dom-Ino house, the Unite represents the application of mass-production techniques; but where the

Dom-Ino represents the principle in its most basic form, the Unite is a masterful expression of scale, complexity, and sophistication④. The disappointments of the 1920s and the upheavals of the 1930s had only strengthened Le Corbusier in his faith that a great new age of the machine was about to dawn. In the plans for the Unite he realized that promise of a collective beauty which had been his aim in the Dom-Ino design; he achieved a collective grandeur which the Dom-Ino houses had only hinted at; and finally, he foresaw for all the residents of the Unite a freedom and abundance beyond even that which he had planned for the elite of the Contemporary City. The apartments in the Unite are not assigned on the basis of a worker's position in the industrial hierarchy but according to the size of his family and their needs. In designing these apartments, Le Corbusier remarked that he "thought neither of rich nor of poor but of man." He wanted to get away both from the concept of luxury housing, in which the wasteful consumption of space becomes a sign of status, and from the concept of Existenzminimum, the design of workers' housing based on the absolute hygienic minimums. He believed that housing could be made to the "human scale," right in its proportions for everyone, neither cramped nor wasteful. No one would want anything larger nor get anything smaller.

Words and Expressions

juxtaposition [ˌdʒʌkstəpə'ziʃən] n. 并置;并列;邻近;毗连
syndicalist ['sindiklist] n. 工会组织主义者;工团主义者
sphere [sfiə] n. (活动)范围;(研究)领域
synthesis ['sinθisis] n. 综合;合成
authoritarian [ɔːˌθɔri'tɛəriən] adj. 权力主义的;独裁主义的
libertarian [ˌlibə'tɛəriən] adj. 自由意志论者的;鼓吹思想和行动自由的
predecessor ['priːˌdisesə] n. 前任[辈];祖先
coordination [kəuˌɔːdi'neiʃən] n. 同等;同位;对等;协调
anarchic [æ'nɑːkik] adj. 无政府主义的;无法无天的

marketplace ['mɑˌkit'pleis] n. 市场
preordain ['priˌɔː'dein] v. 命中注定；预先规定
reconstruction ['riːkən'strʌkʃən] n. 重建；改造；翻修
elite [eɪ'liːt] n. 精英；精华；中坚
prefect ['priːfekt] n. (古罗马的)行政长官；高级文武官员；(法国的)省长
elector [i'lektə(r)] n. 选举者；有选举权的人
lucidly ['luːsidli] adv. 清透地；透明地
formulation [ˌfɔːmju'leiʃən] n. 有系统而确切地陈述或说明；设计；规划
underlay ['ʌndə'lei] v. 铺在……的下面；从下面支撑[垫起]
highrise ['hɑirɑiz] adj. 高耸的
culmination [kʌlmi'neiʃ(ə)n] n. 巅峰；最高点
grandeur ['grændʒə] n. 伟大；高贵；庄严；富丽堂皇
hygienic [hɑi'dʒiːnik] adj. 卫生的；保健的；清洁的
cramped [kræmpt] adj. 狭窄的；局促的；难辨认的
The Radiant City "光明城市"理论
total administration 总体管理
productive capacity 生产能力
Ebenezer Howard 埃比尼泽·霍华德(1850～1928)(20世纪英国著名社会活动家、城市学家、风景规划与设计师，"花园城市"之父，英国"田园城市"运动创始人)
Frank Lloyd Wright 弗兰克·劳埃德·赖特(1869～1959)，美国建筑师
the Machine Age 机器时代(介于一战与二战之间的工业文明时代)
industrial process 工业生产过程
motive forces 动力
division of labor 劳动力的分工
full range 全范围
apartment block 公寓楼
mass-production 大量生产
absolute minimum 绝对极小值

Difficult Sentences

① The Radiant City retained the most important principle of the Contemporary City: the juxtaposition of a collective realm of order and administration with an individualistic realm of family life and participation.

光明城理论保持了现代城市构想中最重要的原则:让充斥着秩序和管理的集体王国与以家庭生活和分享为特征的个人空间完美地结合。

② The Radiant City was a more daring and difficult synthesis than the Contemporary City. In his effort to realize the contradictory elements of syndicalism, Le Corbusier made the Radiant City at once more authoritarian and more libertarian than its predecessor.

光明城理论比现代城市理论更为大胆、更加难以实现。为了努力实现与辛迪加斯特中相互抵触的基本要素,柯布西耶使光明城理论在创设之初就比现代城市理论更加自治、更加强调自由意志。

③ This plan for Le Corbusier was more than a collection of statistics and instructions; it was a social work of art. It brought to consciousness the complex yet satisfying harmonies of an orderly productive world. It was the score for the great industrial orchestra. The plan summed up the unity that underlay the division of labor in society; it expressed the full range of exchange and cooperation which is necessary to an advanced economy.

柯布西耶的这个计划不仅仅是数字和规程的组合,而是一个社会艺术品。它使人们了解了富有生产力的秩序社会中的复杂多元的却又令人满意的和谐,它是伟大的工业交响乐的华美乐谱。这个计划概括了社会劳动分工背后的和谐统一,表达了发达经济所必备的全方位交流与合作。

④ Like the Dom-Ino house, the Unite represents the application of mass-production techniques; but where the Dom-Ino represents the principle in its most basic form, the Unite is a masterful expression of scale, complexity, and sophistication.

像多米诺住宅一样,光明城的建筑体现了大批量生产技术的应用,不同的是多米诺住宅是对其最基本的展现,而光明城的建筑则是其规模性、复杂性和精密性更精彩的表达。

Phrases and Patterns

1. This was a crucial extension of the concept of... 这是对……概念的重要延伸

    The Radiant City is a crucial extension of Le Corbusier's utopian perspective, which had much in common with the Contemporary City—clearance of the historic cityscape and rebuilding utilizing modern methods of production.

    光明城市是柯布西耶乌托邦思想的重要延伸,与现代城市有异曲同工之处,都是提倡拆除旧有的城市建筑,运用现代生产理念重建城市。

    Urban Planning Play is about the imagination of fantasized space. It is a crucial extension of the concept of mental maps, we might say that only the child most to have to the future city plan critique right.

    城市计划游戏是关于人们对幻想空间的想象,是心灵地图概念的重要延伸,也许可以说只有儿童才最具有对未来城市计划批判的发言权。

2. It brought sth. to consciousness 使某事为人所知

    The vertical street, the skyscraper, the death of the street, and a catering section in the basement in each apartment building brought Le Corbusier's daring notions into consciousness by the experts of that age.

    互相垂直交叉的街道、摩天大楼、旧有街道的颠覆、每幢公寓大楼地下室中的娱乐餐饮中心,这一切都使当时的专家们了解了柯布西耶的大胆创意。

    Through the child, the artist and the art educator's interaction, the activity of "Mental Maps and Urban Planning Play" has brought developing images of utopia city to people's consciousness.

    "心灵地图和城市计划游戏"通过儿童与美术教育者、艺术家的互动活动,使人们对关于乌托邦式城市的发展映象问题有了一定的了解。

Questions

1. What kind of balance and harmony did Le Corbusier attempt to achieve in the theory of Radiant City?
2. In regulating corporation and achieving coordination, how is the Radiant City different from the Contemporary City?
3. How did Le Corbusier refute the notion that "planning is natural economic order"?
4. Compared to the Dom-Ino house, what advantages does the Radiant City have?

2.7　Broadacre City
广亩城市

A good plan is the beginning and the end, because every good plan is organic. That means that its development in all directions is inherent and inevitable.

Frank Lloyd Wright, "In the Cause of Architecture"

In the late 1920s, Wright expanded his plan for a new Usonian city until it became a complete alternative society—Broadacre City. He read widely in social theory and economics, seeking the proper form for all the institutions of the new civilization. The ideal city was a useful intellectual tool; it enabled him to show the workings of government, education, religion, the economy, and the home as integral parts of the total environment he wished to create. The Great Depression gave an added urgency to his work and provided him with the enforced leisure to pursue it[①]. The stock-market crash of 1929 strengthened his conviction that the nation needed a radical change both in its physical and in its economic organization. Wright first advanced a summary of his plan in the Kahn Lectures he delivered at Princeton University in 1930. The complete plan was expounded in a book, The *Disappearing City*, published in 1932.

Wright's book depicted a time when the great urban centers were not merely "disappearing"; they had already ceased to exist. This, Wright believed, was inevitable. In the age of the automobile and the telephone the great cities were doomed: they were "no longer modern." The expensive concentration of people was merely wasteful when modern means of communication could overcome distance. Nor was there any further need for the large, centralized organizations which were based in the cities. Their functions could be accomplished far more economically in decentralized units spread over the countryside.

Wright gave little attention to the mechanics of this process. He was convinced that the big city was as obsolete as the horse-and-carriage, and therefore destined to be replaced by something better. Like so many other Americans of his time, Wright was fascinated by the automobile, convinced of its potential to revolutionize modern life and blind to its limitations[2]. He assumed that modern man had an inherent right to own a car and to burn as much gasoline in driving it as he desired. He knew only that the automobile had created the possibility of new communities based on a new mastery of time and space. Thus, the only questions were: what form would these communities take, and what opportunities for a new American civilization did they offer?

Wright's essential insight was that decentralization, if taken to its logical extreme, could create the material conditions for a nation of independent farmers and proprietors. If properly planned, cities could spread over the countryside and still not lose their cohesion or efficiency. The diffusion of population would create conditions for the universal ownership of land. The world of concentrated wealth and power would be replaced by one in which the means of production would be widely held③. The most advanced technology thus pointed the way for a revival of the democratic hopes of the eighteenth century: Edison and Ford would resurrect Jefferson. The individuality which Wright had been preaching would have its base in the very structure of the country. A society of proprietors, Wright believed, was a society of independent men—a democracy. "When every man, woman, and child," he proclaimed, "may be born to put his feet on his own acres, then democracy will have been realized."

Broadacre City was thus a juxtaposition of the past and the future: the ideal of Jeffersonian democracy given new meaning in terms of the technology of the future. This hybrid provided the standards of efficiency and humanity against which Wright judged the cities of the present and, not surprisingly, found them wanting④. "To look at the plan of any great city is to look at the cross-section of some fibrous tumor," he remarked. Wright's critique of the modern city was often intemperate in tone, and occasionally incoherent in substance.

Words and Expressions

organic [ɔː'gænik] adj. 有组织的;有系统的
decentralized [diː'sentrəlaizd] adj. 分散的
mechanics [mi'kæniks] n. 结构;构成法;技巧
proprietor [prə'praiətə] n. 所有者;业主
revival [ri'vaivəl] n. 苏醒;更[再]生,复活[兴];再流行
resurrect [ˌrezə'rekt] v. 使复活;复兴
hybrid ['haibrid] n. 混合;融合
cross-section ['krɔs'sekʃən] n. 横截[断]面;剖面图
fibrous ['faibrəs] adj. 纤维状的;坚韧的
tumor ['tjuːmə(r)] n. 肿块;肿瘤
critique [kri'tiːk] n. 批评;批判;评论;鉴定
intemperate [in'tempərit] adj. 过度的;激烈的
broadacre city 广亩城市(美国建筑帅 F. L. 赖特在20世纪30年代提出的城

市规划思想。他的城市规划的思想基础是：每个独户家庭的周围有一英亩土地，生产供自己消费的食物；用汽车作交通工具，居住区之间有超级公路连接，公共设施沿着公路布置，加油站设在为整个地区服务的商业中心内）

a new Usonian city "美国风"的住宅新体系（Usonian 这个词是借用了 Samuel Butler 的小说《欧洪》〈Erewhon〉中的用语。赖特之所以用 Usonian 而不用 America 的目的是表示这种住宅是未来的美国住宅）

material condition 实质条件

the ownership of land 土地所有权

means of production 生产手段；生产工具；生产资料

Difficult Sentences

① The Great Depression gave an added urgency to his work and provided him with the enforced leisure to pursue it.

经济大萧条使赖特更为急切地推出新作，并且使他更热衷于对此项目的研究。

② Like so many other Americans of his time, Wright was fascinated by the automobile, convinced of its potential to revolutionize modern life and blind to its limitations.

像同时代的其他美国人一样，莱特深深着迷于汽车，对汽车能变革现代生活的潜力深信不疑，对它的局限性则视而不见。

③ Wright's essential insight was that decentralization, if taken to its logical extreme, could create the material conditions for a nation of independent farmers and proprietors. If properly planned, cities could spread over the countryside and still not lose their cohesion or efficiency. The diffusion of population would create conditions for the universal ownership of land. The world of concentrated wealth and power would be replaced by one in which the means of production would be widely held.

赖特的最基本的观点是分散发展，如果按其做最终端的发展，它会为自给自足的农民和小业主提供物质条件。如果发展得当,城市会扩展至农村而不失其内聚力和效率。人口的分散会为土地公有制创造条件。原有的财富和权力集中的社会将会被生产资料普遍共有的社会所取代。

④ Broadacre City was thus a juxtaposition of the past and the future: the ideal of Jeffersonian democracy given new meaning in terms of the technology of the future. This hybrid provided the standards of efficiency and humanity against which Wright judged the cities of the present and, not surprisingly, found them wanting.

因此,广亩城市是过去和未来的并置,是理想的杰斐逊式的民主在未来科技社会中的新的体现形式。这种结合体为赖特评判效率和人性提供了标准,这也就是为什么赖特根据这种标准来评判现在的城市,并发现它们远远不足了。

Phrases and Patterns

1. be destined to do 一定会

   One can survive for long in the memory of the city, will be destined to represent some outstanding ideas, as the representative of the conquest of Rome, Jerusalem representative of beliefs, Athens representatives excellent quality classical art.

   一座长久存在于人们记忆中的城市,必定代表某种杰出的思想,正如罗马代表征服,耶路撒冷代表信仰,雅典代表艺术的杰出品质。

   Emerging from the landscape, and shaped by nature, the design of the National Stadium is destined to create a simple symbolic link—a bridge between old and new, between people and country and China with the world.

   跳脱于美景之外却又浑然天成,国家体育馆的整个设计必然将创造一个质朴的符号链接——一座联结新与旧、人民与国家、中国与世界的桥梁。

2. sb. assumes that... (某人)相信;认为
They assumed that town master planning and design projects in that university have received international recognition.
他们认为,那所大学的造镇计划和设计项目已经得到了国际性认证。
Some professionals assume that designing street landscapes includes plant and tree selections, furniture finishes in appropriate applications.
有些专业人士认为,设计街道景观包括植物的选取、街道商店的装饰与整体艺术的呈现。

Questions

1. What does an ideal city look like in the eyes of Frank Lloyd Wright?
2. Do Frank Lloyd Wright and Le Corbusier stand on the same ground?

2.8 The Living City
活着的城市

Genius is a sin against the mob!
Frank Lloyd Wright, Genius and the Mobocracy

In 1949, Wright published his angriest book. It was ostensibly a tribute to Louis Sullivan, but Wright's eloquent tribute to the Lieber Meister was overshadowed by his aggrieved reflections on Sullivan's tragic neglect by the American people in the last decades of his life. These reflections impelled him to a more intemperate polemic on the neglect of his own genius by the present "mobocracy"[①].

"A nation industrialized beyond proper balance with its own agronomy is a menace to its own peace and the peace of the world," he began. "It is a house in a chronic state of civil war always divided against itself." To maintain order and to pursue those wars which are "the necessary clearing house" for a society where "head and heart, soul and intellect come in constant conflict," some form of centralized control is necessary. "The artificiality of our mechanized society is helplessly drifting toward a bureaucracy so top-heavy that the bureaucracy of Soviet Russia will seem honest and innocent by comparison."

The structure of centralized authority would necessarily make passivity, conformity, and mediocrity ubiquitous among the American people. Wright never had much faith in the average city dweller's capacity to maintain his individuality. In 1914 he had written, "The 'Democracy' of the man in the American street is no more than the Gospel of Mediocrity." Nevertheless, he maintained that the nation had retained a heritage of genuine ideas on which the artist could base his work. If the artist could penetrate the surface of conformity and touch the bedrock of individualism, the man in the street would recognize works created in this spirit as "prophetic expressions of himself" and would cling to them "for salvation."

In the 1930s, Wright hoped that everyone could perform this act of recognition; by 1949, however, he trusted only an elite, the "democratic minority." For the vast majority, mass conformity and bureaucratic dislike of anything irregular would combine to completely exclude imagination and originality. In the mobocracy the genius is not the natural leader but the natural outcast[②]. "The genius does not 'belong'. He will not 'stay in line'." If, as Wright believed, the artist needs a healthy "indigenous" culture in which to work, then "demoralization of the creative instinct—O Lord, be merciful—lies in this universalsed governmental substitution of a falsely-decorated mobocracy for the thought-built democracy we might have." And if, as Wright also believed, society needs the creative artist if it is ever to attain its proper form, then all hope for significant change must die in the mobocracy.

So this new democratic architecture we call organic and is original may again be swamped by the same heedless mobocracy or more likely by official statism (the two gangsterisms do work together) and our hope of organic culture will be left to die with principle in this Western Wasteland!

Wright, as I have said, thought in terms of complete acceptance or rejection. For all his vaunted democracy, he lacked any conception of a genuinely reciprocal contact between the artist and his people. For him the genius was an individual working alone, true to his own goals and standards[3]. Like an architect presenting his drawings to a design competition, the artist-leader presents his prophetic vision to his people as a completed whole. Wright's "democracy" consisted in his belief that the American nation was capable of living up to his standards.

Having despaired in *Genius and the Mobocracy*, he regained his faith before he died. In one sense this was inevitable, because his harsh judgment of his country implied an equally harsh judgment of himself. Wright was imbued with the idea of a pervasive "spirit of the age"; since the artist could never alienate himself from that spirit, his society's failings inevitably became his own. Wright, finally, could not accept either himself or his country as failures. Moreover, the publication of *Genius and the Mobocracy* coincided, ironically, with a real rebirth of Wright's architectural practice. This new phase in his creative career has been initiated in 1935 by the great Edgar Kaufmann house, "Fallingwater," The commission to build the Johnson Wax Company administration building, awarded the following year, was his first major project since the Imperial Hotel. The fame of these two structures was spread by an influential retrospective of Wright's work at the Museum of Modern Art in New York in 1940. After the war he received commissions from every area of the country. When Wright turned eighty in 1947 he was entering the most productive decade of his life.

He was becoming a national institution; he could hope that Broadacre City would become a national institution as well. In his ninetieth year he completely rewrote (for the fourth time) the book he had published in 1932 as *The Disappearing City*. The city had not disappeared in the intervening twenty-five years: the urban areas and their suburbs had grown, and the countryside had been depopulated. Nevertheless, Wright still asserted that decentralization was "innate necessity." He left the theory virtually unchanged. Even the defense of Henry George was retained. Broadacre City remained one man's vision of the future, unaltered by practice. The vision seemed remote, but Wright was confident that "our nation is learning. ... A new city is as inevitable as sunrise tomorrow though rain may fall." This last affirmation of Broadacres appeared in 1958 as *The Living City*. Wright died April 9, 1959.

Words and Expressions

mob [mɔb] *n.* 暴民；暴徒；下层民众
mobocracy [mɔ'bɔkrəsi] *n.* 暴徒统治；暴民政治
ostensibly [ɔs'tensəbli] *adv.* 外表地；表面上地
tribute ['tribju:t] *n.* 表示尊敬或赞美的言辞或行为
aggrieved [ə'gri:vd] *adj.* 愤愤不平的；感到委屈的
polemic [pɔ'lemik] *n.* 争[辩]论；论战；攻击；驳斥
agronomy [əg'rɔnəmi] *n.* 农学；农艺学
artificiality [ˌɑ:tifiʃ'æliti] *n.* 人工；不自然之物；人造物
bureaucracy [bjuə'rɔkrəsi] *n.* 官僚主义；官僚政治；官僚机构
top-heavy [tɔp'hevi] *adj.* 头重脚轻的
passivity [pæ'sivit] *n.* 被动；消极情绪[状态]；服从；忍受
conformity [kən'fɔ:miti] *n.* 相似；一致；遵从；顺从；整合
mediocrity [ˌmi:di'ɔkriti] *n.* 普通；平凡；平凡的人[能力]
ubiquitous [ju:'bikwitəs] *adj.* 无所不在的；普遍存在的
gospel ['gɔspəl] *n.* 福音；主义；信条

bedrock ['bed'rɔk] n. 基本事实[原理];最低点[额];最小量
prophetic [prə'fetik] adj. 预言的;预示的;先知的
demoralization [di'mɔrəlɑiziʃən] n. 道德败坏;纪律松弛;士气消沉
statism ['steitiz(ə)m] n. 中央集权下的经济统制
gangsterism ['gæŋstərizəm] n. 犯罪;歹徒及其犯罪行为
vaunted ['vɔ:ntid] adj. 自夸的;大肆吹嘘的;自负的
conception [kən'sepʃən] n. 观念;想法;构思;构想
reciprocal [ri'siprəkəl] adj. 相互的;互补的;有来有往的
failing ['feiliŋ] n. 缺点;过失;失败
retrospective [ˌretrəu'spektiv] n. 回顾;回忆
affirmation [ˌəfə:'meiʃən] n. 断言;肯定;证实;批准
Louis Sullivan 路易斯·沙利文(美国最有影响力的建筑师之一)
clearing house 票据交换所
city dweller 城市居民
be imbued with 充满
coincide with 与……相符
The Edgar Kaufmann house 考夫曼别墅(流水别墅)(建成于1936年,流水别墅被誉为"绝顶的人造物与幽雅的天然景色的完美平衡",是"20世纪的艺术杰作")
Johnson Wax Company administration building 约翰逊制蜡公司总部办公楼(一幢七层建筑,空间封闭,采用蘑菇形空心圆柱,由下而上逐渐变粗,上部为一圆伞状结构,其间的空档玻璃覆盖,形成一奇特的空间效果)
the Imperial Hotel 东京帝国饭店
Museum of Modern Art 纽约现代艺术馆
Henry George 法国章牌设计师——乔治·亨利

Difficult Sentences

① These reflections impelled him to a more intemperate polemic on the neglect of his own genius by the present "mobocracy."

这些思考使他陷入更为激烈的论辩，为他自己的天分被现在的"下里巴人"所忽视而愤愤不平。

② In the 1930s, Wright hoped that everyone could perform this act of recognition; by 1949, however, he trusted only an elite, the "democratic minority." For the vast majority, mass conformity and bureaucratic dislike of anything irregular would combine to completely exclude imagination and originality. In the mobocracy the genius is not the natural leader but the natural outcast.

20世纪30年代时，赖特希望人人都会认同他的看法；然而到了1949年，他认为只有一小部分的社会精英，即"追求民主的少数人"才会理解他。对于大多数人来说，随波逐流的心态和厌弃任何不中规中矩事物的官僚作风，二者结合起来会全然弃想象力与创新精神而不顾。在暴民统治当道的社会中，天才不是合乎规则的领导者，而是普遍被排斥的放逐者。

③ Wright, as I have said, thought in terms of complete acceptance or rejection. For all his vaunted democracy, he lacked any conception of a genuinely reciprocal contact between the artist and his people. For him the genius was an individual working alone, true to his own goals and standards.

正如前面我所说的，赖特考虑问题总是从极端出发，要么全然接受，要么全盘否定。在他大肆推崇的民主精神中，缺乏艺术家同他的人民之间鱼水互惠的基本概念。在他看来，天才就是一个人奋斗，忠实于自己的目标和标准。

Phrases and Patterns

1. be imbued with 富有

   Series of tourist products shall be carefully designed and developed with a strong element of the Beijing culture but also imbued with the Olympic values.

   我们将会精心设计和开发具有浓郁北京人文特色、反映丰富奥运理念的旅游产品系列。
Imbued with the spirit of "New Beijing, New Olympics", with a seating capacity of 91,000, the stadium will host the opening and closing ceremonies, the track and field competitions and the football finals during the 2008 Olympic Games.
秉承着"新北京,新奥运"的精神,能容纳91,000个座位的国家体育馆将在2008年奥运会期间举行开闭幕式、田径比赛及足球比赛决赛。

2. This new phase has been initiated in... 这一新的时期始于……
Wright's distinctively personal style has been initiated through the turn of the 20th century.
赖特独特的个人风格始自于19和20世纪之交。
The concept of "new towns" in the postindustrial urban context has been initiated in the late 19th century from Ebenezer Howard's idea of the garden city as a radical solution to urban problems.
在后工业时代的都市背景下,"新城市"的理念形成于19世纪末期,源自于埃比尼泽·霍华德为了解决城市问题而提出的激进的花园城市的想法。

Questions

1. According to the passage, which one did Frank Lloyd Wright advocate, centralization or individuality?
2. What made Frank Lloyd Wright assert that his own genius was neglected by the present "mobocracy"?
3. What are the drawbacks of Frank Lloyd Wright's Democracy?
4. List some of Wright's works that make him renowned.

3

Sustainable and Report of the Asia Pacific Urban Forum
可持续发展与亚太城市论坛报告

【本章导读】 可持续发展作为21世纪最重要的经济与环境政策,对城市规划的发展产生重要的影响。本章3.1介绍了可持续发展的具体含义,3.2介绍了3个可持续发展设计和建设的实例。

3.3~3.8是关于亚太城市的专题报告,是联合国国际人居会议中关于居住在亚洲城市专题的讨论结果,具体分析了亚太城市的经济发展、城市管理、媒介、交通、城市空间、住宅等方面对城市发展的影响。

3.1 Sustainable Design and Construction
可持续发展设计和建设

Sustainable design and construction is a holistic, proactive approach to building that maintains and restores the natural qualities of the site, improves energy efficiency and building performance, diminishes environmental degradation, encourages resource conservation and the use of renewable resources, and responds to the needs of developers and their building's occupants[①]. It is based on project planning, which focuses on the long term implications of building design, construction, and operation. It includes services during all phases of design, construction and occupancy, and hinges upon the integration of the project team. The goal of the sustainable construction process is to create buildings that last longer, are more comfortable to live and work in, perform better, and are sensitive to the natural environment.

Sustainable Design and Construction Objectives

The world has been recently <u>confronted with a growing recognition that</u> our methods of living on this planet are reducing our quality of life. These methods may even be destroying the planet's very ability to support our own existence. Meadows, Meadows, and Randers in their study. Beyond the limits, claim that humans' impacts through consumption, misuse of resources, and waste are rapidly leading us toward and exceeding the carrying capacity of the planet. The United Nations sponsored report by the World Commission on the Environment and Development entitled Our Common Future calls for a new approach to development which ensures that "it meets the needs of the present without compromising the ability of future generations to meet their own needs."

The United States is just beginning to become aware of and address these issues, the interdependencies between human and environmental needs, and the economic ramifications of meeting these needs. There are great opportunities to address these issues and create an economically successful development, which maximizes the environmental and human benefits achievable through sustainable design and construction approaches.

Sustainability, as defined by the United Nations World Commission on the Environment and Development, refers to ensuring "our long-term cultural, economic and environmental health and vitality." This concept can guide many decisions made during design and construction. The long term environmental, human and economic impact of design and construction decisions can be weighed, and through this approach a balance between these needs is achieved creating the most sustainable project possible②.

Sustainable Development—Regarding Environmental Ethics

It is clear that the quality of our natural environment is being reduced. Carbon dioxide levels in the atmosphere are rising, stratospheric ozone levels are falling, species are becoming extinct at an alarming rate, landfills are rapidly nearing capacity, and grand natural ecosystems such as tropical and temperate rainforests are systematically disappearing③.

We are not only destroying the life around us, but we are impacting our own lives as well. Air quality in many urban areas is unhealthy, water from many of our rivers and lakes is unfit to swim in or drink, and we will have spent an estimated $90 billion in 1994 dollars to clean up nonfederal superfund sites by the year 2070. A recent phenomena called "Sick Building Syndrome" is causing thousands of people to become sick each year, and could be resulting in billions of dollars in lost productivity and related medical expenses.

All of these crises are the direct result of our day to day choices of where we live, what we consume, how we travel, what we produce, and how we build. By modifying these choices, we can significantly reduce the negative impacts that we have on the natural environment, ourselves and future generations.

Future development should strive to meet the following environmental objectives through appropriate planning and construction.

(1) To provide good stewardship of and minimize environmental impacts on the project site, the surrounding region, and the planet throughout the development and operation of the project.

(2) To integrate the built and natural environments.

(3) To design for resource efficiency and appropriate resource use.

(4) To enhance ecological integrity and preserve biodiversity.

Sustainable Development—Regarding Human Scale

Never before in human history have we as a species been so separated from the natural environment. Nor have we ever before been in a condition where our relationships with each other have been more disjointed. Our society has evolved to a point where concerns for human health and well being is thought of in terms of longevity not quality, and little thought is given to how our day to day choices affect either positively or negatively our emotional, spiritual, and physical well being. We have created a basis of decision making that concentrates solely on short term economics and fails to take into account the effects our decisions have on people.

Concentrating on human scale means that human needs are taken into account and designed into the project at a basic level. The need for a place that is nurturing to people on a physical, emotional and spiritual level should be incorporated into the very essence of the development. Focus can be given to identifying opportunities for people to develop relationship with the natural environment and with other people. Sustainable development projects strive to create the best human environment throughout the course of development by meeting the following objectives.

(1) To provide an enjoyable and nurturing environment for building occupants and project neighbors.

(2) To provide an opportunity for building occupants to connect with the natural environment and learn about the local region, its natural environment, and community, as well as enhance user's physical, emotional and spiritual health and well being.

(3) To design within the regional context, respecting indigenous culture, heritage, and legacy as well as archaeological, geological, and

historical resources.

Sustainable Development—Regarding Economic Return

Often people argue that business, or more accurately business' requirement for profitability, is the cause of environmental degradation. Many people also argue that businesses have little concern for their impacts on human health and well being. Without question, strong cases can be made that profits are often maximized at the expense of human and environmental health and vitality. It can also be demonstrated that more appropriate business decisions can be made that reduce or eliminate negative impacts on environmental and human needs. These decisions can even be made in a way that actually enhances and restores the environment and provides a nurturing, supportive and sustaining place in which people can live, work and play.

Sustainable building projects strive to be such a place, while also providing a reasonable economic return. Through focusing on inherent relationships and interdependencies between the environment, people and economic success, the projects create economic opportunities that are beneficial to the local, regional, and global environment, as well as to the building occupants, local community and society at large. Sustainable building projects capitalize on opportunities to reduce long-term operating costs, improve employee productivity and effectiveness, and create durable, high quality facilities which perform better and last longer. They take advantage of opportunities to not only capture economic benefits in the planning, design, and construction processes, but also create environmental and human benefits as well.

Sustainable developments strive to meet the following economic objectives through the course of development.

(1) To demonstrate that sustainable development is a sound economic investment.

(2) To identify and implement decisions that benefit the environment and people, while meeting the economic requirements of the project.

(3) To achieve an acceptable return on investment.

Words and Expressions

holistic [həʊˈlistik] *adj.* 整体的；全盘的
proactive [ˌprəʊˈæktiv] *adj.* [心理]前摄的
occupant [ˈɔkjuːpənt] *n.* 占有者；居住者
ramification [ˌræmifiˈkeiʃən] *n.* 分枝；分叉；衍生物；支流
vitality [vɑiˈtæliti] *n.* 活力；生命力；生动性
ozone [ˈəuzəun, əuˈz-] *n.* 新鲜的空气；[化]臭氧
ecosystem [iːkəˈsistəm] *n.* 生态系统
integrity [inˈtegriti] *n.* 完整；完全；完整性
longevity [lɔnˈdʒeviti] *n.* 长命；寿命；供职期限，
nurture [ˈnəːtʃə] *vt.* 养育；给与营养物；教养
indigenous [inˈdidʒənəs] *adj.* 本土的
archaeological [ˌɑːkiəˈlɔdʒikəl] *adj.* 考古学的；考古学上的
implement [ˈimplimənt] *vt.* 贯彻；实现
energy efficiency 能量效率
building performance 建筑性能
environmental degradation 环境退化
renewable resources 可再生资源
hinge upon 决定(由……决定)
beyond the limits 越出；超出(范围、限度)
carrying capacity 承载能力
World Commission on the Environment and Development 世界环境与发展委员会
sustainable development 可持续发展
tropical and temperate rainforests 热带和温带雨林
Sick Building Syndrome 病态建筑综合症(建筑内的人员出现急性不舒适症状，症状原因不明，离开建筑以后，症状很快就消

失）

human scale 人类尺度

be incorporated into 加入

capitalize on 利用

Donella H. Meadows, Dennis L. Meadows, Jorgen Randers 美国麻省理工学院的经济学家梅多斯等人

Difficult Sentences

① Sustainable design and construction is a holistic, proactive approach to building that maintains and restores the natural qualities of the site, improves energy efficiency and building performance, diminishes environmental degradation, encourages resource conservation and the use of renewable resources, and responds to the needs of developers and their building's occupants.

可持续发展设计和建设是对建筑的一个全新的、具有前瞻性的理念。这一理念的实施可保持及恢复自然地理特征、提高能源效率和建筑性能、减少环境恶化、加强资源保护和可再生资源的利用以及满足开发商和居住者的需求。

② The long term environmental, human and economic impact of design and construction decisions can be weighed, and through this approach a balance between these needs is achieved creating the most sustainable project possible.

可持续发展的设计和建设理念对环境的保护、人类的生存及经济的发展的长远影响是可以估量的,并且通过这些理念可以使这些因素达到平衡,最终创建最大限度的可持续发展。

③ It is clear that the quality of our natural environment is being reduced. Carbon dioxide levels in the atmosphere are rising, stratospheric ozone levels are falling, species are becoming extinct at an alarming rate, landfills are rapidly nearing capacity, and grand natural ecosystems such as tropical and temperate rainforests are systematically disappearing.

很明显,自然环境正在恶化。大气中二氧化碳的含量过高,平流层中臭氧层减少,一些物种正以惊人的速度濒临灭绝、垃圾堆放处已经快到了极限,以及像热带和温带雨林一样大规模的自然生态环境正在慢慢地消失。

Phrases and Patterns

1. be confronted with a growing recognition that... 越来越多的人意识到……

   The world has been recently confronted with a growing recognition that our methods of living on this planet are reducing our quality of life.
   最近全世界越来越多的人意识到我们的生存方式正在降低自己的生活质量。
   The world has been recently confronted with a growing recognition that our planet is in danger.
   最近全世界越来越多的人意识到我们的星球正处于危险中。

2. It is clear that... 很明显

   It is cleat that we are destroying the life around us
   很明显,我们正在破坏着我们的生活。
   It is cleat that the majority come to recognize the importance of environmental protection.
   很明显,大多数人开始意识到环境保护的重要性。

3. not only ... but also... 不仅……而且……

   They take advantage of opportunities to not only capture economic benefits in the planning, design, and construction processes, but also create environmental and human benefits as well.
   一旦他们利用好了机会,就不仅能在计划、设计、施工的全过程均获经济利益,而且也可以给环境和人类创造利益。

Sustainable development can not only benefit us generation but also our children and grandchildren.

可持续发展不仅可以使我们这一代受益,而且还会造福后代。

Questions

1. What benefits can human obtain through sustainable development?
2. How can sustainable building projects provide economic return?

3.2　Example
实例

Although not a commonly practiced approach to development, several sustainable development demonstration projects already exist. In addition, a wide variety of projects, both commercial and residential in nature, incorporate various sustainable concepts on a more limited scale. This type of approach to development has made significant strides since the late 1980s, and many successful projects have been completed including large scale community developments, commercial office buildings, single family houses, retail banks, light industrial structures, resorts, retreat centers and many others[①]. Described below are three projects, which incorporate unique sustainable design and construction features. These projects, built by Turner Construction Company, are included to demonstrate actual projects that have been successfully built. They have not only achieved significant environmental and human benefits, but they have also proven to be economically competitive with "standard" development approaches.

Duracell Corporate Headquarters, Bethel, Connecticut

Built to house the corporate employees of the Duracell Corporation, this project is a 3 level corporate office building, totaling 308,000 square feet. It includes 195,000 square feet of general office space,

14,000 square feet of laboratories, a conference/training center, a TV production studio, a fitness facility, a dining area and maintenance and circulation areas.

The office facility was designed to blend harmoniously with its wooded 44 acre setting and to convert efficiently to multi-tenant use if required to do so in the future. Turner provided extensive preconstruction input and assisted with siting the building as well as conducting excavation studies in an attempt to minimize environmental and economic impacts on the project. Throughout the project, the integrity of the local natural environment of the site including local forest, wetland and field ecosystems was maintained. Product research, including economic and constructability analysis of available environmentally friendly building products was performed. Through these efforts, over forty environmentally sensitive building products were incorporated into the project. Many recycled content products including top soil, fiberglass insulation, glass tile, hardwoods, gypsum wall board, ceiling files, structural steel and many others were included in the project. Additionally, wood from sustainably managed forests, low volatile organic compound containing paint, and many recyclable products were utilized.

The project also focused on achieving significant energy efficiency. Extensive energy efficient technologies, including gas fired absorption chillers, natural daylighting strategies and other efficient mechanical and lighting technologies were designed into the project[2].

Southern California Gas Co. Energy Resource Center, Los Angeles, California

Built as an energy and building equipment demonstration facility for the Southern California Gas Company, this project consisted of extensive renovation of an existing 32,000 square foot single, story facility and a new addition. The construction included demolition of the middle third of the existing building and constructing a two story addition in its place, which added 15,000 square feet to the project.

Sustainable design and construction was a primary focus for the project. The scope of Turner's preconstruction efforts included extensive research on green building products, including products that were recycled and reused. Products that incorporated recycled content such as carpet tiles, wall covering, linoleum, drywall, wood flooring, rebar, steel studs and many others were identified and incorporated into the project. The project also reused materials from the demolished facility and from other buildings. Reused products included such things as electrical conduit, mechanical and electrical equipment, piping, ductwork, and wood planking. Products that could not be reused were either donated to charitable causes or were recycled.

<u>Special attention was also given to</u> the indoor air quality of the project. Products that were less toxic to the indoor environment were selected. Many products that contained little or no volatile organic compounds were used in place of more toxic alternatives. Such products as paint, flooring, adhesives and other finished materials, that proved to be less toxic to the indoor environment, were installed. Not only were non toxic products favored, but extra measures were taken to increase the use of outside air prior to occupancy, thus flushing toxins out of the space. In addition, dust and moisture build-up were minimized during construction, and extra care was taken to protect ventilation equipment from contamination during construction.

The project incorporated extensive energy efficient measures including energy efficient lighting and mechanical systems. Super efficient windows were installed that reduced heat transmission and allowed maximum daylight to enter the building. Extra insulation was installed in the roof and walls, and reflective roof coatings reduced summer heat gain. The cumulative result of all of the energy efficient strategies reduced the energy consumption of the building by over forty-five percent.

Rose Garden Arena —Portland, Oregon

Turner Construction Company implemented a demolition and construction debris recycling program at the Rose Garden Arena built for the National Basketball Association's Portland Trailblazers, which was the largest recycling effort to date in the United States[3]. The program consisted of a source separated approach to waste handling, that allowed most construction debris to be recycled. Taking advantage of the vast recycling infrastructure available in the City of Portland located in the State of Oregon, Turner was able to recycle gypsum wallboard, cardboard, wood, ferrous metal, land clearing debris, concrete, asphalt, and rubble.

The results of this effort were significant. Through the recycling program, 45,000 tons of materials were eliminated from local landfills, recycled and re-introduced into various manufacturing and building process. The material recycled represented nearly 95% of all the "waste" generated during the project. By utilizing the source separated waste management strategy, the client realized over $190,000 in savings generated from reduced landfill costs and material rebates from the recycled materials. Although Turner was responsible for managing the waste handling on the construction site, source separated recycling would not have been feasible had the local infrastructure not been in place to recycle the materials. The city of Portland played a critical role in making this possible due to a progressive tax scheme which raised the price of garbage disposal to a level that stimulated the recycling industry and allowed recycling to be cost competitive[4]. <u>For further information about</u> these projects of information regarding Turner Construction

Company, call (206) 224-4343 or e-mail icampbell@tcco.com.

Words and Expressions

stride [straid] v. 大步走；跨过；大步行走
convert [kən'və:t] vt. 使转变；转换……
siting ['saitiŋ] n. 建筑工地选择（道路等）定线
excavation [ˌekskə'veiʃən] n. 挖掘；发掘；挖掘成的洞；出土文物
integrity [in'teɡriti] n. 完整；完全；完整性
gypsum ['dʒipsəm] n. [矿]石膏；[农]石膏肥料
chiller ['tʃilə] n. 使寒冷之人或事物；冷却器
integrity [in'teɡriti] n. 完整；完全；完整性
renovation [ˌrenəu'veiʃən] n. 革新
demolition [ˌdemə'liʃən] n. 破坏；毁坏；毁坏之遗迹
linoleum [li'nəuljəm] n. 油布；油毡
rebar [ri'bɑ:] n. 钢筋；螺纹钢筋
ductwork ['dʌktwɛ:k] n. 管道系统
toxic ['tɔksik] adj. 有毒的；中毒的
adhesive [əd'hi:siv] n. 黏合剂
debris ['debri:, 'deib-] n. 碎片；残骸
infrastructure ['infrə'strʌktʃə] n. 下部构造；基础下部组织
asphalt ['æsfælt] n. 沥青
demonstration project 示范项目
community development 地区开发
retail bank 小额银行业务
industrial structure 产业结构
office building 办公楼
general office 总办公处
fitness facility 健身设施
maintenance area 养护面积
circulation area 流通面积
top soil 表土
glass tile 玻璃瓦
volatile organic compound 挥发性有机化合物

natural daylight 自然光
electrical conduit 电缆
flush out of (从隐蔽处)驱逐出去
ferrous metal 黑色[铁类]金属

Difficult Sentences

① This type of approach to development has made significant strides since the late 1980's, and many successful projects have been completed including large scale community developments, commercial office buildings, single family houses, retail banks, light industrial structures, resorts, retreat centers and many others.
自从20世纪80年代末,这种发展的方法已经取得了长足的进步,并且许多成功的项目也完成了,比如大规模的地区开发、商业办公楼、独立家庭住宅、小额银行、轻型产业结构、风景区、退休中心和许多其他的区域。

② Extensive energy efficient technologies, including gas fired absorption chillers, natural daylighting strategies and other efficient mechanical and lighting technologies were designed into the project.
广泛的节省能源的技术包括以煤气为燃料的吸收制冷器、自然采光策略以及其他高效率的机械和照明设备技术已经被设计到项目中。

③ Turner Construction Company implemented a demolition and construction debris recycling program at the Rose Garden Arena built for the National Basketball Association's Portland Trailblazers, which was the largest recycling effort to date in the United States.
特纳建筑公司在为全国篮球协会的波特兰开拓者队建造玫瑰园赛场时,实现了爆破和建筑肥料再利用,这一举措是迄今为止美国规模最大的再循环工程。

④ The city of Portland played a critical role in making this possible due to a progressive tax scheme which raised the price of garbage disposal to a level that stimulated the recycling industry and allowed recycling to be cost competitive.

波特兰市在实现这一举措中起了很大的作用,它开启了一项累进税政策,为垃圾处理筹集了足够的资金促使再循环行业加入价格竞争。

Phrases and Patterns

1. Special attention was also given to... 特别注意……

   Special attention was also given to the indoor air quality of the project.

   本项目特别注意室内空气质量。

   Special attention was given to environmental protection.

   环境保护受到了特别关注。

2. For further information about... 关于……的更多的信息

   For further information about these projects of information regarding Meadows Construction Company, call (206) 142-562 or e-mail icampbell@tcco.com.

   关于梅多斯建筑公司在这些项目上的更多信息可致电(206)142-562或是发送邮件,地址是icampbell@tcco.com。

   For further information about sustainable development, read page 14, paragraph 23.

   关于可持续发展的更多信息,可阅读14页第23段。

Questions

1. Summarize the characteristics of the project built by Duracell Corporate.
2. Summarize the characteristics of the project built by Southern California Gas Co. Energy Resource Center.
3. Summarize the characteristics of the project built by Rose Garden Arena.

3.3 Global Trade Agreements, Economic Reforms and Their Impact on Cities
全球贸易协定和经济改革对城市的影响

It was undeniable that globalization and the policies that many countries of the region had implemented to cope with it had a major impact in many urban centres, particularly since most economic activities in the region were concentrated in urban areas.

Global trade agreements and economic reforms speeded up the process of urbanization and larger cities implied greater demand for services and for investment in infrastructure①. Furthermore, increased urban economic activity made cities even bigger markets which, in turn, made business want to remain in cities.

Those policies resulted in the further promotion of privatization and various forms of public-private partnerships at the city level.

Development was increasingly technology-driven and so led to highly specialized urban economies.

There was a shift from growth through competition towards growth by collaboration. Competition within the region was being replaced by regional collaborations such as APEC, ASEAN and growth triangles.

There were greater demands on natural resources, such as energy, to support large cities and increased substitution of land for urban use from land for agricultural use.

The impact of economic structural adjustment, liberalization of trade, etc. differed by country, by city, among stakeholders, among sectors of the society, between business and city residents. The view's depended on one's vantage point. In some countries it might be positive while in others it might be negative. Also within the same country, the impact might be positive or negative for different stakeholders. In other words, they had country and stakeholder specific effects and, therefore, the means of addressing their impact could not be generalized.

In some ways, those programmes created injustice along with economic growth. It was critical to consider their social impact, particularly on social values. There was a need to ensure support for disadvantaged sectors of the society, for instance in the area of health and education. The need for an equitable, efficient and practical redistribution of the wealth derived from economic growth had to be carefully considered.

Those programmes placed added urgency to addressing the issue of sustainable urban development. Particular concerns included:

· Resource conservation, e. g. land, energy, water;

· Basic needs priorities such as housing, water and sanitation, transportation, pollution control, waste management;

· Effectiveness of urban environmental planning and management systems including financing mechanisms (regional perspectives, environmental accounting);

· Effectiveness of institutional arrangements and interrelationships among and between stakeholders (intergovernmental relationships, public-private partnerships, community participation. etc).

The impacts of those programmes on cities required strengthening the powers and capacities of urban local authorities across the full range of urban management functions and responsibilities, in the political, functional and tax domain. Simultaneously, there was a need for greater transparency, especially in relation to privatization of urban services and to the pricing of those services.

Improving conditions in the cities was likely to make them more attractive to business and people. That put more pressure on the cities. However, business could change locations with some financial cost but people could do so only at a high social cost. Within that context, the strengthening of secondary cities and giving incentives to business that could move would play an important role in attenuating the negative effects of the programmes.

Many problems in the cities arose from a mismatch between the private economic costs and the real social costs. In those cases, an efficient pricing mechanism and an effective taxation system should be used to correct that imbalance.

Very often, rural areas were adversely affected by those programmes. However, since those areas in fact constituted a support system for cities, there was a need for integrated planning at all levels. That also meant that large finance conglomerates and investors, as well as central governments, should be included in the planning process at the local level.

There was a need to compensate for the non-economic effects of those programmes which included a widening political gap between urban and rural areas as well as between competing cities within one country[2]. There was a need to insert a social agenda and environmental concerns into global trade agreements.

Words and Expressions

globalization [ˌgləubəlaiˈzeiʃən] n. 全球化；全球性
implement [ˈimplimənt] v. 执行
urbanization [ˌə:bənaiˈzeiʃən] n. 都市化；文雅化
collaboration [kəˌlæbəˈreiʃən] n. 协作；通敌
liberalization [ˌlibərəlaiˈzeiʃən] n. 自由主义化；使宽大
stakeholder [ˈsteikhəuldə(r)] n. 赌金保管者
simultaneously [siməlˈteiniəsly] adv. 同时地
incentive [inˈsentiv] n. 动机
attenuate [əˈtenjueit] v. 削弱
conglomerate [kɔnˈglɔmərit] v. 聚结
trade agreement 贸易协定
economic reform 经济改革

public-private partnership 公司合营
structural adjustment 结构调整
vantage point 优势地位

Difficult Sentences

① Global trade agreements and economic reforms speeded up the process of urbanization and larger cities implied greater demand for services and for investment in infrastructure.

全球贸易协定和经济改革加速了大中小城市的壮大,尤其是有对服务及基础设施投资需求较大的大城市。

② There was a need to compensate for the non-economic effects of those programmes which included a widening political gap between urban and rural areas as well as between competing cities within one country.

有必要弥补这些措施带来的非经济影响,包括城市与乡村地区之间及本国城市之间日益扩大的政治差异。

Phrases and Patterns

1. It was undeniable that... 不可否认

   It was undeniable that globalization and the policies that many countries of the region had implemented to cope with it had a major impact in many urban centres, particularly since most economic activities in the region were concentrated in urban areas.

   不可否认各国配合全球化实施的政策对许多城市中心有很大的影响,尤其是大多数的经济活动多集中在城市里。

   It was undeniable that globalization lead great benefits to many countries.

   不可否认全球一体化给许多国家带来了很大利益。

2. in turn 反过来

   Furthermore, increased urban economic activity made cities even bigger markets which, in turn, made business want to remain in cities.

此外,城市经济活动与日俱增造就了一个更大的市场,反过来,大市场把商家留在城市里。

Environment did benefit human greatly, in turn, human should do good to the environment.

环境给人类带来了巨大的利益,反过来,人类也应该为环境做些好事。

Questions

1. What are the impacts global trade agreement make on cities?
2. What are the impacts economic reforms make on cities?

3.4 Cities as the Engines of Economic Growth
城市——经济发展的动力

The growth of Asian cities was unparalleled in human history. European and American cities experienced similar growth in the late nineteenth and early twentieth centuries (albeit not at the same intensity and scale). Like many Asia countries at present, wealth was amassed in Western societies by very few. The wealth and income distribution of the United Kingdom in the late nineteenth century <u>was not dissimilar to</u> that of some Asian countries today. The advent of Keynesian economics recognized the wealth generation potential of societies as a whole, and created the platform for social equity that led to the unparalleled rise in production, consumerism and wealth for Western nations[①]. The lesson learned from pre-Keynesian society was that concentration of wealth does not maximize the potential economic wealth of nations. As the developed countries of the world moved once again towards the greater concentration of wealth resulting from structural adjustment, their GDPs had continued to fall, social equity gaps had broadened and social dislocation in the form of crime, homelessness and urban poverty had risen[②]. The growing concentration of wealth in Asian and Pacific cities by a few might be resulting in substantial underachievement in the economic performance of cities.

The group spent a considerable time discussing the need to ensure more efficient and equitable cities. It was generally agreed that the economic growth of cities rested with the creation of a new paradigm or approach to development based on partnerships that forged growth with equity under the umbrella of sustainability. If the latent potential to generate wealth in the communities of the poor, migrants and dispossessed was not unlocked, then the prospects for forging a better society and maximizing the economic growth of cities would be limited. The continued concentration of wealth would only reinforce the growing disharmonies and social unrest emerging in cities. Continued growth that enabled wealth to be accumulated by so few did not maximize the growth potential of cities.

Unless there was a new paradigm to broaden equity and increase wealth in cities, down to the smallest unit of society, that was the family, then the prospects for sustainable development and enhanced economic performance would continue to be limited. It was necessary to learn to leverage the surpluses of the elite and the multinationals of the world, with the grossly untapped or latent potential of the disenfranchised and under class of cities that had great energy, entrepreneurship and desire for social mobility, if enhanced economic performance, greater social stability and sustainable resource management were to be achieved in cities.

The group touched on a number of ways by which the economic structure of cities might be reinvented or re-engineered to achieve more sustainable outcomes for economic wealth and social equity. Those were worth reinforcing in the Habitat Agenda and in national commitments to action plans. Such initiatives included:

· A focus on the transformation of the informal sector at a community level to generate wealth rather than consumption or trade driven enterprises;

· Empowerment of communities to organize the raising of capital in open markets;

· The creation of multilevel and a fourth level of partnerships with multinational and international finance agencies for local economic development;

· Re-engineering the governance of cities and strengthening the role of governments as facilitators rather than executors of public programmes;

· The development of social capital through civic engagement, openness and accountability of government;

· Shifting the focus of economic development away from planning and controlling economic development to the management of development;

· Creating regional partnerships for urban management and development which would enable networked partnerships to develop between cities and nations involving collaboration, sharing and information transfer in research, education, training, policy, capacity-building and other matters of interest to cities in the Asia-Pacific region.

In summary, cities were the engines of economic growth and would play a central role in setting the path for greater social equity and more sustainable forms of economic development in cities in future. But the path for achieving equity and sustainability for the nations and cities In the Asian and Pacific region would not be the same. There were no models for building a sure path for the future for cities or nations. Each city must create its own economic path for the future.

Cities, however, were more than engines of economic growth. They were the measure of civilization and a testimony to one of the highest achievements of mankind. The importance placed by all levels of government, business (both national and international), non-governmental organizations and community based organizations in ensuring that our cities became more sustainable better designed and managed was summed up by that statement③. The commitment to that goal and the need for the paper on "Living in Asian Cities" to share the good points about cities while at the same time acknowledging the mistakes, issues and problems facing the development of cities was what we should take away from the gathering. Only by sharing experiences of urban scenes globally could we learn from each other ways to tackle collaboratively some of the complex issues facing cities. This was the raison d'etre for Habitat II.

Words and Expressions

unparalleled [ʌn'pærəleld] *adj.* 无比的；无双的；空前的

albeit [ɔːl'biːit] *conj.* 虽然

amass [ə'mæs] *vt.* 收集；积聚(尤指财富)

dislocation [ˌdislə'keiʃən] *n.* 混乱；断层；脱臼

underachieve ['ʌndərə'tʃiːv] *v.* 学习成绩不良未能发挥学习潜能

dispossessed [ˌdispə'zest] *adj.* 无依无靠的；被逐出的

leverage ['liːvəridʒ] *n.* 杠杆作用

habitat ['hæbitæt] *n.* (动植物的)生活环境；产地；栖息地；居留地；自生地；聚集处

empower [im'pauə] *v.* 授权与；使能够

testimony ['testiməni] *n.* 证词(尤指在法庭所作的)；宣言；陈述

raison d'etre [reizuŋ'detr] *n.* 存在的目的或理由

wealth and income distribution 财富和收入分配

rest with 取决于；在于

resource management 资源管理

sum up 计算……的总数；概括；总结

Difficult Sentences

① The advent of Keynesian economics recognized the wealth generation potential of societies as a whole, and created the platform for social equity that led to the unparalleled rise in production, consumerism and wealth for Western nations.
凯恩斯经济学出现后,社会财富阶层被认为是一个整体,并给社会平衡提供平台,这个平台可以促成西方国家在生产、消费和财富上空前的增长。

② As the developed countries of the world moved once again towards the greater concentration of wealth resulting from structural adjustment, their GDPs had continued to fall, social equity gaps had broadened and social dislocation in the form of crime, homelessness and urban poverty had risen.
随着发达国家在经济结构的调整,他们再一次把注意力集中在聚集财富上,他们的 GDP 继续下滑,社会平衡的差距继续扩大,此外因犯罪、无家可归及城市的贫穷而带来的社会混乱也继续扩大。

③ The importance placed by all levels of government, business (both national and international), non-governmental organizations and community based organizations in ensuring that our cities became more sustainable better designed and managed was summed up by that statement.
各层政府、公司(包括国际与国内)、非政府组织以及社区组织所强调的重要性,即维护城市的可持续发展、优化设计和管理的重要性,在那个声明中被全面概括出来。

Phrases and Patterns

1. was not dissimilar to 与……相同
   The wealth and income distribution of the United Kingdom in the late

nineteenth century was not dissimilar to that of some Asian countries today.

19 世纪末英国财富和收入的分配与今日的亚洲国家的做法是一样的。

The initiatives taken in China were not dissimilar to that in Western countries in maintaining sustainable development.

中国采取的维持可持续发展的措施和西方国家是一样的。

2. It was generally agreed that... 人们通常认为

It was generally agreed that the economic growth of cities rested with the creation of a new paradigm or approach to development based on partnerships that forged growth with equity under the umbrella of sustainability.

人们通常认为,城市经济发展取决于基于合作并在可持续发展方向的保护下而产生的新方法。

It was generally agreed that environmental protection was crucial to both human health and economic development.

人们通常认为,环境保护对人类健康和经济发展都很关键。

Questions

1. What are the dissimilarities between the growth of Asian cities and that of western cities?
2. Why were cities crucial in economic growth?

3.5 Civic Engagement and the Role of Media
市民的参与与媒体的作用

An initial observation was that expenditure on social and economic programmes might be better directed to effective use of the media to link users to suppliers of goods and services. <u>In that context</u>, three examples were cited as follows:

- Social and economic development example from Japan

(agriculture). In the post-war period in Japan, the media (the national TV network NUK) was successfully used to inform farmers of potential changes in their status in relation to land tenure, to provide them with information on how to formalize new tenure arrangements, and to provide them with information and training in new agricultural modes of production[1]. All of those generated massive improvements in agricultural production and living standards for the rural population.

· Environmental and social welfare example from Japan (Minamata disease). Following the major litigation case against polluting industries resulting from the appearance of the symptoms of Minamata disease, the media played a pivotal role in forcing government and industry to give compensation to affected populations and to take action to prevent further pollution.

· Fablic awareness on housing supply and demand. The government agency responsible for social housing In Japan had been rather ineffectual in meeting large scale housing shortages following the Second World War. From perusing listings for housing in the major newspaper in the United States, it was realized that that media could play an important role in tapping existing supplies for people in need of housing. By using newspaper and other media in a strategic way to inform people requiring housing of potential sources, on the one hand, and by informing suppliers of major categories of housing needs, on the other, they were able to achieve dramatic improvements in housing delivery[2].

A number of ways to maximize the usage of media effectively to foster development of civil society were discussed:

· Specify types of media: press, radio. TV, Internet. Each medium had specific strengths and weaknesses in terms of audience, type of information being dealt with, accessibility of the medium itself and depth in which issues could be presented.

• Identify target groups: Information should be tailored to the interests and needs of the intended audiences. The effectiveness and impact of the message would greatly depend on how well the audience had been defined. In addition, the type of media chosen would depend on the nature of the message, i.e. broadcast media with large circulation might be better suited for public awareness campaigns, whilst instructional material to specific categories of audience would best employ "narrow-cast" media such as magazines, local radio stations, etc. Using local languages whenever possible should also be considered.

• Relationship between citizen groups and the media: In the experience of many civic groups and NGO actors, the press and the media were somewhat reluctant to carry news items and features simply because they were for a "good cause". Moreover, newspaper and broadcast media often had strong links with governments and big businesses. A consumer protection example from the Republic of Korea was cited. A consumer protection group had detected some ingredients in major soya sauce brands that were harmful to health. Their attempts to advertise their grievances in newspapers were thwarted. However, when they presented their story as a litigation against the soya sauce producers to the media rather than as a general warning, the grievances were duly carried. That proved to be a major factor in bringing government action against the producers.

The need for greater sensitization of media to civic problems was considered an important issue. That might require, however, a paradigm shift in thinking. "Bad news is good news" seemed to characterize the stance of the media towards daily events. Many of the local and global problems were dealt with only when they reached a crisis. There was a need to sensitize media professionals to the importance of playing a more positive role in anticipating and preventing the worst occurring by reporting in a more in-depth and timely way on many social and environmental issues③. Too often developmental professionals had neglected specifically targeting and engaging the media in their advocacy work and simply focused on the public at large and governments. The potential of the media to forge a bridge between those two groups was highlighted.

Innovative and alternative media ways to use the media were also discussed: for example, the use of interactive media such as community radio to engage people to work on long-term solutions to local social, economic and environmental problems. Similar uses of the Internet might be highly effective in the coming years to deal with local and national problems. A highly original example of using broadcast media interactively came from Brazil where "soap operas" dealt with important social issues. At certain climactic points in the story, viewers were invited to phone in and vole for a particular outcome of the plot. Tens of thousands of responses were gathered and the script-writers incorporated the viewers' wishes accordingly. That might be a powerful way of reflecting contemporary social values and promoting socially positive attitudes and behaviour④.

Words and Expressions

Minamata [minə'ma:tə] n. 水俣病(汞中毒引起的一种严重神经疾病)
litigation [liti'geiʃən] n. 诉讼；起诉
pivotal ['pivətl] adj. 枢轴的；关键的
ineffectual [ini'fektʃuəl] adj. 无效的；不成功的
peruse [pə'ru:z] v. 细读
tapping ['tæpiŋ] n. 出渣,出钢,出铁
foster ['fɔstə] vt. 养育；抚育；培养；鼓励, 抱(希望)
whilst [wilst] conj. 时时；同时
grievance ['gri:vns] n. 委屈；冤情；不平
thwart [θwɔ:t] vt. 反对；阻碍；横过
sensitize ['sensitaiz] vt. 使变得敏感；使具有感光性

land tenure 土地所有制
agricultural production 农业生产
take action 采取行动；提出诉讼
potential source 位源；势源；电源
in terms of 根据；按照；用……的话；在……方面
target group 目标群
consumer protection 消费者保护（法）
at large 未被捕；详尽；普遍
in relation to 关于

Difficult Sentences

① In the post-war period in Japan, the media (the national TV network NUK) was successfully used to inform farmers of potential changes in their status in relation to land tenure, to provide them with information on how to formalize new tenure arrangements, and to provide them with information and training in new agricultural modes of production.
在战后的日本，媒体（日本国家电视网络 NUK）被用来成功地通知农民土地所有制后他们地位可能发生的变化，此外，媒体还可以在如何实施新的所有制方面给他们提供信息以及新生产方式的培训。

② By using newspaper and other media in a strategic way to inform people requiring housing of potential sources, on the one hand, and by informing suppliers of major categories of housing needs, on the other, they were able to achieve dramatic improvements in housing delivery.
合理的运用报纸和媒体一方面可以帮助需要住房资源的人发布信息，另一方面可以帮助提供房源的人发布信息，这样就能使房屋买卖取得很大的收益。

③ There was a need to sensitize media professionals to the importance of playing a more positive role in anticipating and preventing the worst

occurring by reporting in a more in-depth and timely way on many social and environmental issues.
很有必要训练新闻工作者的敏感性,通过深入及时地报道有关社会和环境事件,使他们能预计并阻止最糟糕的事件的发生。

④ That might be a powerful way of reflecting contemporary social values and promoting socially positive attitudes and behaviour.
可能会有一个更有效的方法,来反映现代社会价值观,推进人们的积极态度及行为。

Phrases and Patterns

1. In that context 在那一点上
   In that context, three examples were cited as follows.
   在那一点上,以下三个例子被引用了进来。
   In that context, China has precedence over other countries in environmental protection.
   在那一点上,中国在环境保护上优于其他国家。

Questions

1. What are the dissimilarities between the growth of Asian cities and that of western cities?
2. What kind of role does media play in urban development?

3.6 Urban Transport and Communications
城市交通

Public Transport

Undoubtedly, there was a need for more and better public transport in Asian and Pacific cities, particularly in the large, dense cities.

The dangers of trying to control public transport fares were highlighted—it was staled that that could backfire and lead to a decline in public transport supply.

A plea was made not to forget the role of buses and other public transport. Mass transit was very important but buses would also continue to play a significant role. There were many cost-effective measures which could be taken to improve bus service, speed and reliability (including bus lanes, bus priority at traffic lights, busways, etc).

Walking and Non-motorized Vehicles

Non-motorized transport (walking, bicycles, tricycles, trishaws, etc) was recognized as an important part of an integrated transport system. Those modes were too often trivialized and not taken seriously as transport modes. Most trips in densely populated cities were short and within the range of non-motorized transport. Pedalled vehicles integrated very well with public transport as feeder modes (e. g. Japan).

Case Studies and Best Practices

Several pleas were made not to forget smaller, intermediate and provincial cities—often the focus was only on the capitals and megacities. Some of the cases mentioned, the successful bus system in Madras, and Curitiba's "surface metro" (which was a busway system) and integration of land-use planning with the transport system were highlighted as useful models.

Singapore's philosophy of restraining private vehicles and promoting public transport was also highlighted. It was pointed out that Singapore began that process in 1974, at a time of low incomes and many years before the rail mass transit system had been built.

The case study of the Islamic Republic of Iran was mentioned, where the extremely low price of gasoline presented a problem by encouraging high demand for car use. Prevalence of old vehicles also caused air pollution problems.

Equity and Accessibility

It was agreed that more attention should he given to creating transport systems accessible to people with disabilities. In particular, all mass transit systems should be built with disabled access from the outset since it was very expensive to retrofit such access later.

It was pointed out that measures to improve access to public transport and the pedestrian environment for people with disabilities also benefited a very large proportion of the population, including frail elderly people, young children, people with luggage, etc[1].

Private transport facilities benefited a privileged minority in most cities, whereas public transport, cycling and pedestrian facilities benefited the majority, and in particular several disadvantaged groups-people living in poverty, many women, children and those who cared for them, the frail elderly and people with disabilities.

It was further indicated that there was a potential for an "enabling" approach in that field such as access to credit for informal sector providers of public transport and that it was necessary to consider equity impacts of any transport policy measures.

Environmental Impacts and Safety

Transport already had huge environmental impacts in the region, despite low per-capita car ownership in most countries[2]. For example, transport accounted for 70 percent of air pollution in many cities of the region. Thus, transport problems were a large factor in the widespread perception of deteriorating quality of urban life throughout the region.

It was also noted that the rate of deaths and injuries from urban transport were very high in much of the region.

Finally, the importance of enforcement in encouraging cleaner vehicles was emphasized.

Strategic and Flexible Planning Approach

There was a need for coordination and integration of: (a) all aspects of transport planning, (b) measures by all levels of government, and (c) transport with land-use and urban planning. It was also noted that a strategic and flexible planning style was more realistic than a master plan approach. In addition, a package of integrated complementary policies was more powerful than isolated measures (such as mass transit alone). The value of public input into urban transport planning was highlighted, with examples from Bangalore and Bangkok.

Land-use control was weak in many countries and transport infrastructure should be planned wisely because of its influence on new development patterns, including the use of road investment to direct development in desirable directions and avoid sensitive areas, thus using infrastructure projects as de facto urban planning tool. Furthermore, intercity and rural transport infrastructure also had an impact on the development of smaller cities and on the overall urban hierarchy of a nation.

Decentralization was mentioned as a way to avoid congested city centres. "Decentral concentration" was suggested as a better policy. Decentral concentration aimed at having metropolitan areas with a number compact centres of activity in addition to the CBD. That avoided: (a) overconcentration on congested central business districts and (b) random dispersal of businesses and activities, which made public transport difficult to supply and encouraged private transport use.

It was pointed out that mega-projects could be problematic in some countries because of weak administrative capabilities.

Rapid Growth in Vehicle Numbers

It was noted that the number of vehicles was growing very rapidly in many cities and that the need to contain congestion and restrain vehicle use sometimes conflicted with aspiration for large national vehicle industries[3].

Huge numbers of motorcycles in many cities of the region presented special issues and problems. Thus, there was a need for better understanding of those implications.

Latent Demand for Travel in Congested Cities

It was pointed out that in large dense cities, there was usually huge "latent demand" for travel. That meant that if new transport infrastructure was built, it would immediately unleash many new trips which had previously been suppressed[4]. New roads in such cities normally became congested very soon after completion. That latent demand implied that neither building roads alone, nor building mass transit alone, would be enough to solve congestion.

Funding for Infrastructure

It was possible to capture some contribution towards the cost of infrastructure from all parties who benefited from it ("value capture" techniques). Various methods were mentioned, including private developer contributions, requirements for developers to build infrastructure, betterment taxes on land owners, special taxes (such as extra fuel lax) to build a public transport improvement fund, etc.

It was noted that the cost of infrastructure could affect housing affordability if standards were set too high.

Demand Side Measures

Some of the policies which could be implemented by local governments included: taxation, congestion pricing, road pricing and targeted subsidies.

It was noted that social cost should be accounted for-not just private costs. Costs and benefits were often too narrowly conceived in cost-benefit analysis.

It was suggested that each level of government had various powers at its disposal and that there was a need for integration and cooperation. Local governments usually had some power over road space allocation, land-use planning, parking supply and parking prices—all of which could he used in transport policy.

Fair and Efficient Road Space Allocation

Private transport modes were much less efficient in terms of use of space than public or non-motorized modes. Therefore reallocation of road space was justified to improve efficiency. Measures included bus lanes, bicycle lanes, high-occupancy-vehicle lanes, busways, bus and bicycle priority measures at traffic lights.

Communications

Communications was mentioned as extremely important to business and communications technology as a potential "safety valve" for transportation demand.

The service level of telecommunications seemed to be improving rapidly in most countries. Technology change and an increased private sector role were given some credit. However, urban-rural and regional equity of access with respect to greater private sector focus was an issue of concern since there was an increasing focus on urban markets.

Words and Expressions

plea [pliː] *n.* 恳求;请求;辩解;借口
busway ['bʌswei] *n.* [电]汇流条通道;配电通道;母线通道
trivialize ['triviəlaiz] *vt.* 使平凡;使琐碎

pedal ['pedl] v. 踩……的踏板
intermediate [ˌintə'miːdjət] adj. 中间的
megacity ['megəˌsiti] n. (人口超过 100 万的)大城市
prevalence ['prevələns] n. 流行
accessibility [ˌæksesi'biliti] n. 易接近；可到达的
retrofit ['retrəˌfit] n. 式样翻新；花样翻新
pedestrian [pe'destriən] n. 步行者
deteriorate [di'tiəriəreit] v. (使)恶化
complementary [ˌkɔmplə'mentəri] adj. 补充的；补足的
de facto [dei'fæktəu] adj. 事实上的；实际的
dispersal [di'pəːsəl] n. 散布；分散；消散；驱散；疏散
latent ['leitənt] adj. 潜在的；潜伏的；隐藏的
unleash ['ʌn'liːʃ] v. 释放
subsidy ['sʌbsidi] n. 补助金；津贴
public transport fare 公共汽车费
mass transit 公共交通；公共交通工具(总称)大量客运
cost-effective 有成本效益的；划算的
bus lane (街道上的)公共汽车专用车道
transport facility 交通运输工具
account for 说明；占；解决；得分
safety valve 安全阀
pedestrian environment 步行交通

Difficult Sentences

① It was pointed out that measures to improve access to public transport and the pedestrian environment for people with disabilities also benefited a very large proportion of the population, including frail elderly people, young children, people with luggage, etc.
据报道，为残疾人士设计的公共交通便利方式以及步行街的建立，同样会使一大群人受益，包括老人、儿童以及提着行李的人们。

② Transport already had huge environmental impacts in the region, despite low per-capita car ownership in most countries.

交通已经对这一地区的环境产生了影响,尽管大多数国家人均拥有车的数量是很低的。

③ It was noted that the number of vehicles was grow in very rapidly in many cities and that the need to contain congestion and restrain vehicle use sometimes conflicted with aspiration for large national vehicle industries.

据报道,汽车的数量在大多数城市里都增长得很快,因此控制交通拥挤、限制汽车的使用,就与大型的国家汽车工业的发展壮大形成了矛盾。

④ That meant that if new transport infrastructure was built, it would immediately unleash many new trips which had previously been suppressed.

这就意味着如果建立新的交通设施,以往大受钳制的交通状况将会立即得到缓解。

Phrases and Patterns

1. It was pointed out that …据报道

    It was pointed out that Singapore began that process in 1974, at a time of low incomes and many years before the rail mass transit system had been built.

    据报道,新加坡于1974年开始了这一过程,这一年正是低收入和公共交通系统建立之前。

    It was pointed out that China has precedence over other countries in environmental protection.

    据报道,中国在环境保护上优于其他国家。

Questions

1. What does accessibility mean to transportation?
2. What is the strategic and flexible planning approach?

3. What are demanded side measures?

3.7 Urban Physical and Social Space
城市的物质空间与社会空间

Most of the planning models used in Asia were derived from the West. However, the Asian space had different characteristics from the Western space[①]. Therefore, attempts should be made to rescue the elements of the Asian space bearing in mind that there was not one single Asian space but a variety of spaces[②].

There was a trend towards multifunctional spaces.

There was also a trend for malls to become the only "community" spaces available, with the resulting changes in patterns of consumption and in cultural values. In addition, foreign investment and international markets affected land-use patterns and consequently, the urban physical and social space.

Social space in modem urban areas was a commodity and issues concerning accessibility of social spaces by different groups should be examined.

Some of the conceptual and political issues which needed to be examined included:

· Who defined a space as private, public, community, etc;

· Differences between mobility and transport;

· The relationship between market development and spatial arrangements, including the tension between overall planning and local needs;

· Security as a concept;

· The division of urban spaces according to economic and ethnic groups, professions, etc.

There was a need for more participation in the planning and organization of urban spaces, NGOs and community should advise governments on the planning process. Public hearings and local development councils could be used for that purpose.

Planning of urban spaces should be made through a process of consultation and collaboration, i. e. give and lake. Culture should be preserved together with the social life and not at the expense of social life.

Urban spaces should be accessible to all, i. e. disabled, elderly, children, women, etc. Lack of access might translate into lack of opportunities such as education.

Legal action and support might be required in cases such as the creation of barrier-free environments, percentage of land reserved for open spaces, housing rights for women, etc.

Words and Expressions

commodity [kə'mɔditi] *n.* 日用品
conceptual [kən'septʃuəl] *adj.* 概念上的
spatial ['speiʃəl] *adj.* 空间的
consultation [ˌkɔnsəl'teiʃən] *n.* 请教；咨询；磋商
bear in mind 记住
patterns of consumption 消费结构
ethnic group 同种同文化之民族
legal action 诉讼
planning models 规划模型

Difficult Sentences

① Most of the planning models used in Asia were derived from the West. However, the Asian space had different characteristics from the Western space.
大多数亚洲国家采用的规划模型的灵感来自于西方。然而，亚洲的空间特点却区别于西方国家。

② Therefore, attempts should be made to rescue the elements of the

Asian space bearing in mind that there was not one single Asian space but a variety of spaces.

因此,应该尽力保存亚洲地区的特色,并牢记除了亚洲地区还有许多其他区域存在。

Phrases and Patterns

1. at the expense of 以牺牲……为代价
   Culture should be preserved together with the social life and not at the expense of social life.
   文化应该和社会生活一起保存下来,而不是以牺牲社会生活为代价的。
   Economic development should be harmonious with environmental protection, not at the expense of it.
   经济发展应该与环境保护和谐发展,而不是以牺牲环保为代价。

Questions

1. What was the trend of Asian space?
2. What are necessary elements in the planning and organization of urban spaces?

3.8 Housing and Urban Indicators
住房和城市的基本情况

A presentation was made on the Housing and Urban Indicators Programme. Its objectives, methodology, database and operational problems in selected Asian countries and in that perspective, the activities being planned to continue the work beyond Istanbul as pan of a programme to develop management techniques and capabilities of city governments were brought out[①]. The main recommendations of the group were:

· The indicators programme was a useful activity that could

strengthen capacity to formulate, manage and implement programmes, especially in the changing environment of government emerging as a facilitator and other actors coming to play a more critical role than in the past. The slowdown in budgetary funds' flow and increased recourse to market-cost funds made it essential to ensure better use of resources and indicators were a facilitating tool to monitor those activities and brine about a better level of coordination and dovetailing of activities than in the past.

• In many cases, the indicators worksheets had initially (and in some cases even now) scared people and the reaction was "It can't be done" The constraint of bringing them out in one language, inadequate explanations and lack of illustrative examples were some of the reasons. Some were of the view that the indicators were too sophisticated to be used at the city level. Promotional activity was missing and no attempt was made to clear doubts whether the data generated and indicators provided would not be used by international agencies against the interests of the countries. What emerged was that regional and subregional workshops and awareness creation and advocacy work should have been given a high priority and just mailing the worksheets was not an effective method of developing the indicators programme.

• The list of indicators should be very compact and many of the indicators on which data were not easily available and did not seem relevant in the Asia-Pacific region might be deleted. Some of them related to land use, house tenure and housing finance. Indicators did not recognize specific local socio-community practices such as extended families, community land holdings, etc.

• Many of the indicators should be developed at the town level and capture town-specific issues. The present package of indicators should be developed at a sufficient level of desegregation, to capture sensitivities of formal and informal settlements, gender issue and income categories and cover also activities like eviction (housing destroyed), quality of life, new urban-related crimes, social development activities, among others.

• The indicators in the different modules should he interlinked and a set of integrated composite indicators should be developed, instead of single-purpose ones. It would be dangerous to use individual indicators to the exclusion of their relationship with other indicators. An operational framework should be developed to interlink the indicators for analytical purposes.

• Over time, indicators should be developed on a time series basis. Basically secondary and regularly available data should be used, and if necessary, supplemented by primary survey data, including quick surveys recommended by UNCHS[2].

• Additional inputs were required to effectively translate national data (say GNP, poverty line, income distribution) into city data, as the latter were normally not available. Also, data in monetary terms had limitations and alternative data had to be developed for effective comparison across projects and over time.

• The main objectives of the Indicators programme should be to facilitate city governments and other actors to manage city activities and to facilitate comparisons of situations within the country or region. Cross-country comparisons across regions should not be the main objective and might be a long-term objective. The impression that those indicators were basically for international comparisons should be removed.

• Focuses on social indicators, particularly on women, children and informal settlements, should be developed as special modules.

• The indicators should be projected as being "user-friendly": simple to develop, easy to understand, readily accessible and applicable to assess situations and suggest solutions. Some norms on "good" and "bad" situations might be developed and disseminated and a brief "indicators interpretation" guide should be made available. The indicators should develop into a rapid urban appraisal package and be used to promote a rapid assessment culture.

• The indicators work should be also linked to national census and similar database development activity.

• An international reporting system for city/town performance might be developed, using the indicators and recommended to city and national governments. The activity should be taken up at the city level through a collaborative endeavour of city governments, NGOs and research and training institutions.

• The global and regional observatory, whose need was strongly endorsed should not, however, remain only a depository of data and information, but should emerge as a global and regional resource centre that should provide technical and human resources to cities/countries to develop the indicator activities, to take up advocacy and promotional work and facilitate the eventual outcome of a "state of the city" report on a regular basis.

All United Nations agencies should collaborate in the indicators activity. At the drafting stage, each specialized agency should be consulted for technical guidance on the appropriateness of the indicators and the promotion and application through their respective programmes[3].

Government participation should be a sine qua non if the indicators were to be accepted and used, ultimately for planning, policy and monitoring purposes.

Words and Expressions

indicator ['indikeitə] *n.* 指示器；[化]指示剂

methodology [meθə'dɔlədʒi] *n.* 方法学；方法论

Istanbul [ˌistæn'buːl] *n.* 伊斯坦布尔(土耳其西北部港市)

formulate ['fɔːmjuleit] *vt.* 用公式表示；明确地表达；作简洁陈述

promotional [prəʊˈməʊʃənəl] *adj.* 增进的；奖励的
subregion [ˈsʌbˌriːdʒən] *n.* (动植物分布的)亚区
desegregation [ˌdiːsegriˈgeiʃən] *n.* 废止种族歧视
eviction [i(ː)ˈvikʃən] *n.* 逐出；赶出
module [ˈmɔdjuːl] *n.* 模数；模块；登月舱；指令舱
supplement [ˈsʌplimənt] *v.* 补充
facilitate [fəˈsiliteit] *vt.* (不以人作主语的)使容易；使便利；推动；帮助；使容易；促进
cross-country [krɔsˈkʌntri; (US) ˈkrɔːs-] *adj.* 越野的；横过田野的
appraisal [əˈpreizəl] *n.* 评价；估价(尤指估价财产；以便征税)；鉴定
endorse [inˈdɔːs] *v.* 在(票据)背面签名；签注(文件)；认可；签署
operational problem 操作问题
housing finance 住宅信贷
time series 时间数列[序列]
UNCHS (abbr. = United Nations Centre for Human Settlement) 联合国人类居住中心
user-friendly [计]用户界面友好的；用户容易掌握使用的
national census 人口普查
draft stage 起草阶段(标准，专利用语)
sine qua non 必要条件；要素

Difficult Sentences

① Its objectives, methodology, database and operational problems in selected Asian countries and in that perspective, the activities being planned to continue the work beyond Istanbul as plan of a programme to develop management techniques and capabilities of city governments were brought out.
目标、方法论、数据库和操作问题已经在所选的亚洲国家实施开了。此次活动正在被规划中，目的是在除伊斯坦布尔之外的其他地区继续改善管理技术及政府能力。

② Over time, indicators should be developed on a time series basis. Basically secondary and regularly available data should be used, and

if necessary, supplemented by primary survey data, including quick surveys recommended by UNCHS.
一段时间以后，指标应该按时间的顺序发展下去。基本上，次要的数据应被利用上，如有必要的话，联合国人类居住中心建议的初级数据也可以加上。

③ At the drafting stage, each specialized agency should be consulted for technical guidance on the appropriateness of the indicators and the promotion and application through their respective programmes.
在开始阶段，每个专项规划组织都应就指标的恰当性进行磋商，给以技术指导，并依照各自的程序加以改进和应用。

Phrases and Patterns

1. among others 除了别的以外
   The present package of indicators should cover also activities like quality of life, and social development activities, among others.
   除了别的以外，现阶段的指标应包括生活质量和社会发展活动。
   Environment is basic to human beings, among other things.
   除了别的因素以外，环境也是人类生存的基础。

2. to the exclusion of 排斥着
   It would be dangerous to use individual indicators to the exclusion of their relationship with other indicators.
   如果只在意一个指标而排斥它与其他指标的联系就会很危险。
   It would be dangerous to focus on economic development to the exclusion of environmental protection.
   如果只在意经济建设而忽视环境保护就会很危险。

Questions

1. What is the indicators programme?
2. What are the main purposes for indicators programme?

4

City for Human Development
适合人类发展的城市

【本章导读】 本章共3篇文章,均在探讨什么样的城市是适宜人类发展的城市。

4.1 是希腊城市规划实践家和人类聚居学理论家道萨迪亚斯(C. A. Doxiadis)通过研究希腊、德国等城镇居民点的实际情况,提出的18个假说。道萨迪亚斯认为未来的城市不仅应该使该城市的居民快乐并安全,还应该给居民创造发展各自潜能的条件。

4.2、4.3 是针对道萨迪亚斯的18个假说中某些问题的讨论,大城市还是小城市更加适合人的居住?人们为什么涌入大城市?现代人的生活模式以及城市污染等等。

4.1　Eighteen Hypotheses
18个假说

Although one of the members of our group opposes the definition that I am using of the goal of the city, I have been impressed from my youth by the definition given by Aristotle, who said that the goal of the city is to make Man(Anthropos), the citizen, happy and safe. I have read a lot in forty years of professional life and found many other definitions. But I have concluded that this is the only one that I can hold to, with one major difference; the population of the ancient Greek world at the time of Aristotle had reached a levelling-off point, and probably Aristotle was not at all concerned about zero growth of population and energy, because they had already reached their maximum. This means that today Aristotle's goals are not sufficient by themselves, because of the colossal explosion of forces in the fields of science, technology, energy, population, etc. It has therefore become imperative that Man (Anthropos) should develop, so that he can manage to remain in balance and therefore feel safe and happy in the new world around him. Just as Man (Anthropos) was obliged to adapt himself to new conditions when he created the first cities, he must adapt himself now that he is building dynapolis, which is turning the metropolis into megalopolis and laying the foundation for Ecumenopolis①. Aristotle was also probably not concerned about the notion of: Where we go from here? But today, we are in an earlier development phase in our civilization and therefore I think we have to add that the goal of the city is to make Man (Anthropos) happy and safe and also to help his human development.

All right but how far forward do we look? Can we consider Man (Anthropos) a thousand years from now? This seems absurd and probably the most we can seriously consider is the next three to five generations. These are the reasons why a decision was made to hold a gathering of a few scientists who are interested in the fate of Man (Anthropos) in order to discuss whether it is within our ability to create a city which will make Man (Anthropos) both happy and secure, as undoubtedly all would want, and which would also help him to develop in a more satisfactory manner, as is being envisaged, or at least anticipated throughout the world.

In order to facilitate the discussion I have drawn up a proposal which faces this problem from the point of view of a craftsman who builds houses and cities, and who feels the need to develop them in a responsible manner.

The report is based on the following hypotheses:

Hypothesis one: We are dealing with a very complex, dynamic system of life on the surface of the earth, where every part has an influence on the others. These influences follow certain principles and laws, some of which we know and some we do not, because of their complexity. But the whole is a dynamically changing system (it was not in the time of Aristotle), that has positive or negative effects on its parts depending on the criteria we use. I want to insist on this. We have to talk about the most complex system created on this earth.

Hypothesis two: Throughout human history, Man (Anthropos) has been guided by the same five principles in every attempt he makes to live normally and survive by creating a settlement which is the physical expression of his system of life[2].

The first principle is maximization of Man's (Anthropos') potential contacts. If the black dots represent clusters of people and somebody wants either to create their capital city, or to supply all of them with goods, or to deliver any services, he will certainly select the location shown. This is true from ancient days to the present; Man (Anthropos) seeks a maximization of potential contacts.

The second principle is the minimization of energy. Biologists and zoologists may be able to show that not only Man (Anthropos), but also animals observe this principle. Actually, a donkey going uphill, tries to discover the best possible path for minimization of energy.

The third principle, which is also probably common to other animals is that we create around us an optimum protective space. When we talk together, when we sleep in bed with the other sex, when we move away from something that annoys us; each time we seek an optimum dimension. This is just as true of city building which always has optimum distances: not maximum or minimum distances but optimum ones.

The fourth principle is that we seek a balance between the five elements that form the human settlements: Nature, Man (Anthropos), Society, Shells, Networks.

 The fifth principle is an optimum synthesis of the previous four principles, based on time and space, on actual conditions and on Man's (Anthropos') ability to create his own synthesis[③]. Fig. 4.1 shows a simple expression: a room. We think it is so simple to create a room but it took Man (Anthropos) tens of thousands of years to achieve it, and it was a great invention. A room is a place in which Man (Anthropos) can maximize his contacts with family and friends with minimum effort (opening a door); he can optimize his protective space (by closing the door); he can optimize his contacts with Nature, Society, Shells and Networks (by adjusting doors and windows to control view, temperature, etc.).

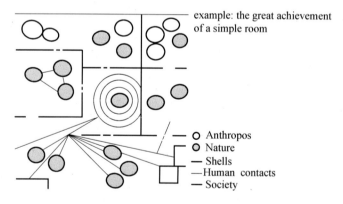

Fig. 4.1 Fifth Principle: Optimization in the Synthesis of All Principles
图 4.1 第五原则:所有原则的综合优化

 Hypothesis three: Man's (Anthropos') attention to his whole system of life is indirect. His main direct interest is his own safely, happiness, and, at times, his development. Balance, on the basis of human satisfaction, is Man's (Anthropos') ultimate goal when dealing with his system of life. Our goal should be to reach a new balance between Man (Anthropos) and Nature corresponding to the many changes which have occurred as a result of Man's (Anthropos') new needs and development. This balance cannot now be expressed only at the village scale (as was the goal ten thousand years ago) or only at the city scale (an additional goal over the last five thousand years), but at all scales from Man (Anthropos) himself to the whole earth. This means that the system of Man (Anthropos), Nature and other elements must all change as they move towards the same goal.

Hypothesis four: The settlements created by Man (Anthropos), guided by the first four principles, have been more successful, and have made their inhabitants happier and able to live longer whenever the fifth principle of a balance between the other four has been well applied. I have chosen a simple example from primitive man showing how he gradually moved from the notion of isolated huts to a sequence of straight walls separating adjacent rooms. This is the sort of way that Man (Anthropos) has resolved many of his problems.

Hypothesis five: Human settlements will be created in the future by Man (Anthropos) guided by his own five principles which should not and cannot be changed by anyone.

Hypothesis six: The big city is inevitable; it is already growing and it is going to grow even more since it has now become a multi-speed city. Our task is to discover and understand why the city is changing at present and where this continuous change will lead. In the past we had isolated cities or villages dependent on human energy. But then came the different systems of mechanized energy—the railway and the automobile—and mankind moved to another type of city: People can now move at higher speeds and in this way their commuting fields, which are parts of their fields of movement (kinetic fields), grow to form systems of cities which give birth to new ones where these kinetic fields overlap. The old, static city is turning first into a dynamic one, the polis into dynapolis, and finally into an urban system.

Hypothesis seven: The future city is going to be much more complex in every respect for very many reasons—from new technology and new dimensions to the three forces which condition its shape. These three forces, which increase the complexity beyond those created by the multi-speed systems, are the attraction of existing urban systems, the existing and new lines of transportation and esthetics.

Hypothesis eight: The future city is going to grow much more than the city of the present because of the growth of (a) population, which will take time to slow down, (b) income and energy and (c) Man's (Anthropos') mobility.

Hypothesis nine: The main crisis of the city is due to a lack of balance between the five elements. There are certainly many reasons for this but the basic ones are the increase in its dimensions (people, area, energy, economy) and the changes in its physical structure.

Hypothesis ten: The inevitable evolution in the structure and the dimensions of today's cities are leading to a universal city, Ecumenopolis. This evolution is going to occur by stages in the next few generations. The spread of present-day urban systems is inevitable. Their foundation stone was laid in 1825 when the first railway ran with passengers in northern England. Urban systems are already 147 years old and they are going to become much larger. The trouble is that we do not understand these facts. We close our eyes in fear and let our urban systems remain without proper structure, leading more and more towards bad conditions and a poor quality of life.

We can easily foresee, that if we avoid any major catastrophe, that we will have to deal with a universal city whose population will tend to be stable in numbers but increasingly more developed intellectually and socially, which will dispose of much greater quantities of energy and achieve greater social interaction.

What is going to happen to Man (Anthropos) within this complex system? We have to consider "Man (Anthropos) within his City", and my next hypothesis states:

Hypothesis eleven: The first goal of human development must be to help the average person develop to the maximum of his potential (as we do now for longevity), and the second must be gradually to increase the level of this potential to its maximum in order to help humanity develop to its utmost.

Hypothesis twelve: The greatest difference which exists in the relationship of Man (Anthropos) and his settlements is the difference between people in varying phases of their life. Any grown-up can walk in the street with cars; even if he has not seen one before he can adjust to them. But a two-year-old cannot. I have been hearing all my life about racial segregation, religious segregation, etc., but the largest difference I have found in the relation of people to the city is by age-groups because a black, a white or a red man can cross the street but their small children cannot. From this, I tried to find how people are divided by age-groups, and here I can cite the divisions in Sanskrit philosophy and those made by Shakespeare and several experts, including Dr. Erikson who is with us. I then took the initiative, not as an expert on Man (Anthropos) but as a builder of cities, to see which phases of our life are related to the city in different ways. We start with the prenatal or fetal phase; then the breast dependent infant; then the toddler, preschool childhood, school age etc., until we reach old age. Having clients of all these ages, 1 could see different needs for each different group.

Hypothesis thirteen: Man (Anthropos) should be given the opportunity to move out as far and to as many places as he needs in every phase of his development. This, for the average person, means to start from the minimum distance—the body of his mother—and to expand to the whole earth or even go beyond it and then, gradually, reduce to the smaller areas corresponding to actual needs and interests. This is an ultimate goal facilitated by modern science and technology.

Hypothesis fourteen: Man (Anthropos) should be given the opportunity to move by himself without any assistance as far out as he wishes and in the best possible way for him and in every phase of his development. I asked myself whether one could speak a bit more clearly about this, and Fig. 4.2 shows two curves, one delineating the areas within which we can move by walking, having an independent natural movement, the other the areas for which we have to use machines. Figs. 4.3, 4.4 and 4.5 show the gradual exposure of the child to his environment. First, only the room as seen from his small bed, then the house and garden, gradually the small street and wider areas.

Hypothesis fifteen: A city must guarantee everybody the best possible development under conditions of freedom and safety and thus it becomes a specific goal to fit the city to Man (Anthropos) in the same way that a tailor fits a suit to our body and not vice versa[④]. We always have to think how the city can best be built to fit human needs. This means that the man-built environment (Shells and Networks) should protect Man (Anthropos) physically from adverse exposures to his physical environment: this also should apply to Nature, with its various aspects all serving Man (Anthropos) as structures and as functions.

Hypothesis sixteen: A City for Human Development must create a system that can challenge every citizen to enjoy it and develop himself to his maximum, and this can only be achieved by a system of quality that transmits the notion of order. This can be done if the system has the proper quality at an optimum level (not too low and not too high and intense) with the larger part of the system representing an order and the

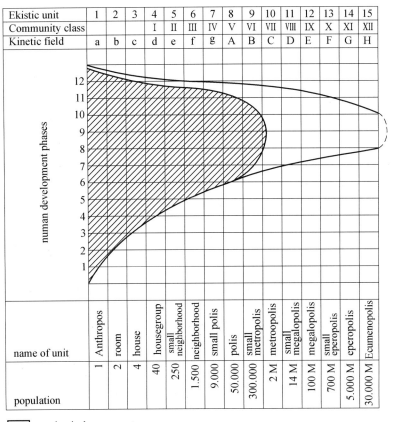

Fig. 4.2 Mobility in Space Conquering the World the Natural Way
图 4.2 空间的灵活性：自然方式征服世界

smaller parts a disorder. We cannot expect civilization to be created within the jungle although a garden can be like a jungle within an orderly system.

The relation of Man (Anthropos) to space is not so simple. For example we can enclose the child in a room but open it at the top (the atrium); open it also to the garden; open it more and more so that we

Fig. 4.3 The Room as the Infant Sees It
图 4.3 婴儿眼中的房间

Fig. 4.4 The Garden as the Infant Sees It
图 4.4 婴儿眼中的花园

can see the complexity of the system related to the energy explosion of the small child.

Hypothesis seventeen: Man (Anthropos) always needs to maximize his potential contacts with people and minimize the energy required, but this has to be accomplished without endangering the quality and quantity

Fig. 4.5 The Home-street
图4.5 乡村街道

of his contacts. This requires a gradual exposure to the city and its people, with an optimum situation for every developmental phase, allowing for the possibility throughout Man's (Anthropos') lifetime of exposure to areas with different types and intensities of contacts. If we have insurmountable boundaries, as in a prison, the energy has no outlet and it may blow up.

Hypothesis eighteen: The task of the city is to help the source of energy—that is the individual—to respond to all challenges and to develop and meet as many new ones as possible. If this can be achieved from the individual's first relationship to his environment, then the source of his energy becomes stronger and can overcome even more hindrances. Such a well developed source of energy will finally be able to conquer the whole space—physical, sensory, intellectual—which surrounds it, although this does not necessarily mean that it can conquer all obstacles within this space. Fig. 4.6 shows that in stage one all the time is spent inside the mother; then most of the time is in the room, then in the home, then school and high school, then downtown business or factory, at some distance away; but the system as a whole emphasizes that we spend nearly 80% of our time inside our home and in the small area around it.

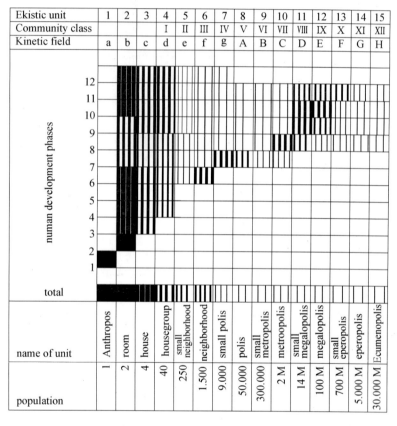

Fig. 4.6 Time Spent in Different Units of Space in Every Phase of Life
图4.6 人生各个阶段不同空间单元的时间

We can proceed and speak about the meaning of each unit of space for every phase of our life. It is clear that the room and the house and the immediate environment are of the greatest importance. If we have noise there, we suffer. If we have noise on the highway which we cross to go to work we care much less.

The importance of space in each different phase of life related to its total importance shows that what really matters are the smaller units. And I began to ask myself, as a builder of houses, whether we are sure what it is we want the small child to see in its early phase. On Fig. 4.7 I put question marks on the walls (the colors, the light). And then let us try to look at the courtyard, as the child sees it. Here the child is safe but it begins to see the sky instead of ceiling; it begins to learn to contact strangers without danger to itself. We can then think of the further units of human scale within which the child can move by itself and the broader units and the broader system of balances up to the whole system corresponding to the world of the young adults who can drive all over it.

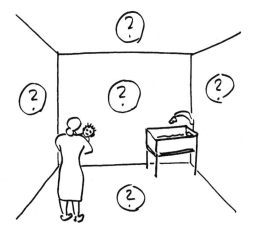

Fig. 4.7 What Kind of Room?
图 4.7 什么性质的房间?

In the past we had centers of power and centers of religion but we dream of a future where hospitable centers for learning and human development in the broadest sense are going to be at least of equal importance with the centers of power. We cannot turn the philosophers into kings but we must always attempt to give them enough power to influence Man (Anthropos).

Words and Expressions

hypotheses [hai'pɔθisi:z] n. 假设；假说
colossal [kə'lɔsl] adj. 巨大的；异常的；非常的
imperative [im'perətiv] adj. 绝对必要的；紧急的；迫切的；不可避免的
dynapolis [dai'næpəlis] n. (交通干线附近的)新兴城市
megalopolis [ˌmegə'lɔpəlis] n. 特大城市(由几个城市和郊区连成的)；特大城市的生活方式；以大城市为中心的人口稠密区
Ecumenopolis [ˌekjumi'nɔpəlis] n. 世界都市观(把世界看做是一个延伸的广大城市)
envisage [in'vizidʒ] v. 正视；面对(事实等)；想象；拟想；展望
facilitate [fə'siliteit] v. 使容易；帮助；促进
craftsman ['krɑ:ftsmən] n. 手艺人；工匠；技工
settlement ['setlmənt] n. 居留地；新建区；住宅区
maximization [ˌmæksəmai'zeiʃən] n. 最大值化；极大值化
minimization ['minimaiˌzeiʃən] n. 小型化；化为最小值；最简化
optimum ['ɔptiməm] n. 最适宜(条件)；最适度
shell [ʃel] n. 薄片；房屋的框架
optimize ['ɔptimaiz] v. 表示乐观；优化
kinetic [kai'netik] adj. 动力(学)的；运动的
polis ['pəulis] n. 古希腊的城邦
esthetics [i:s'θetiks] n. 美学；审美学
mobility [məu'biliti] n. 可动性；流动性；能动性
Sanskrit ['sænskrit] adj. 梵语的；梵文的
prenatal ['pri:'neitl] adj. 出生前的；胎儿期的
fetal ['fi:tl] adj. 胎儿的；胎的
delineate [di'linieit] v. 描……的外形；画……的轮廓；勾画

atrium [ˈɑːtriəm] n. (罗马建筑内部的)中庭;门廊
insurmountable [ˌinsəˈmauntəbl] adj. 不可克服的;难以逾越的
courtyard [ˈkɔːtjɑːd] n. 庭院;院子;天井
zero growth 零增长;不增长
human development 人类发展
optimum dimension 最佳尺寸
optimum distance 最佳距离
optimum synthesis 最优分析
actual conditions 实际情况
direct interest 直接兴趣
multi-speed 多极的;多(种)速(度)的
urban system 城市体系
physical structure 物理结构
foundation stone 基石;基础
complex system 复杂系统
racial segregation 种族分离;种族隔离
Dr. Erikson 加拿大建筑师亚瑟·埃里克森
minimum distance 最小距离
quality and quantity 质与量
source of energy 能源
immediate environment 直接环境
human scale 人类尺度

Difficult Sentences

① Just as Man (Anthropos) was obliged to adapt himself to new conditions when he created the first cities, he must adapt himself now that he is building dynapolis, which is turning the metropolis into megalopolis and laying the foundation for Ecumenopolis.

正如人类在建造了第一座城市时必须使自己适应新的环境一样,他们现在也必须自己适应正在拔地而起的新兴城市,这一切正在把大都市改造成为几个城市相连的特大城市,也逐渐奠定了世界都市观的基础。

② Throughout human history, Man (Anthropos) has been guided by the same five principles in every attempt he makes to live normally and survive by creating a settlement which is the physical expression of his system of life.

纵观整个人类历史,人类一直处于同样的五条原则的指引下,建造能够代表生命的物质存在的容身之所,努力使自己生活得舒适并存续下去。

③ The fifth principle is an optimum synthesis of the previous four principles, based on time and space, on actual conditions and on Man's (Anthropos') ability to create his own synthesis.

第五条原则是对前四条原则的最优分析,根据时间和地点、实际情况、人的基本能力来决定每个人的生存之所的优劣。

④ A city must guarantee everybody the best possible development under conditions of freedom and safety and thus it becomes a specific goal to fit the city to Man (Anthropos) in the same way that a tailor fits a suit to our body and not vice versa.

一座城市必须在自由和保障安全的前提下,确保每个公民的最大限度的发展,因此,就如同裁缝根据我们身体的尺寸量体裁衣一样,使城市适合人的需要也就成为一个明确的目标,但是反过来则不行,即不能让人去适应城市,就像身体不能将就一件衣服一样。

Phrases and Patterns

1. reach the maximum 达到顶点(最高值)
    Wright's masterpiece of the Robie House, built in Chicago in 1909, reached the maximum of his prairie style.
    赖特1909年建于芝加哥的建筑杰作——罗宾别墅,使他的"草原住宅"风格发挥到极致。
    Historically, new towns in Southeast Asia reach the maximum to promote housing and industrial progress while reducing urbanization

pressures by decentralizing employment and population.
历史中,通过分化就业岗位和分散人口的手段,东南亚的新城镇建设最大化地实现了提高住宅质量、推进工业化进程的目的。

2. develop to the maximum of one's potential/ increase the level of one's potential to its maximum 最大地发挥潜能
Students majored in city planning should explore their creativity and develop to the maximum of their potential, so as to make architectural contribution to Chinese culture.
攻读城市设计的学生应当挖掘他们的创造力,最大限度地发挥潜能,以期为中国文化的发展作出建筑领域的贡献。
Limpid Child's eye is imbued with its unique sensibility. The activity can develop to the maximum of its potential, and provide the explanation of the utopia urban development from sociological and psychology point by the artist and educator.
儿童清澈的眼睛赋予其独特的感性心灵,而这项活动可以将其发挥至最大潜力,为艺术家和教育者从社会学、心理学角度阐释乌托邦城市发展提供一条有效途径。

Questions

1. How did Aristotle inspire the author to define the goal of the city?
2. Can you expound the five principles on which Man creates his settlement with your own words?
3. What are the five elements that form the human settlements? How does Man interact with other elements in his settlement?
4. What are the three forces that develop cities and increase their complexity?
5. Do you agree with the eigthteen hypotheses cited by the author? If not, present your viewpoint and support them with examples.

4.2　Great City versus Small City
巨型城市 vs. 微型城市

Here are a few quotations from Doxiadis' original report:

"Because of science and technology the city is changing in a very natural way, but we are still confused and talk about improbable things such as the desirability of the small city, although we know that mankind will always abandon it, and run to the big city①."

Will mankind always run to the big city, and is this forced on us by science and technology? I refuse to believe this. Why do people run to the big city? Doxiadis gives an interesting argument; a minority of "blue people" can find their like in a big city. I admit this only in the case of very undesirable "blue people", such as homosexuals, criminals, drug addicts and drug pushers. They need the big city to hide in! It is true that more desirable "blue people", such as scientists, philosophers, painters also find their like in a big city, but would they not find them easier in smaller places, such as university towns or painters' colonies?

The normal citizen, I believe, runs to the big city mainly because he wants job security. It is easier to find a job, or change it, in a big city, though when the job changes, this leads to the phenomenon of thousands of commuters crossing through the town center every day, from one end of London or New York to the other. A smaller number, especially young ones, drift to the city in search of excitement, but there is hope that this slightly pathological symptom will not always be with us. Many young Swedes already are starting to prefer small towns, or even rural districts, to Stockholm.

I query even more the statement that the drift to the big city <u>is a consequence of</u> science and technology. Certainly, science and technology have enabled crowded multi-million populations to be provided with transport, power, water and food, but how unsatisfactory is the solution of transport! In cities like New York the commuting time is almost independent of the distance. Consequently, it is not the city proper that is growing, but the suburbs②. The populations of the inner cities are already decreasing in the U.S. with well known disastrous consequences for the town finances.

Doxiadis is, of course, right in recognizing the trend towards giant conurbations. But let me ask him (with Lewis Mumford), why he takes a trend for a command? Why does he abandon so lightly the small city, into which his plans would fit so much better? Modern technology can replace commuting by communications, and by the placement of key industries one could make small cities as job-secure as great ones.

There is another argument, which makes me believe that Doxiadis is too rash when saying that "Even if we assume that we could do the impossible and effect an immediate levelling-off of the Earth's population, the urban population would still increase to three times the present size." And "... we should not, and in any case cannot, control the influx of rural people to the urban system." The argument is that crime and drugs are increasing so rapidly, especially in the big cities of the U.S. that responsible parents ought to accept even a small reduction in living standards (which is not at all necessary) to keep their children out of crime and clear of drugs. Small towns (especially newly built ones which have no slums) can be so much more easily policed than big ones.

This question of the unavoidability of the growth of big cities is evidently of the greater importance, and we must thrash it out in the discussion.

Words and Expressions

pathological [pæθə'lɔdʒik(ə)l] *adj.* 病理学的;病理上的

conurbation [ˌkɔnə'beiʃən] *n.* 具有许多卫星城镇的大城市

influx ['inflʌks] *n.* 流入(量);注入(量);汇集;涌进
Doxiadis 道萨迪亚斯(希腊学者、著名城市规划学家首先创立了"人类聚居科学"的理论)
drug addict 吸毒成瘾者;药瘾者
drug pusher 毒品贩子
university town 大学城
inner city 市中心区
Lewis Mumford 刘易斯·芒福德(美国社会学家、城市规划师)
key industry 基础工业
living standard 生活水平

Difficult Sentences

① Because of science and technology the city is changing in a very natural way, but we are still confused and talk about improbable things such as the desirability of the small city, although we know that mankind will always abandon it, and run to the big city.

由于科学和技术所带来的影响,城市必不可免地经历着变化,但我们仍然感到困惑,还在谈及不可能发生的事,如对小城市的向往,虽然我们心里清楚人类总是离弃小城市,奔向大城市。

② I query even more the statement that the drift to the big city is a consequence of science and technology. Certainly, science and technology have enabled crowded multi-million populations to be provided with transport, power, water and food, but how unsatisfactory is the solution of transport! In cities like New York the commuting time is almost independent of the distance. Consequently, it is not the city proper that is growing, but the suburbs.

有种说法认为,移居大城市的热潮是科学和技术发展的必然后果,我对此相当质疑。诚然,科学和技术能为拥挤的数百万人口提供交通、能源、水和食物,但是对于交通运输方面难题的解决是多么的无能为力!在像纽约这样的大城市里,上班通勤所用的时间甚至和距离的远近没有关系。因此,不断发展的不应当是城市,而应当是市郊。

Phrases and Patterns

1. A is a consequence of B B 是造成 A 的原因
   Urban density in Hong Kong is a consequence of hundreds of remote islands and too much mountainous terrain to build on.
   上百个偏远的岛屿以及太多的山地难以盖房,是造成香港人口密集的主要原因。
   Maintenance of existing forests and establishment of new forests is a consequence of the increasing need for the protective and recreational functions of the forests.
   现有森林的维护以及新的森林的开辟,是出于对森林的保护和休养功能的日益增长的需求。

Questions

1. Which one does the author prefer, big city or small city?
2. What are the two arguments mentioned in Doxiadis' report that the author strongly opposes to?

4.3 Economics and Ecology of the City
城市的经济与生态

I am surprised that Doxiadis nowhere seems to mention that the city is for work, not only for habitation. I cannot believe that he thinks only of dormitory towns. I gladly admit that his city is much superior to the usual American "housing development", but this would be measuring from a very low level. John Aldridge, in his book *In the Country of the Young*, speaking of the confusion and aimlessness of American youth writes: "What better can you expect from people who have grown up in housing developments?" Indeed, what other window have these poor people on life and civilization than the school and television?①

The dormitory town is largely an unwelcome creation of the motor car, combined with the economic insecurity which drives people into proximity of big cities. My ideal is a town in which the working place is within walking or at most cycling distance. It is true that modern Man does not like to walk, but perhaps he can learn again. It will do him a lot of good. There is much talk nowadays about people not going to work at all, but doing it at home, at a computer console. This, as well as the other great "future shock" invention, that the housewife should do her shopping at a television screen, and order the goods by pushing some buttons, I consider as unmitigated psychological nonsense. Most people, except perhaps craftsmen and some creative artists, need to get out of the home to do their work, and the housewife needs the walk to the shops and the gossip with others in the shops and markets, or else she will get the typical suburban claustrophobia. But neither is it necessary to travel 10, 20, 30 or more miles to one's working place. The modern light-industry factory need not be ugly; in fact in many small American towns these are the only buildings with some pretension to beauty. They are light, white, pleasant structures, surrounded by well-kept parks.

As regards shops, Doxiadis claims boldly that, "Man can only interact successfully on the ground floors of the city". I hope this does not mean that he approves of the horrible one-floor shopping centers which are now sprouting up in or around the main roads of small American towns? To me they are an architectural eyesore, much worse than the "Emporia" in the English suburbs. Perhaps he has the old-fashioned market place in mind, at the centers of some beautiful German towns? I do hope he will be able to give us a vision of something equally attractive.

The small city must be economically sound; it must not live by exporting labor. In order to assure job-security it must have mainly basic industries which are not too subject to fashions and fluctuations, such as food processing, textiles, clothing, furniture, artistic crafts. Most "modern" industries, such as electronics or aircraft, have too sharp ups and downs.

Ecological soundness can mean very different things. The minimum requirement is of course that the city must not pollute air or water. The problem of pollution has created quite unnecessary heat, because on the whole, in the industrialized countries, it takes only one and one half to two per cent of the GNP to keep air and water clean. If for some industries, such as the paper industry it means an extra cost of 15 ~ 20%, let them add it to the cost of the product! Most of us would be quite happy with that much less paper polluting our writing desks.

But ecological soundness can mean much more than absence of pollution. In a country like Denmark, where agricultural land is already scarce, it may mean strong pressure towards high density town population. Most countries, especially the United States, are still far from this stage, but as I mentioned before, there may be some pressures toward higher density by the wastefulness of oil heating of single, small houses as compared with the ease with which densely populated centers can be provided with central heat. We know how violently the developing countries are reacting to the ecological principles which are now propagandized by the industrialized countries. As they are mostly in hot zones, they can congratulate themselves that at least they will be free from the headache of house heating.

Ecological constraints are, unavoidably, restrictions in the efficiency of production, and they cannot fail to be painful. Unless we are very wise, the greed which is now ruling the industrialized countries will lead to an ecological catastrophe, or, conversely, it may require so much dirigisme that we shall have to give up democracy in the Western sense[②]. In a very thoughtful article, Arnold Toynbee wrote: "... we cannot be sure that even in Britain parliamentary government is going to survive the fearful ordeal of having to revert, on the material plane, to the stable way of life". This is a fearful problem, too enormous to discuss in our small symposium, but we must keep it in the back of our minds.

Words and Expressions

habitation [ˌhæbi'teiʃən] n. 住所；住宅；聚居地
unmitigated [ʌn'mitigeitid] adj. 绝对的；纯粹的；彻头彻尾的
claustrophobia [ˌklɔːstrə'fəubjə] n. 幽闭恐惧症
pretension [pri'tenʃən] n. 矫饰；虚饰；虚荣；做作
eyesore ['aisɔː(r)] n. 刺眼的东西
emporia [em'pɔːriə] n. 商业中心；大百货店
textile ['tekstail] n. 织物；纺织品；纺织原料
propagandize [ˌprɔpə'gændaiz] v. 宣传；传播；(对……)做宣传
dirigisme [ˌdiːriː'ʒiːsm] n. (政府对国民经济)干预或统制(主义)
ordeal [ɔː'diːl] n. 严峻的考验；痛苦的经验；折磨
symposium [sim'pəuziəm] n. 专题讨论会；座谈会；学术报告会
dormitory town 卧城
housing development 住宅新区通常是由同一经营单位设计建造的一群类似的房屋或公寓
computer console 计算机控制台；电脑控制台(计算机的一个组成部分，用于操作员或维护工程师与计算机之间的通信)
future shock 未来冲击，未来震撼(指对未来社会的发展、技术的进步、价值观念及行为准则的变化，担心不能适应而产生的不安情绪。)
exporting labor 劳务输出
food processing 食品加工
high density 高密度
oil heating 油热法
hot zone 断字区
house heating 住房供热

Arnold Toynbee 英国经济历史学家阿诺德·汤因比
parliamentary government 代议政府;议会内阁制;议会政体

Difficult Sentences

① Indeed, what other window have these poor people on life and civilization than the school and television?
的确,除了学校和电视以外,还有什么其他的窗口可以让这些贫苦的人了解生活、展望文明呢?

② Ecological constraints are, unavoidably, restrictions in the efficiency of production, and they cannot fail to be painful. Unless we are very wise, the greed which is now ruling the industrialized countries will lead to an ecological catastrophe, or, conversely, it may require so much dirigisme that we shall have to give up democracy in the Western sense.
不可避免地,生态学所面临的桎梏是高效率生产的有限程度,而且这会一直让人为此头痛不已。除非我们能够很明智,否则它们主宰着工业化国家的人的贪念,必然会导致生态灾难,或者相反,可能会需要政府的介入与干预,而这又会使人们被迫放弃西方概念中的民主。

Phrases and Patterns

1. be sprouting up 涌现
   Recently, a multitude of websites are sprouting up, offering an overall overview of many designers' prolific career and their representative works.
   近来涌现出了大量的网站,全面概述了很多设计者多产的职业生涯以及他们的代表作品。
   Since the 18th century and increasingly since the second half of the 20th century, the demands for transformation of the ancient landscape structures are sprouting up.

从18世纪开始,尤其是从20世纪后50年代以来,要求变革旧有的城市建筑格局的呼声不断涌现。

Questions

1. Why does the author disapprove of the idea of dormitory town?
2. How can a small city achieve its ecnomic and ecological soundness according to the author?

5

City Form
城市形态

【本章导读】 本章5.1~5.10的10篇文章介绍了凯文·林奇的主要城市设计理论。当代著名城市设计师、美国麻省理工学院教授凯文·林奇(Kevin Lynch),把认知心理学引入城市分析和城市设计。他通过多年细心观察和群众调查,对美国波士顿、洛杉矶和新泽西城3座城市作了分析,将城市景观归纳为道路、边界、区域、节点和标志物五大组成因素。通过对五要素的组织,为城市构成一种可意象的景观,清晰、连贯而且有条理。林奇的理论现广泛用于城市设计中。

5.1 Imageable City Form
可意象的城市形态

We have the opportunity of forming our new city world into an imageable landscape: visible, coherent, and clear. It will require a new attitude on the part of the city dweller, and a physical reshaping of his domain into forms which entrance the eye, which organize themselves from level to level in time and space, which can stand as symbols for urban life. The present study yields some clues in this respect.

Most objects which we are accustomed to call beautiful, such as a painting or a tree, are single-purpose things, in which, through long development or the impress of one will, there is an intimate, visible linkage from fine detail to total structure. A city is a multi-purpose, shifting organization, a tent for many functions, raised by many hands and with relative speed①. Complete specialization, final meshing, is improbable and undesirable. The form must be somewhat noncommittal, plastic to the purposes and perceptions of its citizens.

Yet there are fundamental functions of which the city forms may be expressive: circulation, major land-uses, key focal points. The common hopes and pleasures, the sense of community may be made flesh. <u>Above all</u>, if the environment is visibly organized and sharply identified, then the citizen can inform it with his own meanings and connections. Then it will become a true place, remarkable and unmistakable.

To take a single example, Florence is a city of powerful character which has deep hold on the affection of many people. Although many foreigners will at first react to it as cold or forbidding, yet they cannot deny its special intensity. To live in this environment, whatever the economic or social problems encountered, seems to add an extra depth to experience, whether of delight or of melancholy or of belonging②.

The city of course has an economic, cultural, and political history of staggering proportions, and the visual evidence of this past accounts for much of the strong Florentine character. But it is also a highly visible city. It lies in a bowl of hills along the Arno River, so that the hills and the city are almost always inter-visible. On the south, the open country penetrates almost to the heart of the city, setting up a clear contrast, and from one of the last steep hills a terrace gives an "overhead" view of the urban core. On the north, small distinct settlements, such as Fiesole and Settignano, are perched visibly on characteristic hills. From the precise symbolic and transportation center of the city rises the huge and unmistakable dome of the Duomo, flanked by Giotto's campanile, a point of orientation visible in every section of the city and for miles outside of it. This dome is the symbol of Florence.

The central city has district characters of almost oppressive strength: slot-like streets, stone-paved; tall stone and stucco buildings, yellowish-gray in color, with shutters, iron grilles, and cave-like entrances, topped by the characteristic deep Florentine eaves. Within this area are many strong nodes, whose distinctive forms are reinforced by their special use or class of user. The central area is studded with landmarks, each with its own name and story. The Arno River cuts through the whole and connects it to the larger landscape.

To these clear and differentiated forms people have made strong attachments, whether of past history or of their own experience. Every scene is instantly recognizable, and brings to mind a flood of associations. Part fits into part. The visual environment becomes an integral piece of its inhabitants' lives. The city is <u>by no means</u> perfect, even in the limited sense of imageability; nor does all of the city's visual success lie in this one quality. But there seems to be a simple and automatic pleasure, a feeling of satisfaction, presence, and rightness, which arises from the mere sight of the city, or the chance to walk through its streets[③].

Florence is an unusual city. Indeed, even if we no longer confine ourselves to the United States, the highly visible city is still somewhat of a rarity. Imageable villages or city sections are legion, but there may be no more than twenty or thirty cities in the world which present a consistently strong image. Even so, not one of these would encompass more than a few square miles of area. Although the metropolis is no longer a rare phenomenon, yet nowhere in the world is there a metropolitan area with any strong visual character, any evident structure. The famous cities all suffer from the same faceless sprawl at the periphery.

One may reasonably ask, then, if a consistently imageable

metropolis (or even a city), is in fact possible; and whether it would be appreciated if it did exist. Given the lack of examples, it is necessary to argue largely on supposition and by the projection of past events. Men have increased the scope of their perception before, when faced with a new challenge, and there is little reason to see why it could not happen again. There are, furthermore, existing highway sequences which indicate that such a new large-scale organization might be possible.

It is also possible to cite examples of visible form at this larger scale which are not urban examples. Most people can call to mind a few favorite landscapes which have this differentiation, this structure and clear shape that we would like to produce in our living environments. The landscape south of Florence, on the road to Poggibonsi, has this character for mile after mile. The valleys, ridges, and little hills are of great variety, but lead down in a common system. The Appenines bound the horizon in the north and east. The ground, visible over long distances, is cleared and intensively cultivated for a great variety of crops—wheat, olive, grape—each clearly discernible for its own particular color and form. Each fold of the ground is mirrored in the lay of the fields, plants, and paths; each hillock is crowned by some little settlement, church, or tower, so that one could say: "Here is my town, and there is that other." Guided by the geological structure of the natural features, men have achieved a delicate and visible adjustment of their actions. The whole is one landscape, and yet each part can be distinguished from its neighbor.

Sandwich, New Hampshire, might be taken as another example, where the White Mountains sink down into the rolling headwaters of the Merrimac and the Piscataqua Rivers. The forested mountain wall is sharply contrasted with the rolling, half-cultivated country below. To the south the Ossipee Mountains are a final isolated upthrust of hills. Several of the peaks, such as Mr. Chocorua, are of peculiar individual form.

The effect is strongest in the "intervales," the flat plateaus at the very base of the mountains, which ire entirely cleared and which have that strange and powerful sensation of special "place," exactly comparable to the sensation of strong locale in a city like Florence. At the time when all the lower ground was cleared for farming, the entire landscape must have had this quality.

Hawaii might be taken as another more exotic example: with its sharp mountains, highly colored rocks and great cliffs, luxuriant and highly individualized vegetation, contrast of sea and land, and dramatic transitions between one side of the island and another.

These are, of course, personal examples; the reader can substitute his own. Occasionally they are the product of powerful natural events such as on Hawaii; more often, as in Tuscany, they are the product of human modification working for consistent purposes and with common technology on the basic structure provided by a continuous geologic process. If successful, this modification is done with an awareness of the interconnectedness, and yet the individuality, of both natural resources and human purposes.

As an artificial world, the city should be so in the best sense: made by art, shaped for human purposes. It is our ancient habit to adjust to our environment, to discriminate and organize perceptually whatever is present to our senses. Survival and dominance based themselves on this sensuous adaptability, yet now we may go on to a new phase of this interaction. On home grounds, we may begin to adapt the environment itself to the perceptual pattern and symbolic process of the human being.

Words and Expressions

imageable ['imidʒəbl] *adj.* 可成像的;能引起意象的
dweller ['dwelə(r)] *n.* 居住者;居民
noncommittal ['nɔn'kɔmitəl] *adj.* 不明朗的;不承担义务的

Florence [ˈflɔːrəns] n. 佛罗伦萨(意大利都市名)
melancholy [ˈmelənkəli] n. 忧郁
staggering [ˈstæɡəriŋ] adj. 蹒跚的；摇晃的；令人惊愕的
intervisible [ˌintəˈvizəbl] adj. 可通视的
terrace [ˈterəs] n. 梯田；房屋之平顶；露台；阳台；倾斜的平地
duomo [ˈdwɔːmɔː] n. 大教堂；中央寺院
campanile [ˌkæmpəˈniːli] n. 钟楼；钟塔
orientation [ˌɔː(ː)rienˈteiʃən] n. 方向；方位；定位；倾向性；向东方
stucco [ˈstʌkəu] vt. 涂以灰泥；粉刷
encompass [inˈkʌmpəs] v. 包围；环绕；包含或包括某事物
metropolis [miˈtrɔpəlis] n. 首都；主要都市；都会；大主教教区；大城市
metropolitan [ˌmetrəˈpɔlit(ə)n] adj. 首都的；主要都市的；大城市
ridge [ridʒ] n. 背脊；山脊；屋脊；山脉；犁垄
discernible [diˈsɛːnəbl,-ˈzɛː-] adj. 可辨别的
upthrust [ˈʌpˌθrʌst] n. 向上推；向上冲；[地]上冲断层
intervale [ˈintə(ː)veil] n. 丘陵间低地
plateau [ˈplætəu,plæˈtəu] n. 高地；高原；(上升后的)稳定水平(或时期、状态)
exotic [iɡˈzɔtik] adj. 异国情调的；外来的；奇异的
luxuriant [lʌɡˈzjuəriənt] adj. 丰产的；丰富的；肥沃的；奢华的
sensuous [ˈsensjuəs] adj. 感觉上的；给人美感的
perceptual [pəˈseptjuəl] adj. 知觉的；有知觉的
be accustomed to 习惯于
multi-purpose 多用途的；多功能的
focal point 焦点
argue on 辩论[争论]某事
call to mind 回想
sink down 沉落

Difficult Sentences

① A city is a multi-purpose, shifting organization, a tent for many functions, raised by many hands and with relative speed.

一个城市是多用途的、组织多变的、多功能的；是由众人合力迅速建成的。

② To live in this environment, whatever the economic or social problems encountered, seems to add an extra depth to experience, whether of delight or of melancholy or of belonging.

在这样的环境居住，无论遇到什么经济问题或是社会问题，无疑都增加了人们的感性经验，无论是欢喜、忧郁抑或归属感。

③ But there seems to be a simple and automatic pleasure, a feeling of satisfaction, presence, and rightness, which arises from the mere sight of the city, or the chance to walk through its streets.

但是有一种简单、自发的快乐，一种满足感、存在感和充实感，这些都来自于城市的美丽景观，或是偶尔在街头漫步时的所感。

Phrases and Patterns

1. Above all 最重要的是

   Above all, if the environment is visibly organized and sharply identified, then the citizen can inform it with his own meanings and connections.

   最重要的是，如果环境结构合理，特点鲜明，其内涵和关系就会对居民产生影响。

   Above all, environmental protection should become the basic awareness of human beings.

   最重要的是，环境保护应该是人类最基本的意识。

2. by no means 决不

   I'll forgive you this time, but you shall by no means make the mistake again.

   我这次就原谅你，你可不许再犯错误。

   This is by no means a good way to solve the problem.

   这决非解决问题的好办法。

Questions

1. What are the purposes of city form?
2. What are the distinct characteristics of city Florence?
3. What should be the decisive factors in city design?

5.2　Designing the Paths
设计路径

　　To heighten the imageability of the urban environment is to facilitate its visual identification and structuring. The elements isolated above—the paths, edges, landmarks, nodes, and regions—are the building blocks <u>in the process of</u> making firm, differentiated structures at the urban scale. What hints can we draw from the preceding material as to the characteristics such elements might have in a truly imageable environment?

　　The paths, the network of habitual or potential lines of movement through the urban complex, are the most potent means by which the whole can be ordered. The key lines should have some singular quality which marks them off from the surrounding channels: a concentration of some special use or activity along their margins, a characteristic spatial quality, a special texture of floor or facade, a particular lighting pattern, a unique set of smells or sounds, a typical detail or mode of planting. Washington Street may be known by its intensive commerce and slot-like space; Commonwealth Avenue by its tree-lined center.

　　These characters should be so applied as to give continuity to the path. If one or more of these qualities is employed consistently along the line, then the path may be imaged as a continuous, unified element[①]. It may be a boulevard planting of trees, a singular color or texture of pavement, or the classical continuity of bordering facades. The regularity may be a rhythmic one, a repetition of space openings, monuments, or corner drugstores. The very concentration of habitual travel along a path, as by a transit line, will reinforce this familiar, continuous image.

This leads to what might be called a visual hierarchy of the streets and ways, analogous to the familiar recommendation of a functional hierarchy: a sensuous singling out of the key channels, and their unification as continuous perceptual elements. This is the skeleton of the city image.

The line of motion should have clarity of direction. The human computer is disturbed by long successions of turnings, or by gradual, ambiguous curves which in the end produce major directional shifts[2]. The continuous twistings of Venetian calli or of the streets in one of Olmsted's romantic plans, or the gradual turning of Boston's Atlantic Avenue, soon confuse all but the most highly adapted observers. A straight path has clear direction, of course, but so does one with a few well-defined turns close to 90 degrees, or another of many slight turns which yet never loses its basic direction[3].

Observers seem to endow a path with a sense of pointing or irreversible direction, and to identify a street with the destination toward which it goes. A street is perceived, in fact, as a thing which goes toward something. The path should support this perceptually by strong termini, and by a gradient or a directional differentiation, so that it is given a sense of progression, and the opposite directions are unlike[4]. A common gradient is that of ground slope, and one is regularly instructed to go "up" or "down" a street, but there are many others. A progressive thickening of signs, stores, or people may mark the approach to a shopping node; there can be a gradient of color or texture of planting as well; a shortening of block length or a funneling of space may signal the nearness of the city center. Asymmetries may also be used. Perhaps one can proceed by "keeping the park on the left," or by moving "toward the golden dome." Arrows can be used, or all projecting surfaces facing one direction might have a coded color. All these means make the path an oriented element to which other things can be referred. There is no danger of making a "wrong-way" mistake.

If positions along the line can be differentiated in some measurable way, then the line is not only oriented, but scaled as well. Ordinary house numbering is such a technique. A less abstract means is the marking of an identifiable point on the line, so that other places may be thought of as "before" or "after." Several check points improve the definition. Or a quality (such as the space of the corridor) may have a modulation of gradient at a changing rate, so that the change itself has a recognizable form. Thus one could say that a certain place is "just before the street narrows down very rapidly," or "on the shoulder of the hill before the final ascent." The mover can feel not only "I am going in the right direction," but "I am almost there" as well. Where the journey contains such a series of distinct events, a reaching and passing of one sub-goal after another, the trip itself takes on meaning and becomes an experience in its own right.

Observers are impressed, even in memory, by the apparent "kinesthetic" quality of a path, the sense of motion along it: turning, rising, falling. Particularly is this true where the path is traversed at high speed. A great descending curve which approaches a city center can produce an unforgettable image. Tactile and inertial senses enter into this perception of motion, but vision seems to be dominant. Objects along the path can be arranged to sharpen the effect of motion parallax or perspective, or the course of the path ahead may be made visible. The dynamic shaping of the movement line will give it identity and will produce a continuous experience over time.

Any visual exposure of the path, or its goal, heightens its image. A great bridge may do this, an axial avenue, a concave profile, or the distant silhouette of the final destination. The presence of the path may be made evident by high landmarks along it, or other hints. The vital line of circulation becomes palpable before our eyes, and can become the symbol of a fundamental urban function. Conversely, the experience is heightened if the path reveals the presence of other city elements to the traveler: if it penetrates or strikes them tangentially, if it offers hints and symbols of what is passed by. A subway, for example, instead of being buried alive, might suddenly pass through the shopping zone itself, or its station might recall by its form the nature of the city above it[5]. The path might be so shaped that the flow itself becomes sensuously evident: split lanes, ramps, and spirals would allow the traffic to indulge in self-contemplation. All these are techniques of increasing the visual scope of the traveler.

Normally, a city is structured by an organized set of paths. The strategic point in such a set is the intersection, the point of connection and decision for the man in motion. If this can be visualized clearly, if the intersection itself makes a vivid image and if the lie of the two paths with respect to each other is clearly expressed, then the observer can build a satisfactory structure. Boston's Park Square is an ambiguous joining of major surface streets; the junction of Arlington Street and Commonwealth Avenue is clear and sharp. Universally, subway stations fail to make such clear visual joints. Special care must be taken to explain the intricate intersections of modern path systems.

A joint of more than two paths is normally quite difficult to conceptualize. A structure of paths must have a certain simplicity of form to make a clear image. Simplicity in a topological rather than a geometrical sense is required, so that an irregular but approximately right-angled crossing is preferable to a precise trisection. Examples of such simple structures are parallel sets or spindle forms; one-, two-, or three-barred crosses; rectangles; or a few axes linked together.

Paths may also be imaged, not as a specific pattern of certain individual elements, but rather as a network which explains the typical relations between all paths in the set without identifying any particular path. This condition implies a grid which has some consistency, whether direction, topological interrelation, or interspacing. A pure gridiron combines all three, but directional or topological invariance may by themselves be quite effective. The image sharpens if all paths running in one topological sense, or compass direction, are visually differentiated from the other paths. Thus the spatial distinction between Manhattan's Streets and avenues is effective. Color, planting, or detail might serve equally well. Naming and numbering, gradients of space, topography, or derail, differentiation within the net may all give the grid a progressive or even a scaled sense.

There is a final way or organizing a path or a set of paths, which will become of increasing importance in a world of great distances and high speeds. It might be called "melodic" in analogy to music. The events and characteristics along the path—landmarks, space changes, dynamic sensations—might be organized as a melodic line, perceived and imaged as a form which is experienced over a substantial time interval. Since the image would be of a total melody rather than a series of separate points, that image could presumably be more inclusive, and yet less demanding. The form might be the classical introduction – development–climax–conclusion sequence, or it might take more subtle shapes, such as those which avoid final conclusions[6]. The approach to San Francisco across the bay hints at a type of this melodic organization. The technique offers a rich field for design development and experiment.

Words and Expressions

facilitate [fə'siliteit] vt. (不以人作主语的)使容易；使便利；推动；帮助
potent ['pəutənt] adj. 有力的；有效的
facade [fə'sɑːd] n. 正面

continuity [ˌkɔntiˈnju(ː)iti] n. 连续性；连贯性
boulevard [ˈbuːlivɑːd] n. <美>林荫大道
hierarchy [ˈhaiərɑːki] n. 层次；层级
analogous [əˈnæləgəs] adj. 类似的；相似的；可比拟的
endow [inˈdau] v. 捐赠；赋予
irreversible [ˌiriˈvəːsəblˌ-sib-] adj. 不能撤回的；不能取消的
termini [ˈtəːminai] n. 目的地；界标
gradient [ˈgreidiənt] adj. 倾斜的
funnel [ˈfʌnəl] n. 漏斗；烟窗
conceptualize [kənˈseptjuəlaiz] v. 使有概念
asymmetry [æˈsimətri] n. 不对称
modulation [ˌmɔdjuˈleiʃən] n. 调制
kinesthetic [ˌkinisˈθetik, ˌkai-] adj. 肌肉运动知觉的
traverse [ˈtrævə(ː)s] vt. 横过；穿过；经过；在……来回移动；反对；详细研究
tactile [ˈtæktail] n. [心]触觉型
inertial [iˈnəːʃəl] adj. 不活泼的；惯性的
silhouette [ˌsilu(ː)ˈet] n. 侧面影像；轮廓
rectangle [ˈrektæŋgl] n. 长方形；矩形
intersection [ˌintə(ː)ˈsekʃən] n. [数]交集；十字路口；交叉点
invariance [inˈvɛəriəns] n. 不变性；恒定性
subtle [ˈsʌtl] adj. 狡猾的；敏感的；微妙的；精细的；稀薄的
mark off 划分出
light pattern 光图象，(录音)光带 轻型
single out 挑选
ground slope 地面坡度
oriented element 有向元
concave profile (叶片)内弧形面
indulge in 沉湎于

Difficult Sentences

① These characters should be so applied as to give continuity to the path. If one or more of these qualities is employed consistently along the line, then the path may be imaged as a continuous, unified element.

这些特点应该被应用于保持道路的延续性。如果这些特色中的一点或几点被应用到道路建设上,那么道路的延续性和完整性就保持下了。

② The human computer is disturbed by long successions of turnings, or by gradual, ambiguous curves which in the end produce major directional shifts.

人类计算机开始受到一系列缓慢的转变干扰,这些干扰起初并不明显,但最终会产生方向性的重大变化。

③ A straight path has clear direction, of course, but so does one with a few well-defined turns close to 90 degrees, or another of many slight turns which yet never loses its basic direction.

当然一条直路有明确的方向,可是同样的是,一条路即使有几个几乎接近直角的转弯或很多小的弯弯曲曲,也绝对不会失去它的大方向。

④ The path should support this perceptually by strong termini, and by a gradient or a directional differentiation, so that it is given a sense of progression, and the opposite directions are unlike.

道路应该依照这一明显的方向标识性来设计,可以依照坡度的变化、方向的改变,实现一种行进的感觉,而相对的方向涉及要正好不一样。

⑤ A subway, for example, instead of being buried alive, might suddenly pass through the shopping zone itself, or its station might recall by its form the nature of the city above it.

例如地铁,不再被掩盖在地下,而是有可能横跨商业区,也可能出现在地面而成为城市的特色。

⑥ The form might be the classical introduction–development–climax–conclusion sequence, or it might take more subtle shapes, such as those which avoid final conclusions.

形式可能是传统的开端—发展—高潮—结尾的形式,或者可能是更加微妙的形式,例如有些没有给出最后定论的形式。

Phrases and Patterns

1. in the process of 在……过程中
   Human beings play a decisive role in the process of environmental protection.
   人类在环境保护过程中起到了决定性的作用。
   Methods to control contamination are in the process of being tested or tried.
   控制污染的方法正处在被测验的过程中
2. with respect to 关于……
   We were still unsettled with respect to their future plans.
   对于他们有关未来的计划仍然心怀疑虑
   Washington's announcement with respect to the environmental conditioning ended a week of nail-biting.
   美国政府关于环境治理的声明结束了一星期的焦虑不安

Questions

1. Why so paths play a key role in planning a truly imageable environment?
2. What are the means by which one can make the path an oriented element to which other things can be referred?
3. What are the techniques of increasing the visual scope of the traveler?

5.3 Form Qualities
形态特性

These clues for urban design can be summarized in another way, since there are common themes that run through the whole set: the repeated references to certain general physical characteristics. These are the categories of direct interest in design, since they describe qualities that a designer may operate upon. They might be summarized as follows:

(1) Singularity or figure-background clarity: sharpness of boundary (as an abrupt cessation of city development); closure (as an enclosed square); contrast of surface, form, intensity, complexity, size, use, spatial location (as a single tower, a rich decoration, a glaring sign)①. The contrast may be to the immediate visible surroundings, or to the observer's experience. These are the qualities that identify an element, make it remarkable, noticeable, vivid, recognizable. Observers, as their familiarity increases, seem to depend less and less on gross physical continuities to organize the whole, and to delight more and more in contrast and uniqueness which vivify the scene.

(2) Form simplicity: clarity and simplicity of visible form in the geometrical sense, limitation of parts (as the clarity of a grid system, a rectangle, a dome). Forms of this nature are much more easily incorporated in the image, and there is evidence that observers will distort complex facts to simple forms, even at some perceptual and practical cost. When an element is not simultaneously visible as a whole, its shape may be a topological distortion of a simple form and yet be quire understandable.

(3) Continuity: continuance of edge or surface (as in a street channel, skyline, or setback); nearness of parts (as a cluster of buildings); repetition of rhythmic interval (as a street-corner pattern); similarity, analogy, or harmony of surface, form, or use (as in a common building material, repetitive pattern of bay windows, similarity of market activity, use of common signs)②. These are the qualities that facilitate the perception of a complex physical reality as one or as interrelated, the qualities which suggest the bestowing of single identity.

(4) Dominance: dominance of one part over others by means of size, intensity, or interest, resulting in the reading of the whole as a

principal feature with an associated cluster (as in the "Harvard Square area"). This quality, like continuity, allows the necessary simplification of the image by omission and subsumption. Physical characteristics, to the extent that they are over the threshold of attention at all, seem to radiate their image conceptually to some degree, spreading out from a center.

(5) Clarity of Joint: high visibility of joints and seams (as at a major intersection, or on a sea-front); clear relation and interconnection (as of a building to its site, or of a subway station to the street above). These joints are the strategic moments of structure and should be highly perceptible.

(6) Directional Differentiation: asymmetries, gradients, and radial references which differentiate one end from another (as on a path going uphill, away from the sea, and toward the center); or one side from another (as with buildings fronting a park); or one compass direction from another (as by the sunlight, or by the width of north-south avenues). These qualities are heavily used in structuring on the larger scale.

(7) Visual Scope: qualities which increase the range and penetration of vision, either actually or symbolically. These include transparencies (as with glass or buildings on stilts); overlaps (as when structures appear behind others); vistas and panoramas which increase the depth of vision (as on axial streets, broad open spaces, high views); articulating elements (foci, measuring rods, penetrating objects) which visually explain a space; concavity (as of a background hill or curving street) which exposes farther objects to view; clues which speak of an element otherwise invisible (as the sight of activity which is characteristic of a region to come, or the use of characteristic detail to hint at the proximity of another element). All these related qualities facilitate the grasping of a vast and complex whole by increasing, as it

were, the efficiency of vision: its range, penetration, and resolving power.

(8) Motion Awareness: the qualities which make sensible to the observer, through both the visual and the kinesthetic senses, his own actual or potential motion. Such are the devices which improve the clarity of slopes, curves, and interpenetrations; give the experience of motion parallax and perspective; maintain the consistency of direction or direction change; or make visible the distance interval. Since a city is sensed in motion, these qualities are fundamental, and they are used to structure and even to identify, wherever they are coherent enough to make it possible (as: "go left, then right," "at the sharp bend," or "three blocks along this street"). These qualities reinforce and develop what an observer can do to interpret direction or distance, and to sense form in motion itself. With increasing speed, these techniques will need further development in the modern city.

(9) Time Series: series which are sensed over time, including both simple item-by-item linkages, where one element is simply knitted to the two elements before and behind it (as in a casual sequence of detailed landmarks), and also series which are truly structured in time and thus melodic in nature (as if the landmarks would increase in intensity of form until a climax point were reached). The former (simple sequence) is very commonly used, particularly along familiar paths. Its melodic counterpart is more rarely seen, but may be most important to develop in the large, dynamic, modern metropolis. Here what would be imaged would be the developing pattern of elements, rather than the elements themselves—just as we remember melodies, not notes. In a complex environment, it might even be possible to use contrapuntal techniques: moving patterns of opposing melodies or rhythms. These are sophisticated methods, and must be consciously developed. We need fresh thought on the theory of forms which are perceived as a continuity over time, as well

as on design archetypes which exhibit a melodic sequence of image elements or a formed succession of space, texture, motion, light, or silhouette.

(10) Names and Meanings: non-physical characteristics which may enhance the imageability of an element. Names, for example, are important in crystallizing identity. They occasionally give locational clues (North Station). Naming systems (as in the alphabetizing of a street series), will also facilitate the structuring of elements. Meanings and associations, whether social, historical, functional, economic, or individual, constitute an entire realm lying beyond the physical qualities we deal with here. They strongly reinforce such suggestions toward identity or structure as may be latent in the physical form itself.

All of the above-mentioned qualities do not work in isolation. Where one quality is present alone (as a continuity of building material with no other common feature), or the qualities are in conflict (as in two areas of common building type but of different function), the total effect may be weak, or require effort to identify and structure[3]. A certain amount of repetition, redundancy, and reinforcement seems to be necessary. Thus a region would be unmistakable which had a simple form, a continuity of building type and use, which was singular in the city, sharply bounded, clearly jointed to a neighboring region, and visually concave.

Words and Expressions

singularity [ˌsiŋjuˈlæriti] n. 单一；异常；奇异；奇妙；稀有
vivify [ˈvivifai] vt. 给予生气；使复生；使生动；使活跃
distort [disˈtɔːt] vt. 弄歪(嘴脸等)；扭曲；歪曲(真理、事实等)；误报
distortion [disˈtɔːʃən] n. 扭曲；变形；曲解；失真
analogy [əˈnælədʒi] n. 类似；类推
bestowing [biˈstəuiŋ] n. 砖窑中砖堆上层已烧透的砖

cluster ['klʌstə] n. 串；丛
threshold ['θreʃhəuld] n. 开始；开端；极限
subsumption [sʌb'sʌmpʃən] n. 包容；包含
penetration [peni'treiʃən] n. 穿过；渗透；突破
parallax ['pærəlæks] n. 视差
crystallize ['kristəlaiz] v. 明确
alphabetize ['ælfəbitaiz] vt. 依字母顺序排列；以字母表示
concave ['kɔn'keiv] n. 凹；凹面
bounded ['baundid] adj. 有界限的；有限制的
run through 跑着穿过；刺；戳；贯穿；匆匆处理；划掉；挥霍
operate on 操作；运转；开动；起作用；动手术；开刀
less and less 越来越少的；更少的
more and more 越来越多
item by item 逐条；逐项
resolving power （光学仪器等）分辨能力

Difficult Sentences

① Singularity or figure-background clarity：sharpness of boundary (as an abrupt cessation of city development); closure (as an enclosed square); contrast of surface, form, intensity, complexity, size, use, spatial location (as a single tower, a rich decoration, a glaring sign).
单一或轮廓清晰化：界限分明（像城市的发展突然到此戛然而止），封闭式（比如一个封闭的广场），以及表面、外形、强度、复杂性、大小、应用、空间位置的对比（像一个孤立的塔、一处华丽的装饰、一个耀眼的标识）。

② Continuity：continuance of edge or surface (as in a street channel, skyline, or setback); nearness of parts (as a cluster of buildings); repetition of rhythmic interval (as a street-corner pattern); similarity, analogy, or harmony of surface, form, or use (as in a common building material, repetitive pattern of bay windows, similarity of market activity, use of common signs).

连贯性:边缘或表面的连续(如街道上的涵洞、高大的城市建筑物所勾勒出的天空轮廓),各部连贯(如一群楼宇),有规律的间隔重复(如一个街角),相似性,类似或表面、形式、使用上的和谐(如楼体建筑材料的统一,凸窗样式的呼应,购物环境的相似,各处的标识一致)。

③ Where one quality is present alone (as a continuity of building material with no other common feature), or the qualities are in conflict (as in two areas of common building type but of different function), the total effect may be weak, or require effort to identify and structure.

如果一个特点单独出现(比如楼体的材料没有任何共同特色)或者各个特点相互矛盾(就像拥有同样楼型的两个地区却发挥不同的功能),那么整体的效果就会降低,或是很难辨识和构建。

Phrases and Patterns

1. by means of 通过
   Dominance of one part over others is achieved by means of size, intensity.
   一个部分优于另外其他部分是通过它的大小、强度达到的。
   They were able to position the yacht by means of radar.
   他们能够用雷达测定快艇的方位。

2. to the extent 在某种程度上
   The measurement of the extent of something includes one from side to side.
   宽度、广度的测量包括从一边到另一边长度的测量。
   Snow sometimes blocks up a road to such an extent that the town authorities have to break a path.
   有时大雪塞途,市政当局不得不另辟一条通道。

Questions

1. What does singularity mean as one of the qualities that a designer may operate upon?
2. What does visual scope mea as one of the qualities that a designer may operate upon?
3. What does time series mean as one of the qualities that a designer may operate upon?

5.4 The Sense of the Whole
整体的感知

In discussing design by element types, there is a tendency to skim over the interrelation of the parts into a whole. In such a whole, paths would expose and prepare for the districts, and link together the various nodes. The nodes would joint and mark off the paths, while the edges would bound off the districts, and the landmarks would indicate their cores. It is the total orchestration of these units which would knit together a dense and vivid image, and sustain it over areas of metropolitan scale[①].

The five elements—path, edge, district, node, and landmark—must be considered simply as convenient empirical categories, within and around which it has been possible to group a mass of information. To the extent that they are useful, they will act as building blocks for the designer. Having mastered their characteristics, he will have the task of organizing a whole which will be sensed sequentially, whose parts will be perceived only in context. Were he to arrange a sequence of ten landmarks along a path, then one of these marks would have an utterly different image quality than if it were placed singly and prominently at the city core.

Forms should be manipulated so that there is a strand of continuity between the multiple images of a big city: day and night, winter and summer, near and far, static and moving, attentive and absent-minded[2]. Major landmarks, regions, nodes, or paths should be recognizable under diverse conditions, and yet in a concrete, rather than an abstract way. This is not to say that the image should be the same in each case. But if Louisburg Square in the snow has a shape that matches Louisburg Square in midsummer, or if the Stale House dome by night shines in a way that recalls that dome seen in the day, then the contrasting quality of each image becomes even more sharply savored because of the common tie. One is now able to hold together two quite different city views, and thus to encompass the scale of the city in a way otherwise impossible: to approach the ideal of an image which is a total field,

While the complexity of the modern city calls for continuity, it also furnishes a great delight: the contrast and specialization of individual character. Our Study hints at an increasing attention to detail and to uniqueness of character, as familiarity develops. Vividness of elements, and their precise tuning to functional and symbolic differences, will help to provide this character. Contrast will be heightened if sharply differentiated elements are brought into close and imageable relation. Each element then takes on an intensified character of its own.

Indeed, the function of a good visual environment may not be simply to facilitate routine trips, nor to support meanings and feelings already possessed. Quite as important may be its role as a guide and a stimulus for new exploration. In a complex society, there are many interrelations to be mastered. In a democracy, we deplore isolation, extol individual development, hope for ever-widening communication between groups. If an environment has a strong visible framework and highly characteristic parts, then exploration of new sectors is both easier and more inviting. If strategic links in communication (such as museums or libraries or meeting places) are clearly set forth, then those who might otherwise neglect them may be tempted to enter.

The underlying topography, the pre-existing natural setting, is perhaps not quire as important a factor in imageability as it once used to be. The density, and particularly the extent and elaborate technology of the modern metropolis, all tend to obscure it. The contemporary urban area has man-made characteristics and problems that often override the specificity of site. Or rather, it would be more accurate to say that the specific character of a site is now perhaps as much the result of human action and desires as of the original geological structure. In addition, as the city expands, the significant "natural" factors become the larger, more fundamental ones, rather than the smaller accidents. The basic climate, the general flora and surface of a large region, the mountains and major river systems, take precedence over local features. Nevertheless, topography is still an important element in reinforcing the strength of urban elements: sharp hills can define regions, rivers and strands make strong edges, nodes can be confirmed by location at key points of terrain. The modern high-speed path is an excellent viewpoint from which to grasp topographic structure at an extensive scale.

The city is not built for one person, but for great numbers of people, of widely varying backgrounds, temperaments, occupations, and class. Our analyses indicate a substantial variation in the way different people organize their city, in what elements they most depend on, or in what form qualities are most congenial to them[3]. The designer must therefore create a city which is as richly provided with paths, edges, landmarks, nodes, and districts as possible, a city which makes use of not just one or two form qualities, but of all of them. If so, different observers will all find perceptual material which is congenial to their own particular way of looking at the world. While one man may recognize a street by its brick pavement, another will remember its sweeping curve, and a third will have located the minor landmarks along its length.

There are, moreover, dangers in a highly specialized visible form; there is a need for a certain plasticity in the perceptual environment. If there is only one dominant path to a destination, a few sacred focal points, or an ironclad sec of rigidly separated regions, then there is only one way to image the city without considerable strain. This one may suit neither the needs of all people, nor even the needs of one person as they vary from time to time. An unusual trip becomes awkward or dangerous; interpersonal relations may tend to compartment themselves; the scene becomes monotonous or restrictive.

We have taken as signs of good organization those parts of Boston in which the paths chosen by interviewees seemed to spread out rather freely. Here, presumably, the citizen is presented with a rich choice of routes to his destination, all of them well structured and identified. There is a similar value in an overlapping net of identifiable edges, so that regions big or small can be formed according to taste and need. Nodal organization gains its identity from the central focus and can fluctuate at the rim. Thus it has an advantage of flexibility over boundary organization, which breaks down if the shape of regions must change. It is important to maintain some great common forms: strong nodes, key paths, or widespread regional homogeneities. But within this large framework, there should be a certain plasticity, a richness of possible structures and clues, so that the individual observer can construct his own image: communicable, safe, and sufficient, but also supple and integrated with his own needs.

The citizen shifts his place of residence more frequently today than ever before, from area to area, from city to city. Good imageability in his environment would allow him to feel quickly at home in new surroundings. Gradual organization through long experience can less and less be relied upon. The city environment is itself changing rapidly, as techniques and functions shift. These changes are often disturbing to the citizen emotionally, and tend to disorganize his perceptual image. The techniques of design discussed in this chapter may prove useful in maintaining a visible structure and a sense of continuity even while massive changes are occurring. Certain landmarks or nodes might be retained, thematic units of district character carried over into new construction, paths salvaged or temporarily conserved.

Words and Expressions

orchestration [ˌɔːkiˈstreiʃən, -ke-] n. 管弦乐编曲；管弦乐作曲法
manipulate [məˈnipjuleit] vt. (熟练地)操作；巧妙地处理
savor [ˈseivə] vt. 加调味品于；使有风味；尝到或闻到；尽情享受
stimulus [ˈstimjuləs] n. 刺激物；促进因素；刺激；刺激
deplore [diˈplɔː] v. 表示悲痛
extol [iksˈtɔl] v. 赞美
obscure [əbˈskjuə] vt. 使暗；使不明显
flora [ˈflɔːrə] n. 花神
terrain [ˈterein] n. 地形
sacred [ˈseikrid] adj. 神的；宗教的；庄严的；神圣的
ironclad [ˈaiənˈklæd] adj. 装甲的；打不破的
compartment [kəmˈpɑːtmənt] n. 间隔间；车厢
monotonous [məˈnɔtənəs] adj. 单调的；无变化的
restrictive [risˈtriktiv] adj. 限制性的
overlapping [ˌəuvəˈlæpiŋ] n. 重叠；搭接
fluctuate [ˈflʌktjueit] vi. 变动；波动；涨落；上下；动摇
thematic [θiːˈmætik] adj. 词干的；题目的；主题的；论题的
salvage [ˈsælvidʒ] vt. 海上救助；抢救；打捞；营救
skim over 掠过；滑过；浏览
mark off 划分出
to the extent that 达到这种程度以至……
building block (儿童游戏用的)积木
call in 调用

set forth 阐明;宣布;提出;陈列;出发;把(会议等)提前动身
take precedence over 优先于
from time to time 有时
break down 毁掉;制服;压倒;停顿;倒塌;中止;垮掉;分解
be congenial to 志趣相投

Difficult Sentences

① It is the total orchestration of these units which would knit together a dense and vivid image, and sustain it over areas of metropolitan scale.
这些因素结合起来完美地构筑成密集的、生动的形象,并能在大都市的广袤地界持久地维持这一形象。

② Forms should be manipulated so that there is a strand of continuity between the multiple images of a big city: day and night, winter and summer, near and far, static and moving, attentive and absent-minded.
可以巧妙地处理形式以使大城市的各个层次形成一系列的连续性:白天和夜晚,冬天和夏天,远还是近,静止还是活动,专注还是心不在焉。

③ Our analyses indicate a substantial variation in the way different people organize their city, in what elements they most depend on, or in what form qualities are most congenial to them.
我们的分析表明了不同的人群组建城市的迥异方式,他们生存的基础或喜欢的特色都有很大的不同。

Phrases and Patterns

1. In addition 此外

   In addition, as the city expands, the significant "natural" factors become the larger, more fundamental ones, rather than the smaller accidents.

此外,随着城市的发展,"自然"的重要因子开始更加凸显,成为更重要的要素,而不是可有可无、微乎其微的东西。

In addition, Delphi 2.0 makes it easy for customer to create application to meet the requirement to get the window95 logo.

另外,为了满足能够使用 Windows95 徽标的要求,Delphi2.0 使客户创建应用程序更加简便。

2. If so 假如这样的话

If so, different observers will all find perceptual material which is congenial to their own particular way of looking at the world.

假如是这样的话,不同的观察者将会从各自的看世界的角度去搜寻感知的素材。

Is steel plate purchasable? If so purchase price and delivery time expect.

能否购得钢板? 若可能,约何时发货,价格如何。

Questions

1. How can a city build a sense of whole?
2. How can designer create a city for great numbers of people, of widely varying backgrounds, temperaments, occupations, and class?

5.5　Metropolitan Form

大都市形态

　　The increasing size of our metropolitan areas and the speed with which we traverse them raise many new problems for perception. The metropolitan region is now the functional unit of our environment, and it is desirable that this functional unit should be identified and structured by its inhabitants[①]. The new means of communication which allow us to live and work in such a large interdependent region, could also allow us to make our images commensurate with our experiences. Such jumps to new levels of attention have occurred in the past, as jumps were made in the functional organization of life.

Total imageability of an extensive area such as a metropolitan region would not mean an equal intensity of image at every point. There would be dominant figures and more extensive backgrounds, focal points, and connective tissue. But, whether intense or neutral, each part would presumably be clear, and clearly linked to the whole. We can speculate that metropolitan images could be formed of such elements as high-speed highways, transit lines or airways, large regions with coarse edges of water or open space; major shopping nodes; basic topographic features; perhaps massive, distant landmarks.

The problem is none the less difficult, however, when it comes to composing a pattern for such an entire area. There are two techniques with which we are familiar. First, the entire region may be composed as a static hierarchy. For example, it might be organized as a major district containing three sub-districts, which each contain three sub-sub-districts, and so on. Or as another example of hierarchy, any given part of the region might focus on a minor node, these minor nodes being satellite to a major node, while all the major nodes are arranged to culminate in a single primary node for the region.

The second technique is the use of one or two very large dominant elements, to which many smaller things may be related: the sitting of settlement along a sea-coast, for example; or the design of a linear town depending on a basic communication spine[②]. A large environment might even be radially related to a very powerful landmark, such as a central hill.

Both these techniques seem somewhat inadequate to the metropolitan problem. The hierarchical system, while congenial to some of our habits of abstract thinking, would seem to be a denial of the freedom and complexity of linkages in a metropolis. Every connection must be made in a roundabout, conceptual fashion: up to a generality and back to a particular, even though the bridging generality may have little to do with the real connection. It is the unity of a library, and libraries require the constant use of a bulky cross-referencing system.

Dependence on a strong dominant element, while giving a much more immediate sense of relation and continuity, becomes more difficult as the environment increases in size, since a dominant must be found that is big enough to be in scale with its task, and has enough "surface area" so that all the minor elements can have some reasonably close relation to it. Thus one needs a big river, for example, that winds enough to allow all settlement to be fairly near its course.

Nevertheless, these are two possible methods, and it would be useful to investigate their success in unifying large environments. Air travel may simplify the problem again, since it is (in perceptual terms) a static rather than a dynamic experience, an opportunity to see a metropolitan area almost at a glance.

Considering our present way of experiencing a large urban area, however, one is drawn coward another kind of organization: that of sequence, or temporal pattern. This is a familiar idea in music, drama, literature, or dance. Therefore it is relatively easy to conceive of, and study, the form of a sequence of events along a line, such as the succession of elements that might greet a traveler on an urban highway. With some attention, and proper tools, this experience could be made meaningful and well shaped.

It is also possible to handle the question of reversibility, i. e., the fact that most paths are traversed in both directions. The series of elements must have sequential form taken in either order, which might be accomplished by symmetry about the midpoint, or in more sophisticated ways[3]. But the city problem continues to raise difficulties. Sequences are not only reversible, but are broken in upon at many points. A carefully constructed sequence, leading from introduction, first statement, and development to climax and conclusion, may fail utterly if a driver enters it directly at the climax point. Therefore it may be necessary to look for sequences which are interruptible as well as reversible, that is, sequences which still have sufficient imageability even when broken in upon at various points, much like a magazine serial. This might lead us from the classic start–climax–finish form to others which are more like the essentially endless, and yet continuous and variegated, patterns of jazz.

These considerations refer to organization along a single line of movement. An urban region might then be organized by a network of such organized sequences, any proposed form being tested to see it each major path, in each direction and from each entry point, was possessed of a formed sequence of elements. This is conceivable when the paths have some simple pattern such as radial convergence. It becomes more difficult to image where the network is a diffuse and intersecting one, as in a gridiron. Here the sequences work in four different directions throughout the map. Although on a much more sophisticated scale, this is akin to the problem of timing a progressive traffic-light system over a network.

It is even conceivable that one might compose in counterpoint along these lines, or from one line to another. One sequence of elements, or "melody," might be played against a counter-sequence. Perhaps, however, such techniques would wait upon a time when there is a more attentive and critical audience.

Even this dynamic method, the organization of a network of formed sequences, does not yet seem ideal. The environment is still not being treated as a whole but rather as a collection of parts (the sequences) arranged so as not to interfere with each other[④]. Intuitively, one could imagine that there might be a way of creating a whole pattern, a pattern that would only gradually be sensed and developed by sequential experiences, reversed and interrupted as they might be. Although felt as a whole, it would not need to be a highly unified pattern with a single center or an isolating boundary. The principal quality would be sequential continuity in which each part flows from the next—a sense of interconnectedness at any level or in any direction. There would be particular zones that for any one individual might be more intensely felt or organized, but the region would be continuous, mentally traversable in any order. This possibility is a highly speculative one; no satisfactory concrete examples come to mind.

Perhaps this pattern of a whole cannot exist. In that case, the previously mentioned techniques remain as possibilities in the organization of large regions: the hierarchy, the dominant element, or the network of sequences. Hopefully, these techniques would require no more than the metropolitan planning controls now sought for other reasons, but this also remains to be seen.

Words and Expressions

traverse ['trævə(:)s] vt. 横过；穿过
perception [pə'sepʃən] n. 感知；感觉
inhabitant [in'hæbitənt] n. 居民；居住者
interdependent [ˌintə(:)di'pendənt] adj. 相互依赖的；互助的
commensurate [kə'menʃərit] adj. 相称的；相当的
speculate ['spekjuˌleit] vi. 推测；思索；做投机买卖
transit ['trænsit] vt. 横越；通过；经过
culminate ['kʌlmineit] v. 达到顶点
inadequate [in'ædikwit] adj. 不充分的；不适当的
congenial [kən'dʒi:njəl] adj. 性格相似的；适意的
linkage ['liŋˌkidʒ] n. 连接
generality [ˌdʒenə'ræliti] n. 一般性
temporal ['tempərəl] adj. 时间的；当时的；暂时的，
conceive [kən'si:v] vt. 构思；以为；持有

reversibility [ri,vəːsə'biliti] *n.* 可逆性；可取消
variegated ['vɛərigeitid] *adj.* 杂色的；斑驳的；多样化的
convergence [kən'vɜːdʒəns] *n.* 集中；收敛
diffuse [di'fjuːz] *v.* 散播；传播；漫射
intersect [,intə'sekt] *vi.* (直线)相交；交叉
conceivable [kən'siːvəbl] *adj.* 可能的；想得到的；可想象的
counterpoint ['kauntəpɔint] *n.* 对应物
attentive [ə'tentiv] *adj.* 注意的；专心的；留意的
intuitive [in'tjuː(ː)itiv] *adj.* 直觉的
speculative ['spekjulətiv, -leit-] *adj.* 投机的
focal point 感兴趣的中心
transit line 运输线
shopping node 购物节点
primary node 主要节点
start-climax-finish form 开端—高潮—结尾形式

Difficult Sentences

① The increasing size of our metropolitan areas and the speed with which we traverse them raise many new problems for perception. The metropolitan region is now the functional unit of our environment, and it is desirable that this functional unit should be identified and structured by its inhabitants.
随着大都市地区规模的不断扩大和其中运动速度的不断提高，人们的感知过程也产生了许多新的问题。大都市区域如今已成为环境中的功能单元，我们期望这种功能单元能够得到居民的认同和共建。

② The second technique is the use of one or two very large dominant elements, to which many smaller things may be related: the sitting of settlement along a sea-coast, for example; or the design of a linear town depending on a basic communication spine.
其二，是利用一个或两个非常巨大的主导元素，让许多小一点的

元素与之发生联系,比如沿海居住区的选址,或是依靠一条交通干线发展起来的线型城镇。

③ It is also possible to handle the question of reversibility, i. e., the fact that most paths are traversed in both directions. The series of elements must have sequential form taken in either order, which might be accomplished by symmetry about the midpoint, or in more sophisticated ways.

我们也完全有可能解决可逆性的问题,即在大多数双行道上,元素系列必须在两个方向都具有次序性的特征。这有可能通过中心对称或其他一些更为复杂的方法来实现。

④ Even this dynamic method, the organization of a network of formed sequences, does not yet seem ideal. The environment is still not being treated as a whole but rather as a collection of parts (the sequences) arranged so as not to interfere with each other.

即使是这种动态方法,即成形序列的网络组织,似乎也并不十分理想。在此环境仍没有被作为一个整体来对待,而只是作为众多部分的集合,以避免相互之间的干扰。

Phrases and Patterns

1. When it comes to sth. /doing sth. 当涉及(做)某事时

   The problem is none the less difficult, however, when it comes to composing a pattern for such an entire area.

   然而,当涉及为整个地区创造一种模式时,这个问题依然很困难。

   When it comes to space, we can refers to Barbara Phillips' words, "after years of neglect, space is a hot topic in social theory and philosophy."

   当我们谈到空间时,我们可以参考菲利浦·巴伯拉的话,"多年来,空间被人们所忽视,而现在它是社会理论和哲学的一个热门话题。"

2. conceive of 想出

Therefore it is relatively easy to conceive of, and Study, the form of a sequence of events along a line, such as the succession of elements that might greet a traveler on an urban highway.

因此,要构思并研究排列在同一条线上一系列事件的形式要相对容易一些,比如在城市高速公路上展现在旅行者面前的一连串要素。

The paper introduces the concept of "negative growing" to make an answer of these questions and conceive of a future developmental mode on the shrinking area.

本方案引入"负生长"概念来对城市衰退地区的问题进行解答,同时对未来的发展模式作出设想。

Questions

1. What are two possible methods to unify large environments? Make comments on these two methods.
2. What are the functions of hierarchy dominant element and the network of sequences in the organization of large cities?

5.6 The Process of Design
设计过程

Any existing, functioning urban area has structure and identity, even if only in weak measure. Jersey City is a long step upward from pure chaos. If it were not, it would be uninhabitable. Almost always, a potentially powerful image is hidden in the situation itself, as in the Palisades of Jersey City, its peninsular shape, and its relation to Manhattan. A frequent problem is the sensitive reshaping of an already existing environment: discovering and preserving its strong images, solving its perceptual difficulties, and, above all, drawing out the structure and identity latent in the confusion[①].

At other times, the designer faces the creation of a new image, as when extensive redevelopment is underway. This problem is particularly significant in the suburban extensions of our metropolitan regions, where vast stretches of what is essentially a new landscape must be perceptually organized. The natural features are no longer a sufficient guide to structure, because of the intensity and scale of the development being applied to them. At the present tempo of building, there is no time for the slow adjustment of form to small, individualized forces. Therefore we must depend far more than formerly on conscious design: the deliberate manipulation of the world for sensuous ends. Although possessed of a rich background of former examples of urban design, the operation must now proceed at an entirely different scale of space and time.

These shapings or reshapings should be guided by what might be called a "visual plan" for the city or metropolitan region: a set of recommendations and controls which would be concerned with visual form on the urban scale[2]. The preparation of such a plan might begin with an analysis of the existing form and public image of the area, using the techniques rising out of this study which are detailed in Appendix B. This analysis would conclude with a series of diagrams and reports illustrating the significant public images, the basic visual problems and opportunities, and the critical image elements and element interrelations, with their detailed qualities and possibilities for change.

Using this analytical background, but not limited thereby, the designer could proceed to develop a visual plan at the city scale, whose object would be to strengthen the public image. It might prescribe the location or preservation of landmarks, the development of a visual hierarchy of paths, the establishment of thematic units for districts, or the creation or clarification of nodal points. Above all, it would deal with the interrelations of elements, with their perception in motion, and with the conception of the city as a total visible form.

Substantial physical change may not be justified on this esthetic score alone, except at strategic points. But the visual plan could influence the form of physical changes which occur for other reasons. Such a plan should be fitted into all the other aspects of planning for the region, to become a normal and integral part of the comprehensive plan. Like all the other parts of this plan, it would be in a continuous state of revision and development.

The controls employed to achieve visual form at the city scale could range from general zoning provisions, advisory review, and persuasive influence over private design, to strict controls at critical points and to the positive design of public facilities such as highways or civic buildings[3]. Such techniques are not in principle very different from controls used in the pursuit of other planning objectives. It will probably be more difficult to gain an understanding of the problem and to develop the necessary design skill than it will be to obtain the necessary powers, once the objective is clear. There is much to be done before far-reaching controls are justified.

The final objective of such a plan is not the physical shape itself but the quality of an image in the mind. Thus it will be equally useful to improve this image by training the observer, by teaching him to look at his city, to observe its manifold forms and how they mesh with one another. Citizens could be taken into the street, classes could be held in the schools and universities, the city could be made an animated museum of our society and its hopes. Such education might be used, not only to develop the city image, but to reorient after some disturbing change. An art of city design will wait upon an informed and critical audience. Education and physical reform are parts of a continuous process.

Heightening the observer's attention, enriching his experience, is one of the values that the mere effort to give form can offer. To some degree, the very process of reshaping a city to improve its imageability may itself sharpen the image, regardless of how unskillful the resulting physical form may be. Thus the amateur painter begins to see the world around him; the novice decorator begins to take pride in her living room and to judge others. Although such a process can become sterile if not accompanied by increasing control and judgment, even awkward "beautification" of a city may in itself be an intensifier of civic energy and cohesion④.

Words and Expressions

uninhabitable [ˌʌnin'hæbitəbl] adj. 不适于人居住的
peninsular [pi'ninsjulə] adj. 半岛(状)的(居民); 形成半岛的
sensitive ['sensitiv] adj. 敏感的; 灵敏的; 感光的
suburban [sə'bə:bən] adj. 郊外的; 偏远的
tempo ['tempəu] n. (音乐)速度、拍子; 发展速度
conscious ['kɔnʃəs] adj. 有意识的; 有知觉的; 故意的; 羞怯的
deliberate [di'libəreit] adj. 深思熟虑的; 故意的;
interrelation [ˌintə(:)ri'leiʃən] n. 相互关系
clarification [ˌklærifi'keiʃən] n. 澄清; 净化
substantial [səb'stænʃəl] adj. 坚固的; 实质的; 真实的
esthetic [i:s'θetik] adj. 感觉的
integral ['intigrəl] adj. 完整的; 整体的
advisory [əd'vaizəri] adj. 顾问的; 咨询的; 劝告的
manifold ['mænifəuld] adj. 多种形式的; 多方面的
mesh [meʃ] vt. 啮合; 编织
animated ['ænimeitid] adj. 活生生的; 活泼的; 愉快的
informed [in'fɔ:md] adj. 见多识广的
novice ['nɔvis] n. 新手; 初学者
sterile ['sterail] adj. 贫瘠的; 不育的; 不结果的
intensifier [in'tensifaiə] n. 使更激烈之物; 增强剂
Jersey City 泽西市
public facilities 公共设施
civic building 市政建筑

take pride in 以……为傲

Difficult Sentences

① A frequent problem is the sensitive reshaping of an already existing environment: discovering and preserving its Strong images, solving its perceptual difficulties, and, above all, drawing out the structure and identity latent in the confusion.

一个经常出现的课题就是如何对敏感的现状环境进行改造,其中包括发现和保留强烈的意象元素,克服一些感知上的难点等等,总之就是从模糊混乱之中提取出潜在的结构和个性。

② These shapings or reshapings should be guided by what might be called a "visual plan" for the city or metropolitan region: a set of recommendations and controls which would be concerned with visual form on the urban scale.

这种成形和改造的过程,应该由所谓城市或大都市区域的"视觉规划"来进行控制,其实也就是一组与城市尺度的视觉形态相关的管理和建议。

③ The controls employed to achieve visual form at the city scale could range from general zoning provisions, advisory review, and persuasive influence over private design, to strict controls at critical points and to the positive design of public facilities such as highways or civic buildings.

对城市范围内视觉形态进行的控制,可以说既包括一般的分区规定、咨询评估、对单体设计的评审影响,也包括对关键点的严格控制以及对快速路、城市房屋等公共设施的参与设计。

④ Although such a process can become sterile if not accompanied by increasing control and judgment, even awkward "beautification" of a city may in itself be an intensifier of civic energy and cohesion.

尽管改造过程如果不伴随着越来越多的管理和评价可能会成为徒劳,但即使是一个笨拙的城市"美化"过程,其自身也可能成为城市能量和凝聚力的增强剂。

Phrases and Patterns

1. proceed to 继续

   Using this analytical background, bur not limited thereby, the designer could proceed to develop a visual plan at the city scale, whose object would be to strengthen the public image.

   设计师采用这种分析的背景,但并不能局限于此,他能够继续在城市范围内打造一种视觉计划,其目的在于强化公共形象。

   Poetry in fact is able to concretize those totalities which elude science, and may therefore suggest how we might proceed to obtain the needed understanding.

   事实上诗歌可以将这些整体具体化,它们可以避开科学,因此可以表明我们可能如何继续获得所需要的理解。

2. in the pursuit of 追求

   Such techniques are not in principle very different from controls used in the pursuit of other planning objectives.

   在原则上,这些技术与在追求其他设计目标中使用的控制手段大致相同。

   In the pursuit of the workability of the end result of city design, we can bring into full play the advantages of the two, making it possible for the content of the two to be truly integrated with one another

   在追求城市设计最终成果的可应用性过程当中,我们可以充分发挥二者的优势,促进二者内容的真正融合。

   Maybe we have lost something in the mere pursuit of living, and we should try to find the purest self and regain passion and dream is what we might do.

   在单纯追求生存的过程中我们失去了一些东西,我们应该试着去找到最纯真的自我,重获激情、梦想才是我们可能做的。

Questions

1. How to understand "any existing, functioning urban area has structure and identity"?
2. How to make city "an animated museum of our society and its hopes"?

5.7 Specifying Form or Performance
指定形态或性能

  Criteria, standards, and performance dimensions are means by which models are evaluated, but they are not models in themselves, except where they become detailed enough to specify form (such as a prescribed setback)①. Policies and strategies may include models, but, since they are decisions about future actions, they must include much more, and they may not employ models at all. The process of design always uses models, although a basic model may be obscured by a surface innovation, or an alien model may be converted to some surprising new purpose. The use of models is not <u>confined to</u> the creation of new places, but is equally important in the management and remodeling of existing places.

  There are two ways of setting form rules: by prescription or by specifying performance. Models are more like the former than the latter: "make a bay window," rather than "make it possible for someone in the room to see up and down the street."② But the distinction is not as clear as it seems. Both statements are only a piece of a much longer means-ends continuum. The bay window can be made in many forms and requires detailed instructions for its construction, while looking up and down the street is instrumental to other more general ends, such as sociability or security. Nevertheless, any particular prescription (or model) is instrumental <u>relative to</u> its associated performance statement, and usually the performance statement stops short of describing a recognizable environmental form.

Since performance statements are more abstract and general than models, they must be features of any general theory. They are also touted as the best way to write regulations and guidelines, since they hold fast to the underlying effect that is wanted, while leaving the means flexible and open to innovation. But performance standards may not always be preferable in realistic situations. They require rather elaborate, usually post facto, tests to see if they are being adhered to. By leaving room for innovation, they are likely to increase the uncertainty of design, and thus the time and effort it requires, as well as to increase the burden on those who will implement the new form. Even though a new form satisfies the required basic performance, it may have unpredicted side effects, or fail to fit in with other elements of the environment[3]. For example, if the degree of summer shade required is specified (instead of specifying trees), the unexpected solution may be a series of opaque metal panels which are ugly, cause a massive disruption of the land, and cast an unpleasant shade in the winter as well as in the summer. Customary prototypes are relatively easy to specify and construct, are likely to fit with other customary parts, and will have well-known consequences. Thus, while performance statements are the building blocks of general theory, they may or may not be useful as direct guides to action. They tend to be more apt in regard to key elements, where the gain in flexibility and innovation is well worth the cost and risk entailed in their use. In more routine design and evaluation, people work directly from a stock of implicit or fuzzy environmental models: culs-de-sac, fire escapes, foundation plantings, ranch houses, highway cross sections, civic centers, shopping malls, front yards, park landscapes, rear entrances, side-yard setbacks, suburban districts—the list is enormous and yet quite familiar. To be of any use, a theory must be able to connect its statements to these ordinary and indispensable mental pictures, while explaining the way in which their usefulness depends on the concrete situation in which any design finds itself.

The most useful model is one in which the dependence on the situation in which it is to be applied is carefully stated, and in which the expected performance of the model is also specified. Then the model is open to test and improvement. These are the characteristics embodied in the elaborate series of environmental models developed by Christopher Alexander, which he calls "patterns."④ Similarly, where public regulations or guidelines are prepared, the reasoning behind them should also be laid bare, so that they are fully open to political correction. A hybrid regulation may specify an acceptable, conventional form (such as a wall detail or a street cross section), and also specify the performance wanted, so that those being regulated may propose a new form for the purpose, if they are willing to suffer the detailed testing of performance that will be required.

Words and expressions

dimension [di'menʃən] n. 尺寸；尺度；维(数)；度(数)；元
evaluate [i'væljueit] vt. 评价；估计；求……的值
setback ['setbæk] n. 顿挫；挫折；退步；逆流
specify ['spesifai] vt. 指定；详细说明；列入清单
obscure [əb'skjuə] adj. 暗的；朦胧的；模糊的；晦涩的
innovation [ˌinəu'veiʃən] n. 改革；创新
alien ['eiljən] adj. 外国的；相异的；背道而驰
prescription [pri'skripʃən] n. 指示；规定；命令；处方；药方
instrumental [ˌinstru'mentl] adj. 仪器的；器械的；乐器的
sociability [ˌsəuʃə'biliti] n. 好交际；社交性；善于交际
recognizable ['rekəgnaizəbl] adj. 可认识的；可辨认的
underlying [ˌʌndə'laiiŋ] adj. 在下面的；根本的；潜在的

preferable ['prefərəbl] adj. 更可取的；更好的；更优越的
elaborate [ɪ'læbərət] adj. 精心制作的；详细阐述的；精细
opaque [əu'peik] adj. 不透明的；不传热的；迟钝的
panel ['pænl] n. vt. 面板；嵌板；嵌镶板
disruption [dis'rʌpʃən] n. 中断；分裂；瓦解；破坏
prototype ['prəutətaip] n. 原型
entail [in'teil] vt. 使必需；使蒙受；使承担
fuzzy ['fʌzi] adj. 有绒毛的；模糊的；失真的
ranch [ræntʃ, rɑːntʃ] n. 大农场
embodied [im'bɔdi] vt. 使具体化；包含；收录
bay window 凸窗
be instrumental to 对……有益
side effect 副作用
in regard to 关于
cross section 交互区

Difficult Sentences

① Criteria, standards, and performance dimensions are means by which models are evaluated, but they are not models in themselves, except where they become detailed enough to specify form (such as a prescribed setback).
规定标准和性能指标是用来评估典范的手段，但它们自己本身不是典范，除非它们已经足以详细到有特定的形态(如对建筑退台的规定)。

② There are two ways of setting form rules: by prescription or by specifying performance. Models are more like the former than the latter: "make a bay window," rather than "make it possible for someone in the room to see up and down the street."
有两个制定空间形态的方法：一个是通过描述，另一个则是通过指定性能。城市的典范更像是前者而不是后者，例如，"做一个角窗"，而不是"使在房间里的人能够看清街道的前前后后"。

③ By leaving room for innovation, they are likely to increase the uncertainty of design, and thus the time and effort it requires, as well as to increase the burden on those who will implement the new form. Even though a new form satisfies the required basic performance, it may have unpredicted side effects, or fail to fit in with other elements of the environment.

通过为创新留有空间,性能描述可能会增加设计的不确定性,所以它所要求的时间、精力也增加了那些想要实现新形态的人的负担。即使一个新的形态满足了基本性能的要求,也可能产生不可预见的副作用,或是无法和空间中的其他元素相契合。

④ Then the model is open to test and improvement. These are the characteristics embodied in the elaborate series of environmental models developed by Christopher Alexander, which he calls "patterns."

这种模式是可以去测试和改进的。这些就是体现于克里斯托夫·亚历山大发展出来的环境典范架构中的特征。

Phrases and patterns

1. confine to 限制

   The use of models is not confined to the creation of new places, but is equally important in the management and remodeling of existing places.

   这种模式的使用并没有被局限在新场所的创造上,在现有场所的管理和重塑方面也同样重要。

   The driver shouldn't be confined to the road itself; field boundaries, local roads, established businesses and residences all constitute the important cultural aspect of the landscape and the journey.

   驾驶者不应该被限制于公路本身,田野的边界、当地的公路、已存在的企业和居民都构成了地形和旅途的重要文化方面。

2. relative to 相对于

Nevertheless, any particular prescription (or model) is instrumental relative to its associated performance statement.

然而,任何特定的规定(或模式)相对于它的相关性能陈述都是有帮助的。

Relative to the passage, a road is not only a passage, but also the outdoor space for people to contact. People can appreciate the surroundings in the cities through it. Therefore, road is the important factor of urban space.

相对于通道而言,道路不仅仅是通道,还是人们交往活动的室外空间。人们通过它可以观赏城市的外部环境。因此,道路是城市空间的重要组成要素。

Relative to the other areas in Dominica, the site of Roseau Inner City is flat. Therefore it has been possible to develop a grid there.

相对于多米尼克的其他地区来说,罗素中心城区比较平坦。因此,我们可能在那里设计一种网格。

Questions

1. Why the use of model is important in the management and remodeling of existing places?
2. Compare the two ways of setting form rules.
3. What's the most useful model mentioned in the passage?

5.8 The Baroque Network Model
巴洛克典型型制

Look at the baroque axial network as one example of a model often used in the past to guide designs for new as well as for old cities. This is a coherent and well developed idea about city form.

It states that one may organize any complex and extended landscape in the following way: choose a set of commanding points throughout a terrain, and site important symbolic structures at those points. Connect these foci by major streets, wide enough to carry arterial traffic, and shaped as visual approaches to the symbolic points, or nodes[①]. The borders of these streets should be controlled to give them a sense of unity, <u>by means of</u> special planting and furniture, as well as height, facade, and use restrictions. Once that is done, a more intricate, less controlled pattern of streets and buildings of varied type can occupy the interior triangles between the linking arteries. The model has some particular advantages. It is a simple, coherent idea that can be rapidly employed in a great range of complex landscapes. Major L'Enfant, using the model at a time when it had been well developed, was able to survey, design, lay out, clear, acquire materials, auction off lots, and commence construction on the future city of Washington—all in nine months and with the aid of two surveyors. The model told him just what to look for and how to decide. If the resulting city is not as clear and vivid as he hoped, it is due in part to his ill-advised overlay of the baroque model with an unevenly spaced grid. Even more, it was <u>due to</u> the subsequent management of Washington's development, which never followed his model of powerful central control, and indeed could not have done so.

Given effective central control, the model works well in organizing extended, irregular landscapes, whether virgin or developed (for example, Paris under Haussman). It creates a memorable general structure without imposing control on every part and without requiring an unattainable level of capital investment[②]. It is, in fact, a strategy for the economical application of central power. It produces strong visual effects and lays the groundwork for public symbolism. In other words, it is a useful way to achieve sensibility, and to apportion public and private control. In one respect, at least, it is a flexible form, since changes can occur within the blocks created by the linkage network without disturbing the general pattern in any way. Yet while local flexibility is achieved, more general changes in use and flow are difficult to make, since the nodes and their links are permanent, symbolic features, and they must retain their significance.

As an access system, it is a workable strategy for opening up an existing circulatory maze and performs reasonably well for traffic moving from focal point to focal point (tourists or processions), or for flows which are local, using low-speed, maneuverable, space-efficient modes, such as horseback, bicycle, or foot. However, the form is difficult to traverse by high-speed, long-distance, space-demanding vehicles. Extended movement must follow an erratic route from point to point, and each point is a peak of congestion, where many routes converge[3].

While visually quite powerful at the intermediate scale of a central city or a large park or garden, the irregular triangular network can be very confusing at more extended scales. The foci and all the links between them must be recognizable and memorized. General cognitive strategies of direction or overall pattern cannot be applied. Finally, while the model emphasizes certain uses, such as the symbolic public ones or the commercial activities which favor the arterial frontages, it has very little to say about ordinary houses or workplaces.

Thus this particular concept can be analyzed in terms of appropriate situation and expected performance along the various dimensions. It has a wide, but far from universal, usefulness. It is an idea which has developed over several centuries, first in the royal hunting forests (where the primary motives were the visual tracking of game and quick access to it), and then in the planning of papal Rome (where the motive was to enhance and control the processional movements of pilgrims)[4]. Subsequent to L'Enfant, Haussmann used the model in Paris to improve access in the central city, to create profitable new building sites, and to displace and control the working class. Historically, it has always been an elite model: a way of using the city as an expression of central power and a strategy for attaining visual magnificence and control within available means. For that purpose, it works.

Words and Phrases

axial ['æksiəl,-sjəl] *adj.* 轴的；轴向的
coherent [kəu'hiərənt] *adj.* 一致的；连贯的
landscape ['lændskeip] *n.* 风景；地形；前景
commanding [kə'mɑːndiŋ] *adj.* 指挥的；发号施令的
foci ['fəusɑi] *n.* 焦距；配光
arterial [ɑː'tiəriəl] *adj.* 动脉的
furniture ['fəːnitʃə] *n.* 家具；设备；储藏物
intricate ['intrikit] *adj.* 复杂的；错综的；难以理解的
interior [in'tiəriə] *adj.* 内部的；内的
artery ['ɑːtəri] *n.* 动脉；要道
auction ['ɔːkʃən] *vt.* 拍卖
overlay [ˌəuvə'lei] *n.* 覆盖；覆盖图
grid [grid] *n.* 格子；栅格
subsequent ['sʌbsikwənt] *adj.* 后来的；并发的
impose [im'pəuz] *vt.* 征税；强加；以……欺骗
unattainable [ˌʌnə'teinəbl] *adj.* 难到达的；做不到的
sensibility [ˌsensi'biliti] *n.* 敏感性
apportion [ə'pɔːʃən] *v.* 分配
workable ['wəːkəbl] *adj.* 可经营的；可使用的
circulatory [sɛːkjʊ'leitəri] *adj.* 循环的
maze [meiz] *vt.* 使迷惘；使混乱
maneuverable [mə'nuːvərəbl] *adj.* 容易操作的；有机动性的
erratic [i'rætik] *adj.* 不稳定的；奇怪的
congestion [kən'dʒestʃən] *n.* 拥塞；充血
cognitive ['kɔgnitiv] *adj.* 认知的；认识的；有感知的
papal ['peipl] *adj.* 罗马教皇的
pilgrim ['pligrim] *n.* 圣地朝拜者；朝圣
baroque network model 巴洛克典型型制

commanding point 操控点
symbolic point 焦点
auction off 拍卖
Paris under Haussman 奥斯曼的巴黎改造计划

Difficult Sentences

① It states that one may organize any complex and extended landscape in the following way: choose a set of commanding points throughout a terrain, and site important symbolic structures at those points. Connect these foci by major streets, wide enough to carry arterial traffic, and shaped as visual approaches to the symbolic points, or nodes.

它认为人们可以把任何一个复杂和大范围的地形用下列方式加以组织:在规划范围内选择一组控制点,并在这些控制点上设立重要的象征性物体。将这些控制点用大道连接起来,大道要足够宽,用以承担主要的交通功能,并把这些大道的空间设计成能看到那些主要象征物和节点的序列。

② Given effective central control, the model works well in organizing extended, irregular landscapes, whether virgin or developed (for example, Paris under Haussman). It creates a memorable general structure without imposing control on every part and without requiring an unattainable level of capital investment.

如果能保证有效的集中管理权利,巴洛克模式能够很好地组织一个大规模和不规则的地形建设,无论是未开发的土地还是已开发的土地(如奥斯曼改造的巴黎),都有良好成效,它能创造出一个令人印象深刻的城市结构,而不至于对每一个细部都强加控制,也不用依靠天文数学般的投资费用。

③ However, the form is difficult to traverse by high-speed, long-distance, space-demanding vehicles. Extended movement must follow an erratic route from point to point, and each point is a peak of congestion, where many routes converge.

然而,高速、远距离、大型的交通工具很难在这种形式中存在。扩展运动必须采取从一个点到另一个点的不确定的路线,而且每一个点都是一个交通拥堵集中点,因为许多路线在那些点交汇。

④ It is an idea which has developed over several centuries, first in the royal hunting forests (where the primary motives were the visual tracking of game and quick access to it), and then in the planning of papal Rome (where the motive was to enhance and control the processional movements of pilgrims).

这是一种几个世纪以来形成的观点,首先设计皇家狩猎场(在那里它的主要功能是对猎物的可视追踪和快速接近猎物),接着是设计教皇制罗马城(在那里它的动机是加强和控制朝圣者的游行运动)。

Phrases and patterns

1. by means of 通过

   The borders of these streets should be controlled to give them a sense of unity, by means of special planting and furniture, as well as height, facade, and use restrictions.

   我们应该通过特殊的植物、家居装饰,还有高度,正面外观或使用一些制约条件控制街道的界限以制造一种整体感,

   Being qualitative totalities of a complex nature, places cannot be described by means of analytic, "scientific" concepts.

   作为复杂自然的定性整体,场所不能用分析的、"科学的"概念来描述。

2. due to 因为

   Even more, it was due to the subsequent management of Washington's development, which never followed his model of powerful central control, and indeed could not have done so.

   此外,是由于华盛顿发展的后继管理,没有遵循巴洛克有力中心

控制的模式,事实上本不该如此。

On the other hand, due to the discovery and exploration of new continents, people showed great interest in study of geography.

另一方面,由于对于新大陆的发现和探索,人们对地理研究表示了极大兴趣。

Questions

1. Summarize the term "the baroque network model".
2. What's the functions of "the borders of streets"?
3. How to understand the baroque network model uses city as an expression of central power?

5.9 An Imaginary Model
一个虚构的模式

Is it possible to think of a model which deals with form, process, and associated institutions in one whole? Examples are rare. The familiar model of an isolated dwelling, a nuclear family, and private land ownership connects form and institution, but not process. The trailer camp as a way of housing refugees or temporary labor connects form with process[①]. But the form is not well developed, and the process is banal and truncated: no more than here today and gone tomorrow. So we are forced to imagine a model of this kind, even though it must be an unripe one. This imaginary model might be called an "alternating net":

The basic pattern is one in which the major arterials form an open, irregular grid, sufficiently widely spaced that there is ample open space within the interstices. The arterial frontage is occupied by a relatively dense and continuous set of land uses. Orthogonal to the arterial grid, and offset half an interval from it, is a grid of similar pattern which is restricted to pedestrians, cyclists, horsemen, boaters, and other slow and backward travelers. Its frontages are occupied by recreational uses, as well as by uses catering to these peculiar people. Both grid systems, while irregular in detail in order to be able to conform to the land and its history, are regular grids in the topological sense. That is, each grid consists of two sets of continuous, mutually intersecting lines, which maintain their sequential order with respect to each other[2]. These rights-of-way were originally laid down by some regional planning authority. In the blocks between these two grid systems, the land is farmed, wooded, waste, or occupied by small, relatively self-sufficient groups, who put a low value on access. This interior land is serviced by a shifting, mazelike system of low-capacity lanes, penetrating inward from one or the other of the two grids.

The arterial "fast" grid system is owned, and immediate frontage is controlled, by a public body, while the fronting uses are individually held. The "slow" grid, while open to the public, is managed by local frontage associations. Both rights-of-way are permanent, although their structures and management are not. The interstitial land is individually owned, or is held by small communitarian groups, and is relatively free of public control, although the density of use must be kept low. Densities are moderately high along the arterials, and the uses, while regulated, are finely mixed. Uses along the slow grid are also mixed, but are low in intensity, and with a greater predominance of recreational activity.

Minor adaptations can easily be made along these lines, or shallow additions can be extended into the interstitial lands near their borders. On initiative of the regional authority, and by agreement of the majority of the fronting owners and frontage associations, a periodic reversal of the two grid systems can be made, to accommodate major changes. That is, a single "slow" line, or portion of it, can be taken over for public management as a new arterial. As this new channel is completed, the parallel arterial is closed down and ceded to local frontage associations.

Uses on each old line are abandoned, or take up new sites on the appropriate renewed line. The old arterials are cleared for their new recreational use, while a few interesting landmarks are saved and reused. The ample open space along the old recreational way provides for a new order of movement and intensive use. Thus the settlement maintains a permanent reserve of circulation space and may gradually accumulate a "layering" of notable structures saved from successive epochs. However, any truly permanent symbolic features are located on neither line, but in the interstices just off the line, so that they can be maintained without disturbance③.

This concocted model refers at once to map pattern, flow pattern, the grain of use and density, the distribution of control, and a cyclical pattern of change and how it is implemented. Presumably, these elements are fitted one to another. The motives are adaptability (albeit a somewhat convulsive one) and good generalized access, combined with a high degree of access to open space and a sharp grain of local access, as well as a wide variety of density and activity and a diversity of modal choice. An efficient means of central control is allied to a convenient way of escaping that central control. The model produces three widely different yet connected habitats (the arterial frontage, the "slow" frontage, and the rural interior), and a strong sense of time, via the cycling of the grids and the retention of the permanent symbolic locations. It seems to be suited to a low-density landscape, rich in land and in transport vehicles.

It has its antecedents in the street village, the "section" grid of the American midwest, the baroque axial network, and many exurban areas of the United States, whose new houses have reoccupied the roadsides of the old farming communities while letting the backlands return to forest. The trick of renewal via alteration has other precedents: I have already cited the periodic rebuilding of the Shinto temple at Ise. In the proposed model, however, the administrative difficulties in reversing the use of the two grid systems simultaneously might be formidable. Since the model is untested, its true performance is unknown, as well as whether it would be desired by any group, or whether it conceals destructive incompatibilities④. Speculative as it is, and vulnerable to criticism (as it should be), it serves to illustrate what is meant by a model that deals with form, process, and management all working together.

Words and Phrases

institution [ˌinstiˈtjuːʃən] n. 公共机构；协会；制度
dwelling [ˈdweliŋ] n. 住处
temporary [ˈtempərəri] adj. 暂时的；临时的；临时性
banal [bəˈnɑːl] adj. 平凡的；陈腐的；老一套的
truncate [ˈtrʌŋkeit] v. 截去尖端；修剪(树等)；把……截短
interstice [inˈtəːstis] n. 空隙；裂缝
orthogonal [ɔːˈθɔgənl] adj. 直角的；直交的
offset [ˈɔːfset] vt. 弥补；抵消；用平版印刷
interval [ˈintəvəl] n. 间隔；距离；幕间休息
pedestrian [peˈdestriən] adj. n. 徒步的；呆板的；通俗的；步行者
cyclist [ˈsaiklist] n. 骑脚踏车的人
conform [kenˈfɔːm] vt. 使一致；使遵守；使顺从
sequential [siˈkwinʃəl] adj. 连续的；有顺序的；结果的
interstitial [ˌintə(ː)ˈstiʃəl] adj. 空隙的；裂缝的
communitarian [kəˌmjuːniˈtɛəriən] n. 共产主义社会的成员
initiative [iˈniʃiətiv] n. 主动
accommodate [əˈkɔmədeit] vt. 供应；使适应；调节
cede [siːd] vt. 放弃
circulation [ˌsəːkjuˈleiʃən] n. 循环；流通
cyclical [ˈsiklik(e)l] adj. 轮转的；循环的
adaptability [əˌdæptəˈbiliti] n. 适应性
ally [əˈlai, æˈlai] v. 结盟；与……有关联
habitat [ˈhæbitæt] n. 居留地；聚集处

retention [ri'tenʃən] *n.* 保持力
exurban [eks'ɛːbən] *adj.* 城市远郊的
precedent [pri'siːdənt] *n.* 先例
formidable ['fɔːmidəbl] *adj.* 强大的；令人敬畏的；可怕的；艰难的
administrative [əd'ministrətiv] *adj.* 管理的；行政的
incompatibility ['inkəmˌpætə'biliti] *n.* 不两立；不相容
trailer camp 活动房营地
housing refugee 住房难民
alternating net 交互网
grid system 栅格系统
topological sense 拓扑结构
frontage association 临街建筑

Difficult Sentences

① Is it possible to think of a model which deals with form, process, and associated institutions in one whole? Examples are rare. The familiar model of an isolated dwelling, a nuclear family, and private land ownership connects form and institution, but not process. The trailer camp as a way of housing refugees or temporary labor connects form with process.

是不是可能想出一种将形式、过程和相关制度结合成一个整体的模式呢？这种例子很少。我们熟悉孤立的房子、核心家庭和私有土地所有权的模式将形式和制度联系起来，但不包括过程。活动房集中地，作为难民和暂时性劳动工人的一种居住方式将形式和过程联系起来。

② Both grid systems, while irregular in detail in order to be able to conform to the land and its history, are regular grids in the topological sense. That is, each grid consists of two sets of continuous, mutually intersecting lines, which maintain their sequential order with respect to each other.

这两种方格系统，虽然为了符合土地和其历史条件，在细节上不规则,但是从整体来看是规则的网格,即每一种网格包括两套连续的、相互交叉的路线,这样可以保持相互之间的连续的秩序。

③ Thus the settlement maintains a permanent reserve of circulation space and may gradually accumulate a "layering" of notable structures saved from successive epochs. However, any truly permanent symbolic features are located on neither line, but in the interstices just off the line, so that they can be maintained without disturbance.

因此,这个群落永久保存了循环空间并可能逐渐积累历经数年而保存下来的显著结构的一个层面。然而,真正永久的象征性的特征不在任何一条路线上,而是在路线旁边的空隙间,这样,这些象征性的特征才可以不受打扰地被保存下来。

④ The trick of renewal via alteration has other precedents: I have already cited the periodic rebuilding of the Shinto temple at Ise. In the proposed model, however, the administrative difficulties in reversing the use of the two grid systems simultaneously might be formidable. Since the model is untested, its true performance is unknown, as well as whether it would be desired by any group, or whether it conceals destructive incompatibilities.

通过改造进行革新的秘诀有其他先例:我已经引用了伊势岛神道寺的阶段性重建的例子。然而在所提议的模式中,在颠倒使用两种方格系统的过程中,行政部门所面临的阻力是很大的。因为这种模式没有被测试过,它的真实性能也无从得知,同样,它是否会满足某一社会群体的需要,或是否隐藏着破坏性的不相容也都是一个未知数。

Phrases and patterns

1. cater to 满足;迎合

   Its frontages are occupied by recreational uses, as well as by uses catering to these peculiar people.

它的正面要满足于娱乐用途,此外,还要迎合特殊人群的需求。

Any enterprise which wants to develop its products must be able to meet a certain demand of consumers; the sale of its products must be able to cater to consumers' psychology.

任何企业要想要开发新产品都必须能满足消费者的某种需求,产品的销售也必须能迎合消费者的消费心理。

2. It seems to 好像;似乎

It seems to be suited to a low-density landscape, rich in land and in transport vehicles.

这种模式似乎适用于低密度地形、地域宽阔或交通工具多的情况。

It seems to be rarely found in the urban city interiors. Mostly the countryside homes adopt these kind of themes.

这好像很少出现在城市内部区域中,反而大多数的农村住房都采取了这样的主题形式。

Questions

1. What's the relationship between form, process and institutions?
2. Summarize the "two grid systems" in the passage.

5.10 City Design
城市设计

Design is the playful creation and strict evaluation of the possible forms of something, including how it is to be made. That something need not be a physical object, nor is design expressed only in drawings. Although attempts have been made to reduce design to completely explicit systems of search or synthesis, it remains an art, a peculiar mix of rationality and irrationality[①]. Design deals with qualities, with complex connections, and also with ambiguities. City design is the art of creating possibilities for the use, management, and form of settlements or their significant parts. It manipulates patterns in time and space and has as its justification the everyday human experience of those patterns. It does not deal solely with big things, but also with policies for small things—like seats and trees and sitting on front porches—wherever those features affect the performance of the settlement. City design concerns itself with objects, with human activity, with institutions of management, and with processes of change.

City design may be engaged in preparing a transit or a shoreline plan, a comprehensive regional access study, a development strategy, a new town, a suburban extension, or a regional park system. It may develop prototypes for houses or workplaces, a policy for bus shelters, or a neighborhood analysis. It may seek to protect neighborhood streets, revitalize a public square, improve lighting, planting, or paving, set regulations for conservation or development, build a participatory process, write an interpretive guide, or plan a city celebration②. It uses techniques of its own: area diagnoses, framework plans, sequential strategies, conservation zones, illustrative designs, design liaison and service, development controls and guides, process rules, place monitoring, and the creation of new place institutions. Its peculiar features are the consequences of the scale and complexity of its domain, the fluidity of events, and the plurality of actors, as well as its imperfect and overlapping controls③.

Having laid out this splendid array of subject matter and technique, I should also admit that city design is rarely practiced—or, more often, it is mispracticed as big architecture or big engineering: the design of whole towns as single physical objects, extended site plans or utility networks, to be built to precise plan in a predetermined time. True city design never begins with a virgin situation, never foresees a completed work. Properly, it thinks in terms of process, prototype, guidance, incentive, and control and is able to conceive broad, fluid sequences along with concrete, homely details. It is a scarcely developed art—a new kind of design and a new view of its subject matter. A well-developed stock of models which integrated process and form would be of immense value to it. These models and theoretical constructs must be sufficiently independent and simple, however, to allow for that continuous recasting of aims, analyses, and possibilities that is inherent in the conduct of city design.

Words and Phrases

playful ['pleiful] *adj.* 好玩的；嬉戏的；十分有趣的；顽皮的
physical ['fizikəl] *adj.* 身体的；物质的；自然的；物理的
rationality [ˌræʃə'næliti] *n.* 合理性；唯理性
irrationality [ɪˌræʃə'nælətɪ] *n.* 不合理
ambiguity [ˌæmbi'gjuːiti] *n.* 含糊；不明确
justification [dʒʌstifi'keɪʃ(ə)n] *n.* 认为有理；认为正当；理由；辩护；释罪
transit ['trænsit] *n.* 经过；通行；运输；转变
porch [pɔːtʃ] *n.* 门廊；走廊
revitalize ['riː'vaitəlaiz] *v.* 新生
participatory [pɑː'tɪsɪpeɪtəri, pə-] *adj.* 供人分享的
interpretive [in'təːpritiv] *adj.* 作为说明的；解释的
liaison [li(ː)'eizɑːn, -zən] *n.* 联络
complexity [kəm'pleksiti] *n.* 复杂(性)；复杂的事物；复杂性
fluidity [flu(ː)'iditi] *n.* 流动性；流质；流度
plurality [pluə'ræliti] *n.* 复数；较大数；多数；兼职
overlap ['əuvə'læp] *v.* (与……)交叠
incentive [in'sentiv] *n.* 动机
inherent [in'hiərənt] *adj.* 固有的；内在的；与生俱来的
recast ['riː'kɑːst] *v.* 重铸；彻底改动；重做；重新铸造
engage in 从事于；涉及
bus shelter 公共汽车候车站
conservation zone 保护区
along with 连同……一起

allow with 考虑到

Difficult Sentences

① Design is the playful creation and strict evaluation of the possible forms of something, including how it is to be made. That something need not be a physical object, nor is design expressed only in drawings. Although attempts have been made to reduce design to completely explicit systems of search or synthesis, it remains an art, a peculiar mix of rationality and irrationality.

设计是通过有趣的创造和严格的评价来形成任何事物的形态,其中也包括成形的整个过程和形式。这种事物不一定是物质的东西,设计手段也不仅局限于绘画这一种形式。虽然人们已经尝试将设计简化为寻找综合的完全明确的体系,但它仍是一种艺术,一种理性和非理性的奇特组合。

② It may develop prototypes for houses or workplaces, a policy for bus shelters, or a neighborhood analysis. It may seek to protect neighborhood streets, revitalize a public square, improve lighting, planting, or paving, set regulations for conservation or development, build a participatory process, write an interpretive guide, or plan a city celebration.

城市设计可能会为房屋或工作场所提出原型,为公共汽车候车亭提出一种建筑原则,或为周边地区提供规划分析。它可能尽力去保护临近的街道,为公共广场注入活力,改善照明、植被或甬路,为建筑风格的保存或发展设定规则,建立一种参与性的过程,写一份说明性的准则或策划一次城市庆祝活动。

③ Its peculiar features are the consequences of the scale and complexity of its domain, the fluidity of events, and the plurality of actors, as well as its imperfect and overlapping controls.

城市设计独特的特征是它所涉及领域的规模和复杂性,事件的流动性,参与要素的多重性,它所控制机制的不完善性和重叠性综合作用的结果。

Phrases and patterns

1. make attempt to 努力做

   Although attempts have been made to reduce design to completely explicit systems of search or synthesis, it remains an art, a peculiar mix of rationality and irrationality.

   虽然人们已经努力将设计变为寻找或综合的明确体系,但设计仍然是一种艺术,一种理性和非理性的结合。

   Based on the development of urban design and visual design in computer science, he made attempt to put forward some views on the visual urban design.

   在回顾传统的城市设计与计算机可视化发展的基础上,他尝试提出了对城市设计可视化的一些认识。

2. allow for 考虑到

   These models and theoretical constructs must be sufficiently independent and simple, however, to allow for that continuous recasting of aims, analyses, and possibilities that is inherent in the conduct of city design.

   然而,考虑到目标、分析以及城市规划进展中必然存在的连续的改变,这些模式和理论建筑必须非常独立且简单。

   In general "theme and variation" allows for the expression of individual identity within a system of manifest common meanings.

   总的来说,"主题"和"变化"在明显的共同意义中考虑到了个体属性的表达。

Questions

1. Define the term "Design" and "City design".
2. What's the content of "City design" mentioned in the passage?

6

Place
场所

【本章导读】 挪威的建筑理论家诺伯格·舒尔茨(Norberg-Schulz)系统地创立了建筑现象学,提出建筑现象是环境现象的反映,并提出"场所"的概念。舒尔茨认为任何独立存在的事物都有自己的守护神,场所也一样,它是由自然环境和人造环境所结合的有意义的整体,具有自己的独特气氛,场所所聚集到的意义构成了"场所的精神"。本章6.1~6.9选取的9篇文章详细说明了什么是场所,什么是空间,什么是场所精神这几个核心问题。

6.1 The Phenomenon of Place
场所现象

Being qualitative totalities of a complex nature, places cannot be described by means of analytic, "scientific" concepts. As a matter of principle science "abstracts" from the given to arrive at neutral, "objective" knowledge. What is lost, however, is the everyday life-world, which ought to be the real concern of man in general and planners and architects in particular. Fortunately a way out of the impasse exists, that is, the method known as phenomenology[①].

Phenomenology was conceived as a "return to things", as opposed to abstractions and mental constructions. So far phenomenologists have been mainly concerned with ontology, psychology, ethics and to some extent aesthetics, and have given relatively little attention to the phenomenology of the daily environment. A few pioneer works however exist, but they hardly contain any direct reference to architecture. A phenomenology of architecture is therefore urgently needed.

Some of the philosophers who have approached the problem of our life-world, have used language and literature as sources of "information". Poetry in fact is able to concretize those totalities which elude science, and may therefore suggest how we might proceed to obtain the needed understanding. One of the poems used by Heidegger to explain the nature of language, is the splendid A Winter Evening by Georg Trakl. The words of Trakl also serve our purpose very well, as they make present a total life-situation where the aspect of place is strongly felt[②].

A WINTER EVENING
Window with falling snow is arrayed,
Long tolls the vesper bell,
The house is provided well,
The table is for many laid.
Wandering ones, more than a few,
Come to the door on darksome courses.
Golden blooms the tree of graces
Drawing up the earth's cool dew.
Wanderer quietly steps within;
Pain has turned the threshold to stone.
There lie, in limpid brightness shown,
Upon the table bread and wine.

We shall not repeat Heidegger's profound analysis of the poem, but rather point out a few properties which illuminate our problem. In general, Trakl uses concrete images which we all know from our everyday world. He talks about "snow", "window", "house", "table", "door", "tree", "threshold", "bread and wine", "darkness" and "light", and he characterizes man as a "wanderer". These images, however, also imply more general structures. First of all the poem distinguishes between an outside and an inside. The outside is presented in the first two verses of the first stanza, and comprises natural as well as man-made elements. Natural place is present in the falling snow, which implies winter, and by the evening. The very title of the poem "places" everything in this natural context. A winter evening, however, is something more than a point in the calendar. As a concrete presence, it is experienced as a set of particular qualities, or in general as a Stimmung or "character" which forms a background to acts and occurrences. In the poem this character is given by the snow falling on the window, cool, soft and soundless, hiding the contours of those objects which are still recognized in the approaching darkness. The word "falling" moreover creates a sense of space, or rather: an implied presence of earth and sky. With a minimum of words Trakl thus <u>brings a total natural environment to life.</u> But the outside also has man-made properties. This is indicated by the vesper bell, which is heard everywhere, and makes the "private" inside become part of a comprehensive, "public" totality.③ The vesper bell, however, is something more than a practical man-made artifact. It is a symbol, which reminds us of the common values which are at the basis of that totality. In Heidegger's words: "The tolling of the evening bell brings men, as mortals, before the divine".

    The inside is presented in the next two verses. It is described as a house, which offers man shelter and security by being enclosed and "well provided". It has however a window, an opening which makes us experience the inside as a complement to the outside. As a final focus within the house we find the table, which "is for many laid". At the table men come together, it is the centre which more than anything else constitutes the inside. The character of the inside is hardly told, but anyhow present. It is luminous and warm, in contrast to the cold darkness outside, and its silence is pregnant with potential sound. In general the inside is a comprehensible world of things, where the life of "many" may take place. In the next two stanzas the perspective is deepened. Here the meaning of places and things comes forth, and man is presented as a wanderer on "darksome courses". Rather than being placed safely within the house he has created for himself, he comes from the outside, from the "path of life", which also represents man's attempt at "orientating" himself in the given unknown environment④.

Words and Phrases

qualitative [ˈkwɔlitətiv] adj. 性质上的；定性的
totality [təuˈtæliti] n. 全体；总数
analytic [ˌænəˈlitik] adj. 分析的；解析的
architect [ˈɑːkitekt] n. 建筑师
phenomenology [fiˌnɔmiˈnɔlədʒi] n. 现象学
impasse [æmˈpɑːs, im-] n. 僵局
psychology [saiˈkɔlədʒi] n. 心理学；心理状态
ethics [ˈeθiks] n. 道德规范
approach [əˈprəutʃ] n. 接近；方法；途径；通路
concretize [kɔnˈkri(ː)taiz] vt. 使具体化；使有形化
elude [iˈljuːd, iˈluːd] v. 躲避
vesper [ˈvespə] n. 薄暮；晚祷
illuminate [iˈljuːmineit] vt. 照明；照亮；阐明；说明
characterize [ˈkæriktəraiz] vt. 表现……的特色；刻画的……性格
stanza [ˈstænzə] n. 节；演出期；比赛中的盘
comprise [kəmˈpraiz] v. 包含；由……组成
contour [ˈkɔntuə] n. 轮廓；周线；等高线
artifact [ˈɑːtifækt] n. 人造物品
shelter [ˈʃeltə] n. v. 掩蔽处；保护；庇护所掩蔽；躲避

constitute ['kɔnstitjuːt] vt. 制定(法律);建立(政府);组成;任命
orientate ['ɔːrienteit] v. 向东;朝向
luminous ['ljuːminəs] adj. 发光的;明亮的
arrive at 得出
conceive as 被认为
Georg Trakl 特拉克尔(人名)
vesper bell 晚祷钟

Difficult Sentences

① Being qualitative totalities of a complex nature, places cannot be described by means of analytic, "scientific" concepts. As a matter of principle science "abstracts" from the given to arrive at neutral, "objective" knowledge. What is lost, however, is the everyday life-world, which ought to be the real concern of man in general and planners and architects in particular. Fortunately a way out of the impasse exists, that is, the method known as phenomenology.
作为复杂自然的定性整体,场所不能用分析的、"科学的"概念来描述。作为一种从既定环境中"抽象"出来的原理科学,它最终得出中立的、"客观的"知识。然而,所失去的是日常生活的东西,这应该是一般人所真正关心的,特别是设计者和建筑师所关心的。幸运的是,现在我们已经有了摆脱目前的这种困境的方法,这就是"现象学"。

② One of the poems used by Heidegger to explain the nature of language, is the splendid A Winter Evening by Georg Trakl. The words of Trakl also serve our purpose very well, as they make present a total life-situation where the aspect of place is strongly felt.
海德格尔用来解释语言本质的一首诗,是特拉克尔的一首极好的诗《冬夜》。特拉克尔的语言恰当地说明了我们的目的,他的诗呈现了一幅完整的生活画面,我们能从中强烈地感受到场所的含义。

③ But the outside also has man-made properties. This is indicated by the vesper bell, which is heard everywhere, and makes the "private" inside become part of a comprehensive, "public" totality. The vesper bell, however, is something more than a practical man-made artifact. It is a symbol, which reminds us of the common values which are at the basis of that totality.

但外部环境也有人造产物的印迹。这一点可以从在每一个角落都能听见的晚祷钟声看出来,这样它使得"私有的"内部场所变成了全面的"公共整体"的一部分。然而,晚祷钟声不仅仅是一种人工制品,它是一个象征,随时提示我们在整体基础上的共同价值。

④ Here the meaning of places and things comes forth, and man is presented as a wanderer on "darksome courses". Rather than being placed safely within the house he has created for himself, he comes from the outside, from the "path of life", which also represents man's attempt at "orientating" himself in the given unknown environment.

在这里,场所和事件的含义得以浮现,人被描述为在"黑暗途中"的一个徘徊者。人没有被妥善地安置在他为自己造的房子里,他从外面来,从"人生之路"来,这也体现了人企图将自己"定位"在既定的未知环境里。

Phrases and patterns

1. bring sth. / sb. to life 给某人、某物以活力
   With a minimum of words Trakl thus brings a total natural environment to life.
   用最简洁的语言,特拉克尔将一幅自然环境的画面描绘得栩栩如生。
   He is able to, through his fiction; bring to life a panoramic view of a troubled China in the early 1930s.

他通过小说描绘出一幅20世纪30年代前半期中国社会大动荡的全景图。

The story was based on a play. Popular songs, dances, and fabulous sets and costumes were then used to bring the words to life.

其故事来自剧本。然后采用流行歌曲、舞蹈、精彩的布景及服装将文字描述生动地呈现出来。

2. in contrast to 与之相对比

It is luminous and warm, in contrast to the cold darkness outside, and its silence is pregnant with potential sound.

和外面冰冷的黑暗相比较,它是光明的、温暖的,在它的沉默中孕育的是潜在的声音。

In contrast to wide medians, narrows are often found in low speed environment.

与宽中线相比,窄中线经常出现在低速通行的环境中。

Questions

1. Define the term "Phenomelogy" and why "Phnomelogy of architecture" is urgently needed?
2. How to understand the meaning of "place" in "A Winter Evening"?
3. How to understand Heidegger's words "The tolling of the evening bell bring men, as mortals, before the divine"?

6.2　Space
空间

"Space" is certainly no new term in architectural theory. But space can mean many things. In current literature we may distinguish between two uses: space as three-dimensional geometry, and space as perceptual field. None of these however are satisfactory, being abstractions from the intuitive three-dimensional totality of everyday experience, which we may call "concrete space". Concrete human actions in fact do not take place in an homogeneous isotropic space, but in a space distinguished by qualitative differences, such as "up" and "down". In architectural theory several attempts have been made to define space in concrete, qualitative terms. Giedion, thus uses the distinction between "outside" and "inside" as the basis for a grand view of architectural history. Kevin Lynch penetrates deeper into the structure of concrete space, introducing the concepts of "node" ("landmark"), "path", "edge" and "district", to denote those elements which form the basis for men's orientation in space[①]. Paolo Portoghesi finally defines space as a "system of places", implying that the concept of space has its roots in concrete situations, although spaces may be described by means of mathematics. The latter view corresponds to Heidegger's statement that "spaces" receive their being from locations and not from "space". The outside-inside relation which is a primary aspect of concrete space, implies that spaces possess a varying degree of extension and enclosure. Whereas landscapes are distinguished by a varied, but basically continuous extension, settlements are enclosed entities. Settlement and landscape therefore have a figure-ground relationship. In general any enclosure becomes manifest as a "figure" in relation to the extended ground of the landscape. A settlement loses its identity if this relationship is corrupted, just as much as the landscape loses its identity as comprehensive extension. In a wider context any enclosure becomes a centre, which may function as a "focus" for its surroundings. From the centre space extends with a varying degree of continuity (rhythm) in different directions. Evidently the main directions are horizontal and vertical, that is, the directions of earth and sky. Centralization, direction and rhythm are therefore other important properties of concrete space. Finally it has to be mentioned that natural elements (such as hills) and settlements may be clustered or grouped with a varying degree of proximity[②].

All the spatial properties mentioned are of a "topological" kind, and correspond to the well-known "principles of organization" of Gestalt theory. The primary existential importance of these principles is confirmed by the researches of Piaget on the child's conception of space.

Geometrical modes of organization only develop later in life to serve particular purposes, and may in general be understood as a more "precise" definition of the basic topological structures③. The topological enclosure thus becomes a circle, the "free" curve a straight line, and the cluster a grid. In architecture geometry is used to make a general comprehensive system manifest, such as an inferred "cosmic order".

Any enclosure is defined by a boundary. Heidegger says: "A boundary is not that at which something stops but, as the Greeks recognized, the boundary is that, from which something begins its presencing". The boundaries of a built space are known as floor, wall and ceiling. The boundaries of a landscape are structurally similar, and consist of ground, horizon, and sky④. This simple structural similarity is of basic importance for the relationship between natural and man-made places. The enclosing properties of a boundary are determined by its openings, as was poetically intuited by Trakl when using the images of window, door and threshold. In general the boundary, and in particular the wall, makes the spatial structure visible as continuous or discontinuous extension, direction and rhythm.

Words and Phrases

geometry [dʒi'ɔmitri] n. 几何学
abstraction [æb'strækʃən] n. 提取
intuitive [in'tju(:)itiv] adj. 直觉的
homogeneous [ˌhɔməu'dʒi:njəs] adj. 同类的；相似的；均一的，均匀的
isotropic [ˌaisəu'trɔpik] adj. 等方性的
landmark ['lændmɑ:k] n. （航海）陆标；地界标；里程碑；划时代的事

denote [di'nəut] vt. 指示；表示
extension [iks'tenʃən] n. 延长；扩充；范围
settlement ['setlmənt] n. 群落
identity [ɑi'dentiti] n. 同一性；身份；一致
centralization ['sentrəlɑi'zeiʃən] n. 集中；中央集权化
rhythm ['riðəm, 'riθəm] n. 节奏；韵律
proximity [prɔk'simiti] n. 接近；亲近
curve [kə:v] vt. n. 弯；使弯曲；曲线；弯曲
manifest ['mænifest] adj. 显然的；明白的
cosmic ['kɔzmik] adj. 宇宙的
boundary ['bɑundəri] n. 边界；分界线
discontinuous ['diskən'tinjuəs] adj. 不连续的；间断的；中断的
similarity [ˌsimi'læriti] n. 类似；类似处
three-dimensional geometry 三维几何学
grand view 宏观视角
figure-ground relationship 人物—背景关系
cosmic order 宇宙顺序

Difficult Sentences

① In architectural theory several attempts have been made to define space in concrete, qualitative terms. Giedion, thus uses the distinction between "outside" and "inside" as the basis for a grand view of architectural history. Kevin Lynch penetrates deeper into the structure of concrete space, introducing the concepts of "node" ("landmark"), "path", "edge" and "district", to denote those elements which form the basis for men's orientation in space.

在建筑理论上，人们曾数次尝试用具体的、定性的术语去定义空间。因此,基提恩使用"外部"和"内部"的区别作为审视建筑史宏观视角的基础。凯文·林奇向更深层次探究了具体空间的结构,引用"节点"("地标")、"道路"、"边"、"区"的概念去指示构成人们空间定位基础的那些因素。

② Evidently the main directions are horizontal and vertical, that is, the directions of earth and sky. Centralization, direction and rhythm are therefore other important properties of concrete space. Finally it has to be mentioned that natural elements (such as hills) and settlements may be clustered or grouped with a varying degree of proximity.
非常明显,主要方向是水平和垂直方向,即天和地的方向。因此,中心化、方向和节奏是具体空间的其他重要特征。最后,需要提及的是自然因素(如山)和住宅区必须以不同程度的"临近性"群集或组合起来。

③ Geometrical modes of organization only develop later in life to serve particular purposes, and may in general be understood as a more "precise" definition of the basic topological structures.
组织的几何模式只是后来为了服务于特定的目的而在生活中形成的,一般来说可以被理解为基本拓扑结构的更"精确"的定义。

④ Heidegger says: "A boundary is not that at which something stops but, as the Greeks recognized, the boundary is that, from which something begins its presencing". The boundaries of a built Space are known as floor, wall and ceiling. The boundaries of a landscape are structurally similar, and consist of ground, horizon, and sky.
海德格尔说:"界限不是事物停止的地方,而就像希腊人认识到的那样,界限是事物出现的地方。"一个已建空间的界限就是地板、墙和天花板。一种地形的界限在结构上是与其相似的,是由地面、水平线、天空组成的。

Phrases and patterns

1. root in 根植于;来源于
   Paolo Portoghesi finally defines space as a "system of places", implying that the concept of space has its roots in concrete situations, although spaces may be described by means of mathematics.
   保罗·波多盖希最终将空间定义为"场所体系",意思是虽然空间可以通过数学手段来描述,但是空间的概念来源于具体的环境。

This transformation let people see Japanese companies' decision and action to root in China.

这种转变让人看到日本企业要在中国扎根的决心和行动。

2. It has to be mentioned that... 必须要提的是

Finally it has to be mentioned that natural elements (such as hills) and settlements may be clustered or grouped with a varying degree of proximity.

必须要提的是,自然因素(如山)和住宅区必须以不同程度的"临近性"群集或组合起来。

It has to be mentioned that the structure of a place is not a fixed and eternal state.

必须要提的是场所的结构不是一种固定的、永恒不变的状态。

Questions

1. What is "concrete space" and what are its properties?
2. What's the relationship between "outside" and "inside"?
3. How to understand "boundary" posed by Heidegger?

6.3　The Character of Place
场所的性格

"Character" is at the same time a more general and a more concrete concept than "space". On the one hand it denotes a general comprehensive atmosphere, and on the other the concrete form and substance of the space-defining elements. Any real presence is intimately linked with a character. A phenomenology of character has to comprise a survey of manifest characters as well as an investigation or their concrete determinants. We have pointed out that different actions demand places with a different character. A dwelling has to be "protective", an office "practical", a ball-room "festive" and a church "solemn"①. When we visit a foreign city, we are usually struck by its particular character, which becomes an important part of the experience. Landscapes also possess character, some of which are of a particular "natural" kind. Thus we talk about "barren" and "fertile", "smiling" and "threatening" landscapes. In general we have to emphasize that all places have character, and that character is the basic mode in which the world is "given". To some extent the character of a place is a function of time; it changes with the seasons, the course of the day and the weather, factors which above all determine different conditions of light.

The character is determined by the material and formal constitution of the place. We must therefore ask: how is the ground on which we walk, how is the sky above our heads, or in general; how are the boundaries which define the place. How a boundary is depends upon its formal articulation, which is again related to the way it is "built". Looking at a building from this point of view, we have to consider how it rests on the ground and how it rises towards the sky.

Particular attention has to be given to its lateral boundaries, or walls, which also contribute decisively to determine the character of the urban environment. We are indebted to Robert Venturi for having recognized this fact, after it had been considered for many years "immoral" talk about "facades"②. Usually the character of a "family" of buildings which constitute a place, is "condensed" in characteristic motifs, such as particular types of windows, doors and roofs. Such motifs may become "conventional elements", which serve to transpose a character from one place to another. In the boundary, thus, character and space come together, and we may agree with Venturi when he defines architecture as "the wall between the inside and the outside"③.

Except for the intuitions of Venturi, the problem of character has hardly been considered in current architectural theory. As a result, theory has to a high extent lost contact with the concrete life-world. This is particularly the case with technology, which is today considered a mere means to satisfy practical demands. Character however, depends upon how things are made, and is therefore determined by the technical realization ("building"). Heidegger points out that the Greek word techne meant a creative "re-vealing" (Entbergen) of truth, and belonged to poiesis, that is, "making". A phenomenology of place therefore has to comprise the basic modes of construction and their relationship to formal articulation. Only in this way architectural theory gets a truly concrete basis.

Words and Expressions

intimate ['intimit] *adj.* 亲密的；隐私的
atmosphere ['ætməsfiə] *n.* 大气；空气；气氛
investigation [in‚vesti'geiʃən] *n.* 调查；研究
determinant [di'tə:minənt] *adj.* 决定性的
protective [prə'tektiv] *adj.* 给予保护的；保护的
solemn ['sɔləm] *adj.* 庄严的；隆重的；严肃的
barren ['bærən] *adj.* 不生育的；不孕的；贫瘠的
fertile ['fə:tail; 'fə:til] *adj.* 肥沃的；富饶的；能繁殖的
constitution [‚kɔnsti'tju:ʃən] *n.* 宪法；构造；体质
articulation [ɑ:‚tikju'leiʃən] *n.* 清晰度
lateral ['lætərəl] *adj.* 横(向)的；侧面的
immoral [i'mɔrəl] *adj.* 不道德的；邪恶的
motif [məu'ti:f] *n.* 主题；主旨；动机；图形
conventional [kən'venʃənl] *adj.* 惯例的，常规的，习俗的，传统的
transpose [træns'pəuz] *vt.* 调换；颠倒顺序；移项
be struck by 被……打动
the course of the day 日夜更迭
lateral boundary 边线
be indebted to 感谢

Difficult Sentences

① A phenomenology of character has to comprise a survey of manifest characters as well as an investigation or their concrete determinants. We have pointed out that different actions demand places with a different character. A dwelling has to be "protective", an office "practical", a ball-room "festive" and a church "solemn".

场所性格的现象学必须包括对明显特征的调查,还有调查研究或者是他们的具体决定因素的研究。我们已经指出不同的行为决定了不同的特征。一个房屋必须是"保护性"的住所,是一个"实用的"办公室,是一个"欢乐的"舞厅,还是一个"神圣的"教堂。

② Particular attention has to be given to its lateral boundaries, or walls, which also contribute decisively to determine the character of the urban environment. We are indebted to Robert Venturi for having recognized this fact, after it had been considered for many years "immoral" talk about "facades".

我们应该特别注意它的边线,或者墙,这些也至关重要地决定了城市环境的特征。我们非常感谢感谢罗伯特·文丘里,因为他已经认识到了这个事实,多年来,这个事实一直被人们认为是对于"建筑物正面"的"不道德"论调。

③ Such motifs may become "conventional elements", which serve to transpose a character from one place to another. In the boundary, thus, character and space come together, and we may agree with Venturi when he defines architecture as "the wall between the inside and the outside".

这些主题可能会变成"常规因素",将一种特征从一个场所调换到另一个场所。这样,在界限内,特征和空间一起出现。我们可以赞同文丘里对建筑的定义,他将建筑定义为"内部和外部之间的墙"。

Phrases and patterns

1. link with 与之联系

    Any real presence is intimately linked with a character.

    任何真实的"存在"都是与一种特征密切联系的。

    Labor relations will link with trade relations and state relations in scope. It will evaluate social and political problems.

    劳动关系在范围上将把贸易关系和国家关系连接起来。它将会评价社会问题和政治问题。

2. to some extent 从某种程度上说

    To some extent the character of a place is a function of time; it changes with the seasons, the course of the day and the weather, factors which above all determine different conditions of light.

    在一定程度上,场所的特征是一种时间的功能,它随季节的循环、日夜的更迭、天气的变化、最能够影响光线条件的因素而变化。

    So far phenomenologists have been mainly concerned with ontology, psychology, ethics and to some extent aesthetics.

    到目前为止现象学家主要关心的是存在论、心理学、道德规范,某种程度上还有美学。

    The central services of that broadcasting company to some extent feed off the regional stations.

    那家广播公司中央台的业务在某种程度上是依靠地方台供应材料的。

Questions

1. Define the term "character" and "phenomenology of character"?
2. What are the elements that determine "character"?

6.4　The Structure of Place
场所的结构

The structure of place becomes manifest as environmental totalities which comprise the aspects of character and space. Such places are known as "countries", "regions", "landscapes", "settlements" and "buildings". Here we return to the concrete "things" of our everyday life-world, which was our point of departure, and remember Rilke's words: "Are we perhaps here to say..." When places are classified we should therefore use terms such as "island", "promontory", "bay", "forest", "grove", or "square", "street", "courtyard", and "floor", "wall", "roof", "ceiling", "window" and "door".

Places are hence designated by nouns. This implies that they are considered real "things that exist", which is the original meaning of the word "substantive". Space, instead, as a system of relations, is denoted by prepositions. In our daily life we hardly talk about "space", but about things that are "over" or "under", "before" or "behind" each other, or we use prepositions such as "at", "in", "within", "on", "upon", "to", "from", "along", "next". All these prepositions denote topological relations of the kind mentioned before. Character, finally, is denoted by adjectives, as was indicated above. A character is a complex totality, and a single adjective evidently cannot cover more than one aspect of this totality. Often, however, a character is so distinct that one word seems sufficient to grasp its essence. We see, thus, that the very structure of everyday language confirms our analysis of place[①].

Countries, regions, landscapes, settlements, buildings (and their sub-places) form a series with a gradually diminishing scale. The steps in this series may be called "environmental levels". At the "top" of the series we find the more comprehensive natural places which "contain" the man-made places on the "lower" levels. The latter have the "gathering" and "focusing" function mentioned above. In other words, man "receives" the environment and makes it focus in buildings and things. The things thereby "explain" the environment and make its character manifest. Thereby the things themselves become meaningful. That is the basic function of detail in our surroundings. This does not imply, however, that the different levels must have the same structure. Architectural history in fact shows that this is rarely the case②. Vernacular settlements usually have a topological organization, although the single houses may be strictly geometrical. In larger cities we often find topologically organized neighbourhoods within a general geometrical structure, etc. We shall return to the particular problems of structural correspondence later, but have to say some words about the main "step" in the scale of environmental levels: the relation between natural and man-made places.

Man-made places are related to nature in three basic ways. Firstly, man wants to make the natural structure more precise. That is, he wants to visualize his "understanding" of nature, "expressing" the existential foothold he has gained. To achieve this, he builds what he has seen. Where nature suggests a delimited space he builds an enclosure; where nature appears "centralized", he erects a Mal; where nature indicates a direction, he makes a path. Secondly, man has to complement the given situation, by adding what it is "lacking". Finally, he has to symbolize his understanding of nature (including himself). Symbolization implies that an experienced meaning is "translated" into another medium. A natural character is for instance translated into a building whose properties somehow make the character manifest. The purpose of symbolization is to free the meaning from the immediate situation, whereby it becomes a "cultural object", which may form part of a more complex situation, or be moved to another place. All the three relationships imply that man gather the experienced meanings to create for himself an imago mundi or microcosmos which concretizes his world. Gathering evidently depends on symbolization, and implies a transposition of meanings to another place, which thereby becomes an existential "centre".

Visualization, complementation and symbolization are aspects of the general processes of settling; and dwelling, in the existential sense of the word, depends on these functions. Heidegger illustrates the problem by means of the bridge; a "building" which visualizes, symbolizes and gathers, and makes the environment become a unified whole. Thus he says: "The bridge swings over the stream with case and power. It does not just connect banks that are already there, the banks emerge as banks only as the bridge crosses the stream. The bridge designedly causes them to lie across from each other. One side is set off against the other by the bridge. Nor do the banks stretch along the stream as indifferent border strips of the dry land. With the banks, the bridge brings to the stream the one and the other expanse of the landscape lying behind them. It brings stream and bank and land into each other's neighborhood. The bridge gathers the earth as landscape around the stream". Heidegger also describes what the bridge gathers and thereby uncovers its value as a symbol. We cannot here enter into these details, but want to emphasize that the landscape as such gets its value through the bridge. Before, the meaning of the landscape was "hidden", and the building of the bridge brings it out into the open. "The bridge gathers being into a certain 'location' that we may call a 'place'. This 'place', however, did not exist as an entity before the bridge (although there were always many 'sites' along the river-bank where it could arise), but comes-to-presence with and as the bridge". The existential purpose of building (architecture) is therefore to make a site become a place, that is, to uncover the meanings potentially present in the given environment[3].

The structure of a place is not a fixed, eternal state. As a rule places change, sometimes rapidly. This does not mean, however, that the genius loci necessarily changes or gets lost. Later we shall show that taking place presupposes that the places conserve their identity during a certain stretch of time. Stabilitas loci is a necessary condition for human life. How then is this stability compatible with the dynamics of change? First of all we may point out that any place ought to have the "capacity" of receiving different "contents", naturally within certain limits. A place which is only fitted for one particular purpose would soon become useless. Secondly it is evident that a place may be "interpreted" in different ways. To protect and conserve the genius loci in fact means to concretize its essence in ever new historical contexts. We might also say that the history of a place ought to be its "self-realization". What was there as possibilities at the outset, is uncovered through human action, illuminated and "kept" in works of architecture which are simultaneously "old and new". A place therefore comprises properties having a varying degree of invariance.

In general we may conclude that place is the point of departure as well as the goal of our structural investigation; at the outset place is presented as a given, spontaneously experienced totality, at the end it appears as a structured world, illuminated by the analysis of the aspects of space and character④.

Words and Expressions

departure [di'pɑːtʃə] n. 启程；出发；离开
promontory ['prɔməntəri] n. 岬；隆起；海角
grove [grəuv] n. 小树林
substantive ['sʌbstəntiv] adj. 独立存在的；真实的；有实质的；大量的，
preposition [ˌprepə'ziʃən] n. 介词
distinct [dis'tiŋkt] adj. 清楚的；明显的；截然不同的；独特的

essence ['esns] n. 基本；[哲]本质
correspondence [ˌkɔris'pɔndəns] n. 相应；通信；信件
visualize ['vizjuəlaiz, 'viʒuəlaiz] vt. 形象；形象化；想象
foothold ['futhəuld] n. 立足处
complement ['kɔmplimənt] n. vt. 补足物；补助；补足
symbolize ['simbəlaiz] vt. 象征；用符号表现
experienced [ik'spiəriənst] adj. 富有经验的
transposition [ˌtrænspə'ziʃən] n. 调换；变换
designedly [di'zainidli] adv. 故意地；特意地；有计划地
expanse [iks'pæns] n. 宽阔的区域；宽阔；苍天；膨胀扩张
existential [ˌegzis'tenʃəl] adj. 有关存在的
potential [pə'tenʃ(ə)l] adj. 潜在的；可能的
presuppose [ˌpriːsə'pəuz] v. 预示
conserve [kən'səːv] vt. 保存；保藏
stability [stə'biliti] n. 稳定性
compatible [kəm'pætəbl] adj. 协调的；一致的；兼容的
dynamic [dai'næmik] adj. 动力的；动力学的；动态的
interpret [in'təːprit] v. 解释；说明
spontaneous [spɔn'teinjəs, -niəs] adj. 自发的；自然产生的
environmental totality 环境整体
point of departure 出发点
genius loci 场所精神；一个地方的风气或特色
be compatible with 与……共存

Difficult Sentences

① A character is a complex totality, and a single adjective evidently cannot cover more than one aspect of this totality. Often, however, a character is so distinct that one word seems sufficient to grasp its essence. We see, thus, that the very structure of everyday language confirms our analysis of place.
特征是一个复杂的总体，很明显，一个单独的形容词仅仅能覆盖这个总体的一个侧面。然而，一个特征经常是如此特别，一个词

好像又已经足够能够抓住它的本质。这样,我们看到,正是日常用语的结构证实了我们对于场所的分析。

② In other words, man "receives" the environment and makes it focus in buildings and things. The things thereby "explain" the environment and make its character manifest. Thereby the things themselves become meaningful. That is the basic function of detail in our surroundings. This does not imply, however, that the different levels must have the same structure. Architectural history in fact shows that this is rarely the case.

换句话说,人"接受"环境并使环境集中表现在建筑物和物体上。因此,物体"解释"了环境并使得它的特征更为明显。因此,物体本身也变得更有意义,那是我们周围环境中细目的基本功能。然而,这并不能说明不同的等级必须有相同的结构。事实上,建筑史表明这种情况极其罕见。

③ This "place", however, did not exist as an entity before the bridge (although there were always many "sites" along the river-bank where it could arise), but comes-to-presence with and as the bridge. The existential purpose of building (architecture) is therefore to make a site become a place, that is, to uncover the meanings potentially present in the given environment.

然而,这个"场所"在桥出现之前作为一个实体是不存在的(虽然沿着河岸两侧一直有很多"场所"能够出现的场地),但是这个场所随着桥的出现而出现,并且最后化身为桥。因此,建筑物(建筑)的存在目的就是使一个场地变成一个场所,即发现既定环境中存在的潜在意义。

④ In general we may conclude that place is the point of departure as well as the goal of our structural investigation; at the outset place is presented as a given, spontaneously experienced totality, at the end it appears as a structured world, illuminated by the analysis of the aspects of space and character.

总的来说,我们可以得出结论,场所是出发点,也是我们结构研究的目标;最初场所是一个既定的、自发的经验总体,后来它成为一个由空间和特征方面的分析所阐明的结构世界。

Phrases and patterns

1. compatible with 与……一致;兼容

   How then is this stability compatible with the dynamics of change?
   那么这种稳定性是如何与变化的动态共存的呢?
   The beauty of art must be fair and reasonable. "Be fair" is to be compatible with the way of the world, and "be reasonable" is to be compatible with reason, ethics and the mental standards of human society, that is, to be compatible with the law of objective reality.
   艺术的美必须是"合情合理"的。"合情"就是合乎人之常情;"合理"就是合乎事理,合乎伦理,合乎人类社会的道德规范,也就是客观事物发展的规律。

2. It is evident that... 很明显

   Secondly it is evident that a place may be "interpreted" in different ways.
   第二,很明显,一个场所可以用不同的方式来"理解"。
   It is evident that differing color holds considerable importance within the black community and is measurably influencing self-esteem, prestige, and marital status。
   很明显,不同的肤色在黑人社区内有着相当重要的意义,它会明显地影响自尊、威望和婚姻状况。

Questions

1. Which words are usually used to denote "place", "space" and "character"?
2. How are man-made places related to nature?
3. How is stability compatible with the dynamics of change?

6.5 The Spirit of Place
场所精神

Genius loci is a Roman concept. According to ancient Roman belief every "independent" being has its genius, its guardian spirit. This spirit gives life to people and places, accompanies them from birth to death, and determines their character or essence. Even the gods had their genius, a fact which illustrates the fundamental nature of the concept. The genius thus denotes what a thing is, or what it "wants to be", to use a word of Louis Kahn. It is not necessary in our context to go into the history of the concept of genius and its relationship to the daimon of the Greeks. It suffices to point out that ancient man experienced his environment as consisting of definite characters. In particular he recognized that it is of great existential importance to <u>come to terms with</u> the genius of the locality where his life takes place. In the past survival depended on a "good" relationship to the place in a physical as well as a psychic sense. In ancient Egypt, for instance, the country was not only cultivated in accordance with the Nile floods, but the very structure of the landscape served as a model for the lay-out of the "public" buildings which should give man a sense of security by symbolizing an eternal environmental order[①].

During the course of history the genius loci has remained a living reality, although it may not have been expressively named as such. Artists and writers have found inspiration in local character and have "explained" the phenomena of everyday life as well as art, referring to landscapes and urban milieus. Thus Goethe says: "It is evident, that the eye is educated by the things it sees from childhood on, and therefore Venetian painters must see everything clearer and with more joy than other people"[②].

Still in 1960 Lawrence Durrell wrote: "As you get to know Europe slowly, tasting the wines, cheeses and characters of the different countries you begin to realize that the important determinant of any culture is after all the spirit of place".

Modern tourism proves that the experience of different places is a major human interest, although also this value today tends to get lost. In fact modern man for a long time believed that science and technology had <u>freed</u> him <u>from</u> a direct dependence on places.

This belief has proved an illusion; pollution and environmental chaos have suddendly appeared as a frightening nemesis, and as a result the problem of place has regained its true importance.

We have used the word "dwelling" to indicate the total man-place relationship. To understand more fully what this word implies, it is useful to return to the distinction between "space" and "character". When man dwells, he is simultaneously located in space and exposed to a certain environmental character. The two psychological functions involved, may be called "orientation" and "identification". To gain an existential foothold man has to be able to orientate himself; he has to know where he is. But he also has to identify himself with the environment, that is, he has to know how he is a certain place.

The problem of orientation has been given a considerable attention in recent theoretical literature on planning and architecture. Again we may refer to the work of Kevin Lynch, whose concepts of "node", "path" and "district" denote the basic spatial structures which are the object of man's orientation[3]. The perceived interrelationship of these elements constitute an "environmental image", and Lynch asserts: "A good environmental image gives its possessor an important sense of emotional security". Accordingly all cultures have developed "systems of orientation", that is, "spatial structures which facilitate the development of a good environmental image". "The world may be organized around a set of focal points, or be broken into named regions, or be linked by remembered routes". Often these systems of orientation are based on or derived from a given natural structure. Where the system is weak, the image-making becomes difficult, and man feels "lost". "The terror of being lost comes from the necessity that a mobile organism be oriented in its surroundings". To be lost is evidently the opposite of the feeling of security which distinguishes dwelling. The environmental quality which protects man against getting lost, Lynch calls "imageability", which means "that shape, color or arrangement which facilitates the making of vividly identified, powerfully structured, highly useful mental images of the environment". Here Lynch implies that the elements which constitute the spatial structure are concrete "things" with "character" and "meaning". He limits himself, however, to discuss the spatial function of these elements, and thus leaves us with a fragmentary understanding of dwelling. Nevertheless, the work of Lynch constitutes an essential contribution to the theory of place. Its importance also consists in the fact that his empirical studies of concrete urban structure confirm the general "principles of organization" defined by Gestalt psychology and by the researches into child psychology of Piaget[④].

Without reducing the importance of orientation, we have to stress that dwelling above all presupposes identification with the environment. Although orientation and identification are aspects of one total relationship, they have a certain independence within the totality. It is evidently possible to orientate oneself without true identification; one gets along without feeling "at home". And it is possible to feel at home without being well acquainted with the spatial structure of the place, that is, the place is only experienced as a gratifying general character. True belonging however presupposes that both psychological functions are fully developed. In primitive societies we find that even the smallest environmental details are known and meaningful, and that they make up complex spatial structures. In modern society, however, attention has almost exclusively been concentrated on the "practical" function of orientation, whereas identification has been left to chance. As a result true dwelling, in a psychological sense, has been substituted by alienation. It is therefore urgently needed to arrive at a fuller understanding of the concepts of "identification" and "character".

Identification and orientation are primary aspects of man's being-in-the-world. Whereas identification is the basis for man's sense of belonging, orientation is the function which enables him to be that homo viator, which is part of his nature. It is characteristic for modern man that for a long time he gave the role as a wanderer pride of place. He wanted to be "free" and conquer the world. Today we start to realize that true freedom presupposes belonging, and that "dwelling" means belonging to a concrete place.

Words and Expressions

guardian [ˈgɑːdjən] n. 护卫者；保护人；监护人
accompany [əˈkʌmpəni] vt. 陪伴；伴奏
fundamental [ˌfʌndəˈmentl] adj. 基础的；基本的
suffice [səˈfɑis] vi. 足够；有能力
locality [ləuˈkæliti] n. 位置；地点
survival [səˈvɑivəl] n. 幸存；幸存者；残存物
cultivate [ˈkʌltiveit] vt. 培养；耕作
inspiration [ˌinspəˈreiʃən] n. 灵感
phenomena [fiˈnɔminə] n. 现象
milieu [ˈmiːljəː] n. 周围；环境
Venetian [viˈniːʃən] adj. 威尼斯的
illusion [iˈluːʒən, iˈljuː-] n. 幻想
chaos [ˈkeiɔs] n. 混乱；混沌
frightening [ˈfrɑitəniŋ] adj. 令人恐惧的；引起突然惊恐的
distinction [disˈtiŋkʃən] n. 区别；差别
organism [ˈɔːgənizəm] n. 生物体；有机体

fragmentary ['frægməntəri] *adj.* 由碎片组成的；断断续续的
empirical [em'pirikəl] *adj.* 完全根据经验的；经验主义的
gratifying ['grætifaiiŋ] *adj.* 悦人的；令人满足的
psychological [ˌsaikə'lɔdʒikəl] *adj.* 心理(上)的
identification [ai‚dentifi'keiʃən] *n.* 辨认；鉴定；证明
give life to 为……注入活力
system of orientation 定位系统
mobile organism 移动机制
Gestalt psychology 格式塔心理学
child psychology of Piaget 皮亚杰儿童心理学

Difficult Sentences

① In the past survival depended on a "good" relationship to the place in a physical as well as a psychic sense. In ancient Egypt, for instance, the country was not only cultivated in accordance with the Nile floods, but the very structure of the landscape served as a model for the lay-out of the "public" buildings which should give man a sense of security by symbolizing an eternal environmental order.

在过去,生存要取决于在物质上和精神上与场所保持良好的关系。例如,在古埃及,全国不仅要按照尼罗河的洪水来袭规律来耕作,而且地形的结构也成为公共建筑物设计的模式,公共建筑物通过象征一种永恒的环境次序给人一种安全感。

② Artists and writers have found inspiration in local character and have "explained" the phenomena of everyday life as well as art, referring to landscapes and urban milieus. Thus Goethe says: "It is evident that the eye is educated by the things it sees from childhood on, and therefore Venetian painters must see everything clearer and with more joy than other people".

艺术家们和作家们已经在当地的特征中找到了灵感并解释了日常生活的现象和艺术,这指的是地形和城市环境。因此,歌德说:"非常明显,眼睛是被人从童年起看到的事物训练出来的,因此,威尼斯的画家必须比其他人更清楚、更愉悦地看待每一件事情。"

③ The problem of orientation has been given a considerable attention in recent theoretical literature on planning and architecture. Again we may refer to the work of Kevin Lynch, whose concepts of "node", "path" and "district" denote the basic spatial structures which are the object of man's orientation.

定位的问题在近期的规划和建筑理论著作中被给予了极大的关注。我们需要再次提及凯文·林奇的著作,他的概念"节点"、"道路"和"区域"指示了基本的空间结构,这些也是人定位的目标。

④ Its importance also consists in the fact that his empirical studies of concrete urban structure confirm the general "principles of organization" defined by Gestalt psychology and by the researches into child psychology of Piaget.

它的重要性还在于这样一个事实,他对于具体城市结构的经验主义研究证实了由格式塔心理学和皮亚杰儿童心理学定义的一般的"组织原则"。

Phrases and patterns

1. come to term with/term with 与……达成一致

   In particular he recognized that it is of great existential importance to come to terms with the genius of the locality where his life takes place.

   尤其是他意识到要与他生活地点的特色相一致有重要的存在意义。

   The road design should term with the landscape character and respond to the shape of the landform and patterns of natural and farmed vegetation cover.

   公路设计应该与地形特征一致,应该根据地形、自然的范式与植被种植相呼应。

2. free from ... 将..从……解脱出来

In fact modern man for a long time believed that science and technology had freed him from a direct dependence on places.

事实上,长久以来现代人认为科学和技术已经解除了人对场所的直接依赖。

The purpose of symbolization is to free the meaning from the immediate situation, whereby it becomes a "cultural object", which may form part of a more complex situation, or be moved to another place.

象征的目的是将意义从当前的情况中脱离出来,因此它变了一种"文化产物",它可能会成为一种更为复杂的环境的一部分,或者被移入另外一个场所。

Questions

1. What's the spirit of place (Genius loci) in this passage?
2. What's your understanding of "dwelling"?
3. What's the relationship between "orientation" and "identification"?

6.6 Natural and Manmade Place
自然场所与人造场所

When discussing the natural and manmade place, we gave a general survey of their basic meanings and structural properties. The natural meanings were grouped in five categories, which sum up man's understanding of nature. Evidently man interacts with these meanings. He is a "thing" among "things": he lives among mountains and rocks, rivers and trees; he "uses" then and has to know them. He also lives with the "cosmic order": with the course of the sun and the cardinal points. The directions of the compass are not mere geometry, but qualitative realities which follow man everywhere. In particular, man is related to the "character" of things. From the initial animistic stage he gradually develops a conscious or unconscious understanding that there exists an Ubereinstimmung, a correspondence, between his own psychic states and the "forces" of nature. Only thus he may obtain a personal "friendship" with things, and experience the environment as meaningful. He cannot be friends with scientific "data", but only with qualities. Man also lives with "light" and is tuned by light. Personal and collective attitudes ("mentalities") are in fact influenced by the environmental "climate". Finally man lives in "time", which means that he lives with the changes of the other four dimensions. He lives with the rhythms of day and night, with the seasons and in history[①].

Man's dependence on nature has long been recognized. Hegel starts his "Philosophy of History" with a chapter on the "Geographic Basis of World History", and wants to define the "natural type of the locality, which is closely related to the type and character of the people which is born from this soil. This character is the way peoples appear and find their place in world history". Herder introduced the concept "climate" to cover the entire natural and manmade environment, and characterized man's life as "climatic". He added, however, that climate does not "force" man; rather it "tends" and "disposes". Arnold Toynbee interpreted the relationship between man and his environment as a "challenge and response". To a high extent Toynbee understands "environment" as physical nature. All these great historians thus recognized the importance of the natural environment, but simultaneously they stressed man's ability to "respond" and to shape his world[②]. Man does not obviously only "build" nature, but also builds himself, society and culture, and in this process he may interpret a given environment in different ways.

To achieve a full understanding of "dwelling" and the relationship between man and nature, the concept of alienation is introduced to illustrate the psychological aspect of it. Alienation is in our opinion first of all due to man's loss of identification with the natural and man-made things which constitute his environment. This loss also hinders the process of gathering, and is therefore at the root of our actual "loss of place". Things have become mere objects of consumption which are thrown away after use, and nature in general is treated as a "resource". Only if man regains his ability of identification and gathering, we may stop this destructive development. The first step to take is to arrive at a full understanding of the objects of identification and gathering, that is, an understanding of the concept of thing. Thereby we shall also be able to define the nature of man-made meanings and their relation to natural meanings. Again we have to ask Heidegger for help. In his essay The Thing, he uses a jug as example, and asks for the "jugness" of the jug. "The jug's jug-character consists in the poured gift of the pouring out... The giving of the outpouring can be a drink. The spring stays on in the water of the gift. In the spring the rock dwells, and in the rock dwells the dark slumbers of the earth, which receives the rain and the dew of the sky. In the water of the spring dwells the marriage of sky and earth... In the gift of water, in the gift of wine, sky and earth dwell. But the gift of the outpouring is what makes the jug a jug. In the jugness of the jug, sky and earth dwell..." "The jug's essential nature, its presencing... is what we call a thing". Heidegger takes the function of the jug, the pouring, as his point of departure. He defines the pouring as a gift and asks what is here "given". Water and wine are given, and with them earth and sky. The jug is understood as an artifact which serves a purpose. Its function, however, forms part of a life which takes place between earth and sky. The jug participates in this taking place; yes, it is part of the place in which life is concretized. The function of real things is therefore to concretize or "reveal" life in its various aspects. If a thing does not do that, it is not a thing but a mere commodity. We dwell poetically when we are able to "read" the revealing of the things which make up our environment. Things are made with the purpose of revealing; they gather world, and may themselves be gathered to form a microcosmos④.

Words and Expressions

survey [səː'vei] *v.* 测量；调查；俯瞰
structural ['strʌktʃərəl] *adj.* 结构的；建筑的
category ['kætigəri] *n.* 种类；别
evidently ['evidəntli] *adv.* 明显地；显然
cardinal ['kɑːdinəl] *adj.* 主要的；最重要的
compass ['kʌmpəs] *n.* 罗盘；指南针；圆规
geometry [dʒi'ɔmitri] *n.* 几何学
initial [i'niʃəl] *adj.* 最初的；词首的；初始的
unconscious [ʌn'kɔnʃəs] *adj.* 不省人事；未发觉的；无意识的
psychic ['sɑikik] *adj.* 精神的
mentality [men'tæliti] *n.* 智力；精神；心理
geographic [ˌdʒiə'græfik] *adj.* 地理学的；地理的
rind [rɑind] *n.* 外壳
dispose [dis'pəuz] *v.* 处理；处置；部署
isolate ['ɑisəleit] *vt.* 使隔离；使孤立
consciousness ['kɔnʃəsnis] *n.* 意识；知觉；自觉
reflection [ri'flekʃən] *n.* 反射；反省；沉思
omission [əu'miʃən] *n.* 省略
alienation [ˌeiliə'neiʃən] *n.* 疏远；转让
consumption [kən'sʌmpʃən] *n.* 消费；消费量
destructive [dis'trʌktiv] *adj.* 破坏(性)的
outpour [ɑut'pɔː] *v.* (使)泻出；(使)流出
poetical [pəu'etikəl] *adj.* 诗的；理想化的
tenet ['tiːnet, 'tenit] *n.* 原则
Hegel ['heigl] *n.* 黑格尔
climatic [klɑi'mætik] *adj.* 气候上的
structural property 结构特征

cardinal points 方位基点
initial animistic stage 万物有灵阶段
four dimensions 四维空间
Herder 赫尔德(人名)
Arnold Toynbee 阿诺德·汤因比(人名)

Difficult Sentences

① Personal and collective attitudes ("mentalities") are in fact influenced by the environmental "climate". Finally man lives in "time", which means that he lives with the changes of the other four dimensions. He lives with the rhythms of day and night, with the seasons and in history.

个人和集体的态度(心理)事实上受到环境"大气候"的影响。最终,人是生活在"时间"当中,这意味着他的生活随着其他的四度空间的变化而变化。他生活在日夜的交替中,四季的轮回中,活在历史当中。

② Arnold Toynbee interpreted the relationship between man and his environment as a "challenge and response". To a high extent Toynbee understands "environment" as physical nature. All these great historians thus recognized the importance of the natural environment, but simultaneously they stressed man's ability to "respond" and to shape his world.

阿诺德·汤因比将人与环境的关系理解为"挑战"与"回应"。在很大程度上,汤因比将"环境"理解为物质自然。因此,所有伟大的历史学家都认识到了自然环境的重要性,但同时他们也强调人有能力对他的世界作出"回应"并有能力去塑造这个世界。

③ We dwell poetically when we are able to "read" the revealing of the things which make up our environment. Things are made with the purpose of revealing; they gather world, and may themselves be gathered to form a microcosmos.

当我们能够"读懂"组成我们环境的物体所揭示的内涵时,我们就仿佛生活在诗化世界中。物体是以揭示为目的而被造就的;它们聚集了世界,同时它们自身也被聚集在一起而形成了微观世界。

Phrases and patterns

1. In particular 特别;尤其

   I specialize in city planning, in particular, I hold special interest in how to apply theory and technology of "digital city" into the modern city planning.

   我主攻城市规划,尤其对如何将"数字城市"理论及技术应用于现代城市规划感兴趣。

   The book provides the readers with modern city planning theories, in particular, the development process of landscape ecological planning theory is a hot research issue.

   此书为读者呈现了各种现代城市规划理论,其中,景观生态规划理论尤其成为热点研究问题。

2. arrive at... 得出……

   It is therefore urgently needed to arrive at a fuller understanding of the concepts of "identification" and "character".

   因此,我们更为急迫地需要得出对于"认同"和"特征"这两个概念的全面理解。

   He ought to arrive at an ever deeper understanding of the fact that environmental protection and conservation are of utmost importance to many planning systems across the world.

   他应该更为深刻地理解这个事实,环境保护对于全世界很多的规划体系来说都是举足轻重。

Questions

1. In your opinion, what's the relationship between man and his

environment?
2. What's the function of real things?
3. How do you interpret Heideggar's metaphor of "jug" and "jugness"?

6.7 Meaning of Place
场所的意义

But the function of man-made things (places) goes beyond the manifestation of simple rootedness. The concept of gathering implies that natural meanings are brought together in a new way, in relation to human purposes. Natural meanings are thus abstracted from their natural context, and as elements of a language they are com-posed to form a "new", complex meaning which illuminates nature as well as man's role within the totality[①]. Evidently such a composition may also comprise elements which are invented by man. We have already mentioned how man makes a land-mark or a house, which a posteriori are used to "understand" his environment. To be meaningful, however, the inventions of man must have formal properties which are structurally similar to other aspects of reality, and ultimately to natural structures. If this is not the case, they would isolate themselves within a purely artificial world, and lose contact with reality. The basic kinds of structural similarity ought to be described in terms of our categories "space" and "character". Natural and man-made space are structurally similar as regards directions and boundaries. In both, the distinction between up and down is valid, as well as the concepts of extension and enclosure. The boundaries of both kinds of space are moreover to be defined in terms of "floor", "wall", and "ceiling". Natural and man-made space may thus represent each other reciprocally. The same holds true for natural and human characters, as was understood by the Greeks. The man-made forms which concretize characters obviously do not imitate the analogous natural forms, but we have again to ask for common structural properties.

"Gathering" means that things are brought together, that is, that they are moved from one place to another. This transposition is in general done by means of symbolization, but it may also consist in a concrete displacement of buildings and things. Whereas moving by means of symbolization is a creative act of interpretation and translation, concrete displacement is passive, and mostly connected with the wish for getting a "cultural alibi". The Greek polis was based on a creative transposition of meanings. The meanings which are revealed in certain natural places, were translated into buildings and moved to the city, through the erection of similar buildings there[2]. It is a grand conception, indeed, to visualize the qualities of a landscape by means of a man-made structure, and then to gather several landscapes symbolically in one place! We have seen that the genius loci of Rome stems from such a gathering.

Obviously meanings are moved because they are of general interest, that is, because they are part of "truth". The symbols which make truth manifest constitute culture. Culture means to transform the given "forces" into meanings which may be moved to another place. Culture is therefore based on abstraction and concretization. By means of culture man gets rooted in reality, at the same time as he is freed from complete dependence on a particular situation. We understand that the given economic, social, political and cultural conditions do not produce the meanings concretized by a man-made place. The meanings are inherent in the world, and are in each case to a high extent derived from the locality as a particular manifestation of "world". The meanings may however be used by the economic, social, political and cultural forces. This use consists in a selection among possible meanings. The selection therefore tells us about the actual conditions, but the meanings as such have deeper roots. In general they are covered by our four categories "thing", "order", "character" and "light". Traditionally these categories have been associated with earth, sky, man and spirit, respectively. They thus correspond to what Heidegger calls the "fourfold" (das Geviert)③. Dwelling consists in "preserving" the fourfold, which in general means to "keep the fourfold in that with which mortals stay: in things". The nature of a thing resides in its gathering. The jug gathers earth and sky, and the bridge gathers the earth as landscape around the stream. In general things gather world and thereby reveal truth. To make a thing means the "setting-into-work" of truth. A place is such a thing, and as such it is a poetical fact.

The making of places we call architecture. Through building man gives meanings concrete presence, and he gathers buildings to visualize and symbolize his form of life as a totality. Thus his everyday life world becomes a meaningful home where he can dwell. There are many kinds of buildings and settlements. What they gather varies according to the building task and the situation. Vernacular architecture, that is, farms and villages, brings the immediate meanings of the local earth and sky into presence. Hence it is "circumstantial" and intimately connected with a particular situation. Urban architecture, instead, has a more general value, as it is based on symbolization and transposition. Urban architecture therefore presupposes a formal language, a "style". In the town, "foreign" meanings meet the local genius, and create a more complex system of meanings. The urban genius is never merely local; although the examples of Prague, Khartoum and Rome have taught us that the local character plays a decisive role in giving the settlement its particular identity④. Urban gathering may be understood as an interpretation of the local genius, in accordance with the values and need of the actual society. In general we may say that the meanings which are gathered by a place constitute its genius loci.

Architecture is born from the dialectic of departure and return.

Man, the wanderer, is on his way. His task is to penetrate the world and to set its meanings into work. This is the meaning of the word settle. A settlement sets truth into a work of architecture. To set-into-work here means to build the boundary or "threshold" from which the settlement begins its presencing. The threshold is the meeting of "outside" and "inside", and architecture is hence the incarnation of the meeting. "The place-searching and place-forming characters of plastic incarnation" here find their "look" and at the same time man finds his "outlook". Thus the threshold is the "gathering middle", where things appear in "limpid brightness".

Words and Expressions

manifestation [ˌmænifes'teiʃən] n. 显示；表现；示威运动
element ['elimənt] n. 要素；元素；成分；元件
composition [kɔmpə'ziʃən] n. 写作；作文；成分；合成物
ultimately ['ʌltımətlı] adv. 最后；终于；根本
valid ['vælid] adj. [律]有效的；有根据的，正当的
extension [iks'tenʃən] n. 延长；扩充；范围
enclosure [in'kləuʒə] n. 围住；围栏；围场
reciprocal [ri'siprəkəl] adj. 互惠的；相应的；倒数的；彼此相反的
property ['prɔpəti] n. 财产；所有物；所有权；性质；特性
displacement [dis'pleismənt] n. 移置；转移；取代；置换；位移
alibi ['ælibai] n. [律]犯罪现场；辩解；托词
erection [i'rekʃən] n. 直立；竖起；建筑物
symbolical [sim'bɔlikl] adj. 表示象征的；符号的
manifest ['mænifest] adj. 显然的；明白的
inherent [in'hiərənt] adj. 固有的；内在的；与生俱来的
reside [ri'zaid] vi. 居住
vernacular [və'nækjulə] adj. 本国的
circumstantial [ˌsəːkəm'stænʃəl] adj. 依照情况的
presuppose [ˌpriːsə'pəuz] v. 预示
Prague [prɑːg] n. 布拉格

immediate [iˈmiːdjət] *adj.* 直接的；紧接的；紧靠的；立即的
dialectic [ˌdaiəˈlektik] *adj.* 辩证的
wanderer [ˈwɔndərə(r)] *n.* 流浪者；徘徊者
penetrate [ˈpenitreit] *vt.* 穿透；渗透；看穿；洞察
incarnation [ˌinkɑːˈneiʃən] *n.* 赋予肉体；具人形；化身
go beyond 超出
in relation to 关于；涉及；与……相比
derive from 得自；由来；衍生
vernacular architecture 地方性建筑

Difficult Sentences

① Natural meanings are thus abstracted from their natural context, and as elements of a language they are composed to form a "new", complex meaning which illuminates nature as well as man's role within the totality.
因此，自然含义从它们的自然背景中被提炼出来，而且作为语言的成分，它们被组合形成"新的"、复杂的意义，这些意义说明了本质，也说明了人在整体世界中的角色。

② The Greek polis was based on a creative transposition of meanings. The meanings which are revealed in certain natural places were translated into buildings and moved to the city, through the erection of similar buildings there.
希腊的城邦是在意义的创造性转换基础上建立的。某些自然场所中所展示的含义被转换到了建筑物上，并通过在城市里建立相似的建筑物而被搬到了城里。

③ In general they are covered by our four categories "thing", "order", "character" and "light". Traditionally these categories have been associated with earth, sky, man and spirit, respectively. They thus correspond to what Heidegger calls the "fourfold" (das Geviert).
一般来说，他们由四种范畴所覆盖——"物体"、"顺序"、"特征"和"光"。从传统意义上讲，这些范畴分别和"大地"、"天空"、

"人"和"精神"相联系。因此,它们和海德格尔所定义的"四重"相一致。

④ In the town, "foreign" meanings meet the local genius, and create a more complex system of meanings. The urban genius is never merely local; although the examples of Prague, Khartoum and Rome have taught us that the local character plays a decisive role in giving the settlement its particular identity.

在城镇中,"外来"意义遇到了本地精神,创造了一种更为复杂的意义体系。虽然布拉格、喀土穆和罗马的例子都已经告诉我们,地方特色在赋予住宅区特殊属性中起到了重要作用,但是城市的精神绝不仅仅局限于本土。

Phrases and patterns

1. hold true 适用;有效

   The same holds true for natural and human characters, as was understood by the Greeks.
   这同样也适用于自然和人文特征,就像是希腊人理解的那样。
   I believe those principles hold true for everyone, everywhere.
   我相信,这些道理在任何地方、对任何人都是至理名言。

2. in accordance with 和……一致

   Urban gathering may be understood as an interpretation of the local genius, in accordance with the values and need of the actual society.
   城市的聚合可以被理解为地方特色的一种阐释,这与现实社会的价值和需要是一致的。
   In ancient Egypt, for instance, the country was not only cultivated in accordance with the Nile floods, but the very structure of the landscape served as a model for the lay-out of the "public" buildings.
   例如,在古埃及,全国不仅要按照尼罗河的洪水来袭规律来耕作,而且地形的结构也成为公共建筑物的设计的模式。

Questions

1. Summarize the means of transposition.
2. How to understand the sentence "the meanings which are gathered by a place constitute its genius loci"?
3. What does "set-into-work" mean in this passage?

6.8 Identity of Place
场所的特性

Places where natural and man-made elements form a synthesis are the subject-matter of a phenomenology of architecture. The primary relationship between the two kinds of elements is denoted by the world location. Where does man locate his settlements? Where does nature form places which "invite" man to settle? The question has to be answered both in terms of space and character. <u>From the spatial point of view</u> man needs an enclosure, and accordingly tends to settle where nature offers a defined space. From the point of view of character, a natural place which comprises several meaningful things, such as rocks, trees and water, would represent an "invitation". We have in fact seen that Rome was founded in a place where these elements were present. Some times the conditions may be favourable both with regard to space and character, other times only one of the two needs is naturally satisfied (or even none). Where the actual conditions are favourable, visualization becomes the most important means of place concretization, whereas a location where nature offers less, has to be "improved" by complementation and symbolization[①].

In a very general sense, the surface relief of the earth slopes down towards the sea. Except for a few isolated internal basins (possibly of volcanic origin), a "normal" country is always directed towards the sea. On an extended plain this direction is obviously less strongly felt than in a valley. In general, the movement of the land corresponds to a system of rivers (and lakes) which visualize the spatial pattern. When the river approaches the sea, the valley usually opens up and becomes an amphitheatrical bay. The location of human settlements are to a high extent determined by these conditions. Spaces such as plains, valleys and bays have given rise to characteristic types of settlements, and mostly a river, a confluence, or a shore have been used for spatial fixation. The endings of numerous place names express this state of affairs: "ford", "port", "mouth", "gate", "haven", "bridge". When the surface relief of a hill landscape gets accentuated, however, the natural places are found on the tops and crests of the hills rather than in the bottom of the valleys. We see thus that the scale of the surface relief may influence location. A top is obviously also often chosen because it forms a natural centre to the surrounding landscape. Another general factor which influences location is the direction of the sun. A slope exposed to the south is evidently more favourable than a northern one, and in many parts of Europe it is therefore common that farms and villages are situated on the north side of the valleys. Sometimes exposure and natural space collaborate to create very favorable conditions for settlement, other times they are contradictory and some kind of compromise becomes necessary.

If man-made places are at all related to their environment, there ought to exist a meaningful correspondence between natural conditions and settlement morphology[2]. The basic problem to be solved by a settlement is how to gather the surrounding landscape. How do we, in terms of space, gather a plain, a valley, an undulating series of hills, or a bay? Evidently, each of these situations are open to different interpretations. The simplest, vernacular, solution consists in a direct adaptation to the natural space. In a defined valley this would mean to form a row parallel to the direction of the land, that is, along the natural path of communication. This pattern is found in many countries, for instance in the narrow valleys of Telemark and Setesdal in Norway, where the row-tun is the dominant type of rural settlement. An urban valley-settlement, instead, represents a centre which gathers the surrounding space. This is achieved by introducing an axis across the valley, mostly in connection with a ford or a bridge-point③. The centre thus formed is still a function of local circumstances without "cosmic" implications. When the Romans used a site of this kind, however, they usually placed their cardo-decumanus axes on one side of the river, reducing thus the importance of the local space (London, Paris, Cologne, Ratisbon, Turin, etc.). The Roman colonial settlement therefore represented an absolute system, albeit of natural derivation, rather than a gathering of the local landscape. This is particularly evident in Florence where the Roman axes were turned at an angle to the river and the valley. During the Middle Ages the boundary of the urban enclosure was turned back to correspond with the river. Another example of "place-free", "cosmic" orientation is the traditional east-west axis of the Christian church, which in many Mediaeval towns contradicts the dominant directions of the urban tissue.

The identify of a place is determined by location, general spatial configuration and characterizing articulation. As a totality we experience for instance a place as "a dense cluster of enclosed stone houses in a hill side", or as "a continuous row of brightly coloured veranda houses around a small bay", or as "an ordered group of half-timbered gable houses in a valley". Location, configuration and articulation do not always contribute in the same measure to the final result. Some places get their identity from a particularly interesting location, whereas the man-made components are rather insignificant. Others, instead, may be situated in a dull landscape, but possess a well-defined configuration and a distinct character. When all the components seem to embody basic existential meanings, we may talk about a "strong" place. The three cities analyzed above, are such strong places, although Khartoum leaves something to be desired as regards characterizing articulation. The elements, however, are there, and the "strength" of the place could easily be improved if the genius loci is understood and respected[4].

In any case a strong place presupposes that there exists a meaningful correspondence between site, settlement and architectural detail. The man-made place has to know "what it wants to be" relative to the natural environment. Such a correspondence can be achieved in many different ways. We have already mentioned the vernacular "adaptation" and the urban "interpretation". The possibilities of interpretation are evidently determined by the site itself and by the historical circumstances which may both favour a certain approach of the "romantic", "cosmic" or "classical" type. Moreover an interpretation is always open to individual variations. In general settlements are therefore characterized by basic motifs which are varied according to the circumstances. Theme and variation is in fact a basic means of artistic concretization. The "theme" represents a general complex of meanings, and the "variations" its circumstantial realization. Such themes may be a particular type of building as well as motifs of "critical" importance. Well-known examples are the Italian palazzo, the French hôtel of the cour d'honneur type, and the Central European Bürgerhaus. The entrance is also in most settlements a characteristic motif of "thematic" importance. American towns are thus distinguished by the varied repetition of conspicuous porches. In general "theme and variation" allows for the expression of individual identity within a system of manifest common meanings. Thus it conserves the "spirit" of the place without making it become a life-less straightjacket.

Words and Expressions

phenomenology [fi͵nɔmi'nɔlədʒi] n. 现象学
primary ['praiməri] adj. 第一位的；主要的；初级的；根源的
location [ləu'keiʃən] n. 位置；场所；特定区域
spatial ['speiʃəl] adj. 空间的
favorable ['feivərəbl] adj. 赞成的；有利的；赞许的；良好的
complementation [͵kɔmplimen'teiʃən] n. 互补
symbolization [͵simbəlɑi'zeiʃən;-li'z-] n. 象征；符号表现
internal [in'tə:nl] adj. 内在的；国内的
basin ['beisn] n. 盆；盆地；水池
relief [ri'li:f] n.（痛苦等的）减轻；（债务等的）免除；救济，安慰；浮雕
amphitheatrical [͵æmfiθi'ætrikl] adj. 圆剧场式的
confluence ['kɔnfluəns] n. 汇合
fixation [fik'seiʃən] n. 定置；固定；定色
ford [fɔ:d] n. 浅滩
haven ['heivn] n. 港口；避难所
accentuate [æk'sentjueit] v. 重读；强调；着重强调
crest [krest] n. 鸟冠；顶部；顶峰；浪头
collaborate [kə'læbəreit] vi. 合作；通敌
axis ['æksis] n. 轴
correspond [kɔris'pɔnd] vi. 符合；协调；通信；相当；相应
Christian ['kristjən] n adj. 基督徒；信徒；基督教的；信基督教的
Mediaeval [͵medi'i:vəl] adj. 中古的；中世纪的
tissue ['tisju:] n. 薄的纱织品；薄纸；[生]组织；连篇
contradict [kɔntrə'dikt] vt. 同……矛盾；同……抵触
veranda [və'rændə] n. 阳台；走廊
gable ['geibl] n. 尖顶屋两端的山形墙
insignificant [͵insig'nifikənt] adj. 无关紧要的；可忽略的；无意义的
embody [im'bɔdi] vt. 具体表达；使具体化；包含；收录
adaptation [͵ædæp'teiʃən] n. 适应；改编；改写本
variation [͵vɛəri'eiʃən] n. 变更；变化；变异；变种
thematic [θi:'mætik] adj. 词干的；题目的；主题的；论题的

distinguish [dis'tiŋgwiʃ] v. 区别；辨别
conspicuous [kən'spikjuəs] adj. 显著的
porch [pɔːtʃ] n. 门廊；走廊
straightjacket ['streɪtˌdʒækɪt] n. 紧身衣
subject matter 主题
surface relief 地势
give rise to 引起
bridge-point 渡口
albeit of 虽然

Difficult Sentences

① Some times the conditions may be favourable both with regard to space and character, other times only one of the two needs is naturally satisfied (or even none). Where the actual conditions are favourable, visualization becomes the most important means of place concretization, whereas a location where nature offers less, has to be "improved" by complementation and symbolization.
有时，条件可能对于空间和特征都有利，有时可能只对这两种需求中的一种有利（甚至一种都没有）。在现实条件有利的地方，形象化成为使空间具体化的最重要的手段，然而在自然条件贫瘠的地方，人们必须通过补偿和象征来"改善"。

② If man-made places are at all related to their environment, there ought to exist a meaningful correspondence between natural conditions and settlement morphology
如果人造场所完全和他们的环境相关联，那就应该在自然条件和住宅形态学间存在一种有意义的对应。

③ An urban valley-settlement, instead, represents a centre which gathers the surrounding space. This is achieved by introducing an axis across the valley, mostly in connection with a ford or a bridge-point
相反，城市山谷群落代表了聚集周围空间的一个中心。这是通

过引入一根穿过山谷的轴线实现的,它主要和一个浅滩或一个渡口相连接。

④ The elements, however, are there, and the "strength" of the place could easily be improved if the genius loci is understood and respected.

然而,这些元素在那里,只要场所精神被理解和尊重,场所的"力量"就可以被增强。

Phrases and patterns

1. from the point of view of 从……的角度来看

   From the spatial point of view man needs an enclosure, and accordingly tends to settle where nature offers a defined space.

   从空间的角度来看,人需要一个围场,因此趋向于在自然提供的限定空间内定居。

   From the point of view of character, a natural place which comprises several meaningful things, such as rocks, trees and water, would represent an "invitation".

   从特征的角度来看,由几个有意义的事物如岩石、树木和水等等组成的自然场所将代表一种"邀请"。

2. consists in 在于

   The simplest, vernacular, solution consists in a direct adaptation to the natural space.

   最简单的,"当地的"解决方法在于直接适应自然场所。

   This transposition is in general done by means of symbolization, but it may also consist in a concrete displacement of buildings and things.

   这种位置的转变一般是通过象征实现的,但是它可能也存在于建筑物和事物的具体移位。

Questions

1. How does the scale of the surface relief influence location?

2. What are the determinants of the identity of a place?
3. Comment on "theme" and "variation".

6.9　History of Place
场所的历史

　　Our discussion of the identity of a place has already brought us close to the problem of constancy and change. How does a place preserve its identity under the pressure of historical forces? How can a place adapt to the changing needs of public and private life? The common laissez faire attitude of today implies a rejection of the first question and a blind acceptance of adaptation to change. We have tried to show, however, that human identity presupposes the identity of place, and that stabilitas loci therefore is a basic human need. The development of individual and social identity is a slow process, which cannot take place in a continuously changing environment①. We have every reason to believe that the human alienation so common today, to a high extent is due to the scarce possibilities of orientation and identification offered by the modern environment. Piaget's researches in fact show that a mobile world would tie man to an egocentric stage of development, while a stabile and structured world frees his mental powers②. Our analysis of the cities of Prague, Khartoum and Rome have moreover shown that it is possible to preserve the genius loci over considerable periods of time without interfering with the needs of successive historical situations.

　　What kind of changes does history ask for? In general they may be grouped in three categories: practical changes, social changes, and cultural changes. All these changes have physical (environmental) implications. As the cultural and social changes become manifest through their physical implications, we may consider the problem of change in "functional" terms, and ask: How can the genius loci be preserved under the pressure of new functional demands? What happens for instance when new or larger streets become necessary? The example of Prague has taught us that a system of paths may develop during history in conformity with the structure of the natural place. We may also remind of Rome, where the breaking through of Corso Vittorio Emanuele (after 1886) fairly well respected the continuity and scale of the traditional Roman street, whereas the sventramenti carried out under Fascism introduced a new and "foreign" urban pattern, although the aim was to restore the "greatness" of the Imperial capital. We understand, thus, that it makes sense to talk about "good" and "bad" changes.

As one gets to know different countries; talking with people, eating with people, feeling with people, reading their literature, listening to their music and using their places, one beings to realize that the correspondence of man and place has not changed much throughout history. The local human attitude is surprisingly constant, and we must agree with Hegel when he says that it determines the people's "place in world history". We can therefore repeat that the basic existential contents are not produced by changing economical, social and political conditions. The existential contents have deeper roots, and the changing conditions only ask for ever new interpretations. The crucial question therefore is: "How is it possible to remain an Italian, a Russian, or a German under this regime?" Regimes come and go, the place persists, and with it a particular kind of human identity. When we have realized this fact, we should start to improve the world by taking care of our places, rather than by abstract planning and anonymous building. Thus we may leave utopia behind and return to the things of our everyday life-world[3].

Creative participation means to concretize the basic meanings under ever new historical circumstances. Participation, however, can only be obtained "by great labor". The "threshold" which is the symbol of participation, is in fact "turned to stone" by "pain". Participation presupposes sympathy with things, to repeat the word of Goethe, and sympathy necessarily implies suffering. In our context sympathy with things means that we learn to see. We have to be able to "see" the meanings of the things that surround us; be they natural or man-made. Things always tell several stories; they tell about their own making, they tell about the historical circumstances under which they were made, and if they are real things, they also reveal truth. The ability of a thing to reveal truth depends upon how it is made, and the next thing to learn is therefore making. Seeing and making are united in inspiration and concretization. Thus Louis Kahn said: "Inspiration is the moment of possibility when what to do meets the means of doing it". Seeing and making constitute the basis of dwelling.

The results of creative participation constitute man's existential foothold, his culture. They make manifest what he has managed to make out of his existence. Some of the results illuminate a wider range of phenomena than others, and deserve the name "work of art"[4]. In the work of art man praises existence. In his Ninth Elegy and his Sonnets to Orpheus, Rilke develops the image of man as a praising singer. We remember his question: "Are we perhaps here to say: house, bridge, fountain, gate, jug, fruit tree, window, at best: column, tower...", and hear his answer: "Praise to the Angel our world, not the untellable.

You can't impress him with grand emotion. In the cosmos where he so powerfully feels, you're only a newcomer. Then show his some simple thing, grown up through generations till it became ours, and lives near our hands and in our eyes. Tell him of things and he'll stand astonished, as you stood beside the rope-maker in Rome, or with the Nile potter. Show his how joyful a thing can be, how innocent and ours, how even lamenting sorrow can take purely its own form, serve as a thing, or die as a thing—and in ecstasy escape beyond the violin. And these things, that live only in passing, understand that you praise them; fugitive, they look to us, the most fugitive, for rescue. They want us entirely to transform them in our invisible hearts into—oh, infinitely—into us! Whoever we finally are".

Words and Expressions

constancy ['kɔnstənsi] n. 不屈不挠；坚定不移
rejection [ri'dʒekʃən] n. 拒绝
continuously [kən'tɪnjʊəsli] adv. 不断地；连续地
scarce [skɛəs] adj. 缺乏的；不足的；稀有的；不充足的
egocentric [ˌiːgəʊ'sentrɪk] adj. 自我中心的；利己主义的
successive [sək'sesiv] adj. 继承的；连续的
interfere [ˌɪntə'fiə] vi. 干涉；干预；妨碍；打扰
practical ['præktikəl] adj. 实际的；实践的；实用的
implication [ˌɪmpli'keiʃən] n. 牵连；含意；暗示
Fascism ['fæʃizəm] n. 法西斯主义
imperial [im'piəriəl] adj. 皇帝的
throughout [θru(ː)'aut] prep. 遍及；贯穿
content [kən'tent] n. 内容；容量
interpretation [inˌtəːpri'teiʃən] n. 解释；阐明
crucial ['kruːʃiəl, 'kruːʃəl] adj. 至关紧要的
regime [rei'ʒiːm] n. 政体；政权；政权制度
anonymous [ə'nɔniməs] adj. 匿名的
utopia [juː'təupjə, -piə] n. 乌托邦；理想的完美境界
sympathy ['simpəθi] n. 同情；同情心
foothold ['fʊthəʊld] n. 立足处
range [reindʒ] n. 范围；射程
unreliable ['ʌnri'laiəbl] adj. 不可靠的
cosmos ['kɔzmɔs] n. 宇宙
generation [ˌdʒenə'reiʃən] n. 产生；发生
astonish [əs'tɔniʃ] vt. 使惊讶
lamenting [lə'mentiŋ] adj. 悲伤的；悲哀的
fugitive ['fjuːdʒitiv] adj. 逃亡的；无常的；易变的

invisible [in'vizəbl] adj. 看不见的；无形的
laissez faire 自由主义
blind acceptance 盲目接受
stabilitas loci 稳定性
egocentric stage 自我中心阶段
interfere with 打扰
in conformity with 与……一致
work of art 艺术作品

Difficult Sentences

① We have tried to show, however, that human identity presupposes the identity of place, and that stabilitas loci therefore is a basic human need. The development of individual and social identity is a slow process, which cannot take place in a continuously changing environment.

然而，我们已经尝试着证明人的属性预示了场所的属性，因此，稳定性是人的一个基本需求。个人和社会属性的发展是一个缓慢的过程，不可能在一种持续变化的环境中进行。

② Piaget's researches in fact show that a mobile world would tie man to an egocentric stage of development, while a stabile and structured world frees his mental powers.

皮亚杰的研究事实上告诉我们，多变的世界会将人束缚在个人发展的自我中心阶段，而稳定的、有组织的世界才可能释放人的精神力量。

③ Regimes come and go, the place persists, and with it a particular kind of human identity. When we have realized this fact, we should start to improve the world by taking care of our places, rather than by abstract planning and anonymous building. Thus we may leave utopia behind and return to the things of our everyday life-world.

政体不断更替，但场所却亘古不变，其特有的某种人的属性也没有改变。当我们意识到这样一个事实时，我们应该开始通过爱护我们的场所、而不是通过抽象的设计和毫无特色的建筑来改善这个世界。这样，我们可以抛弃乌托邦式的空想，回到我们日常生活中的世界当中。

④ The results of creative participation constitute man's existential foothold, his culture. They make manifest what he has managed to make out of his existence. Some of the results illuminate a wider range of phenomena than others, and deserve the name "work of art".

创造性参与的结果构成了人的存在立足点，即他的文化。文化使得人设法在他的存在中创造的东西更加明显。一些成果较其他成果而言能说明更多的现象，我们把它们称作"艺术作品"。

Phrases and patterns

1. adapt to 使适应

   How can a place adapt to the changing needs of public and private life?

   一个场所如何能够适应公共生活和个人生活不断变化的需要呢？

   We analyze the different engineering tendering and bidding systems in Guangzhou and Macao, and put forward some countermeasures and suggestions, so as to provide some reference for mainland companies to adapt to adapt to the international practice.

   我们分析了广州与澳门在工程招投标制度方面的差异，提出了一些对策和建议，为内地企业适应国际惯例提供参考。

2. in conformity with 与……一致

   The example of Prague has taught us that a system of paths may develop during history in conformity with the structure of the natural place.

   布拉格的例子已经告诉我们，道路体系是在历史中与自然场所的结构不断地整合一致的过程中逐渐形成的。

   The process of social history is in conformity with law and purpose is an idea of idealism. Being in conformity with human purpose and laws is the difference between human activities and the animals' instinctive activities, and is the essence of the real man。

社会历史过程契合规律性和目的性是一种理想的状态。规律性与目的性是人的活动区别于动物本能活动的特性,也是现实的人的本质。

Questions

1. What kind of changes does history ask for?
2: What's the relationship between seeing and making?
3. Will the place preserve its identity under the pressure of historical forces? Give your reasons.

7

Townscape
街道美学

【本章导读】 日本建筑理论家芦原义信多年来致力于街道、广场空间的研究,对日本及意大利、法国、德国等西欧国家的建筑环境与街道、广场等外部空间进行了深入细致的分析比较,从而归纳出东西方在文化体系、空间观念、哲学思想以及美学观念等方面的差异,并对如何接受外来文化和继承民族传统问题,提出了许多独到见解。本章7.1~7.3选取的3篇文章说明了在城市空间中街道与建筑的关系,论述了街道在城市中的角色和作用,比较了日本街道与西欧街道的异同。

7.1 Streets
街道形态

In the history of cities the awareness of and affection for streets is strongest in the Latin countries of western Europe and conspicuously weak in Japan—Italians in particular make the street an integral part of their daily life. For them it exists not simply to carry traffic but as a central arena of the community[①]. Bernard Rudofsky notes that the porticos of Bologna provide much more than shelter from the elements, they are the site of a time-honored custom:

The Bolognese, running back and forth under the colonnades all day long, still would not want to miss the formal promenade that takes place twice a day opposite the Dome under the Portico del Pavaglione. At noon and in the early evening hours, large crowds mill through this vastest of the city's corridors, and it is impossible not to meet one's friends.

Clearly the street is a crucial element of the Italian way of life and an expression of the bonds among the inhabitants of its cities. Rudofsky goes on to note that the English are rather less attached to their streets:

Surely, the English are not a desirable model for an urban society. No other nation developed such a fierce devotion to country life as they did. And with good reason; their cities have been traditionally among Europe's least wholesome. Englishmen may be intensely loyal to their towns, but the street—the very gauge of urbanity—does not figure large in their affections[②]. By preference, they take refuge in the beery atmosphere of the pub. Lord Tennyson spoke for the many when he declaimed: "I loath the squares and streets, and the faces that one meets".

The piazza is an urban open space loved by Italians specifically for meeting people. The English park, on the other hand, is intended for solitary relaxation. In Japan exterior spaces like parks or squares have historically held little interest. Interior space was treated with great refinement and aesthetic sensitivity, but the same sophistication did not extend to exterior space.

When a traveler finds himself in a new city, the first thing he looks for is a map, one that will provide a detailed guide to the names of the streets and squares. As Jane Jacobs has written: "Think of a city, and what comes to mind? Its streets. If a city's streets look interesting, the city looks interesting; if they look dull, the city looks dull." Indeed, the streets are the scale upon which a traveler judges a city. The French word rue and the Italian word via have their own particular associations, invoking the image of a city and arousing the itch to travel.

The names of streets are important, inseparable attributes of the life of a city. And yet in Japan streets are seldom named, save in a few cities like Kyoto, planned and endowed with pleasant street names in ancient times, or Sapporo, built more recently, which has a New York-style numbering system based on the cardinal directions. In most Japanese cities it is customary to indicate an address by reference to numbers <u>corresponding to</u> established community areas or blocks. The practice of naming on the basis of an area <u>rather than</u> a street derives from the same thinking that produced the architecture of the floor③. In Europe, where architectural concepts are oriented to the wall, it follows quite reasonably that addresses be indicated for houses numbered in linear succession along the streets upon which they face. The Japanese practice of naming and numbering <u>in terms of</u> discrete areas is quite unusual in the world today. Its strong orientation to the block or area unit, rather than to the street, again demonstrates the deeply rooted consciousness of inside versus outside and of architecture as stemming from the "floor".

Words and Expressions

conspicuously [kən'spikjuəsli] *adv.* 显著地；超群地
arena [ə'riːnə] *n.* 竞技场；舞台
portico ['pɔːtikəu] *n.* [建]（有圆柱的）门廊，柱廊
Bologna [bə'ləunjə] *n.* 博洛尼亚（意大利城市）
colonnade [ˌkɔlə'neid] *n.* 柱廊
corridor ['kɔridɔː] *n.* 走廊
wholesome ['həulsəm] *adj.* 卫生的；有益的；健康的；有益健康的
gauge [gedʒ] *n.* 标准尺；规格；量规，量表
urbanity [əː'bæniti] *n.* 有礼貌；文雅
refuge ['refjuːdʒ] *n.* 庇护；避难；避难所
declaim [di'kleim] *v.* 巧辩；演讲；高声朗读

loath [ləuθ] *adj.* 不情愿的；勉强的
piazza [pi'ætsə] *n.* 广场；走廊；露天市场
aesthetic [əi:s'θetik] *adj.* 美学的；审美的；有审美感的
sophistication [sə,fısti'keıʃən] *n.* 强词夺理；诡辩；混合
via ['vɑiə,'vi:ə] *prep.* 经；通过；经由
invoke [in'vəuk] *v.* 调用
itch [itʃ] *n.* 发痒；渴望
inseparable [əin'sepərəbl] *adj.* 不能分的
save [seiv] *prep.* 除……之外
Kyoto [ki'əutəu] *n.* 京都(曾是日本古都)
Sapporo [sə'pɔ:rəu] *n.* 札幌[日本北海道西部城市]
time-honored 历史悠久的；老字号的

Difficult Sentences

① In the history of cities the awareness of and affection for streets is strongest in the Latin countries of western Europe and conspicuously weak in Japan—Italians in particular make the street an integral part of their daily life. For them it exists not simply to carry traffic but as a central arena of the community.
在城市的历史中，对街道的意识和感情最强烈的是西欧的拉丁民族，而特别弱的则是日本人。特别是意大利人，街道就是他们日常生活中不可分割的一部分，对他们来说，街道的存在不只是为了满足交通的需要，而是作为社区的中心地带而存在。

② Surely, the English are not a desirable model for an urban society. No other nation developed such a fierce devotion to country life as they did. And with good reason; their cities have been traditionally among Europe's least wholesome. Englishmen may be intensely loyal to their towns, but the street-the very gauge of urbanity-does not figure large in their affections.
的确，就城市社会而言，英国人不是一个令人满意的典范。没有一个其他国家像英国人那样对乡村生活表现出如此强烈的热爱。

出于某些不可规避的理由,他们的城市在欧洲国家中是最不完善的。英国人对城镇也许很忠诚,但他们对于街道——都市化的主要标志——却不怎么热衷。

③ In most Japanese cities it is customary to indicate an address by reference to numbers corresponding to established community areas or blocks. The practice of naming on the basis of an area rather than a street derives from the same thinking that produced the architecture of the floor.

在大多数日本城市,人们习惯参考早已建立的社区区域或街区的编号说明地址。这种根据区域而不是街道来命名地址的习惯做法,是"人走之处即成道路"这一自发村落形态的延续。

Phrases and Patterns

1. correspond to 与……相符;与……一致

   Street names corresponding to street characteristics are named by experts.

   与街道特色相符的街道名称是专家起的。

   Road construction should correspond to the overall plan of the city.

   街道的建设应该符合城市的整体规划。

2. rather than 而不是

   I prefer to live in a peace and quiet community rather than a thriving and busy residential district.

   我宁愿居住在宁静、和睦的社区,而不愿住在繁华、忙碌的城市住宅区。

   The main purpose of developing townscape construction is beautifying the appearance of a city rather than providing a good chance for the business owner to reap lots of benefits from the projects.

   发展城市风景建设的主要目的是美化城市而不是为生意人提供获得大量利润的机会。

3. in terms of 根据;按照

A 200-year-old building is very old in terms of American history.
从美国历史来看,200 年的建筑是很古老的了。

The sign——an exclamation mark in a red triangle--indicates danger in terms of UK road traffic signs.
根据英国道路交通标志,红色三角中有一个叹号的标志表示危险。

Questions

1. What are the different attitudes of different countries towards the street?
2. Summarize the main idea of the passage.

7.2 Buildings
建筑的布局

As a general rule building sites face directly on a street. The composition and character of a townscape <u>take shape</u> from the spatial conception and design of the boundary area adjoining the street. Let us examine, then, how the relationship of streets and buildings in urban space determines the townscape①.

Some years ago I lived for a period of time in the beautiful residential area along the harbor in Sydney, Australia, known as Rose Bay. This is an area dominated by one- or at most two-story private homes, separated from the street by carefully manicured lawns and colorful flowerbeds. Their meticulously tended gardens seem to be intended more for people passing by than for the residents themselves, for the front yards are largely hidden from view inside the houses but open and plainly visible from the street, contributing generally to the attractiveness of the entire neighborhood. This suburban, "garden-city" style of townscape is typical of residential areas all over the United States and in parts of Europe. I remember with particular fondness the streets of suburban Honolulu, where there is a striking stretch from the Waikiki area to Kahala Avenue passing in front of Diamond Head. Lush lawns stretch back from wide sidewalks and flowering trees and shrubs are scattered across the lawns and around the houses.

In the residential areas of Japan's major cities, by contrast, space that corresponds to a front yard visible from the street is extremely rare. The houses, most of which are built in the traditional style of wooden post-and-beam construction, are so open that some kind of surrounding wall seems necessary both for privacy and safety[②]. If the site has a north entrance, the garden will invariably be on the south and therefore difficult to see from the street. If the site has a south entrance, there will be a high wall so that the bedroom and living room are not exposed to the street. Thus, even if there is a garden, it is seldom visible and plays a negligible role in the townscape.

Let us now explore the differences between the front yards of the western townscape and the gardens of Japanese houses in terms of the territories of space. While in both cases the entire site obviously belongs to the owner of the house, in the western-style residence, it would appear that the front yard is consciously included in the external, public order rather than the internal, private one. In other words, in terms of spatial territory, the front yard is conceived of as part of the street. In Japan, on the other hand, the garden is consciously part of the private, internal order belonging to the resident. A wall provides an explicit dividing line between the public and the private spaces, indicating that the garden is not intended to make a contribution to the composition of the townscape. Because of this the townscapes of Japanese residential areas, even those occupied by the wealthy, seem much less attractive than the open atmosphere of western-style residential areas.

Let us look, however, at a type of townscape that is fundamentally different from either of these examples. In Greece and Italy houses are generally of stone masonry construction, and built directly on the street; there are no front yards. Any left-over ground surface around the stone buildings is paved and used as part of the street. The street is determined by the shape of the buildings, now opening wide, now becoming narrow, turning at odd angles, and intersecting itself as it pleases③.

Words and Expressions

adjoining [ə'dʒɔiniŋ] *adj.* 邻接的；隔壁的
urban ['ə:bən] *adj.* 城市的；市内的
dominate ['dɔmineit] *v.* 支配；占优势
manicured [mænikjuəd] *adj.* (花园，草坪)修剪整齐的
meticulous [mɪ'tɪkjʊləs] *adj.* 小心翼翼的
tend [tend] *v.* 趋向；往往是；照管；护理
suburban [sə'bə:bən] *adj.* 郊外的；偏远的
Honolulu [ˌhɔnə'lu:lu:] *n.* 火奴鲁鲁(即"檀香山"，美国夏威夷州的首府和港市)
Waikiki ['waɪkɪˌki:,ˌwaɪkɪ'ki:] *n.* 怀基基海滩[美国夏威夷州]
lush [lʌʃ] *adj.* 青葱的；味美的；豪华的；繁荣的
scattered ['skætəd] *adj.* 离散的，分散的
invariably [ɪn'veərɪəb(ə)lɪ] *adv.* 不变地；总是
negligible ['neglɪdʒəbl] *adj.* 可以忽略的，不予重视的
conceive [kən'si:v] *vt.* 构思，以为，持有
explicit [iks'plisit] *adj.* 外在的，清楚的，直率的，(租金等)直接付款的
masonry ['meisənri] *n.* 石工术，石匠职业
intersect [ˌɪntə'sekt] *vi.* (直线)相交，交叉
townscape ['taunskeip] *n.* 城市风景画；城市风景
left-over 剩余的
post-and-beam 梁和柱

Difficult Sentences

① As a general rule building sites face directly on a street. The composition and character of a townscape take shape from the spatial conception and design of the boundary area adjoining the street. Let us examine, then, how the relationship of streets and buildings in urban space determines the townscape.

依照常规,建筑物要面对街道。城市景观的构成和特征形成于空间观念和毗连街道的边界地区的设计。下面让我们研究一下城市里街道和建筑物的关系是如何影响城市风景的。

② In the residential areas of Japan's major cities, by contrast, space that corresponds to a front yard visible from the street is extremely rare. The houses, most of which are built in the traditional style of wooden post-and-beam construction, are so open that some kind of surrounding wall seems necessary both for privacy and safety.

与此相反,在日本大城市的居民区,那种在街道上就能看得到的前院空地是罕见的。大多数房屋都是以传统方式建成的梁和柱的木质结构,是开放性的住宅,因此为保障私密性和安全性,道路与用地之间多建围墙。

③ In Greece and Italy houses are generally of stone masonry construction, and built directly on the street; there are no front yards. Any left-over ground surface around the stone buildings is paved and used as part of the street. The street is determined by the shape of the buildings, now opening wide, now becoming narrow, turning at odd angles, and intersecting itself as it pleases.

在希腊和意大利,房屋通常是石结构,直接建造在街道上并且没有前院。石结构建筑之外的剩余地面全部铺装作为街道使用。街道是由建筑物的形态决定的,这里宽阔,那里又狭窄,还净是一些急转的岔道和随意的交叉道。

Phrases and Patterns

1. take shape (开始)成形;形成;体现

   Three design drawings of new World Trade Center take shape from the careful consideration of the architects.

建筑师们经过缜密思考之后出台了新世贸中心大楼的三种设计图。

The idea of good quality planning and design of the city took shape in the latter half of the twentieth century in America.

在美国,高品质城市设计的理念形成于20世纪下半叶。

2. make a contribution to 作出贡献

Many architects, engineers and design consultants made great contributions to schematic design.

许多建筑师、工程师和设计顾问为图示设计作出了很大的贡献。

The landscape designers make great contributions to mapping out the reasonable plan of the city.

城市风景设计者为规划合理的城市设计作出了巨大贡献。

Questions

1. How does the relationship of streets and buildings in urban space determine the townscape?
2. What are the differences between the front yards of the western townscape and the gardens of Japanese houses in terms of the territories of space?
3. Which type of townscape is fundamentally different from either of these examples?

7.3 The Type of Townscape
街道美学的类型

At first, one might think these streets are quite the same as the expressionless, walled-in streets of Japan. Yet the exterior walls of houses, unlike the fences that line Japan's streets, have doors and windows that promote continuity between inside and outside, permitting the scene of human activity to overflow into the street. This is part of the delightful flavor of these townscapes, inhabited by ordinary, simple folk. The spatial structure is completely different from that of the western "garden-city" townscape with its suburban-style front yards, and yet it, too, presents a richly human quality. In spots where the street widens, people stop and talk as they would in a square; they put out chairs to do their mending, and relax in the cool of the evening. In terms of the territories of space, this demonstrates how the private, internal order of the home permeates the outer, public order of the street in the form of regular daily activities like mending and evening relaxation. In other words, the street is partly included in the internal order[1]. In a townscape of the garden-city type with its front yards, the external order of the street permeates the internal order; in that of Greece and Italy, it is the reverse, the internal order flowing out into the external one. Both townscapes have their advantages and disadvantages, but they are especially memorable for their attractiveness and human warmth.

Another type of townscape is that which contains patios or inner gardens, as found in Spain or the Islamic countries. Spain's townscapes generally resemble those of Greece or southern Italy. They have an atmosphere of remarkable unity, with brownish-yellow Spanish roof tiles used throughout and walls painted white with lime. Unlike Italy, outdoor activities of a private nature take place in the courtyards of each home, so the streets are not so necessary as a forum of activity. In fact, save for the bright foliage and plants hung on the walls around the inner gardens that may be glimpsed through the open gateways, these streets seem quite desolate.

Japan, too, has townscapes composed of houses built directly on the street. Some well-known examples are the townhouses of Kyoto, the inns of Tsumago, and the shops of Hida Takayama. Today these townscapes, whose character has been preserved for generations, are gaining new recognition. On close inspection the individual buildings are somewhat different, but the use of common building techniques and carpentry imparts a sense of unity and shared values that sustains the whole. A townscape in the true sense is one <u>brought into being</u> by common qualities, and it is on that basis that a town or community establishes itself in the affections of its residents[2].

The townhouses of Kyoto front right on the streets and contribute to the townscape with wonderfully functional, as well as attractive, wooden lattices that mark the boundary between the street and the buildings. These lattices impart a sense of fluidity between the inner and outer order and help to animate the townscape in much the same way as do the doors and windows of the buildings in Italy. Visually, the lattice functions like a one-way mirror, in that it is possible to see from the dark side to the light side but not vice versa. During the day one can see the street from within the houses, but from outside it is difficult to see inside.

Where the vertical bars are made more rectangular in depth, the lattice is stronger and more concealing. These lattices link the houses to the streets before them, protecting the privacy of the residents, on the one hand, and fostering close community relations on the other[3].

The typical townhouses of Kyoto are located on streets 6.5 meters wide, and their average height is 5 meters, so the distance/height (D/H) ratio equals 1.3. These proportions of the exterior space conform to the human scale, a scale in which one immediately feels at home. The streets of Kyoto are straight and 90 meters or less in length, and anything that happens there is easily visible. As a townscape whose design promotes an intermingling of internal and external orders and a sense of community, Kyoto is an outstanding example. Children playing out in the street are within their mothers' sight through the wooden lattices; daily activities and events—sweeping, care of potted plants, sprinkling the streets to keep down the dust, and passing festival processions—make the street a lively place where children grow up in immediate contact with society and the physical world outside the home.

In every country, as industrialization advances, the attachments that grow out of a sense of community are gradually fading. Young people increasingly choose the anonymity and impersonality of big city living to eschew the watchful eyes of close neighbors④. In Japan residential areas are filling with huge company apartment complexes, where the corporate organizational hierarchy reaches out even to the home life of employees, and public housing complexes, where people must dwell in concrete boxes situated in a townscape they can have no voice or role in creating. Many societal problems arise when children grow and develop in inhuman urban environments such as these. Careful thought must be given to how, despite the growing dehumanization of contemporary society, we can restore a truly human way of life and how we can make more attractive and liveable the urban environments in which we live.

Words and Expressions

  expressionless [ɪk'spreʃənlɪs] adj. 无表情的
  overflow ['əuvə'fləu] v. (使)泛滥;(使)溢出;(使)充溢
  permeate ['pə:mieit] v. 弥漫;渗透;透过;充满
  patio ['pɑ:tiəu] n. 天井;院子
  tile [tail] n. 瓦片;瓷砖
  forum ['fɔ:rəm] n. 古罗马城镇的广场(或市场);论坛;法庭;讨论会
  desolate ['desəlit] adj. 荒凉的;无人烟的
  inspection [in'spekʃən] n. 检查;视察
  impart [im'pɑ:t] vt. 给予(尤指抽象事物);传授;告知;透露
  sustain [səs'tein] vt. 支撑;撑住;维持;持续
  lattice ['lætis] n. 格子
  fluidity [flu(:)'iditi] n. 流动性;流质;变移性;流度
  animate ['ænimeit] v. 鼓舞
  vertical ['və:tikəl] adj. 垂直的;直立的;顶点的
  rectangular [rek'tæŋgjulə] adj. 矩形的;成直角的

conform [kən'fɔːm] v. 使一致；使遵守；使顺从；符合；相似；适应环境
intermingle [ˌintə(ː)'miŋgəl] n. 混合
anonymity [ˌænə'nimiti] n. 匿名；作者不明（或不详）
eschew [is'tʃuː] vt. 避开；远避
inhuman [in'hjuːmən] adj. 野蛮的
brownish-yellow 黄褐色

Difficult Sentences

① In terms of the territories of space, this demonstrates how the private, internal order of the home permeates the outer, public order of the street in the form of regular daily activities like mending and evening relaxation. In other words, the street is partly included in the internal order.

从空间领域的角度来说，这是把居住这一私密的内部秩序的一部分，以修缮和夜晚纳凉的形式渗透到街道这一公共的外部秩序之中。换句话说，街道被部分地包括在内部秩序中。

② On close inspection the individual buildings are somewhat different, but the use of common building techniques and carpentry imparts a sense of unity and shared values that sustains the whole. A townscape in the true sense is one brought into being by common qualities, and it is on that basis that a town or community establishes itself in the affections of its residents.

仔细审视就会发现每个建筑物都稍微有所不同，但是使用普通的建造技术和木工奇巧给人一种统一协调的感觉。城市景观的真正含义是它的普遍特性，它的基础在于居民对它的钟爱之情。

③ Where the vertical bars are made more rectangular in depth, the lattice is stronger and more concealing. These lattices link the houses to the streets before them, protecting the privacy of the residents, on the one hand, and fostering close community relations on the other.

垂直的栏栅更加高大和方正，格构式门窗更加结实稳固、更具隐蔽功能。一方面，格构式门窗将房屋和街道连接起来，保护居民的隐私；另一方面，培养了亲密的近邻关系。

④ In every country, as industrialization advances, the attachments that grow out of a sense of community are gradually fading. Young people increasingly choose the anonymity and impersonality of big city living to eschew the watchful eyes of close neighbors.

无论哪个国家都在向工业化发展,上述的近邻观念正在趋向崩溃。越来越多的年轻人选择隐姓埋名、人情冷淡的大城市居住,避开亲密邻居的关注目光。

Phrases and Patterns

1. bring into being 使存在;使出现

   A townscape in the true sense is one brought into being by common qualities.

   城市景观的真正含义是它的普遍特性。

   A thoughtful landscape designer bring into being the easier landscape maintenance.

   一位考虑周到的景观设计者使景观的维护变得更加容易。

2. contact with 接触;联络

   Landscape designers contact with the clients at first, design the landscapes, and gain the customers' approval to begin the installation.

   景观设计者首先和委托人联络,然后设计景观,获得客户认可后开始布景。

   After the building designers contact with the computer, they find that they can finish their tasks efficiently by using computer.

   当建筑设计者接触计算机后,他们发现利用计算机能高效率地完成工作。

Questions

1. What are the differences of townscape between Japan and western "garden-city" type?
2. What are the functions of lattices?
3. What does the writer worry about?

8

The Architecture of the City
城市建筑学

【本章导读】 建筑与城市是紧紧联系在一起的,城市是众多有意义的和被认同的事物(urban facts)的聚集体,它与不同时代不同地点的特定生活相关联。本章主要论述了建筑与城市的关系,不单单从建筑的角度来讨论建筑,而是把建筑放在城市这个大范围内去考虑,从生态学、心理学、类型学等多角度来衡量。最后,建筑又反过来影响城市的规模,城市的规模并不重要,因为其意义和质量并不取决于规模,而是取决于城市的实际建设和单体建筑。

8.1 Urban Artifacts
城市建筑体

In beginning a study of the city, we find ourselves confronted with two very different positions. These are best exemplified in the Greek city, where the Aristotelian analysis of urban reality is counterposed to that of Plato's Republic①. This opposition raises important methodological questions. I <u>am inclined to</u> believe that Aristotelian planning, insofar as it was a study of artifacts, decisively opened the road to the study of the city and also to urban geography and urban architecture. Yet doubtless we cannot explain certain experiences without availing ourselves of both these levels of analysis. Certainly ideas of a purely spatial type have at times notably modified, in form and through direct or indirect interventions, the times and modes of the urban dynamic.

There exists a mass of impressive studies to refer to in the elaboration of an urban theory, but it is necessary to gather these studies from the most disparate places, then to avail ourselves of what they suggest about the construction of a general frame of reference, and finally to apply this knowledge to a specific urban theory. Without here outlining such an overall frame of reference for the history of the study of the city, we can note that two major systems exist: one that considers the city as the product of the generative-functional systems of its architecture and thus of urban space, and one that considers it as a spatial structure. In the first, the city is derived from an analysis of political, social, and economic systems and is treated from the viewpoint of these disciplines; the second belongs more to architecture and geography. Although I begin with this second viewpoint, I also draw on those facts from the first which raise significant questions.

In this work, then, I will refer to writers from diverse fields who have elaborated theses that I consider fundamental (not, of course, without certain qualifications). However, there are not a great many works which I find valuable, considering the mass of material available; and in any case let me observe generally that if an author or a book does not play an important part in an analysis, or if a point of view does not constitute an essential contribution to a work of research, it is meaningless to cite it. Therefore I prefer to discuss only the works of those authors who seem to be fundamental for a study of this kind. The theories of some of these scholars, in fact, constitute the hypotheses of my study. Wherever one chooses to lay the groundwork for an autonomous urban theory, it is impossible to avoid their contributions.

There are also certain fundamental contributions that I would have liked to consider except that they are naturally beyond the scope of this discussion, for example the profound intuitions of Fustel de Coulanges and Theodor Mommsen. In the case of the first of these writers I refer in particular to the importance he ascribes to institutions as truly constant elements of historical life and to the relationship between myth and institution. Myths come and go, passing slowly from one place to another; every generation recounts them differently and adds new elements to the patrimony received from the past; but behind this changing reality, there is a permanent reality that in some way manages to elude the action of time. We must recognize the true foundation of this reality in religious tradition. The relationships which man found with the gods in the ancient city, the cults that he consecrated to them, the names under which he invoked them, the gifts and the sacrifices made to them were all tied to inviolable laws. The individual man had no power over them.

I believe that the importance of ritual in its collective nature and its essential character as an element for preserving myth constitutes a key to understanding the meaning of monuments and, moreover, the implications of the founding of the city and of the transmission of ideas in an urban context[2]. I attribute an especial importance to monuments, although their significance in the urban dynamic may at times be elusive. This work must be carried forward; I am convinced that in order to do so, it will be necessary to probe into the relationship between monument, ritual, and mythological elements along the lines indicated by Fustel de Coulanges. For if the ritual is the permanent and conserving element of myth, then so too is the monument, since, in the very moment that it testifies to myth, it renders ritual forms possible.

Such a study should, once again, begin with the Greek city, which offers many significant insights concerning the meaning of the urban structure, and which at its origins had an inseparable relationship with the mode of being and behavior of human beings. The researches of modern anthropology on the social structure of primitive villages also raise new issues relative to the study of urban planning; they demand a study of urban artifacts according to their essential themes. The existence of such essential themes implies a foundation for the study of urban artifacts, and requires a knowledge of a larger number of artifacts and an integration of these artifacts in time and space—more precisely, a clarifying of those forces that are at work in a permanent and universal way in all urban artifacts.

Let us consider the relationship between an actual urban artifact and the utopian idea of the city. Generally this relationship is studied within a limited period of history, within a modest framework, and with results that are usually questionable. What are the limits within which we can integrate such limited analyses into the larger framework of the permanent and universal forces at play in the city? I am convinced that the polemics that arose between utopian socialism and scientific socialism during the second half of the nineteenth century constitute important scholarly material, but we cannot consider only their purely political aspects; these must be measured against the reality of urban artifacts or else we will perpetuate serious distortions. And this must be done for the full range of urban artifacts. What we see in actuality are the application and extension of only partial conclusions to the history of the city. Generally, the most difficult historical problems of the city are resolved by dividing history into periods and hence ignoring or misunderstanding the universal and permanent character of the forces of the urban dynamic; and here the importance of a comparative method becomes evident.

Thus, in their obsession with certain sociological characteristics of the industrial city, urban scholars have obscured a series of extremely important artifacts which can enrich urban science with a contribution as original as it is necessary③. I am thinking, for example, of the settlements and colonial cities founded by Europeans particularly after the discovery of America. Little exists on this topic; Gilberto Freyre, for example, discusses the influence of certain urban and building typologies that the Portuguese brought to Brazil and how these were structurally linked to the type of society established in Brazil. The relationship between the rural and latifundist families in the Portuguese colonization of Brazil was associated with the theocracy conceived by the Jesuits and, together with the Spanish and French influence, was enormously important in the formation of the South American city. I consider such research to be very important for the study of urban utopias and the construction of the city.

Words and Expressions

Aristotelian [ˌærɪstə'tiːlɪən] adj. n. 亚里士多德的, 亚里士多德学派的；亚里士多德学派的人

counterpose ['kaʊntə'pəʊz] vt. 使对立

Plato ['pleɪtəʊ] n. (427~347BC, 古希腊哲学家)柏拉图

inclined [ɪn'klaɪnd] adj. 倾向……的

avail [ə'veɪl] v. 有益于；有帮助；有用，有利

intervention [ˌɪntə(ː)'venʃən] n. 干涉

ascribe [əs'kraɪb] vt. 归因于；归咎于

cult [kʌlt] n. 礼拜；祭仪；一群信徒；礼拜式

consecrate ['kɒnsɪkreɪt] vt. adj. 用做祭祀；献给；使神圣；被献给神的；神圣的

elusive [i'ljuːsɪv] adj. 难懂的；难捉摸的；易忘的

utopian [juː'təʊpjən] adj. 乌托邦的；理想化的

polemics [pɒ'lemɪks] n. 辩论术；辩论法

obsession [əb'seʃən] n. 迷住；困扰

typology [taɪ'pɒlədʒi] n. 类型学；血型学；体型学；象征学

Difficult Sentences

① These are best exemplified in the Greek city, where the Aristotelian analysis of urban reality is counterposed to that of Plato's Republic.
这在希腊的城市中得到了充分的体现,在那里亚里士多德学派对城市现实的分析与柏拉图的共和国思想相对立。

② I believe that the importance of ritual in its collective nature and its essential character as an element for preserving myth constitutes a key to understanding the meaning of monuments and, moreover, the implications of the founding of the city and of the transmission of ideas in an urban context.
我认为,仪式具有集体的属性和作为保护神话要素的基本特征。仪式的这种重要性不仅是理解纪念物意义的关键,而且也是理解城市的建立以及城市思想传递意义的关键。

③ Thus, in their obsession with certain sociological characteristics of the industrial city, urban scholars have obscured a series of extremely important artifacts which can enrich urban science with a contribution as original as it is necessary.
由于研究城市的学者们沉醉于工业城市中的某些特征,因此在他们的研究中,对一系列极为重要且必然会创造性地丰富城市科学的城市建筑体却变得模糊不清。

Phrases and Patterns

1. be inclined to 倾向于;趋向于
   The planners are inclined to blend symbols and letters in their landscape plan.
   规划者倾向于在景观设计图中混合使用符号和文字。
   At present, the dressing room is inclined to be included in the private living area in American.
   现在,美国的私人起居区域内往往还内建一个更衣室。

2. be derived from 起源于
The bright idea of indoor design of the host is derived from an ancient painting.
主人室内设计的灵感来源于一幅古老的油画。
The experience of making the drawing of the city blueprint is derived from the practice.
绘制城市蓝图的经验来自于实践。

Questions

1. What are the two major systems in the history of the study of the city?
2. What does the passage mainly study?
3. What are the limits within which we can integrate such limited analyses into the larger framework of the permanent and universal forces at play in the city?

8.2 Urban Ecology and Psychology
城市生态学和心理学

I now wish to introduce into this discourse some observations on ecology and psychology, the latter in its application to urban science. Ecology as the knowledge of the relationships between a living being and his environment cannot be discussed here. This is a problem which has belonged to sociology and natural philosophy ever since Montesquieu, and despite its enormous interest, it would take us too far afield.

Let us consider only this question: how does the locus urbis, once it has been determined, influence the individual and the collective? This question interests me here in the ecological sense of Sorre: that is, how does the environment influence the individual and the collective? For Sorre, this question was far more interesting than the opposite one of how man influences his environment. With the latter question, the idea of human ecology changes meaning abruptly and involves the whole history of civilization. We already responded to this question, or to the system that the two questions form, when at the beginning of this study we defined the city as a human thing par excellence.

But as we have said, even for ecology and the urban ecology to which we refer, this study has meaning only when the city is seen in the entirety of its parts, as a complex structure. The historically determined relationships and influences between man and the city cannot be studied by reducing them to a schematic model of the city as in the urban ecology models of the American school from Park to Hoyt①. These theories can offer some answers, as far as I can see, relative to urban technics, but they have little to contribute to the development of an urban science founded on artifacts and not on models.

That the study of collective psychology has an essential part in the study of the city seems undeniable. Many of the authors to whom I feel closest in this work base their studies on collective psychology, which in turn is linked to sociology. This linkage has been amply documented. Collective psychology has bearing upon all the sciences where the city as an object of study is of primary importance.

Valuable information also may be obtained from the experiments conducted under the banner of Gestalt psychology, as undertaken by the Bauhaus in the domain of form and as proposed by the American school of Lynch②. In this book, I have particularly made use of some of Lynch's conclusions with respect to the residential district, as confirmation of the distinctive character of different districts within the city. There have been, however, some inappropriate extensions of the methods of experimental psychology; but before addressing these I should touch briefly on the relationship between the city and architecture as technics.

In speaking of the constitution of an artifact and of its memory, I am thinking of these problems largely in terms of their collective nature;

they pertain to the city, and thus to its collective citizenry. I maintain that in an art or a science the principles and means of action are elaborated collectively or transmitted through a tradition in which all the sciences and arts are operating as collective phenomena. But at the same time they are not collective in all their essential parts; individuals carry them out. This relationship between a collective artifact, which is necessarily an urban artifact, and the individual who proposes and single-handedly realizes it can only be understood through a study of the technics by which the artifact is manifested. There are many different technics; one of them is architecture, and since this is the object of our study, we must here be concerned with it above all, and with economics and history only to the extent that they are manifested in the architecture of the city.

The relationship in architecture between the collective urban artifact and the individual is unique with respect to the other technics and arts. In fact, architecture presents itself as a vast cultural movement: it is discussed and criticized well beyond the narrow circle of its specialists; it needs to be realized, to become part of the city, to become "the city". In a certain sense, there is no such thing as buildings that are politically "opposed," since the ones that are realized are always those of the dominant class, or at least those which express a possibility of reconciling certain new needs with a specific urban condition. Thus there is a direct relationship between the formulation of certain proposals and the buildings that arise in the city.

But it is equally obvious that this relationship can also be considered in its separate terms. The world of architecture can be seen to unfold and be studied as a logical succession of principles and forms more or less autonomous from the reality of locus and history[3]. Thus, architecture implies the city; but this city may be an ideal city, of perfect and harmonious relationships, where the architecture develops and constructs its own terms of reference. At the same time, the actual architecture of this city is unique; from the very first it has a characteristic—and ambiguous—relationship that no other art or science possesses. In these terms we can understand the constant polemical urge of architects to design systems in which the spatial order becomes the order of society and attempts to transform society.

Yet outside of design, even outside of architecture itself, exist urban artifacts, the city, monuments; monographs on single works in particular periods and environments demonstrate this. In his study of Florence in the Age of Humanism, Andre Chastel demonstrates clearly all the links between civilization and art, history, and politics which informed the new vision of Florence (as also Athens, Rome, and New York) and the arts and processes that were shaping it.

If we consider Palladio and the historically determined cities of the Veneto in which we find his work, and how the study of these cities actually transcends Palladio the architect, we find that the concept of locus from which we began these arguments acquires its full meaning; it becomes the urban context, and is identifiable as a single artifact. Again we can ask, where does the singularity reside? It resides in the single artifact, in its material, the succession of events that unfolds around it, and the minds of its makers; but also in the place that determines it—both in a physical sense and above all in the sense of the choice of this place and the indivisible unity that is established between it and the work.

The history of the city is also the history of architecture. But we must remember that the history of architecture is at most one point of view from which to look at the city. The failure to understand this has led to much time spent in studying the city and its architecture in terms of its images, or else an attempt to study the city from the standpoint of other sciences, for example psychology. But what can psychology tell us if not that a certain individual sees the city in one way and that other individuals see it in another? And how can this private and uncultivated vision be related to the laws and principles from which the city first emerged and through which its images were formed? If we are concerned with the city architecturally from more than a stylistic point of view, it does not make sense to abandon architecture and occupy ourselves with something else. Indeed, no one would entertain the idea that when the theoreticians tell us that buildings must respond to criteria of firmness, commodity, and delight, they must explain the psychological motives behind this principle.

When Bernini speaks disdainfully of Paris because he finds its Gothic landscape barbarous, we are hardly interested in Bernini's psychology; instead we are interested in the judgment of an architect who on the basis of the total and specific culture of one city judges the structure of another city[④]. Similarly, that Mies van der Rohe had a certain vision of architecture is important not for ascertaining the "taste" or the "attitude" of the German middle class relative to the city, but for allowing us to appreciate the theoretical basis, the cultural patrimony of Schinkelesque classicism, and other ideas with which this is connected in the German city.

The critic who discusses why a poet has used a particular meter in a certain place in his poetry is considering what compositional problem has presented itself to the poet on a specific occasion. And thus in studying this relationship he is concerned with literature, and possesses all the means necessary for grappling with this problem.

Words and Expressions

ecology [i(ː)ˈkɔlədʒi] *n.* 生态学

Montesquieu [ˌmɔntesˈkjuː] *n.* 孟德斯鸠(Charles, 1689~1755, 男爵, 法国政治哲学家、法学家、启蒙思想家)

den [den] n. 兽穴；洞穴(舒适的)私室(作学习或办公用)穴居居住或藏在洞穴里
par [pɑ:] n. adj. 同等；(股票等)票面价值；票面的；平价的；平均的
Gestalt [gə'ʃtɑ:lt] n. [心]完全形态；完形
pertain [pə(:)'tein] v. 适合；属于
manifest ['mænifest] v. 出现, 表明；证明
reconcile ['rekənsail] vt. 使和解；使和谐；使顺从
autonomous [ɔ:'tɔnəməs] adj. 自治的
ambiguous [æm'bigjuəs] adj. 暧昧的；不明确的
polemical [pə'lemikəl] adj. 辩论法；辩论术；好辩的；挑起争端的
monograph ['mɔnəugrɑ:f] n. 专论
Veneto ['venetɔ:] n. 威尼托区[意大利行政区名]
singularity [,singju'læriti] n. 单一；异常；奇异；奇妙；稀有
reside [ri'zaid] vi. 居住
disdainfully [dis'deinfuli] adv. 轻蔑地
barbarous ['bɑ:bərəs] adj. 野蛮的；残暴的；粗野的；(声音)刺耳的；沙哑的
ascertain [,æsə'tein] vt. 确定；探知
grappling ['græpliŋ] n. (打捞用的)抓机；爪钩

Difficult Sentences

① The historically determined relationships and influences between man and the city cannot be studied by reducing them to a schematic model of the city as in the urban ecology models of the American school from Park to Hoyt.

在研究由历史决定的人们与城市之间的关系和影响时，我们不能通过将其缩减为图解般的城市模式这种方法来进行(这种模式出现在从帕克到霍伊特这些美国学者所提出的城市生态模式之中)。

② Valuable information also may be obtained from the experiments conducted under the banner of Gestalt psychology, as undertaken by the Bauhaus in the domain of form and as proposed by the American school of Lynch.

从在格式塔心理学旗帜指导下所做的实验中(例如包豪斯在形式领域中的实践和美国林奇学派的实验),我们也许能获得一些有价值的资料。

③ But it is equally obvious that this relationship can also be considered in its separate terms. The world of architecture can be seen to unfold and be studied as a logical succession of principles and forms more or less autonomous from the reality of focus and history.

但是同样显而易见的是这种关系可分开来考虑。建筑世界是可以展现在我们面前的,可作为一系列合乎逻辑的原理和形式来研究,这或多或少独立于现实的焦点和历史的尘埃。

④ When Bernini speaks disdainfully of Paris because he finds its Gothic landscape barbarous, we are hardly interested in Bernini's psychology; instead we are interested in the judgment of an architect who on the basis of the total and specific culture of one city judges the structure of another city.

当博尼尼轻蔑地谈起巴黎时——因为他认为巴黎的哥特式景观是没有文化蕴涵的——我们对博尼尼的心理几乎一点不感兴趣;我们感兴趣的是建筑师的判断,他们以一个城市整体文化和特殊文化来判断另一个城市的建筑。

Phrases and Patterns

1. far afield 远离;在远处

    We get a lot of tourists from Europe, and some from even further afield.

    我们的游客很多来自欧洲,有些来自甚至更远的地方。

    The natural scenery of the rural area which is far afield from the city is really attractive.

    远离城市的乡村自然景观真的很吸引人。

2. with respect to 关于;至于

With respect to the street and transportation problem, we will discuss further in the next meeting.

关于街道和交通问题,我们将在下次会议上进一步讨论。

With respect to the sculptures of city, the related department should lay much stress on it.

关于城市雕塑,相关部门应给予高度重视。

Questions

1. Where does the singularity reside?
2. What's the relationship in architecture between the collective urban artifact and the individual?
3. How to understand the history of architecture is at most one point of view from which to look at the city.

8.3　The Development of Industry
工业的发展

　　In the preceding section we pointed out several distortions which have characterized the study of the city: the over importance <u>attributed to the development of industry</u> seen in a generic and conventional way with respect to the real dynamic of urban artifacts, the abstracting of problems out of the actual context of the city, and the confusion that certain moralistic attitudes have introduced, preventing the formation of a scientific habit of thought in urban studies[①]. Although most of these distortions and prejudices do not issue from a single source and do not amount to a clearly systematic set of ideas, they are responsible for many ambiguities and it is worthwhile to consider certain aspects of them at greater length.

　　A number of the arguments that have been arbitrarily invented to explain the genesis of the modern city are to be found as the premises of various technical and regional studies. These tend to turn on the problematical nature of the term city today; the problem arises, it is argued, essentially out of the city's physical and political homogenization following the rise of industrialism. Industry, the source of every evil and every good, becomes the true protagonist in the transformation of the city.

According to these arguments, the change wrought by industry is characterized historically by three phases. The first phase, and thus the origin of the transformation of the city, is marked by the destruction of the fundamental structure of the medieval city, which was based on an absolute identity between the place of work and the place of residence, both being within the same building. Thus began the end of the domestic economy as a unified entity of production and consumption. This destruction of the basic form of life of the medieval city led to a chain of reactions whose ultimate ramifications would come to be measured fully in the city of the future. Contemporaneously, workers' housing, mass housing, and rental housing appeared; only at this point did the housing problem emerge as an urban and social problem. The distinctive sign of this phase in spatial terms, then, was the enlargement of the urban surface, with the house and the work place beginning to be slightly separated in the city.

The second phase, which was the decisive one, was characterized by a progressive expansion of industrialization. It engendered a definitive separation of house and work place and destroyed their former relationship to the neighborhood. The appearance of the first types of collective work was accompanied by a choice of housing that was not always in the immediate vicinity of the work place. Parallel to this evolution was the separation between work places that produced merchandise and those that did not. Production and administration were distinguished, and the division of labor in its most precise meaning began. From this division of work places the "downtown", in the

English sense of the word, originated, creating specific interdependencies between offices that had increasing need for reciprocal contact. The central administration of an industrial complex, for example, sought to have banking, administration, and insurance as neighbors rather than production places. At first, when there was still sufficient room, this concentration came about in the center of the city.

The third phase of the city's transformation began with the development of means of individual transportation and the full efficiency of all means of public transportation to the work place. This development must have resulted not only from an increased technical efficiency but also from the economic participation of public administrations in transportation services. The choice of the place of residence became increasingly independent of the place of work. Meanwhile, as the service activities, which still tended to be located in the center, developed and acquired a primary importance, the search for housing outside the city in the adjacent countryside grew ever stronger. Work and its location came to play an increasingly subordinate role in the choice of housing. The citizen moved into any part of the territory he wished, giving rise to the phenomenon of the commuter. The relationship of residence and work now became fundamentally bound up with time; they became Zeitfunktion.

An explanation of this type contains a continuous mixture of true and false elements; it has its most evident limitations in its description of artifacts, lapsing into a sort of "naturalism" of the urban dynamic whereby the actions of men, the constitution of urban artifacts, and the political choices that the city makes are all assumed to be involuntary②. It results in a consideration of certain legitimate, and technically important, urban proposals (for example, the real problems of decongestion and the work-residence relationship) as ends rather than means, virtually as principles and laws rather than instruments. Above all it makes a number of confused assumptions, based on a facile and schematic mixture of points of view, assertions, systems of interpretation, and disparate methods③.

Words and Expressions

moralistic [mɔrə′lıstık;(US)mɔːr-] *adj.* 道学的;说教的; 教训的
genesis [′dʒenisis] *n.* 起源
premise [′premis] *n.* 前提; 立前提
homogenization [ˌhəumədʒənɑi′zeiʃən] *n.* (均)匀化; 均质化;同质化;纯一化
protagonist [prəu′tægənist] *n.* (戏剧, 故事, 小说中的)主角; 领导者;积极参加者
wrought [rɔːt] *adj.* 做成的; 形成的; 精炼的
ramification [ˌræmifi′keiʃən] *n.* 分支; 分叉; 衍生物; 支流
contemporaneous [kənˌtempə′reinjəs] *adj.* 同时期的; 同时代的
engender [in′dʒendə] *v.* 造成
vicinity [vi′siniti] *n.* 邻近; 附近; 接近
adjacent [ə′dʒeisənt] *adj.* 邻近的; 接近的
commuter [kə′mjuːtə] *n.* 通勤者; 经常往返者
lapse [læps] *n.* 失误; 下降;流逝;丧失; 过失
legitimate [li′dʒitimit] *adj.* 合法的;合理的; 正统的
decongestion [ˌdiːkən′dʒestʃən] *n.* (城市等)拥挤的消除(或缓解)
facile [′fæsɑıl;(US)′fæsl] *adj.* 易做到的; 易得到的;不花力气的; 敏捷的; 流畅的; (性格)柔顺的; 温和的; 容易的
schematic [ski′mætik] *adj.* 示意性的

Difficult Sentences

① In the preceding section we pointed out several distortions which have characterized the study of the city: the over importance attributed to the development of industry seen in a generic and conventional way with respect to the real dynamic of urban artifacts, the abstracting of problems out of the actual context of the city, and the confusion that certain moralistic attitudes have introduced, preventing the formation of a scientific habit of thought in urban studies.

在前一部分中,我们已经指出了城市研究中的几种误解:以一般和习惯的方法来过分强调工业发展的重要性,轻视城市和建筑体的真正动力;脱离城市具体情况来抽象看问题;某些道德态度所引起的困惑阻碍了城市研究中科学思维习惯的形成。

② An explanation of this type contains a continuous mixture of true and false elements; it has its most evident limitations in its description of artifacts, lapsing into a sort of "naturalism" of the urban dynamic whereby the actions of men, the constitution of urban artifacts, and the political choices that the city makes are all assumed to be involuntary.

这种解释是一系列正确和错误论点的混合体,其最明显的局限性在于它对建筑体的描述之中,这使它对城市的动力作出某种"自然主义"的解释,从而把人的作用、城市建筑体的形成和城市所做的政治选择都认为是被动的。

③ Above all it makes a number of confused assumptions, based on a facile and schematic mixture of points of view, assertions, systems of interpretation, and disparate methods.

尤其,它在以轻易和图解的方式混合众多观点的基础上,产生了一些令人困惑的假设、论断、陈述体系和不同的方法。

Phrases and Patterns

1. attribute to 把……归因于;把……归咎于
   People attribute the improvement of air quality to planting trees.
   人们把空气质量的提高归因于植树。
   Some people tend to attribute their success to external causes such as luck.
   有些人往往把他们的成功归因于运气之类的外部原因。

2. result in 结果是;导致

The rapid development of industry results in serious environmental pollution.
工业的快速发展导致严重的环境污染。
Improper transplanting results in the death of the plants.
不适当的移植导致植物的死亡。

Questions

1. According to the passage, the change brought by industry is characterized historically by three phases. What are they?
2. What are the characteristic of each phase?

8.4　Urban Scale
　　城市规模

　　A correct treatment of the problem of scale ought to begin with the subject of the field or area of study and intervention. I have already discussed this in the first chapter of this book and again in my discussion of locus and quality in urban artifacts. Naturally this study of the field can also be applied in other senses, for example in the sense of operative scale. Here I intend to speak of scale only in the sense of what has been seen by some to be a "new urban scale."

　　It is logical that the extraordinary development of cities in recent years and the problems of the urbanization of the population, of concentration, and of the growth of the urban surface have taken on prime importance in the eyes of urbanists and all social scientists studying the city. This phenomenon of increased size is common to large cities and is noticeable to some degree everywhere; in some cases it has had extraordinary ramifications. Thus, in defining the region of the northeast coast of the United States between Boston and Washington and between the Atlantic and the Appalachians, Gottmann used the term megalopolis, already coined and described by Mumford. But if this is the most sensational case of increased urban scale, no less important instances of expansion exist in the large European cities.

These expansions constitute phenomena in themselves and must be studied as such; the various hypotheses of the megalopolis have brought to light interesting material which will undoubtedly be useful for further studies of the city①. In these terms, the hypothesis of the city-region may truly become a working hypothesis, and it will become increasingly valuable the more it serves to illuminate situations that preceding hypotheses have been unable to explain completely②.

What we want to contest, however, is that this "new scale" can change the substance of an urban artifact. It is conceivable that a change in scale modifies an urban artifact in some way; but it does not change its quality. Terms such as urban nebula may be useful in the technical language, but they explain nothing; however, even the inventor of the term stresses that he uses it "to explain the complexity and the lack of clarity of [the city's] structure," disputing in particular the thesis of a school of American ecologists for whom "the old notion of city as structured nucleus, defined in space and distinct from the neighboring area, is a dead concept" and who envision "the nucleus dissolving, forming a more or less colloidal fabric, the city being absorbed by the economic region or even the whole nation."

The American geographer Ratcliff, coming from a different point of view from ours, has also disputed and rejected the popular thesis that metropolitan problems are problems of scale. To reduce metropolitan problems to problems of scale means to ignore completely the existence of a science of the city, in other words to ignore the actual structure of the city and its conditions of evolution. The reading of the city I have proposed here with reference to primary elements, historically constituted urban artifacts, and areas of influence permits a study of the growth of the city in which such changes of scale do not affect the laws of development.

It seems to me that the inappropriate interpretation of the "new scale" by architects can also be explained through certain suggestions of a more figurative nature. It is worth recalling how at the outset of the debate Giuseppe Samona cautioned architects against the error of too easily being led by a perception of increased urban scale to gigantism in their projects. "It is absolutely <u>out of the question</u> in my opinion," he declared, "to nurture any idea of gigantic spatial parameters. In truth we find ourselves, as at all times, in a situation that, from a general point of view, presents man and his space in well-balanced proportion, and in a relationship analogous to that of the ancients, except that in today's relationship all the spatial measures are greater than were the more fixed ones of fifty years ago."③

Words and Expressions

locus ['ləukəs] *n.* 地点；所在地
megalopolis [ˌmegə'lɔpəlis] *n.* 巨大都市；人口稠密地带
nucleus ['nju:kliəs] *n.* [nuclear 的复数；见 nuclear]核子
envision [in'viʒən] *vt.* 想象；预想
colloidal [kə'lɔidl] *adj.* 胶状的；胶质的
perception [pə'sepʃən] *n.* 理解；感知；感觉
gigantism ['dʒaigæntizəm] *n.* [医]巨人症
parameter [pə'ræmitə] *n.* 参数；参量；<口>起限定作用的因素

Difficult Sentences

① These expansions constitute phenomena in themselves and must be studied as such; the various hypotheses of the megalopolis have brought to light interesting material which will undoubtedly be useful for further studies of the city.
这些规模扩展的自身构成了现象，我们应当如此来研究它们；有关大城市的各种假设使人们发现了令人感兴趣的材料，这种材料

对进一步研究城市无疑是有帮助的。

② In these terms, the hypothesis of the city-region may truly become a working hypothesis, and it will become increasingly valuable the more it serves to illuminate situations that preceding hypotheses have been unable to explain completely.

从这方面看,城市区域这个假设也许会真正成为有效的假说。随着其价值的不断增长,它更多地被用来说明以往假说不能完全解释的情况。

③ "It is absolutely out of the question in my opinion," he declared, "to nurture any idea of gigantic spatial parameters. In truth we find ourselves, as at all times, in a situation that, from a general point of view, presents man and his space in well-balanced proportion, and in a relationship analogous to that of the ancients, except that in today's relationship all the spatial measures are greater than were the more fixed ones of fifty years ago."

他断言,"就我看来,任何想要发展巨型空间参数的做法都是绝对行不通的。从一种普遍的观点来看,我们和所有时候都一样,处在这样一种与古代类似的环境之中:人类与其生活空间之间有着良好而平衡的比例关系,只是在今天的环境中,所有的空间尺度都要大于50年前那些更为固定的空间尺度。"

Phrases and Patterns

1. take on 呈现

   The development of means of individual transportation and public transportation take on the city's transformation.
   个人交通工具和公众的交通工具的发展呈现了城市的变化。
   The streets and buildings take on the architectural style of a city.
   街道和建筑物呈现了一个城市的建筑风格。

2. out of the question 不可能的;办不到的

   It is out of the question that he will finish his project two month early.

他将提前两个月完成项目是不可能的。

The plan of hanging gardens designed only by one person is out of the question.

悬挂式花园的规划只由一个人设计是办不到的。

Questions

1. How to understand a "new urban scale"?
2. Summarize the main idea of this passage.

8.5 The Size of a City
城市的尺度

  To choose between the techniques of either artisanal or industrial culture is not a simple question of choosing between past and future; on the contrary, it is a problem that we face every day. I should like to underline the radical difference between the civilisation of artisans and that of industrial culture①. To my mind, industrial civilisation does not have its own proper existence; it exists only as a moment of hypertrophy and of fragmentation of artisanal culture, of its technology and of its instruments and tools. The city, its elements and parts, were the principal instruments of artisanal culture. The construction of the artisanal city is at the same time both a means and an end. Instead, the finality of urban industrial development seems to correspond with the extinction of humanity.

  If we speak of public space, we speak of its quality, of its type, of its measurements, of its proportions. If order and measure are proper to every divine creation, it must therefore also be true for every human creation. Without measure and without form, terrestrial things cannot exist; they exist only as sickness, disorder, uproar. A body either too big or too small is a monster or a dwarf.

Similarly, formless and ill-dimensioned piazzas, streets and courtyards cannot survive. The problem of measure and form as regards the relationship between the city and countryside, between urban space and agricultural land, depends on whether measure and form become instruments of industrial or of artisanal production.

For an urban society, a small fertile island can be a paradise. For a suburban society, no land and no continent is big enough to still its greed, to soothe its misery. The city always defines its limits, it distinguishes urban space from rural land. On the contrary, suburban sprawl aggresses both city and countryside and proclaims urbi et orbi. "What is yours will be mine".

When distinct, city and countryside form a happy marriage. They create a heritage of building, culture, language, knowledge, of instruments and goods. Instead, suburban sprawl is based on a marriage of convenience and, lacking any roots, it repudiates heritage, traditions and cultures. It conquers both city and countryside in order to destroy them. The suburb hates itself: it knows that it is neither countryside nor city and wants to conquer the world because it cannot be at peace with itself.

The city needs no suburb to live. The suburb cannot live without a city. The suburb without a city is like a cancer without a body. A suburb built 100 miles away from a city will do everything to attack its victim: it will erect vast infrastructures and mobilise colossal machines in such a manner as to realise its objectives of destruction. The suburb strangles the city surrounding it and kills the city, tearing out its heart. A suburb can only survive, it cannot live. It can survive like a parasite, consuming both city and countryside. No city and no countryside, however rich and fertile, can survive besieged by a suburb.

The city grows like a family, multiplying itself: the suburb grows instead from its own body, by tentacular expansion. The city is always limited in size and number but the suburb knows no limits: it has no centre or form, it is only a fragment. The city is the ideal state, the mean between the tyranny of the village and the tyranny of the metropolis.

The plan of the city can be good or bad independent of the quality of its architecture, its climate and vegetation. Well constructed buildings cannot enhance a suburb into a city, just as the poorest slums cannot denigrate the quality of good urban design.

A good plan is both of a formal and moral nature. A good plan is the correct description of a city's (immovable) real estate (l'immobilier). The tragic irony of zoning lies in the fact that it mobilises, so to speak, immovable and fixed values (real estate). Thus a good city plan defines not only lines on the ground but it fixes once and for all: a) types and volumes (measures and proportions) of buildings, b) types and volumes of public spaces (streets and squares) and c) distribution of functions (private and public). The city plan is a cultural and political synthesis, it is the sine qua non of a city's existence. To modify the legislation of a plan means modifying a society's life. It follows from this that a complex agglomeration of buildings does not necessarily constitute a city. Los Angeles, New York or Magnitogorsk are not cities.

If we start dismembering a human body, we slaughter the individual. That is exactly what zoning does to the body of the city. Even if a city is abandoned for a certain period by its inhabitants, it still continues to survive like a body in an unconscious state; a body which will revive when the spirit regains consciousness[2]. Venice is a city and so it will remain even if it is inhabited by cats and fish. But if it is transformed into business quarters it would then die.

An abandoned city can be as beautiful as Sleeping Beauty; a zoned city can at best be as beautiful as a corpse.

Zoning is the sufficient condition for the physical and spiritual destruction of a society. The city cannot be simply a sum of buildings and functions. A city is an organism with body and soul. The big city is like a family of such autonomous and infinitely varied individuals. If the city does not have the correct measure and right form it will die. And however rich or fertile its territory may be, it will host a poor society. Such a city is like a loose or tight dress which —even if beautiful or precious—is nonetheless useless and will therefore be thrown away. Who could be proud of his beautiful hat if it does not fit him? According to my friend Massimo Scolari, "beautiful objects are the only friends that never betray us".

It is a truly wretched objective indeed that the principal aim of industrial civilisation has been to transform the most beautiful cities into the worst enemies of man. The Italian cities show clearly all that is good and bad in city planning③. Perhaps we would love this country (Italy) all the more if the architecture constructed after 1930 were to vanish; but the majority of architects refuse to think about the profound significance of this fact. I regret to hear that Pierluigi Cervellati, who courageously opposed the destruction of Bologna, was dismissed from his post. The intellectual courage and moral obligation he showed proved unique amidst the general opportunism of the architectural profession.

Zoning in the hands of the planning authorities (Piani Regolalori) is the worst enemy of the Italian city and countryside. And just as Carthago was the first enemy of Rome, I have to repeat yet again: "Ceterum censeo zoning essere deletum".

Today world opinion is watchful about the destiny of Venice; but that is not enough when a few kilometres away someone works to destroy the Veneto, Padua and that which remains of the once "beautiful Italian countryside". The outcome of these plans will be more lethal than ail bombardment and the aggravation they will cause will become apparent only when it is too late.

As I have already said, a good plan must be a valid plan forever. I must be a volumetric, topographical, and moral project: a global cultural project. Nicolini maintains that this is a totalitarian project. But I should remind him that the First duty of every public person is to distinguish that which is universal from that which is particular; this is also the prime objective of philosophy. Totalitarianism assumes many forms but, to my mind, it always flourishes when the particular is mistaken for the universal. "The part substituting for the whole": this is the essence of every dictatorship. The inevitable result is confusion, disorder and tyranny④.

Words and Expressions

artisan [ˌɑːtiˈzæn] n. 工匠；技工
hypertrophy [haiˈpəːtrəfi] n. [医]肥大；过度生长；过度增大
fragmentation [ˌfrægmenˈteiʃən] n. 分裂；破碎
extinction [ikˈstiŋkʃən] n. 消失；消灭；废止
terrestrial [təˈrestriəl] adj. 陆地
uproar [ˈʌprɔː] n. 喧嚣；骚动
piazza [piˈætsə] n. 广场；走廊；露天市场
soothe [suːð] vt. 使(某人)平静；安慰；使(痛苦,疼痛)缓和或减轻
sprawl [sprɔːl] v. 四肢伸开地坐(或卧)；爬行；蔓生；蔓延
repudiate [riˈpjuːdieit] v. 批判
erect [iˈrekt] vt. 盖；使竖立；使直立；树立；建立
mobilise [ˈməubilaiz] v. (=mobilize)动员，赋予可动性
colossal [kəˈlɔsl] adj. 巨大的；庞大的
strangle [ˈstræŋgl] v. 扼死
parasite [ˈpærəsait] n. 寄生虫；食客
besiege [biˈsiːdʒ] vt. 围困；围攻；包围
multiply [ˈmʌltipli] v. 繁殖；乘；增加
tentacular [tenˈtækjulə] adj. 有触手的
tyranny [ˈtirəni] n. 暴政；苛政；专治

denigrate [ˈdenigreit] v. 毁誉
immovable [iˈmuːvəbl] adj. 固定的；不动的；不改变的
zoning [ˈzəuniŋ] n. 分区制
agglomeration [əˌgləməˈreiʃən] n. 结块；凝聚；块
dismember [disˈmembə] v. 肢解
slaughter [ˈslɔːtə] v. 屠宰；残杀；屠杀
corpse [kɔːps] n. 尸体
opportunism [ˈɔpətjuːnizm] n. 机会主义；投机主义
repeal [riˈpiːl] v. 废止；撤销；否定；放弃；废除
lethal [ˈliːθəl] adj. 致命的
aggravation [ˌægrəˈveiʃən] n. 加重（病情、负担、罪行、危机等）；更恶化；恼怒
volumetric [vɔliʊˈmetrɪk] adj. 测定体积的
topographical [ˌtɔpəˈgræfikəl] adj. 地形学的
totalitarian [ˌtəutæliˈtɛəriən] adj. n. 极权主义的；极权主义者
dictatorship [dikˈteitəʃip] n. 专政

Difficult Sentences

① To choose between the techniques of either artisanal or industrial culture is not a simple question of choosing between past and future; on the contrary, it is a problem that we face every day. I should like to underline the radical difference between the civilization of artisans and that of industrial culture.
工艺方面是选择艺匠文化还是工业文化，绝不是选择过去还是未来的简单问题；相反，它是一个我们每天必须面对的问题。我想强调的是艺匠文化和工业文化之间的根本不同。

② Even if a city is abandoned for a certain period by its inhabitants, it still continues to survive like a body in an unconscious state; a body which will revive when the spirit regains consciousness.
即使一个城市在一定时期被他的居民所抛弃，它仍然会存续下去，就像是处于无意识状态的一个躯体，当神经再次获得意识时

它就会复活。

③ It is a truly wretched objective indeed that the principal aim of industrial civilization has been to transform the most beautiful cities into the worst enemies of man. The Italian cities show clearly all that is good and bad in city planning.

工业文化的确令人讨厌,工业文化的主要目的是把美丽的城市变成人类最坏的敌人。意大利城市清楚地展示了在城市规划中工业文化的所有好与坏。

④ Totalitarianism assumes many forms but, to my mind, it always flourishes when the particular is mistaken for the universal. "The part substituting for the whole": this is the essence of every dictatorship. The inevitable result is confusion, disorder and tyranny.

极权主义假定了很多形式,但是在我看来,当把特殊误认为普遍照样会欣欣向荣。部分代替整体:这是每一个专政的本质。不可避免的结果是混乱、无序和暴政。

Phrases and Patterns

1. To my mind 在我看来

   To my mind, using desert plants as the element of the landscape construction is a great challenge.

   在我看来,用沙漠植物作为景观建设的要素是很大的挑战。

   To my mind, architecture and city are closely related to each other.

   在我看来,建筑和城市是紧密联系在一起的。

2. transform …into 把……变成……

   Planters transform the wasteland into greenbelt.

   种植者把荒地变成绿化地带。

   Landscapers transformed shrubs and vines into a beautiful fence.

   园艺师把灌木丛和藤蔓变成一道美丽的围墙。

Questions

1. What's the relationship between city and suburb?
2. What does a good city plan conclude?
3. What are the bad effects of zoning?

9

Urban Stormwater System Plan and Management
城市雨水处理系统设计规划与管理

【本章导读】 澳大利亚作为人类居住干燥地带的代表性国家，它拥有管理稀缺水资源、保护国家独特且完整的生态系统水循环的管理方式。澳大利亚斥巨资在这种极具代表性的干燥环境下进行储水，用以达到城乡供水的需求。对于雨水的处理，澳大利亚经历了从原始的收集方式到现代生态重新利用等阶段。然而尽管城市雨水作为重要的经济资源，得到了越来越多的重视和认可，但是在城市扩建方面，雨水并没有用于增加供给。研究表明，城市雨水可以以高性价比、对环境有益的方式开发出来。水循环是雨水蒸发、地表径流和地下水径流之间复杂的相互作用，节水型城市设计正是源自于城市发展、雨水系统和下游生态系统质量之间的水循环联系。节水型城市设计强调在流域、市郊和住宅群等方面水资源管理，并以多种学科和方法作为基础。尽管如此，如要实行节水型城市设计方案，会面临水管理整体基础设施的长期资金投入。而城市化和农业发展、森林开采使得雨水管理势在必行。土地开发商的雨水管理应与当地的管理计划和流域内的管理计划和谐一致。应该改善现有的雨水处理系统，避免使用自然水道或自然湿地用于雨水处理。在雨水质量改善方面，人工湿地比雨水污染控制池塘更具有优势，并且能够有效去除颗粒和可溶解的污染物。湿地植物还能够吸收营养，作为生长的养料。同时，人工湿地可能会成为众多鸟类和动物的栖息地，但是值得注意的是：人工湿地不同于自然湿地，需要人为干涉下的保护和维护。此外，处理池也得到了广泛利用。

9.1　Introduction to Urban Stormwater Management in Australia
澳大利亚城市雨水管理概述

  Australians live in the driest inhabited continent. Managing scarce water resources requires a complete water cycle approach to protecting the country's unique ecosystems. The variability of rainfall and runoff is more extreme than other parts of the world. Australians have made a large investment in stored water capacity to supply rural and urban users in this climate. While stormwater runoff from the cities is about equal to the amount of drinking quality water that is supplied at considerable cost each year, little stormwater is captured, with most adding to the pollution of waterways[1]. Urban stormwater is defined as runoff from urban areas, including the major flows during and following rain, as well as dry-weather flows. Many factors influence the amount of stormwater and the contaminants that are transported by it, including:

Duration and intensity of rainfall.
Proportion of impervious surfaces.
Shape of the land.
Landuse.
Design and management of stormwater systems.

  In addition to washing contaminants from the atmosphere, rainfall in the form of stormwater runoff flushes material accumulated on surfaces including litter, dust and soil, fertilisers and other nutrients, chemicals and pesticides, micro-organisms, metals, oils and grease into waterways.

  Overall, about 12% of Australia's rainfall finds its way into surface streams. By contrast, in highly urbanised zones up to 90% of the rainfall may flow into the stormwater system. These flows are complemented by dry weather drainage, flows from garden watering, washdowns and illegal discharges. In some systems wet weather overflows from sewerage systems create significant health and environmental impacts on our waterways.

In the past, the prime objective of urban stormwater management has been flood mitigation. Local councils can be held liable for flood damage caused by stormwater.

Traditionally in Australia, stormwater has been transported separately from the sewerage system. Unlike sewage, stormwater has received little, if any, treatment. The aim has been to channel the stormwater as rapidly and invisibly as possible from within our urban areas to the nearest waterway, usually on the coast[2].

The necessity to deal with both the quantity and quality of runoff is now recognised. The "hard" engineering strategy for the management of stormwater is being modified by an increase in the application of Water Sensitive Urban Design (WSUD). This strategy focuses on the sources of runoff and pollution and the tools to contain and reuse the water within urban housing, commercial and industrial areas.

Today we have the tools to focus on Ecological Sustainable Development (ESD) in stormwater management. Stormwater can be treated as a resource that can bring environmental, economic and social benefits to our urban areas. Rather than going to waste and causing pollution, through capture, treatment and reuse, stormwater can become a major alternative to damming more rivers to ensure water supply[3].

Under landuse planning, development control and resource management agencies work to a common, legally formalised hierarchy of mutually consistent planning instruments. Landuse and water allocation plans operate under a catchment planning umbrella that identifies the natural resources issues within particular catchments, the outcomes sought, and strategies for addressing them.

Although urban stormwater and treated wastewater are recognised increasingly as important economic resources, they are not widely used to augment supplies in expanding urban areas. Recent research and demonstration projects have shown that stormwater and treated wastewater can be exploited in a cost effective and environmentally sensitive manner for new urban developments.

In this context:

· Water reclamation can reduce potable water demand by as much as 50%.

· Properly managed stormwater flows provide important flowreturn to streams, offsetting the environmental impact of upstream water supply diversions and reducing the need for costly in-ground stormwater infrastructure.

· The enhanced use of natural drainage corridors and depressions can provide open space, landscaped and recreational areas and conservation benefits increasing the amenity of new urban developments (multiple use corridors).

· Treatment of stormwater and wastewater closer to source, minimises uncontrolled discharge of water containing high suspended solids, nutrients and organic material.

In many cities in Australia, councils are required to develop a Stormwater Management Plan (SMP) to cover capital works, services, asset replacement programs and activities aimed at protecting environmentally sensitive areas and to promote ecological sustainability.

Typically, the SMP identifies:

· The existing and future values of a catchment.

· Stormwater management objectives to protect these values.

· The range of land use constraints.

- The range of corridor or drainage measures related to flow, interception of pollutants, provision of open space and recreation, conservation areas, urban stormwater reuse requirements and retention of the natural values of urban streams.

Words and Expressions

contaminant [kən'tæminənt] n. 污染物;致污物
fertiliser ['fɜːtilaisə] n. 化肥;受精媒介物
sewerage ['suəridʒ] n. 污水;排水设备
hierarchy ['haiəˌrɑːki] n. 层级;等级制度
catchment ['kætʃmənt] n. 流域;集水
augment [ɔgˈmɛnt] v. n. 增加;增大
exploit [ikˈsplɔit] v. n. 开发,开拓;剥削;开采;勋绩;功绩
reclamation [ˌrɛkləˈmeʃən] n. 开垦;收回;再利用;矫正
amenity [əˈmɛnəti] adj. 舒适;礼仪;愉快;便利设施
interception [ˌintəˈsɛpʃən] n. 拦截,截住;截断,截取;侦听,窃听
organic [ɔrˈgænik] adj. 有机的;组织的;器官的;根本的
ecological [ˈikəˈlɑdʒikl] adj. 生态的,生态学的
retention [riˈtɛnʃən] n. 保留;扣留,滞留;记忆力;闭尿
corridor [ˈkɔridɔr] n. 走廊
provision [prəˈviʒn] n. v. 规定;条款;准备;[经] 供应品;供给…食物及必需品

impervious surface 不透水面
water reclamation 污水回收
cost effective 有成本效益的,划算的
stormwater system 雨水系统
sewerage system 排水系统,污水工程系统
impact on 对……冲击,碰撞;影响
social benefit 社会公益;社会收益
environmentally sensitive 对环境有积极影响的;环境易受破坏的
conservation area 保护区
organic material 有机物;有机材料

asset replacement 资产置换

ecological sustainability 生态可持续性

focus on 集中于

drainage measure 排水措施

prime objective 主要目的,首要目标

Difficult Sentences

① Australians have made a large investment in stored water capacity to supply rural and urban users in this climate. While stormwater runoff from the cities is about equal to the amount of drinking quality water that is supplied at considerable cost each year, little stormwater is captured, with most adding to the pollution of waterways.

在这种气候下,澳大利亚投巨资用于储水以供给给城市乡镇。然而,城市雨水流量大约相当于饮用优质水的数量,而这种优质水每年都花费巨大。只有小部分的雨水得以收集,大部分都没有得到利用。

② Unlike sewage, stormwater has received little, if any, treatment. The aim has been to channel the stormwater as rapidly and invisibly as possible from within our urban areas to the nearest waterway, usually on the coast.

不同于污水,只有很少部分的雨水得到处理利用。而且目的也是尽可能快速地从城市排向距离最近的水路,通常是排向海边。

③ Stormwater can be treated as a resource that can bring environmental, economic and social benefits to our urban areas. Rather than going to waste and causing pollution, through capture, treatment and reuse, stormwater can become a major alternative to damming more rivers to ensure water supply.

雨水,可以作为一种能够为城市带来环境,经济和社会效益的资源。而不是污染,破坏环境,通过收集,处理和再利用,雨水可以成为保障水供给的一种主要方法。

Phrases and Patterns

1. be equal to 等于；相当于

    While stormwater runoff from the cities is about equal to the amount of drinking quality water that is supplied at considerable cost each year, little stormwater is captured, with most adding to the pollution of waterways.

    然而，城市雨水流量大约相当于饮用优质水的数量，而这种优质水每年都花费巨大。只有小部分的雨水得以收集，大部分都没有得到利用。

    Deciding on the number of data drives for each RAID array can be rather complex, since the number of drives in an array is not necessarily equal to the number of drives in which data is populated. This is a complex pair of questions to which it is difficult to find definitive answers.

    每个 RAID 阵列的数据驱动器数目的确定可能相当复杂，因为一个阵列中的驱动器数目并不一定等于进行数据填充的驱动器数目。

    But if bank policy is to make loans andinvestments equal to whatever reserves are in excess of legal requirements, the expansion process will be carried on.

    但是，如果银行政策使得贷款以及投资等于无论什么超过法定需要的准备金，就会出现放大过程。

2. recognise 承认；认可

    Although urban stormwater and treated wastewater are recognised increasingly as important economic resources, they are not widely used to augment supplies in expanding urban areas.

    尽管城市雨水，作为重要的经济资源，得到了越来越多的重视和认可，但是在城市扩建方面，雨水并没有用于增加供给。

    This week the president was characteristically haughty and defiant in a

defeat she refused to recognise as such.
本周在面对她所拒绝承认的挫败时,总统表现出其典型的傲慢与无理。
They added that Obama could choose to recognise Iran as a key power in the Middle East and to offer security guarantees and pledges of no regime change strategies.
他们接着说奥巴马可能选择承认伊朗在中东地区是一股重要力量,并提供安全担保,承诺没有颠覆政权的策略。

Questions

1. What is the significance for Australians to manage stormwater?
2. What Australians have done for managing stormwater?

9.2 Water Sensitive Urban Design
节水城市设计

The water cycle is a complex interaction of rainfall, evapotranspiration, overland flow and groundwater flow. Water Sensitive Urban Design (WSUD) grew out of a recognition of the linkages in the water cycle between urban development, stormwater systems and the quality of downstream ecosystems. WSUD is based on a holistic approach to water cycle management and regional natural resource management. These approaches can be linked to catchment management networks and strategies. They feed into planning by individual councils and then into their operational and works programs and forward budget allocations.

The application of water sensitive planning and management principles involves incorporating water resource issues early in the landuse planning process. It addresses water resource management at the catchment, suburban, precinct, cluster and allotment scale. WSUD makes the entire stormwater treatment network part of the urban fabric via multiple use corridors and best management practice (BMP) treatment trains. Vegetated swales, filter strips, extended detention basins and constructed wetlands are all part of fully functioning stormwater treatment systems. It maximises infiltration and on-site storage, treatment and reuse and utilises natural runoff channels where appropriate.

If regulators set a target for permissible allotment discharges of stormwater, then designers will examine options for reusing stormwater in toilets, hot water systems, irrigation systems and infiltration zones. More sustainable landscaping, roof gardens, bioretention, water tanks, better road drainage design and better planning become options for achieving the targets. Reduced stormwater discharge means less stress on creeks and rivers, resulting from reduced erosion, sedimentation and flooding.

WSUD builds on a multi-disciplinary approach. For instance, landscape architects can combine with ecologists to select a range of natural wetland species that enhance pollutant removal and create attractive residential and industrial estates[1]. Planners can incorporate multiple-use corridors to provide stormwater infiltration, filtering and flow paths and dry weather recreation areas. The community can play a role in defining the types of passive recreational pursuits and water features that are most attractive. Engineers can provide designs that function effectively as stormwater management systems, ensuring minimal risk of flooding and disease while protecting ecosystems.

Natural processes which control runoff, are in constant change. Typically, streams change course, natural erosion occurs, and vegetation and soil permeability change with the seasons[2]. When humans alter the land within a catchment, the changes to the natural processes accelerate, creating a need for constructed stormwater management systems. However, if WSUD is implemented then there can be long term savings in overall water management infrastructure. Water utilities faced with the decision to expand water distribution and stormwater infrastructure (headworks) to meet the needs of extra population, need to make a comparison between the lifecycle cost of:

New and existing infrastructure required to meet the (conventional) additional water supply demand and additional stormwater load.

New practices which decrease potable water consumption and stormwater load, and encourage water reuse and environmental sustainability.

Acomparative analysis of economic externalities, such as environmental and social consequences of traditional and WSUD systems, is crucial. Of all landuse changes that affect an area's hydrological cycle, urbanisation is the most important[3]. However, other landuse changes within a catchment such as agriculture, forestry and mining also alter the hydrological cycle and create a need for stormwater management.

Stormwater Management Planning

Best practice stormwater management for land development is implemented by the developer in harmony with the local council's stormwater management scheme and the catchment management plan. Both are based on the principles of ecologically sustainable development. Land developers and builders are generally responsible for ensuring that their development does not result in significant worsening of existing stormwater management problems. Urban land developments should only occur in areas where a land capability assessment has indicated that stormwater management practices are capable of achieving this objective.

Developers are encouraged to improve existing stormwater systems (e. g. degraded creeks) and avoid using natural waterways or natural wetlands for stormwater treatment purposes. Alternatively, development using WSUD principles based on total water cycle management can be attractive to prospective purchasers, increase the value of adjacent land,

and may avoid expensive new infrastructure. The value of land adjacent to stormwater treatment measures, such as water quality control ponds and constructed wetlands, is usually higher than for land adjacent to a conventional drain.

Case Study: WSUD Development Kogarah Town Square, Sydney, NSW

Urban renewal of Kogarah Town Square involves the construction of 220 residential apartments, 225 parking spaces, commercial retail space and a public library. The development is situated on the ridge between the densely urbanised catchments of the Cooks River and the Georges River which flow into Botany Bay. Both the rivers and the Bay are degraded. They are under pressure from increasing urban consolidation, traffic densities and industrial activities.

The project aims to reduce the impact of stormwater through conservation and efficiency by:

Reducing the reliance on mains water.

Managing stormwater quantity and quality through capture, reuse and treatment.

Stormwater filtration will occur through a specially designed garden bed. In periods of high stormwater flow, surge tanks will regulate the water flow prior to discharge into the stormwater system. Of the 7,500 kilolitres of rain that falls on the site annually, 85% is captured and used.

About 60% is used to flush toilets, the remainder to irrigate the gardens in the courtyards, while 25% passes through the gardens and is purified and stripped of most of the nutrients. The reuse scheme separates the dirtiest water from the Town Square pavement and treats it separately from the relatively clean water from the roofs. The water reuse within the development represents a saving in the order of 17% of mains water.

The project has been supported by the Commonwealth's Urban Stormwater Initiative with $629,000 in partnership with Kogarah Council, Sydney Water and the development company, High Trade Pty Ltd.

Words and Expressions

holistic [ho'listik] adj. 整体的;全盘的
precinct ['prisiŋkt] n. 选区;管理区;管辖区
allotment [ə'lɔtmənt] n. 分配;分配物;养家费;命运
detention [di'tenʃən] n. 拘留;延迟;挽留
infiltration [ˌinfil'treʃən] n. 渗透;渗透物
irrigation [ˌiri'geiʃən] n. 灌溉;[临床] 冲洗;冲洗法
erosion [i'rəuʒən] n. 侵蚀,腐蚀
sedimentation [ˌsedimen'teiʃən] n. [矿业][物化] 沉降;[化学] 沉淀
permeability [ˌpɜːmiə'biləti] n. 渗透性;透磁率,导磁系数;弥漫
potable ['pəutəbl] n. adj. 饮料(常复数);适于饮用的;便携的
hydrological [ˌhaidrə'lɔdʒikəl] adj. 水文学的
adjacent [ə'dʒesnt] adj. 邻近的,毗连的
ridge [ridʒ] n. v. 山脊;山脉;屋脊;使成脊状;作垄;成脊状
surge [sɜːdʒ] n. &v. 大浪;汹涌澎湃;巨涌;激增;汹涌;使颠簸
strip [strip] v. 带;条状;脱衣舞;剥夺;剥去;脱去衣服 脱去衣服
holistic approach 整体分析,整体研究,全方位思考
comparative analysis 对比分析,比较分析
economic externality 经济外部性
hydrological cycle 水循环
traffic density 交通密度
groundwater flow 地下水径流
overland flow 表面径流
urban fabric 城市结构,城市肌理
filter strip 滤土带(草带)
budget allocation 预算分配,预算拨款

detention basin 蓄洪水库,滞洪区域,拦洪水库
roof garden 屋顶花园,空中花园
water tank 水箱;水槽
industrial estate 工业区;工业园区
minimal risk 最低风险
soil permeability 土壤渗透性;土壤通透性
feed into 注入,流入;提供原料

Difficult Sentences:

① WSUD builds on a multi-disciplinary approach. For instance, landscape architects can combine with ecologists to select a range of natural wetland species that enhance pollutant removal and create attractive residential and industrial estates.
节水型城市设计以多学科的方法为基础。例如,景观建筑师能够与生态学家相结合,选择一系列自然湿地,用于加强除污,创造吸引人的居住和商业区。

② Natural processes which control runoff, are in constant change. Typically, streams change course, natural erosion occurs, and vegetation and soil permeability change with the seasons.
控制径流的自然过程处在不断变化中。通常,溪流改变河道,发生自然侵蚀,植被和土壤的渗透性也随着季节而变化。

③ A comparative analysis of economic externalities, such as environmental and social consequences of traditional and WSUD systems, is crucial. Of all landuse changes that affect an area's hydrological cycle, urbanisation is the most important.
对于经济外部性,例如传统的和节水型设计系统的环境和社会结果的比较分析是非常重要的。在所有的土地使用中,城镇化最能影响区域的水循环。

Phrases and Patterns

1. in the order of 大约

The water reuse within the development represents a saving in the order of 17% of mains water.

城市设计发展中的雨水再利用节省了大约17%的主要用水。

Large jobs are jobs which will probably take something in the order of a week to complete.

巨大的工作可能需要花一周才能完成。

Even more, we estimate that the effect of this food crisis on poverty reduction worldwide is in the order of seven lost years.

更重要的是,我们估计这次食品危机对全世界的减轻贫困工作造成了大约七年的损失。

2. result in 引起;导致

Land developers and builders are generally responsible for ensuring that their development does not result in significant worsening of existing stormwater management problems.

通常,土地开发商要保确保他们的开发不会导致现有雨水管理问题的急剧恶化。

This supports our view that falling employment and declining incomes will result in consumption growth remaining weak for the foreseeable future.

这也支持了我们的观点,即失业率的上升和收入下降将在可预见的未来导致消费疲软。

This could result in more effective drug combinations, which target both physiological states [in human hosts and laboratory conditions] simultaneously.

这可能导致更有效的药物组合,同时针对[人体和实验室环境下的]各种生理状态。

Questions

1. What problems will be if WSUD is implemented?
2. What developers should do when implementing the stormwater

management?

9.3 Constructed Wetlands
湿地建设

Usually wetlands are developed with one or more of the following objectives in mind:

To improve downstream water quality.

To improve landscape amenity.

To provide recreational opportunities, usually passive.

To create fauna and flora habitat.

To provide opportunities for stormwater harvesting, sometimes combined with aquifer storage and recovery.

To provide a degree of flood retention.

As a general rule, the more constructedwetlands resemble local natural wetlands, the higher the probability that they will develop into healthy ecosystems that are productive diverse and resilient[1]. When an ecosystem is productive, it means that there is a significant biomass of plants and microscopic algae, that take up nutrients and provide habitat and food for animals. When an ecosystem is diverse it has a large range of animal, plant and microbial species, that promote materials transfer and decomposition of organic material.

Wetland ecosystems that are resilient are able to accommodate seasonal variability in inflows and water level changes.

Once established, constructed wetlands should be able to maintain themselves indefinitely through growth and reproduction of all species of plants and animals with minimal ongoing maintenance. Ongoing maintenance of constructed wetlands may need to include some level of litter removal, weed control, fire control and mosquito control to ensure that their aesthetic and amenity functions are not diminished.

Wetland Performance

Water quality improvement in wetlands or basins primarily relies on suitable design, moderate loadings, and adequate residence time. Although stormwater pollution control ponds and wetlands both have value in intercepting and treating stormwater, wetlands have proved to be a superior treatment option on the basis of pollutant removal, lower removal time and a smaller footprint area[②].

Constructed wetlands are suited to removing fine particles and soluble contaminants.

Wetland plants can take up nutrients, use them for growth and release chemicals such as nitrogen into the atmosphere. They can treat heavy metals and break down organic pesticides or kill disease-producing organisms.

Case Study: Stormwater Quality Improvement with Wetlands Port Phillip, Melbourne, Victoria

The rapid growth of south east Melbourne is leading to increased runoff and deterioration in the health of urban waterways. The Victorian Government has set a target of reducing stormwater discharges of nitrogen across Melbourne into Port Phillip Bay by 500 tonnes by 2010. CSIRO research shows that stormwater is the major source of toxicants, pathogens, litter and sediments discharged into the Bay.

Assisted by \$3.5m funding from the Commonwealth's Clean Seas Program, Melbourne Water is constructing a series of 10 wetlands within the Cities of Casey, Kingston and Greater Dandenong. Innovative water sensitive urban design is also being employed in some housing estates and freeway developments.

The wetlands treat the base flows of catchments by bringing the urban runoff back towards the profile of rural runoff. The stormwater is directed through substantial areas of ephemeral, shallow and deep marshes.

The sites will work as part of a treatment train. Primary treatment of sediment and litter is being conducted at source through education campaigns, installation of traps at strategic locations and detention and stilling ponds and carbon filters in front of the pool and riffle and constructed marsh features.

Some 635,000 plants are being established in the wetlands to filter stormwater and create havens for native wildlife and provide an attractive location for recreation in the urban corridors.

Constructed wetlands need to be supported by strong source control measures focused on land management and pollution control. Farmers on the rural urban fringe can contain and treat runoff through detention and reuse ponds. Builders can protect topsoil from erosion by the use of silt fences. Education campaigns with urban residents, industry, and road authorities can prevent wastes and sediment washing into stormwater systems.

Constructed wetlands have become popular with developers as they add an aesthetic element to residential and industrial estates while treating stormwater runoff. However, care needs to be taken that they don't become a site for the establishment and spread of noxious weeds.

Constructed wetlands need to be designed with safety provisions to minimise the risk of children drowning and avoid stagnant pools that may become mosquito breeding grounds. Care also needs to be taken that constructed wetlands do not become a haven for rats and snakes and even crocodiles in tropical urban areas.

These challenges are surmountable with intelligent wetland design. This is occurring in harmony with the move to multiple use corridors in new housing or industrial estates as part of water sensitive urban design (WSUD)[3]. Using this approach, wetlands are sometimes located on small sites to treat runoff from a cluster of houses or effluent or stormwater from industrial sites for recycling.

Many people have been attracted to constructed wetlands because they see them as a "natural" solution to water quality threats to coastal waterways. However, the wetland will require human intervention to protect and maintain it in a highly urbanized environment that has significant differences to a "natural" catchment. Placement of sediment and litter traps in front of wetlands can increase their effectiveness and reduce maintenance requirements.

Occasionally, complete wetland reconstruction may be required due to siltation from urban runoff. When the time comes it can cause angst for local residents. They frequently forget that this was not a natural feature even though the constructed wetland may have attracted a diversity of bird and animal life.

Case Study: Wetlands And Treatment Ponds Cleveland Bay, Townsville, Qld

Improving stormwater quality from tropical catchments draining into the Great Barrier Reef is a major challenge. The 1998 Reefs at Risk Report identified Cleveland Bay as a "high risk" location. It is the only part of the Great Barrier Reef Marine Park where urban development is the major source of pollution. Ross and Louisa Creek discharge to the Bay, part of the Great Barrier Reef World Heritage Area and a dugong protection zone.

The Commonwealth Government has provided $962,500 to a consortium led by Townsville City Council to undertake water quality improvement works on Ross and Louisa Creek.

A lake system located in the upper Ross Creek catchment has recorded the highest levels of Anabaena algal density in Australia. The Creek is being polluted by leachate from contaminated sites, residential and industrial stormwater, litter from the Central Business District and sediment from high intensity rainfall. To manage the problem, low to medium stormwater flows will be treated in stormwater ponds. The ponds will remove heavy metals, organic matter, bacteria and nutrients. Nettech Gross Pollutant Interceptor Traps, permanent water monitoring stations and sediment remediation techniques will be trialed. If successful, they may be used as pollution control measures in other tropical localities.

In Louisa Creek, Townsville City Council is constructing small treatment wetlands, each tailored to specific design constraints, including:

A long dry season.

Low lying catchment.

Limited ground or surface water storage.

Narrow residential and industrial drainage corridors.

Tropical monsoon events.

The need to avoid attracting crocodiles in urban areas.

The need to avoid attracting large waterbirds to the wetlands as it is close to an air force base flight path.

Wetlands are being spaced along the watercourse to split the contaminant load and enhance fisheries habitat values. They also have major bypass channels to cope with tropical storms.

Flow Distribution

One of the more challenging hydraulic and engineering aspects of constructed wetlands is to achieve a distributed flow through macrophyte plant beds.

Channels can easily form, particularly as a result of occasionally high flows. Short-circuiting of the flows within the system can destroy the pollutant removal effectiveness.

Water Harvesting

The feasibility of water harvesting from urban stormwater wetlands rests upon three conditions:

- The water must be of sufficiently high quality for users.
- The water supply must have sufficient reliability and volume to justify the expense of extraction infrastructure.
- Water extraction must not adversely affect the water quality improvement function of the wetland. Water quality improvement rests, to a large degree, on the health of the aquatic vegetation and aquatic plants are sensitive to water level fluctuations.

Case Study: Waterways Nursery Reuse Adelaide, South Australia

Commercial plant nurseries are high users of water. Wastewater containing high levels of nutrients and chemicals often drains into stormwater collection systems. At the Waterways Nursery, a closed loop system will trap rainwater and recycle stormwater and wastewater after treatment in a small on-site wetland and sand filter. A monitoring system will control irrigation to maximise the use of rainwater and reclaimed water.

The Commonwealth's Cleaning Our Waterways Industry Partnership Program is providing over $44,000 to develop this nursery into a demonstration project for the industry.

Words and Expressions

fauna ['fɔnə] *n.* 动物群；[动] 动物区系
flora ['flɔrə] *n.* 植物区系；植物群
aquifer ['ækwifə] *n.* 〈美〉蓄水层；含水土层
resilient [ri'ziliənt] *adj.* 弹回的,有弹力的

diminish [diˈminiʃ] v. 使减少;使变小 减少,缩小;变小
intercept [ˌintəˈsɛpt] v. n. 拦截;截断;窃听;拦截;[数] 截距;截获的情报
soluble [ˈsɑljəbl] v. [化学] 可溶的,可溶解的;可解决的
deterioration [diˌtiriəˈreʃən] n. 恶化;退化;堕落
ephemeral [əˈfɛmərəl] adj. 短暂的;朝生暮死的
sediment [ˈsɛdimənt] n. 沉积;沉淀物
fringe [frindʒ] n. adj. v. 边缘;穗;刘海;边缘的;附加的;加穗于
aesthetic [ɛsˈθɛtik] adj. 美的;美学的;审美的,具有审美趣味的
noxious [ˈnɑkʃəs] adj. 有害的;有毒的;败坏道德的;讨厌的
stagnant [ˈstæɡnənt] adj. 停滞的;不景气的;污浊的;迟钝的
surmountable [səˈmauntəbl] adj. 可克服的;可超越的,可战胜的
effluent [ˈɛfluənt] n. adj. 污水;流出物;废气;流出的,发出的
constructed wetland 人工湿地
microbial species 微生物种类
pollution control 污染控制
organic pesticide 有机农药
education campaign 教育宣传活动
strategic location 战略位置;关键部分
safety provision 安全措施,安全设施
source control 源头控制,源代码管理,源控件
human intervention 人为干涉
high flow 高流动性;填充…过高;洪流
fine particle 细粒,微粒
housing estate 住宅区,居民村,房地产业
base flow [水文] 基流,基本径流;底流;底流基本水流
stilling pond 泄洪道下前池
carbon filter 炭过滤器;[化工] 活性炭过滤器
demonstration project 示范项目,示范工程

Difficult Sentences

① As a general rule, the more constructed wetlands resemble local natural wetlands, the higher the probability that they will develop into healthy ecosystems that are productive diverse and resilient.

通常来讲,人工湿地与地方自然湿地的相似度越高,人工湿地发展成为多产、多样性和高适应性的健康生态系统的可能性就越大。

② Although stormwater pollution control ponds and wetlands both have value in intercepting and treating stormwater, wetlands have proved to be a superior treatment option on the basis of pollutant removal, lower removal time and a smaller footprint area.

在收集和处理雨水方面,尽管雨水污染控制池塘和湿地有着同样的功效,但是,在利用较少的清除时间和较小的占地面积来去除污染物方面,湿地则是一种更好的处理方式。

③ These challenges are surmountable with intelligent wetland design. This is occurring in harmony with the move to multiple use corridors in new housing or industrial estates as part of water sensitive urban design (WSUD).

通过湿地的智能设计,这些问题是可以克服的。这一做法正在通过将新的住宅区和商业区的多用途的通道作为节水型城市设计的一部分得以实现。

Phrases and Patterns

1. on the basis of 根据;以……为基础

   Although stormwater pollution control ponds and wetlands both have value in intercepting and treating stormwater, wetlands have proved to be a superior treatment option on the basis of pollutant removal, lower removal time and a smaller footprint area.

   在收集和处理雨水方面,尽管雨水污染控制池塘和湿地有着同样的功效,但是,就去除污染物,较少的清除时间和较小的占地面积来说,湿地是一个更优越的处理方式。

   We will be dealing with each one of them on the basis of what information they have.

我们将根据他们所掌握的情报信息来一个个地进行处置。

Via reading books, we can not only learn what mankind has achieved, but can also be greatly inspired to develop and innovate on the basis of existing knowledge.

通过读书,我们不仅可以学到人们已经达到的成就,还可以在已有知识的基础上受到启发,从而进一步地发展和创新。

2. as a result of 由于;作为……的结果

Channels can easily form, particularly as a result of occasionally high flows.

河道很容易形成,尤其是在偶尔的洪流时期。

Workers approaching retirement should be saving more, not less, as a result of low rates.

由于低利率,临近退休的工作者应该更多的储蓄,而不是少储蓄。

Partly as a result of these pressures, household debt has declined in recent quarters for the first time since 1951.

部分由于这些压力,家庭债务在最近几个季度已经自1951年以来第一次出现了下降。

Questions

1. Compared to stromwater pollution control pond, what advantages do wetlands have in improving water quality?
2. What problems should be focused on when constructing wetlands?

10

Cities Designed for Winter
寒地城市设计

【本章导读】 随着人类生态意识的增强和对城市可持续发展的科学理解的逐渐深入，气候条件尤其是极端气候条件对城市空间环境的影响越来越受到人们的关注。本章10.1~10.7的7篇文章以寒地城市为例，结合寒地气候的负面影响以及发达国家寒地城市在规划建设方面的一些经验，分析气候因素对城市规划设计的影响。同时，以哈尔滨城市为例进行了深入剖析，从居住环境、城市交通、公共空间等方面，提出了有效改善寒地城市居住品质、塑造积极的冬季城市形象的设计策略。

10.1 Common Problems and Five Emphases
常见的问题以及**5**个要点

There are a number of common problems associated with northern cities in the winter, which are all extremely familiar to residents in these cities, making little elaboration necessary.

(1) Snow and ice can substantially reduce residents' mobility and social interaction, thereby affecting businesses. Driving and walking can become extremely hazardous.

(2) Long and cold winters can have substantial impacts on energy consumption, which can increase heating bills for homes and business,

making area business less competitive.

(3) Weather can affect outdoor activities. Long cold winters can severely restrict residents' outdoor activities for long periods of time.

(4) The winter landscape can be rather gloomy and bleak, and there may be little vegetation and color.

(5) Long winters can affect a person emotionally. One can sense some residents' depression after a long winter.

Many things can be done to overcome these problems, and to make our downtowns and inner cities more livable in the winter. In this paper, five important areas have been selected for discussion:

What Can One Do to Maintain Accessibility in the City?

Better plowing of streets, alleys, and sidewalks in the neighborhoods is essential to maintain accessibility in the city. Through the city's program, our streets are pretty well plowed. Alleys, however, are not as well serviced, which can hinder our mobility in neighborhoods where garages are connected by alleys. With increasingly tight city budgets, private plowing services, or neighborhood cooperation such as the joint purchase of a plowing vehicle, may be worthy of consideration to insure resident mobility. Special attention should be given to the needs of older persons.

Current road design and neighborhood layouts often pay little attention to how snow is plowed and stored. Providing wider roadways and strategic snow-piling areas may make the plowing and storing work easier and more cost effective. More intelligent snow piling could provide snow banks which would act as windbreaks in the winter.

Salt has been used widely in the winter to improve roadway conditions. However, salt corrodes automobiles, kills curb trees, and even destroys garages which, with increasingly tight budgets, require designs for special protection against salt. Regular washing, inspection and maintenance efforts are needed. More fundamentally, an effective substitute for salt needs to be found.

Heated bus shelters may make bus waiting a little more comfortable, yet more frequent bus service would be truly helpful. In northern cities such as Montreal, Toronto, Stockholm, and Sapporo, rapid transit helps to provide essential services and to shape city form. However, in the Twin Cities, rapid transit remains an elusive goal despite many years of planning efforts①.

In the downtown core, skyways can assure easy and comfortable pedestrian accesses. Since their introduction during the 1960s in the Twin Cities, they have become indispensable. Saint Paul and Minneapolis each have more than 30 bridges connecting major retail, office, government, and entertainment centers, and the system is still expanding.

Many American northern cities such as Des Moines, Spokane, and Duluth, have followed the Twin Cities' example in building their skyway system. In Duluth, the long skyways connecting downtown with the convention center have been used as indoor walkways for winter exercise.

Some blame the decline of street level activities on the growth of the skyways, when in fact, without skyways, the two downtowns could hardly compete with suburban centers. With the skyways, one has witnessed the healthy rebirth of two downtowns②.

On more moderate days, people welcome the opportunity to use streets. To increase pedestrian activities on the street level, more interesting shops and better amenities must be provided.

Recently, there has been increasing interest in enclosing the Nicollet Avenue pedestrian mall in downtown Minneapolis. What is emerging is perhaps a two-level pedestrian-way system, which can help to strengthen downtown activities and adapt downtown even more effectively to winter seasons.

How Can One Design Neighborhoods Differently, Taking Winter into Consideration, and Make One's City Energy Efficient?

In renewing downtowns or inner cities, buildings may be properly clustered to save energy and protect residents from strong wind in the winter. Existing buildings may be retrofitted. Earth-sheltered, super-insulated and solar housing may be cost effective. Streets may be vacated and glazed over, and a winter garden created. Solar energy, and return heat from the district heating system, may help to heat the garden in the winter. The North Quadrant Plan prepared by the Lowertown Redevelopment Corporation provides one such example.

To increase livability, a neighborhood commons could be created just off the winter garden. Such a commons may include a grocery, nursery, day care, and school —all connected to apartments by the winter garden or covered walkways. Even a neighborhood hot tub to do away with the winter chill could be included. In a northern Japanese village to this date, on new year's day all villagers strip and get into a hot tub together. What a way to generate neighborhood spirit!

Creative neighborhood design competitions may even encourage the creation of interesting ice sculptures, as in Saint Paul, Sapporo, and Harbin, and snow gardens in selected parks, as Noguchi did in his beautiful earthwork design for Riverside Park in New York City[3]. This could be done throughout the winter, rather than merely at festival times.

How Can One Expand the Cultural, Arts, Recreational, and Entertainment Activities in the Winter?

More outdoor activities, including hockey, skating, cross-country skiing, ice fishing, and snowmobiling, will help to combat " cabin fever", and keep body and mind vigorous and healthy. The magnificent park system in the Twin Cities provides many opportunities for outdoor activities.

More paths for cross-country skiing could be created for recreation, and even for home-to-work trips, perhaps along public parks and riverfronts.

Skating rinks, warming houses, and tobogganing areas would be welcomed by children and adults alike. However, tight municipal budgets can at times trim the operating period for skating.

Perhaps igloos could even be constructed in the neighborhood parks for recreational and educational purposes.

Special consideration should be given to older persons. Their mobility, for example, is a winter problem. Car pools and van systems could be provided to extend sightseeing, socializing, shopping, exercise, and the like. How the sidewalks in front of their houses are cleared after snow is another problem. Whether it could be done through private contract services, neighborhood volunteers and collaboration, or other means, should be considered.

Safe, secure housing in an urban core, at an affordable level, can make it easier for the elderly to get around, and there are many amenities at hand. A skyway system helps to make these amenities accessible. The potential for developing safe, attractive and supportive environments has not yet been fully realized.

More indoor activities, including concerts, plays, poetry readings, cinemas, libraries, and exhibits, can make winter enjoyable. Arts and cultural programs in the Twin Cities are benefitting the people greatly, and are important factors in keeping or attracting business to the area.

More community-wide celebrations (like Saint Paul's Winter Carnival) and other activities, can help to generate lots of winter fun, community spirit, and national publicity. Saint Paul's Ice Palace, built in the winter of 1986 by hundreds of volunteers, stimulated great public interest and civic pride, and was a very successful example.

Incidentally, the introduction of new fabrics, which are of lighter weight but give effective insulation, is crucial to winter clothing. Certainly, winter clothing can be attractively and fashionably designed. Why couldn't more winter fashion shows be initiated?

How Can We Beautify Our Winter Landscape?

Winter landscapes need not be bleak or depressing. Beyond greater use of evergreens, sensitive articulation of the terrain can make the winter landscape more interesting. Warmer colored street lighting can create a warm glow on dark winter nights. Housing exteriors need not be sombre and monotonous. Better articulated building facades, such as with window set-backs, etc., and the intelligent use of colors, can add much interest to buildings and strengthen the identity of a neighborhood.

In the winter, the days are short. People go to work and return home in darkness. If the downtown skyline can be effectively lit, it would become more distinctive, and our daily journey to-and-from work would be that much more interesting. The lighting idea for the skyline was included in the Metro Center '85 plan for downtown Minneapolis, which is one such example. During the Christmas season, lighting can be made far more creative. Selective use of neons, and new technology including laser lights, can make the downtown skyline an exciting palette for artists.

How Can We Combat the Depression Associated with Winter?

For some people, winter can be depressing because of the longer nights and shorter days, the length of the season, and the inconvenience of restricted mobility. There is a need to combat such depression and negative psychology.

If one assures accessibility, participation in diverse arts and sports activities would go a long way to combat depression. At the beginning of each winter, why couldn't special seminars and events be conducted to prepare people psychologically for the season, to think about its positive aspects, and to plan for activities which help them enjoy rather than dread winter? Why couldn't more festivities be held throughout the winter?

Perhaps for others, long winters and shorter days may affect them physiologically, and a remedy such as daily exposure to simulated sunlight panels may be needed. A short vacation in the South during the middle of winter would be therapeutic.

On the other hand, for some long-time residents of the sun belt who never have been to the North in the winter, experiencing our White Christmas can be most memorable and enjoyable. Why couldn't some initiatives, such as sister cities programs (which can facilitate people in the north and south to exchange residences during winter vacations) be explored?④ In 1986, two CBS weathermen, one from Phoenix, the other from Minneapolis, exchanged jobs for one week during the winter. Each gained much insight into the other city, and helped residents in each of the two cities to learn from the other city.

Finally, winter could be and should be enjoyed for its own beauty and serenity. More time could be found for quiet reading and reflection. Many persons choose to live in the north because of this advantage.

What has been described above are some of the common problems, and possible approaches toward solving them. It will be useful at this point to take one community, the Lowertown district in downtown Saint Paul, to examine how it is attempting to address these problems. Before doing that, it will be necessary to give some background on how the program was initiated, what the functions of Lowertown's Redevelopment Program are, and what the basic concept is behind it. How some of the winter city ideas are advanced will then be explained.

Words and Expressions

elaboration [iˌlæbə'reiʃən] n. 苦心经营；苦心经营的结果；详尽的细节
mobility [məu'biliti] n. 活动性；灵活性；迁移率；机动性
hazardous ['hæzədəs] adj. 危险的；冒险的；碰运气的
bleak [bliːk] adj. 寒冷的；阴冷的；荒凉的；凄凉的；黯淡的
hinder ['hində] v. 阻碍；打扰
windbreak ['windbrek] n. 防风林；防风物；防风墙；防风设备
corrode [kə'rəud] v. 使腐蚀；侵蚀
curb [kəːb] n. 路边
amenity [ə'miːniti] n. 舒适；宜人；令人愉快之事物
sculpture ['skʌlptʃə] n. 雕刻；雕刻品；雕塑，雕塑品
riverfront ['rivəfrʌnt] n. (城镇的)河边地区, 河边陆地
tobogganing [tə'bɔgəniŋ] n. 乘橇作滑雪运动
municipal [mju(ː)'nisipəl] adj. 市政的；市立的；地方性的；地方自治的
igloo ['igluː] n. 圆顶建筑
carnival ['kaːnivəl] n. 狂欢节；饮宴狂欢
terrain ['terein] n. 地形
sombre ['sɔmbə(r)] adj. 昏暗的；阴沉的
neon ['niːən] n. [化]氖
dread [dred] n. v. 恐惧；恐怖；可怕的人(或物)；畏惧；惧怕；担心
initiative [i'niʃiətiv] n. 主动
cabin fever (长期独处斗室引起的)幽闭烦躁症

Difficult Sentences

① In northern cities such as Montreal, Toronto, Stockholm, and Sapporo, rapid transit helps to provide essential services and to shape city form. However, in the Twin Cities, rapid transit remains an elusive goal despite many years of planning efforts.
在北部的城市像蒙特利尔、多伦多、斯德哥尔摩、札幌,快速运输帮助提供基本的服务、塑造城市的形态。然而在双胞城,尽管多

年来一直规划建设,快速运输仍不尽如人意。

② Some blame the decline of street level activities on the growth of the skyways, when in fact, without skyways, the two downtowns could hardly compete with suburban centers. With the skyways, one has witnessed the healthy rebirth of two downtowns.

一些人把街道活动越来越少归因于高架天桥越来越多,实际上,没有高架天桥的话,这两个市区绝对比不上市郊中心。有了高架天桥我们就可以看到两个市区健康的发展。

③ Creative neighborhood design competitions may even encourage the creation of interesting ice sculptures, as in Saint Paul, Sapporo, and Harbin, and snow gardens in selected parks, as Noguchi did in his beautiful earthwork design for Riverside Park in New York City.

创造性的居民设计竞赛甚至可能鼓励人们创造出有趣的冰雕,像在圣保罗、札幌和哈尔滨,人们在经由选择的公园进行雪雕创造,其中突出的例子是野口为纽约河畔公园做的美仑美奂的土方工程的设计。

④ On the other hand, for some long-time residents of the sun bell who never have been to the North in the winter, experiencing our White Christmas can be most memorable and enjoyable. Why couldn't some initiatives, such as sister cities programs be explored?

另一方面,对于长期居住在阳光充足地带,从没在冬季时期去过北方的居民来说,经历一个白色圣诞节一定是难以忘怀、令人愉快的。为什么我们就不能探讨一些像联谊城计划这样的倡议呢?

Phrases and Patterns

1. adapt to 适应

The prickly cacti adapt to the arid whether.

多刺的仙人掌适应干燥的气候。

Some southerners have already adapted to the cold whether of the north after several months.

几个月后一些南方人已经适应了北方寒冷的气候。

2. do away with 废除;去掉

We should do away with ridiculous rules and regulations.

我们应该废除荒唐可笑的规章制度。

The ice sculpture and snow sculpture can do away with the tediousness and dullness of winter.

冰雕和雪雕能赶走冬天的沉闷和单调。

Questions

1. What are the common problems associated with northern cities in the winter?
2. What can be done to overcome these problems and to make our downtowns and inner cities more livable in the winter?

10.2　Lowertown—a Case Study
个案研究——圣保罗"低城区"的改造

Lowertown, one-third of the downtown district of Saint Paul, has been undergoing extensive redevelopment since late 1978. Through the initiative of Mayor George Latimer, and a grant of $10 million from the McKnight Foundation, a new urban village has been created.

There are seven key elements to our Redevelopment Program. Within this framework, we have applied, where possible, some of the significant findings uncovered by Winter City studies.

Our concept includes the following key elements:

(1) retains the character of the district through sensitive rehabilitation and in-fill development, rather than massive clearance and urban renewal 12 blocks have been designated as a historic district[①];

(2) creates new job opportunities and minimizes displacement of people and businesses. 5,000 new jobs was the original goal;

(3) creates diverse housing for the widest possible range of income

groups: from affordable single room occupancy to luxury penthouses, from artist lofts to senior citizen housing. 3,000 housing units is our goal;

(4) provides needed amenities, including neighborhood services, restaurants, shops, physical exercise, recreation, and cultural facilities and programs;

(5) easy and convenient pedestrian access to and from the downtown core, good transit service, and freeways to and from all sections of the region;

(6) creates a district where arts flourish rather than diminish during the redevelopment process;

(7) strives for energy conservation, and explores alternative energy sources where feasible.

Above all, the corporation utilizes public/private partnership with the City and business community, rather than heavily relying on federal subsidies. Unlike the Bedford Styvesant Town Corporation created by the Ford Foundation in the 1960s and focusing primarily on housing, or the Downtown Milwaukee Development Corporation focusing mainly on the revitalization of Grand Avenue. LRC has many diverse social and economic objectives. It attempts to build a lively, colorful, diverse community, rather than merely relying on financing of projects. This is perhaps where the program differs from many other redevelopment programs, and permits us to test or apply new knowledge, such as that on winter city living.

In the beginning, the Lowertown program met with skepticism from some, and over-expectation from others. It also ran into the economic recession in the early 1980s, and other problems. Fortunately, the economy has recovered. After more than seven years of effort, the program has gradually overcome its initial problems, and attracted more and more investors from the Twin Cities and around the country.

Often, the recruitment of developers takes a great deal of time. It took a year to convince a leading Philadelphia developer to invest in Lowertown. Once they believed in Saint Paul, they acquired three buildings in successive purchases, and are now making a $50 million investment in Lowertown.

As the corporation develops the "urban village" in Lowertown, it also advances a number of the following Livable Winter City ideas. Some of them were carried over from existing city policies; others were new ideas initiated in Lowertown.

(1) To provide greater accessibility to, from, and within Lowertown, Saint Paul's Skyway system of second-level pedestrian walkways, covering over 30 downtown blocks, was extended to the area. People thus escaped the snow, ice and outdoor temperatures by using the heated walkways connecting the buildings. Thus far, in Lowertown alone, six skyways have been built, one committed, and two others are planned. The skyway connection has been instrumental in helping to reenergize Lowertown.

Recently, the tax credit for the rehabilitation of one historic building in Lowertown was denied by the National Park Service because of the adverse visual impact that the standard Saint Paul skyway bridge could have upon the historic building[2]. An appeal was made, and the credit was reinstated. However, Saint Paul was warned that no additional skyways may be built in the historic district if the rehabilitation tax credits were to be retained.

Preservationists and city planners in the Twin Cities are arranging a joint seminar with the National Park Service's staff to discuss the issues related to this matter and find a reasonable solution whereby the historic character is not adversely affected and downtown vitality is maintained.

(2) District steam heating was extended throughout Lowertown. Thus far, more than 20 buildings have been connected to the system. It

has been estimated that the system can cut by as much as one half the energy consumption of buildings previously served by individual boilers. It also assures these buildings of service, no matter how the energy situation changes in the future.

(3) To minimize the gloom and depressed feeling of winter skies, atriums were added to many buildings to light up indoor spaces. Almost every mixed-use project in Lowertown has such an amenity, including several dramatic indoor places, such as the seven storey galleria at the new Galtier Plaza, which can be actively used in the winter, and the great halls in the Union Depot and the First Trust Center. Without building a superdome, as the Ghermezians did in West Edmonton, downtown Saint Paul is very alive in the winter, as the skyways and the atriums complement each other and form a very livable city.

(4) Twenty of thirty nine buildings in the district were retrofitted so far. This not only preserves these historic landmarks, but also helps to save a great deal of energy, as experiences thus far have proven.

(5) To make winter life easier for those who use daily bus transportation, a number of ornamental metal, glass-walled bus shelters were installed. If they were heated, they would offer even more comfort in the winter[3].

Historic lights were installed for the central nine block area, which provides a warm glow on winter nights and strengthens the area's identity all year around. There are requests to extend this successful program to other parts of Lowertown.

(6) To overcome the restrictions on outdoor exercise imposed by winter climates, a new YMCA with extensive exercise facilities and swimming pool was provided. YMCA membership has quadrupled as a result, and has also proven to be helpful in attracting more new residents to the area.

The Lowertown Program has brought substantial benefits to the community. To date, more than $275 million has been invested, with another $100 million in the advanced planning stage. Aside from the 3,400 construction jobs, when these 35 projects are completed, it will mean 7,900 jobs, or a net increase of 4,300 jobs for the affected blocks. The city's tax base in the area will have more than quadrupled, and over 1,400 housing units will be built. Besides housing, Lowertown projects include offices, a new hotel, YMCA, Farmers Market, restaurants, five cinemas, art galleries, a new television station, a major festival market, and a host of other amenities.

Words and Expressions

penthouse ['penthaus] *n.* 小棚屋；雨篷
revitalization [riːˌvaɪtəlaɪˈzeɪʃən;-lɪˈz-] *n.* 新生；复兴
skepticism ['skeptisizəm] *n.* 怀疑论
recession [rɪˈseʃən] *n.* 撤回；退回；退后；工商业之衰退；不景气
amenity [əˈmiːniti] *n.* 宜人；礼仪
atrium ['ɑːtriəm] *n.* 中庭；心房
galleria [ˌɡæləˈriə] *n.* 风雨商业街廊
quadruple ['kwɔdrupl] *v.* 使成四倍
YMCA (abbr. = Young Men's Christian Association) 基督教青年会

Difficult Sentences

① Retains the character of the district through sensitive rehabilitation and in-fill development, rather than massive clearance and urban renewal 12 blocks have been designated as a historic district.
通过微妙细致的复建和填充式的发展保持区域的特性，而不是大规模的拆毁，其中城市重建的 12 个街区被指定为具有历史意义的地区。

② Recently, the tax credit for the rehabilitation of one historic building in was denied by the National Park Service because of the adverse visual impact that the standard Saint Paul skyway bridge could have upon the historic building.

近来，为重建一个有历史意义的建筑所需要的税款信贷被国家公园服务机构否决了，因为圣保罗天桥对这个有历史意义的建筑有着不利的视觉影响。

③ To make winter life easier for those who use daily bus transportation, a number of ornamental metal, glass-walled bus shelters were installed. If they were heated, they would offer even more comfort in the winter.

为了让每天乘坐公交车的人冬天能过得舒适些，兴建了许多带有装饰性的金属和玻璃墙壁的公交候车棚。如果候车棚能被装上取暖系统的话，就会带给人们更多的舒适。

Phrases and Patterns

1. meet with 偶然遇见；碰到；获得
   Such flowers are rarely met with in the northern country.
   这种花在北方难得一见。
   The design has met with approval.
   这项设计已获批准。
2. so far 迄今为止；就此范围(程度)来说
   The works are doing things no one has so far attempt.
   工人们正在做以前没有人尝试过的事情。
   He has designed just one garden so far.
   他迄今只设计过一个花园。

Questions

1. What are the seven key elements to the Redevelopment Program?
2. Summarize the Livable Winter City ideas.
3. What are the substantial benefits the Lowertown Program has brought to the community?

10.3 Vernacular Agricultural Townships/Villages in Harbin Region: Conscious Response to Nature
哈尔滨本土的农业乡镇/乡村:依照自然条件而建

What those farmers who emigrated from Central China faced first was the harsh climate as well as the scarcity of energy for heating. Under such hard conditions, they were forced to respond to the climatic elements as much as possible through careful design of their settlements by developing south-facing slopes, building greenhouses and maximizing passive solar gain[①].

Settlement Location and Structure

Most of the vernacular villages or towns were built on the sunny slopes, with a mound of trees raised behind the houses to protect the settlements from the North wind chill, and absorb solar heat as much as possible. These vernacular villages or townships usually evolved slowly over long periods of time. In the beginning, there might be only one or two pioneers' houses there. The followers came and built their houses beside the existing ones. They followed the Chinese custom of living close together in the pattern of a village, although their farmland might spread out. It seems that the unfriendly climate made such a kind of community pattern all the more valuable.

It is interesting that this evolutionary development resulted in an extraordinarily similar pattern. At first, they all built along an East-West direction main street, with all the houses facing South. When the main street was somehow long enough, they began to build along a second street in front of or behind the main street (and then the third and the fourth or more went in the same way) while the main street kept expanding. The connecting road between these streets seldom ran straight through the village. One reason was surely to prevent the North cold wind blowing through. For the same reason, at the rear of the settlement, there was usually forest.

The village center was usually in the middle of the main street, providing easy access for all the citizens, with some shopping, recreation, and institutional buildings.

Site Planning

The farmers usually put their houses on the upper-north end of their plots, leaving much of the vacant lot on the south side, where most of the outdoor activities would happen. A relatively narrower back yard with trees and fences gave a little protection for the house from north winds. On the front yard, a few meters just in front of the house was a courtyard, actually the extension of interior living space. Sometimes, a storage area was built on the west side or both west and east sides to form a complete "sun lock" with a much warmer micro-climate than in an ordinary open space. Farther south from the house usually there was a vegetable garden and livestock or haystack areas. Some families might build a simple greenhouse to grow vegetables from early spring. Through these arrangements, most of the daily outdoor activities could occur in a relatively protected space. For some big families, all the four sides might be built up to form a courtyard, sometimes even more than one of them. However, the house on the north side facing the sunny courtyard always used the courts as part of the main living space.

House Design

The individual house usually took the form of a rectangle in plan to get the largest volume with shortest exterior wall. Thick walls surrounded all sides of the house except the south side or the side facing the courtyard. The south exposure wall of the house was glazed with big windows, to allow as much sunshine as possible into the house during daytime. The heating system of the house is the most special feature of the vernacular house. Through the careful design of this system, the fuel used for cooking was also fully used for heating. The residual heat of the cooking fuel was made to flow through the built-in radiator devices as long as possible[2]. There are two kinds of devices: one is a heating wall, which is a hollow wall for the heated air to pass through; another is more important and even now is still widely used in the countryside, called a "kang"; it is a part of a raised floor used as a bed in the night with canals under the surface for the heated air to pass through. In the earlier times, when little other heating energy was available, it was located next to the window, so it is the best heated part of the house, perhaps the only real warm area in winter. People used it as a bed at night, with thick cotton-wadded quilts on to keep warm. During daytime, most family activities used to happen on it. When a guest dropped in, offering the warmer end of a kang to sit in was considered as a special treatment. It was vitally important for small children and the elderly to spend time here in wintertime.

Another device also played some role in adjusting the microclimate of the vernacular house. It is the vegetable cellar dug under the living room floor. It can accumulate heat energy deep into the earth under the floor, and release it in the winter. In the summer, it can cool the room a little, as well.

Special Winter Activities

These farmers not only retreated from the winter elements, but also derived fun from them. This was mostly done through a series of winter activities. Winter is the time when traditional festivals come into focus. The Chinese Spring Festival (about the beginning of February) is the major one. This period was also the winter break time for farmers, when the harshest part of winter is just about to terminate. People developed numerous means to celebrate the festival. Every family used to erect a colorfully decorated "tree" in their yard, and hang out a lantern on it at night. The house was also decorated colorfully inside and out. Color and light were used as important ways to create a warm atmosphere in the harsh winter. People organized outdoor group folk dancing to amuse themselves, which became the major attraction. These activities usually lasted for half a month, until another climax, the Lantern Festival, came, which used to be a great exhibition of all kinds of lanterns, some of them made out of ice. For children, building snowmen, snow shoeing, sleighing, and whirling were the popular activities. All these created a warm, exhilarating atmosphere, mitigating the unfriendly winter effect <u>in a meaningful fashion</u>[③].

People also prepared especially good food for the festival period. This corresponds to the Chinese medicine's view that winter is the most suitable time for people to take tonic and nourishing food to build up a healthy system[④].

Words and Expressions

scarcity ['skɛəsiti] *n.* 缺乏；不足
slope [sləup] *n.* 斜坡；斜面；倾斜
institutional [ˌinsti'tjuːʃənəl] *adj.* 制度上的
microclimate ['maikrəuklaimit] *n.* [气]小气候(指森林、城市、洞穴等局部地区的气候)
haystack ['heistæk] *n.* 干草堆
residual [ri'zidjuəl] *adj.* 剩余的；残留的
radiator ['reidieitə] *n.* 散热器；水箱；冷却器；电暖炉；辐射体
quill [kwil] *n.* 羽茎；大翎毛；羽绒被
retreat [ri'triːt] *v.* 撤退；退却
terminate ['təːmineit] *v.* 停止；结束，终止
erect [i'rekt] *vt.* 使竖立；使直立；树立；建立
lantern ['læntən] *n.* 灯笼；提灯；幻灯；信号；天窗

exhilarating [iɡˈziləreitiŋ] *adj.* 令人喜欢的；爽快的；使人愉快的
mitigate [ˈmitigeit] *v.* 减轻
tonic [ˈtɔnik] *adj.* 激励的；滋补的
cotton-wadded 用棉花填充的
Spring Festival 春节
Lantern Festival 花灯节

Difficult Sentences

① Under such hard conditions, they were forced to respond to the climatic elements as much as possible through careful design of their settlements by developing south-facing slopes, building greenhouses and maximizing passive solar gain.
在这样恶劣的条件下，他们被迫要对气候因素尽可能多地作出反应，尽心地设计他们的住所，开发利用南向的坡地，建造温室，最大化地利用太阳能。

② The heating system of the house is the most special feature of the vernacular house. Through the careful design of this system, the fuel used for cooking was also fully used for heating. The residual heat of the cooking fuel was made to flow through the built-in radiator devices as long as possible.
房屋的取暖系统是本地房屋的最具特色的地方。经过对取暖系统的精心设计，燃料在用来做饭的同时也用来取暖。做饭剩余的燃料热量通过内置的散热装置还可以尽可能长时间地利用。

③ For children, building snowmen, snow shoeing, sleighing, and whirling were the popular activities. All these created a warm, exhilarating atmosphere, mitigating the unfriendly winter effect in a meaningful fashion.
对孩子来说，堆雪人、穿雪鞋、滑雪橇、抽陀螺都是受欢迎的活动。所有的这些创造了一个温暖的、令人愉快的氛围，以一种有意义的方式减轻了冬天气候带来的不利影响。

④ This corresponds to the Chinese medicine's view that winter is the most suitable time for people to take tonic and nourishing food to build up a healthy system.

这符合中国医学的观点,冬天是进补和吃有营养的食物养出健康身体的最佳时间。

Phrases and Patterns

1. provide... with 装备;供给

   In the past, northerners must provide houses with chimneys.

   在过去,北方人必须给房子装烟囱。

   Activity centers provide old people with all kinds of entertainment activities in winter.

   活动中心在冬季为老年人提供多种多样的娱乐活动。

2. in a... fashion 以……方式

   Landscape designers plan the whole city in an orderly fashion.

   景观设计者把整个城市规划的井井有条。

   They settle heating problems in an effective fashion.

   他们以有效的方法处理取暖问题。

Questions

1. How to understand "Conscious Response to Nature" in Harbin Region?
2. Discuss the following aspects in detail— 1) Settlement 2) Location and Structure 3) Site Planning 4) House Design 5) Special Winter Activities.

10.4 General Structure of Harbin: Compact Pattern and Multiple-function Divisions

哈尔滨总体构架:密集型结构与多功能分区

In consideration of the frigid regional condition, as well as of a land saving demand, the general planning structure of Harbin took the form of compact layout. Except for an industrial administrative division, two county, and four suburban industrial precincts, all six other administrative divisions are concentrated together with rivers, railway, and green belt as separation elements①.

What is important is that each division is a multiple function district, with its own set of housing, shopping and services, schools, and job opportunities. They are developed according to the schemes of the city planning agency. If we take shopping and services development as an example, they are in the form of a net consisting of a number of hierarchical levels of centers. The first is a downtown shopping center. Because railways divide the city into a number of parts, the interconnection between these parts became a problem. One result is that the downtown is split into three parts, of which each is complete but with a different character. The second level is the sub-centre. The third level is the neighborhood centre. The last level is the grocery stores in the clusters of housing or under the apartment buildings. In commercial facility planning in 1985, more emphasis was put on the local levels: the sub-centres were planned to increase from 8 to 18 in number, while the number of neighborhood centres expanded from 30 to 67. Small grocery stores at the housing cluster level were encouraged, too. For the newly developed neighborhoods, national standards demand certain amounts of shopping and services buildings, schools and cultural facilities to be built together with housing. Through such a hierarchy, people's needs for shopping and services can be solved at the local level as much as possible. Daily needs can be solved within easy walking distance, while decreasing the pressure on the downtown and the transportation.

The designs of these centres and subcentres respond to the weather. Underpasses and skyways are provided where traffic is heavy. As a response to weather, Harbin boasts of extremely large department stores, which are at the cores of most centres. Some small shops are interconnected from inside. This allows shopping activities to happen indoors as much as possible in the winter, while not abandoning the streets. Some old markets are in the form of mid-block malls and courtyards where people can stroll inside free of the disturbance of traffic and unfavorable weather elements[②].

In terms of green open space systems, except for the existing city forestry and parks, considering the wind direction in winter, a buffer of trees is planned on the periphery of the city, to act as a shelterbelt.

Words and Expressions

compact ['kɔmpækt] adj. 紧凑的；紧密的；简洁的
frigid ['fridʒid] adj. 寒冷的；冷淡的；(妇女)缺乏性感的
precinct ['priːsiŋkt] n. 区域；围地；范围；界限；选区
hierarchical [ˌhaiə'rɑːkikəl] adj. 分等级的
facility [fə'siliti] n. 容易；简易；灵巧；熟练；便利
underpass ['ʌndəpɑːs] n. 地下道；高架桥下通道
stroll [strəul] v. 闲逛；漫步；跋涉于
disturbance [dis'təːbəns] n. 骚动；动乱；打扰；干扰；骚乱；搅动
buffer ['bʌfə] n. 缓冲器
periphery [pə'rifəri] n. 外围
multiple-function 多功能的

Difficult Sentences

① Except for an industrial administrative division, two county, and four suburban industrial precincts, all six other administrative divisions are concentrated together with rivers, railway, and green bell as separation elements.
  除了一个工业管理区之外，两个城镇、四个郊外工业区域、另外六个管理区都和河流、铁路、绿化带集中在一起，分区而制。

② Some old markets are in the form of mid-block malls and courtyards where people can stroll inside free of the disturbance of traffic and unfavorable weather elements.

一些旧有的市场是以街道中间的步行街和庭院的形式存在,在那里人们可以闲逛漫步,而不受交通和恶劣天气因素的影响。

Phrases and Patterns

1. Except for 除了……外;除去
   The room was dark except for the light coming in through a crack in the door.
   除了从门缝中透过的一丝光亮以外,整个房间是黑漆漆的。
   The winter of Harbin is full of pleasure except for the cold whether.
   哈尔滨的冬天虽说天气寒冷,可是充满无穷的乐趣。

2. act as 起……作用;充当
   The electric wire acts as a fence to keep the animals in.
   这电线起栅栏的作用,把动物关在里面。
   The mountains act as a barrier to keep out wind.
   山岭起屏障作用,能挡风。

Questions

1. What are the four different levels of centers according to the shopping and services development?
2. Explain how the designs of these centres and subcentres respond to the weather.

10.5 Infrastructure Aspects of Harbin: a Few Highlights
哈尔滨基础设施的一些特点

Transportation, snow clearing from the streets, and heating systems are some major issues faced by all winter cities[①]. Now great efforts are put on them in Harbin.

Transportation and Snow Clearing

All over China, the major daily movement methods for citizens are public transportation and bicycles. Bus routes reach each and every neighborhood. The high density neighborhoods make public transportation very efficient. Now a subway system has finished channel construction. Bicycles get special rights-of-way along major roads, sometimes separated from motor vehicles with planting beds. This <u>makes sense</u> especially in the winter when roads are slippery and accidents tend to increase.

In summer, nearly 70 % of people use bicycles, but in winter, because of cold weather and traffic hazards due to slippery roads, some people change to public transportation, resulting in crowding and longer waiting times. To solve the imbalance of public transportation use between summer and winter, the city government takes various approaches, such as flexible working hours to decrease the pressure of rush hours, reducing headways to enhance the public transportation, together with increasing the capacity of and routes for public transportation.

Though Harbin gets <u>much less</u> snow than most other winter cities, severe difficulty is created for transportation. The extremely cold temperature and the pressure of wheels combine to turn the snow into ice right after fresh snowfall. The roads become slippery and accident rates soar. Plowing away snow in good time is definitely important. However, because of the low temperature, salting to melt the snow does not work. To remove the snow from roads as soon as possible, citizens are usually organized to do that manually after a snow storm. Each administrative unit assumes responsibility for a length of street each winter. Mechanization of snow-clearing has been taken as the development direction, and a related program is in effect. On some sloped sites which have more accident hazards, sand is distributed on streets before the plowing can commence.

Heating and Gas System

Heating is a major issue for winter cities, closely related to such highlighted issues as environmental protection and energy saving. Scattered heating methods and coal as the major fuel are still the bigger problems in Harbin[2]. It is not only inconvenient, but low efficiency results in serious pollution. Great effort has been placed to overcome the problems, and centralized heating systems are taken as the development direction. With "planned" development, centralized heating systems have been guaranteed for all the new neighborhoods. However, compared with the whole city, they still account for only a small part.

Changing the types of fuels and scattered heating methods to save energy and decrease pollution has become part of a national policy. Steps are being taken towards the centralization of heating systems and to full use of gas for cooking. In Harbin, utilization of after-heat from existing power plants as a source for large area central heating systems is being developed[3]. Two alternative plans have been proposed in the city's heating system planning. One is building two more heat and power plants together with existing power plants, forming a heating system pattern that relies mainly on the heat and power plants' after-heat while using neighborhood central heating systems as back-up. Another relies mainly on moderate-temperature hot water from mini-nuclear plants while using regional heating systems as auxiliary sources. Now feasibility analysis and comparisons of the two approaches are in progress.

Only a small portion of families have piped gas for cooking, while others get canned gas or still use coal. This causes a lot of inconvenience to peoples' lives, especially during the winter. Now the extension projects of gas plants and piping systems are going on. Middle range plans are to build a new gas plant with the daily productivity of 1,600,000 cubic meters on the site of a nearby coal mine. The major transmission pipe will be 245 kilometers long. When these projects are finished they will make life much more convenient and reduce the pollution which is most pronounced during winter.

Words and Expressions

hazard ['hæzəd] *n.* 冒险；危险；冒险的事
manually ['mænjuəli] *adv.* 用手
auxiliary [ɔ:g'ziljəri] *adj.* 辅助的；补助的
pronounced [prə'naunst] *adj.* 显著的；明确的

Difficult Sentences

① Transportation, snow clearing from the streets, and heating systems are some major issues faced by all winter cities.
交通运输、清除街道上的积雪和供暖系统是城市冬季所面临的一些主要的问题。

② Heating is a major issue for winter cities, closely related to such highlighted issues as environmental protection and energy saving. Scattered heating methods and coal as the major fuel are still the bigger problems in Harbin.
供暖是冬季城市的一个主要问题，它与环境保护、能源节约这样的突出的问题密切相关。在哈尔滨分散供暖的方法以及做主要燃料用的煤仍然是个大问题。

③ Steps are being taken towards the centralization of heating systems and to full use of gas for cooking. In Harbin, utilization of after-heat from existing power plants as a source for large area central heating systems is being developed.
人们正在采取一些方法逐渐实现集中供热以及充分利用煤气做饭。在哈尔滨尝试利用现有发电站的余热为更广泛的地区提供

集中供热系统的资源。

Phrases and Patterns

1. makes sense 讲得通；有意义。
   In my opinion, the abstract sculpture in the center of the city doesn't make sense.
   在我看来,城市中心的抽象雕塑毫无意义。
   This hedge is set back too far from the sidewalk to function as an outdoor wall and pedestrians have cut across the corner, destroying the lawn, that is to say, the design of this outdoor wall doesn't make sense.
   这排用做室外墙的树篱离人行道太远,路人抄近路穿过拐角,破坏了草坪,也就是说这个室外墙的设计没有意义。

2. much less 更不用说；更何况
   He hadn't been to Harbin, much less see the ice sculpture.
   他没来过哈尔滨,更谈不上看冰雕了。
   They didn't learn architecture, much less design building structure.
   他们没学过建筑学,更不用说设计建筑结构了。

Questions

1. What are the highlights in Transportation and Snow Clearing?
2. What are the highlights in Heating and Gas System?

10.6 Residential Environment of Harbin
哈尔滨的居住环境

In winter cities, home is the last refuge and the most important element. Careful planning and design for residential environment is a key point for improving livability in winter cities.

To improve the winter livability of residential environments as well as other aspects, we must start from the country's basic social and economic conditions, and the corresponding general demand and possibilities of housing development. The country has just begun to recover from continuous political upheaval and economic disability; funds available for public housing development are quite limited, and therefore keeping low construction costs is significant. Until now, the housing in our country has been basically "public", although reforms have begun towards the direction of commercialization to improve the investment efficiency. Because of the long time of a stagnated state of housing development and a rapid increase of population, the shortage condition is terribly serious. Providing enough quantity of housing as soon as possible has the utmost priority. The national goal for urban housing is that by the end of this century, each family is to have an apartment, and average living space of 8 square meters per person. However, land is scarce in China compared with her huge population, and saving land is a basic policy of the nation. All urban housing must be high density while certain fundamental living environment standards must be guaranteed. National "Neighborhood Planning and Design Standards" stipulate the quality and quantity standard of the neighborhood, such as land use quota, infrastructure and shopping, services, schools, location, sunshine and ventilation, open space and green, etc. According to the basic conditions mentioned above, for a considerable period of time, multi-storey (5 to 7) walk-up apartment buildings will be the basic urban housing type, to get the high density and keep low construction cost. Pooling funds for "planned development" according to neighborhood theory and hierarchical models is the basic method for all new housing development[①].

Harbin's housing condition is even more serious among the large cities of the country. Located at high latitude, it confronts more challenges on meeting all the goals than other cities, such as higher insulation, heating demand, and sunshine demand that is difficult to achieve in the condition of high density and low sunlight angles during the winter.

Because of the tremendous energy input in the winter environment, together with the economical considerations, efforts are inevitably put more on the individual buildings and the interior environments first, often with the sacrifice of outdoor open spaces[2]. The insulation of buildings receive tremendous attention. The National " Civil Building Energy-Saving Standard (heating necessary for residential building portion)" stipulates the insulation behavior standard and heat absorption standard for different areas. Harbin, as other cities that need heating during winter, redesigned its typical construction details, with new techniques and products for high quality insulation being invented and applied. In terms of building design, the layout and parameters of apartment buildings, such as shape, number of storeys, etc. are often decided according to the insulation standards. The area of exterior wall is reduced to the least to minimize the heat loss.

Few cold region dwellers do not know how important sunshine is to them during the winter, especially to such user groups as the old and infants who are most vulnerable and less capable of going outside for sunshine. According to research about housing sanitation by the Harbin Architectural and Civil Engineering Institute and Harbin Medical Institute in the 1970s quite a few physical diseases happened among children and the elderly, such as osteomalacia and arthritis highly related to the lack of sunshine and activity, to say nothing of the psychological influences. However, because of the lengthy extreme weather, nearly half a year is not suitable for daily outdoor activities in Harbin. Introduction of sunshine for families throughout the coldest period of winter is highly desired by citizens, and has become a most important standard in neighborhood and building design. The national standard for neighborhood design is that not less than one hour of sunshine into south-oriented first floor rooms is guaranteed on the Winter Solstice day. In the building design, guaranteeing each family <u>at least</u> one south exposure orientation is a common practice.

It has become common knowledge that the key for the elderly to retain health and long life lies in activity; for children to grow up healthily also depends on outdoor activities and sunshine. Since most of the open spaces located in the neighborhood are unused for months in the winter, how to extend the outdoor activity season is another major issue related to winter residential environment. To improve the microclimate of these open spaces, put them under intense control of residents, and increase the accessibility of them are some measures to help reach these goals.

The traditional housing type in Harbin is mainly the three or four storey town house, built along the periphery of a small block or around a courtyard, leaving the space in the middle as communal open space. The gallery and staircases to each family facing the yard, which play an important role in organizing the spaces, reduce the wind chill in the winter, and are used as communication places for residents living around the yard. In the 1950s large numbers of plan-developed neighborhoods usually took the form of five storey apartment buildings. Staircases and corridors were placed inside, but still kept the form of courtyards. Comparatively, the south exposure rooms got best sunshine conditions, and are most popular. With the interiors receiving more emphasis, and because of industrialized construction demands and economical considerations, the neighborhoods built later were changed into the pattern of row after row of slab blocks with the court-yard being lost[3]. They were built all over the country. However, with the rapid increase of urban population and abundant development, land is getting more and more scarce, and densities higher and higher. The result is the sacrifice of sunshine quality, dull neighborhood form, and unfriendly outdoor space with severe windchill in the winter.

Under such conditions, great effort is put on the research and design of neighborhoods which are efficient in land use and livable under different local conditions. The old courtyard form is being re-evaluated. Its merits such as land-saving and better outdoor environment get more and more attention. The research and experiments about neighborhood patterns suitable to Harbin region, performed by a few faculty members in the Urban Planning and Design Program of Harbin Architectural and Civil Engineering Institute, are quite interesting. They give comprehensive consideration to the natural condition and urban pattern of Harbin, land use efficiency as well as indoor and outdoor environment quality with particular consideration to winter. Based on the character of Harbin region that the radiation effect and height angle of sun in a few hours around noon are not much different during the winter, and 15 to 20 or even 30 degrees deviation from south direction is not much different for rooms to receive satisfactory sunshine, the apartment buildings are arranged in two directions deviated from south while the sunshine standard is fulfilled. The courtyard pattern and the friendly outdoor environment to the neighborhood is achieved through such arrangement. Sun pockets are formed at the corner of two buildings and wind is buffered out. It also gets good land use efficiency.

At the individual building level, some effort has been made as well. The balconies are glazed into a greenhouse during the winter. The stepped form of apartments was tried to increase the private courtyards on the roofs, which is easy to access and proved to be in much heavier use in the winter than the ordinary open space. In the assignment of apartments, families with elderly or handicapped members get priority for first floor with private courtyards.

Words and Expressions

refuge ['refjuːdʒ] n. 庇护；避难；避难所
upheaval [ʌp'hiːvəl] n. 剧变
stagnate ['stægneit] v. （使）淤塞；（使）停滞；（使）沉滞；（使）变萧条
stipulate ['stipjuleit] v. 规定；保证
quota ['kwəutə] n. 配额；限额
ventilation [venti'leiʃən] n. 通风；流通空气
insulation [ˌinsju'leiʃən] n. 绝缘
stipulate ['stipjuleit] v. 规定；保证
parameter [pə'ræmitə] n. 参数；参量；<口>起限定作用的因素
vulnerable ['vʌlnərəb(ə)l] adj. 易受攻击的；易受……的攻击
sanitation [sæni'teiʃnə] n. 卫生；卫生设施
osteomalacia [ˌɔstiəumə'leiʃiə] n. [医] 骨软化
arthritis [aː'θraitis] n. 关节炎
solstice ['sɔlstis] n. [天] 至；至日；至点
periphery [pə'rifəri] n. 外围
scarce [skɛəs] adj. 缺乏的；不足的；稀有的；不充足的
merit [merit] v. 有益于
deviation [ˌdiːvi'eiʃən] n. 背离
balcony ['bælkəni] n. 阳台；包厢；（戏院）楼厅
handicapped ['hændikæpt] adj. 残废的
Winter Solstice 冬至
Civil Engineering 土木工程

Difficult Sentences

① Pooling funds for "planned development" according to neighborhood theory and hierarchical models is the basic method for all new housing development.
根据邻近理论和分等级的模式集合基金为"有计划的发展"投资，这是所有的新住宅开发的基本方法。

② Because of the tremendous energy input in the winter environment, together with the economical considerations, efforts are inevitably put more on the individual buildings and the interior environments first, often with the sacrifice of outdoor open spaces.

因为在冬季要作出巨大的能源投入,另外再出于经济上的考虑,人们的注意力不可避免地首先放在私人住宅和内部环境上,往往没有顾及户外空间。

③ Because of industrialized construction demands and economical considerations, the neighborhoods built later were changed into the pattern of row after row of slab blocks with the court-yard being lost.

出于工业化建筑的要求和节约的考虑,后建的居民区住宅变成了一排排的混凝土路面的街区模式,传统的院落逐渐消失。

Phrases and Patterns

1. compare with 与……相比

   The outdoor space compared with the indoor space isn't regarded highly.

   与室内空间相比,室外空间并不被重视。

   Responsible engineers always compare buildings which is ongoing with the working drawing.

   负责任的工程师总是把正在建设的建筑物和施工图纸加以比较。

2. at least 至少

   This program requires at least two months.

   这个项目至少需要两个月。

   Residential Environment should be peace and quiet at least.

   居住环境至少应该和睦安静。

Questions

1. Summarize how to improve the Residential Environment.
2. How to solve the problem of sunshine?

10.7 Winter Image and Activities in Open Spaces: Match the Summer with Winter
开放空间的冬季景观和活动:冬夏交融

With its moderate temperature, beautiful tree-lined boulevards, moderate-scaled street-scape with exotic style buildings, Shonghua River swimming and boating facilities, ten kilometer long waterfront esplanade, Sun Island picnic forest, as well as such famous activities as Summer in Harbin Concert Series, Harbin is always a charming city in the summer[①]. It not only provides great conditions for citizens to fully experience the brief summer life after a long coarse winter, but also attracts large numbers of tourists.

However, when the long and fierce winter comes, most of the charm associated with summer is gone. Most people are confined to the home or to limited interior recreation facilities, dreaming about the summer, and leave the outdoor spaces almost dead[②]. How one can improve the image of winter in open spaces so that they could keep attracting people during the winter becomes a special issue for winter cities. In Harbin, the efforts are mainly made toward minimizing the negative image of winter while exploring the positive one and activity opportunities as much as possible.

Color and light play important roles in dealing with the winter image. When the winter comes, most leaves have fallen, and grass is faded. The land is either covered with stark white snow or appears as only grayish pavement or earth. The buildings stand out from the trees. In such a situation, the forms of buildings and other hard landscaping elements are heightened in their impact. The winterscape most likely appears colorless and lifeless. Bringing back color into open spaces, especially onto buildings, which usually take most of the area of peoples' vision, is important to make winter appear less harsh.

Harbin has the tradition to use warm and bright colors on buildings. Bright yellow is the prevailing color of the city. Now, more and more new types of facing materials and weather-resistant plasters are produced, so more color is available. In the massively built neighborhood, each building is provided with a slightly different warm color, enriching the visual environment and enhancing the identity of each building.

Colorful decorations of streets with flags, lettering, lighting, windows, etc., especially in the pedestrian areas, play an important role, too. They create a warm atmosphere. During the winter night, brightness and color of street lights become significant. Warm-color bulbs are used all over the city. Efforts are also made to increase the use of evergreen trees on streets.

Special winter related attractions are also placed into public spaces to match those related with summer. For example, planting sculpture is a traditional attraction during summer on squares, front yards, and streets. In the winter, ice sculpture is used to replace them, usually in the same image. In these ways, the environment does not lose its charm because of the passing of summer.

Winter brings a lot of inconvenience to people's lives, but it also provides some unique fun. White snow-covered trees and land, fascinating icicles, delicate snow flakes, and various ice- and snow-related sports activities attract many people. They must be considered an advantage for winter cities, and public works should fully utilize them, keep them as public space, and make public open spaces lively communication places for people—even in winter.

In Harbin, such efforts are made. The annual Ice and Snow Festival, the biggest winter festival in China, is the major attraction of the season. It is held in the park. Trees or other special structures are sprayed with water, forming a fascinating winter world, canals are turned into ice rinks, children's play facilities are built with ice blocks, and the most attractive feature, hundreds of ice-carved lanterns, turn the winter night into a fascinating and hilarious scene. Some "mago" ice structures are as high as 15 meters. The festival itself lasts for a few days, but the ice-carved lantern show usually can last nearly three months.

The sport events held on the river are more significant to the winter life of citizens. Held by different organizations, they keep the river attractive and lively at least on the sunny winter days. Tobogganing down the slope of the river bank attracts crowds of children; ice-sailing is a popular sport for young people; icy-water swimming is the deed of the brave and attracts many viewers, horse-driven sleds provide a chance for urban dwellers to experience a little old countryside life, ice-skating, snow-shoes are all popular activities. To go farther from the city, one has also the opportunity to ski and even hunt.

Besides the ice-snow activities, a variety of events associated with those traditional festivals as Spring Festival and Lantern Festival, and the yearly held kite contest in the early spring are all chances for people to get out.

These winter activities and improved environment not only enhance winter life a great deal, but also stimulate the economic well-being of the city which used to be handicapped by the winter[3]. In the past, only summer was the popular season for tourists; now, as the reputation of the Ice and Snow Festival gets known, winter becomes even more popular. Last winter, the number of tourists only from foreign countries reached 23 thousands. The festivals also attracted many businessmen to Harbin. Exhibitions and trade shows are usually held to foster such activities. The winter becomes a resource for the city's economy.

Words and Expressions

boulevard ['buːlivaːd] *n.* <美>林荫大道

exotic [igˈzɔtik] *adj.* 异国情调的；外来的；奇异的
waterfront [ˈwɔːtəfrʌnt] *n.* 水边地码头区；滨水地区
esplanade [ˌespləˈneid] *n.* 平坦的空地；游憩场；散步路
stark [staːk] *adj.* 刻板的；十足的；赤裸的；荒凉的
heighten [ˈhaitn] *v.* 提高；升高
prevailing [priˈveiliŋ] *adj.* 占优势的；主要的；流行的
pedestrian [peˈdestriən] *adj.* 徒步的
icicle [ˈɔisikl] *n.* 垂冰；冰柱
sled [sled] *n.* 雪橇；摘棉
handicapped [ˈhændikæpt] *n. adj.* 残疾人；身体有缺陷的人；残废的
Ice and Snow Festival 冰雪节

Difficult Sentences

① With its moderate temperature, beautiful tree-lined boulevards, moderate-scaled street-scape with exotic style buildings, Shonghua River swimming and boating facilities, ten kilometer long waterfront esplanade, Sun Island picnic forest, as well as such famous activities as Summer in Harbin Concert Series. Harbin is always a charming city in the summer.
温暖宜人的气温，美丽而郁郁葱葱的林荫大道，到处都是异国情调的建筑物的不大不小的街景，松花江游泳和划船设施，万米长堤的江边步行街，太阳岛野餐树林，还有远近闻名的哈尔滨消夏系列音乐会，使得夏天的哈尔滨始终是一座迷人的城市。

② However, when the long and fierce winter comes, most of the charm associated with summer is gone. Most people are confined to the home or to limited interior recreation facilities, dreaming about the summer, and leave the outdoor spaces almost dead.
然而，当漫长而寒冷的冬季到来的时候，夏季所具有的魅力都消失了。大多数人被限制在家中或仅能从事有限的室内娱乐项目，人们怀念夏天，室外空间也没了生机。

③ These winter activities and improved environment not only enhance winter life a great deal, but also stimulate the economic well-being of the city which used to be handicapped by the winter.

这些冬季活动和不断改善的环境不仅大大提高了冬季生活质量，也刺激了经济的发展与繁荣，而在以往经济只能受困于冬季的季节因素。

Phrases and Patterns

1. confine to 局限于

   He confines his remarks to scientific management.

   他所讲的仅限于科学管理问题。

   They confine their topic to the outdoor art and man-made landscape.

   他们把话题限定在室外艺术和人造景观上。

2. match with 相配；相称

   The modern sculpture, combined with the fountain, matches with the residential surrounding.

   这个现代雕塑，再加上喷泉，与居住环境很相称。

   Landscape construction should match with the level of city development.

   景观建设应该与城市发展水平相称。

Questions

1. How can we improve the image of winter in open spaces so that they could keep attracting people during the winter?
2. What's the unique fun of winter in Harbin?
3. What is the major attraction of the winter season in Harbin? And explain in detail.

PART TWO
ACADEMIC INFORMATION

第二部分 专业学术信息

1. Academic Journals
专业学术期刊

（1）《城市规划》《China City Planning Review》
　　刊期：月刊
　　主办单位：中国城市规划学会
　　国内刊号：CN 11-2378/TU 国际刊号：ISSN 1002-1329
　　社址：北京市三河路9号中国城市规划设计研究院内小西楼
　　邮编：100037
　　电子邮件：cityplan@public.east.cn.net
　　联系电话：010-68343253

（2）《城市规划学刊》
　　刊期：双月刊
　　主办单位：同济大学建筑城市规划学院
　　国内刊号：CN31-1360/TU 国际刊号：ISSN1000-3363
　　社址：上海四平路1239号
　　邮编：200092
　　电子邮件：upforum@shtel.net.cn
　　联系电话：021-65983507 021-55570632
　　传真：021-65983507

（3）《国际城市规划》
　　刊期：双月刊
　　主办单位：中国城市规划设计研究院
　　国内刊号：CN11-5583/TU
　　社址：北京市三河路9号中国城市规划设计研究院 学术信息中心
　　邮编：100037
　　电子邮件：dofup@public.bta.net.cn
　　联系电话：010-68343240
　　传真：010-68343219

(4)《城市发展研究》
　　刊期:双月刊
　　主办单位:中国城市科学研究会
　　国内刊号:CN11-3504/TU
　　社址:北京百万庄建设部内
　　邮编:100835
　　电子邮件:urbanstudies@mail.cin.gov.cn；ebuds@263.net
　　联系电话:010-68394055
　　传真:010-68313149
(5)《规划师》
　　英文名称:Planners
　　刊期:月刊
　　主办单位:广西城乡规划设计院
　　国内刊号:CN45-1210/TU 国际刊号:ISSN1006-0022
　　社址:广西南宁市华东路39号
　　邮编:530011
　　电子邮件:planner@21cn.net
　　联系电话:0771-5863624
　　传真:0771-5884012
(6)《城乡建设》
　　刊期:月刊
　　主办单位:中华人民共和国建设部
　　国内刊号:CN 11-1618/D 国际刊号:ISSN 1002-8455
　　社址:北京市百万庄三里河路9号
　　邮编:100037
　　电子邮件:cxjs1956@126.com
　　联系电话:010-68393235
　　传真:010-68393235
(7)《小城镇建设》
　　刊期:月刊

主办单位:中国建筑设计研究院
国内刊号:CN 11-4418/TU 国际刊号:ISSN 1002-8439
社址:北京市西城区车公庄大街19号
邮编:100044
联系电话:010-68314486

(8)《现代城市研究》
刊期:月刊
主办单位:南京城市科学研究会
国内刊号:CN 32-1612/TU 国际刊号:ISSN 1009-6000
社址:南京市广州路183号
邮编:210024
电子邮件:Editor@ mur. cn urbnrech@ 163. com
联系电话::025-83730794、83730851
传真:025-83278113

(9)《城市建筑》
刊期:半月刊
主办单位:哈尔滨工业大学建筑设计研究院/哈尔滨工业大学建筑学院
国内刊号:CN23-1528/TU
社址:哈尔滨市南岗区海河路202号
邮编:150090
电子邮件:ua@ ua2004. com
联系电话:0451-86283778
传真:0451-86289326

(10) BERKELEY PLANNING JOURNAL
ISSN：1047-5192
Dept. of City & Regional Planning 228 Wurster Hall #1850
University of California Berkeley, CA 94720-1850
email：bpj@ berkeley. edu

(11) JOURNAL OF PLANNING EDUCATION AND RESEARCH

ISSN: 0739-456X

Department of City and Regional Planning, University of California
Berkeley, CA 94720-1850

email: jpereditors@berkeley.edu

(12) CRITICAL PLANNING

ISSN: 1522-9807

UCLA Department of Urban Planning, School of Public Affairs,
3250 Public Policy Building,
Los Angeles, CA 90095-1656

email: critplan@ucla.edu

(13) ENVIRONMENT AND PLANNING A

Monthly

ISSN: 0308-518X

PION LTD, 207 BRONDESBURY PARK, LONDON, ENGLAND, NW2 5JN

(14) ENVIRONMENT AND PLANNING B-PLANNING & DESIGN

Bimonthly

ISSN: 0265-8135

PION LTD, 207 BRONDESBURY PARK, LONDON, ENGLAND, NW2 5JN

(15) ENVIRONMENT AND PLANNING C - GOVERNMENT AND POLICY

Bimonthly

ISSN: 0263-774X

PION LTD, 207 BRONDESBURY PARK, LONDON, ENGLAND, NW2 5JN

(16) ENVIRONMENT AND PLANNING D-SOCIETY & SPACE

Bimonthly

ISSN: 0263-7758

PION LTD, 207 BRONDESBURY PARK, LONDON,

ENGLAND, NW2 5JN
(17) EUROPEAN PLANNING STUDIES
ISSN: 1469-5944 (electronic) 0965-4313 (paper)
Publication Frequency: 10 issues per year
email: tf. enquiries@ informa. com
(18) INTERNATIONAL JOURNAL OF URBAN AND REGIONAL RESEARCH
Quarterly
ISSN: 0309-1317
BLACKWELL PUBL LTD, 108 COWLEY RD, OXFORD, ENGLAND, OX4 1JF
(19) JOURNAL OF THE AMERICAN PLANNING ASSOCIATION
Quarterly
ISSN: 0194-4363
AMER PLANNING ASSOC, 1313 EAST 60 STREET, CHICAGO, USA, IL, 60637-2891
(20) THE JOURNAL OF ARCHITECTURAL AND PLANNING RESEARCH
Quarterly
ISSN: 0738-0895
LOCKE SCIENCE PUBL CO INC, 117 WEST HARRISON BLDG SUITE 640-L221, CHICAGO, USA, IL, 60605
(21) JOURNAL OF URBAN DESIGN
3 issues per year
ISSN 1357-4809, Online ISSN: 1469-9664
(22) PLANUM: THE EUROPEAN JOURNAL OF PLANNING
ISSN: 1723-0993
Email: staff@ planum. net
(23) LANDSCAPE AND URBAN PLANNING
Bimonthly

ISSN: 0169-2046

ELSEVIER SCIENCE BV, PO BOX 211, AMSTERDAM, NETHERLANDS, 1000 AE

(24) URBAN STUDIES

Monthly

ISSN: 0042-0980

OUTLEDGE JOURNALS, TAYLOR & FRANCIS LTD, 4 PARK SQUARE, MILTON PARK, ABINGDON, ENGLAND, OXFORDSHIRE, OX14 4RN

(25) ENVIRONMENT AND URBANIZATION

Semiannual

ISSN: 0956-2478

SAGE PUBLICATIONS LTD, 1 OLIVERS YARD, 55 CITY ROAD, LONDON, ENGLAND, EC1Y 1SP

(26) EUROPEAN URBAN AND REGIONAL STUDIES

Quarterly

ISSN: 0969-7764

SAGE PUBLICATIONS LTD, 1 OLIVERS YARD, 55 CITY ROAD, LONDON, ENGLAND, EC1Y 1SP

2. Academic Conferences
专业学术会议

(1) 城市规划年会

一年一度的城市规划年会是中国城市规划学会最主要的学术活动,也是我国城市规划领域最高规格的学术交流活动和城市规划行业的盛会。年会出版年会论文集,并择优在《城市规划》杂志刊登。近几年年会主题如下:

2001年,主题:面向全面小康的城市规划

2002年,主题:高速城镇化进程中的规划建设问题

2004年,主题:面向全面小康的城市规划

2005年,主题:健康城市化
2006年,主题:规划五十年
2007年,主题:面向和谐社会的城市规划
2008年,主题:生态文明视角下的城乡规划
(2) 国际规划大会

世界规划师大会是由国际城市与区域规划师学会(ISOCARP)发起举办的,大会每年选择不同的主题在不同的国家举行。我国2007年正式加入国际城市与区域规划师学会,2008年9月了在大连举办第44届国际规划大会,会议的主题是"城市集约增长:可持续的城市化之路"。

(3) 全国建筑与规划研究生年会

全国建筑与规划研究生年会始于2002年,是在全国多所大学的建筑院系的积极倡导和大力支持下设立,旨在通过全国建筑相关院校研究生之间、研究生群体与社会之间的交流与合作,推动我国建筑与规划专业教育的发展与进步的学术交流活动。

第一届年会于2003年在东南大学胜利召开;

第二届年会于2004年在重庆大学召开,有来自全国23所建筑相关院校的研究生代表参与;

第三届年会于2005年在西安建筑大学召开,全国26所建筑院校的研究生汇聚古城西安;

第四届年会于2006年在天津大学举行,年会主题:表·情——走入设计的外在与内涵;

第五届年会于2007年在北京建筑工程学院举行,本次交流年会共有来自清华大学、同济大学、香港大学、香港中文大学等32所高校参会。

(4) EBRA环境行为学会国际研讨会

EBRA环境行为学会国际研讨会由环境行为学会(EBRA)主办,会议接受的论文全文(英语全文)结集正式出版。近几年研讨会举办地点、主题如下:

第5届,2002年,上海,主题:都市的文化、空间与品质

第 6 届,2004 年,天津,主题:舒适宜人的空间环境
第 7 届,2006 年,大连,主题:变化中的和谐
第 8 届,2008 年,北京,主题:关注不同人群的生活品质

3. Academic Websites
专业学术网站

(1) http://www.planning.org.cn/ 中国城市规划学会
(2) http://www.china-up.com/ 中国规划行业信息网
(3) http://www.cnup.com 中国城市规划网站
(4) http://www.upla.cn/ 城市规划网
(5) http://www.cin.gov.cn/ 中华人民共和国住房和城乡建设部
(6) http://www.caupd.com/index.asp 中国城市规划设计研究院
(7) http://www.cacp.org.cn/ 中国城市规划协会
(8) http://www.ccpd.cnki.net/ 中国城建数字图书馆
(9) http://www.cityup.org 城市规划与交通网
(10) http://www.plansky.net 规划空间站
(11) http://www.abbs.com.cn/ ABBS 建筑论坛
(12) http://www.far2000.com/ 自由建筑报道
(13) http://www.planning.org/ APA 美国规划师联合会
(14) http://www.acsp.org/ 美洲规划院校联合会(ACSP)
(15) http://www.aesop-planning.com/ 欧洲规划院校联合会(AESOP)
(16) http://www.hku.hk/cupem/apsa/index.htm 亚洲规划院校联合会(APSA)
(17) http://www.china-designer.com/ 中国建筑与室内设计师网
(18) http://www.drcnet.com.cn/DRCNET.Channel.Web/ 国务院发展研究中心
(19) http://www.chinacsw.com/ 中国城市网
(20) http://www.city-plan.cn/ 城市规划博客

（21） http://www.dpchina.com/ 规划建设网
（22） http://www.cityok.net/ 中国宜居城市网
（23） http://www.turenscape.com/ 土人景观
（24） http://www.xdcad.net/ 晓东论坛
（25） http://www.bjghw.gov.cn/ 北京市规划委员会
（26） http://www.shghj.gov.cn/ 上海城市规划
（27） http://www.njghj.gov.cn/ 南京城市规划
（28） http://www.upp.gov.cn/ 哈尔滨城市规划局
（29） http://www.asla.org/ 美国风景园林师协会
（30） http://www.onla.org 俄亥俄州苗圃和风景协会
（31） http://www.architectureasia.com 亚洲建筑师
（32） http://www.landdesign.com/ 景观设计网
（33） http://www.laclub.net/ 景园世界
（34） http://www.la-bbs.com/21 度景观论坛
（35） http://www.sweco.se/templates/Page__8551.asp SWECO 景观设计中心
（36） http://www.4dld.com/ 4D 景观设计
（37） http://www.edaw.com/ 易道
（38） http://www.elandscape.cn/厄伊斯及怀特景观建筑事务所
（39） http://www.crja.com/（马来西亚）建筑有限公司
（40） http://www.aia.org/ 美国建筑师学会
（41） http://www.raic.org/ 加拿大皇家建筑师学会
（42） http://www.ribanw.org.uk/ 英国皇家建筑师学会
（43） http://www.nai.nl/ 荷兰建筑师学会
（44） http://www.raia.com.au/ 澳大利亚皇家建筑师学会
（45） http://www.landscape-architecture.com/ 欧洲景观规划建筑交流网
（46） http://eserver.org/art/ 艺术与建筑
（47） http://www.beltcollins.com 贝尔高林
（48） http://www.wsatkins.com 英国阿特金斯

（49）http://www.jaodesign.com 美国龙安
（50）http://www.l-i.org.uk 欧盟园林基金会
（51）http://www.alca.org 全美景观承包联合会
（52）http://ssl.green-mall.com.tw 台湾景观专业网
（53）http://www.landscapeweb.com.tw 全球景观咨询网
（54）http://www.csla.ca 加拿大园林协会
（55）http://www.aildm.com.au 澳大利亚园林设计及管理专业网站
（56）http://www.efla.org 英国园林学会
（57）http://www.sila.org.sg 新加坡园林学会
（58）http://www.hkia.org 香港建筑师学会
（59）http://www.jgarden.org 日本公园网
（60）http://www.landscape-architecture.com/ 欧洲景观规划建筑交流网

4. Academic Associations and Organizations 专业学会与组织

（1）中国城市规划学会

城市规划领域的全国性学术团体，其业务范围包括：就城市规划问题开展国际国内学术活动，推广先进技术，参与论证、咨询与决策，编辑出版学术刊物、专著、科普读物和其他出版物，开展继续教育，维护城市规划工作者合法权益，表彰奖励先进。

学会的前身是1956年在北京成立的中国建筑学会城乡规划学术委员会，"文化大革命"期间中断活动，1978年8月在兰州恢复重建，1986年1月经中国科协批准改称中国城市规划学会，1990年12月在四川什坊召开成立大会，1992年经建设部、民政部批准正式注册。历任理事长分别是王文克、曹洪涛、郑孝燮、吴良镛、周干峙。

学会下设组织、青年、学术和编辑出版四个工作委员会，区域规划与城市经济、居住区规划、风景环境规划设计、历史文化名城规划、城市规划新技术应用、小城镇规划、国外城市规划、工程规划、城市生态规划建设、城市设计、城市安全与防灾11个专业学术委员会。学会办事机构为秘书处,下设编辑部、咨询部和联络部。历任秘书长为安永瑜、周干峙、夏宗玕、石楠。

学会会刊是《城市规划》、《China City Planning Review(城市规划英文版)》。

(2) 中国城市规划协会

中国城市规划协会是城市规划行业全国性社会团体,其英文名称为 CHINA ASSOCIATION OF CITY PLANNING,缩写为"CACP"。1994年在国家民政部登记注册成立,业务主管部门为中华人民共和国建设部。

中国城市规划协会是由团体会员、个人会员、名誉会员组成的社会团体。全国共有团体会员400多个,主要是城市规划、城市勘测行业的机构和地方城市规划协会。个人会员包括专家、社会知名人士和有关部门负责人。名誉会员为对中国城市规划事业作出贡献和给予物质、技术支援的海内外团体和个人。

中国城市规划协会的宗旨是遵守宪法、法律和国家有关方针政策,弘扬社会公德,维护会员合法权益,反映会员愿望,密切行业的横向联系,发挥行业与政府之间的纽带作用,促进行业建设与发展。

中国城市规划协会坚持为政府和会员单位服务的方针,依据章程广泛开展行业管理和交流,同时承担业务主管部门委托的行业管理职能。已分别承担了城市规划甲级设计单位资质评审和年检、部级优秀城市规划设计项目评选、城市规划技术公告征集、城市规划设计单位体制改革政策研究、注册规划师和行政管理法规培训等方面的具体组织与实施工作。

中国城市规划协会积极开展国际交流与合作,先后与法国、美国、加拿大等国的城市规划部门的有关机构建立了工作关系,进行了人员培训、业务交流与合作。

中国城市规划协会愿与国内外城市规划组织和机构建立广泛的合作关系,共同为城市规划事业的发展作出贡献。

(3) 国际城市与区域规划师学会(ISOCARP)

国际城市与区域规划师学会是一个成立于1965年的全球性资

深职业规划师的团体组织，目前由来自于70多个国家和地区的团体会员和个人会员组成。ISOCARP是一个联合国、联合国人居中心和欧洲理事会承认的非政府组织，拥有联合国教科文组织的正式咨询地位。由该学会主办的国际大会是其最主要的学术活动，大会每年选择不同的主题在不同的国家和地区举行。

我国的城市规划学会2007年5月由国务院正式批准加入国际城市与区域规划师学会，按照一国一会的原则，中国城市规划学会是作为中国在该组织的正式代表。

PART THREE
GLOSSARY

第三部分 专业词汇

A

abstraction [æb'strækʃən] n. 抽象化；空想；抽象派作品
abundance [ə'bʌndəns] n. 丰富；充足；富裕
accentuate [æk'sentjueit] v. 重读；强调；着重强调
accessibility [ˌækəsesi'biliti] n. 易接近；可到达的
accommodate [ə'kɔmədeit] vt. 供应；使适应；调节
accompany [ə'kʌmpəni] vt. 陪伴；伴奏
accreditation [əˌkrediteiʃən] n. 委派；信赖；鉴定合格
adaptability [ədæptə'biliti] n. 适应性
adaptation [ˌædæp'teiʃən] n. 适应；改编；改写本
adhesive [əd'hiːsiv] n. 黏合剂
adjacent [ə'dʒeisənt] adj. 邻近的；接近的
adjoining [ə'dʒɔiniŋ] adj. 邻接的；隔壁的
administrative [əd'ministrətiv] adj. 管理的；行政的
advisory [əd'vaizəri] adj. 顾问的；咨询的；劝告的
advocacy ['ædvəkəsi] n. 拥护；鼓吹；辩护
aerodrome ['ɛərədrəum] n. 飞机场；航空站
aesthetic [aiːs'θetik] adj. 美学的；审美的；有审美感的
affirmation [əfəː'meiʃən] n. 断言；肯定；证实；批准
agglomeration [əˌglɔmə'reiʃən] n. 结块；凝聚；块
aggravation [ˌægrə'veiʃən] n. 加重（病情、负担、罪行、危机等）；更恶化；恼怒
aggrieved [ə'griːvd] adj. 愤愤不平的；感到委屈的
agronomy [əg'rɔnəmi] n. 农学；农艺学
albeit [ɔːl'biːit] conj. 虽然
Algiers [æl'dʒiəz] n. 阿尔及尔（阿尔及利亚首都）
alibi ['ælibai] n. [律]犯罪现场；辩解；托辞
alien ['eiljən] adj. 外国的；相异的；背道而驰的
alienation [ˌeiliə'neiʃən] n. 疏远；转让
alignment [ə'lainmənt] n. 队列；结盟
allot [ə'lɔt] v. (按份额)分配；分派
alluring [ə'ljuəriŋ] adj. 迷人的；吸引人的；诱惑的

ally [ə'lai, æ'lai] v. 结盟；与……有关联
alphabetize ['ælfəbitaiz] vt. 依字母顺序排列；以字母表示
amass [ə'mæs] vt. 收集；积聚（尤指财富）
ambiguity [ˌæmbi'gju:iti] n. 含糊；不明确
ambiguous [æm'bigjuəs] adj. 暧昧的；不明确的
amenity [ə'mi:niti] n. 宜人；礼仪
amphitheatrical [ˌæmfiθi'ætrikl] adj. 圆剧场式的
ample ['æmpl] adj. 大量的；充足的；丰富的
analogous [ə'næləgəs] adj. 类似的；相似的；可比拟的
analogy [ə'nælədʒi] n. 类似；类推
analytic [ˌænə'litik] adj. 分析的；解析的
anarchic [æ'nɑ:kik] adj. 无政府主义的；无法无天的
animate ['ænimeit] v. 鼓舞
animated ['ænimeitid] adj. 活生生的；活泼的；愉快的
anonymity [ˌænə'nimiti] n. 匿名；作者不明（或不详）
anonymous [ə'nɔniməs] adj. 匿名的
anthropology [ˌænθrə'pɔlədʒi] n. 人类学
antiquarianism ['ænti'kweəriənizəm] n. 古物研究；好古癖
apportion [ə'pɔ:ʃən] v. 分配
appraisal [ə'preizəl] n. 评价；估价（尤指估价财产；以便征税）；鉴定
approach [ə'prəutʃ] n. 接近；方法；途径；通路
arcade [ɑ:'keid] n. 拱廊；有拱廊的街道
archaeological [ˌɑ:kiə'lɔdʒikəl] adj. 考古学的；考古学上的
archetype ['ɑ:kitaip] n. 原始模型；典型
architect ['ɑ:kitekt] n. 建筑师
arena [ə'ri:nə] n. 竞技场；舞台
Aristotelian [ˌærɪstə'ti:liən] adj. n. 亚里斯多德的，亚里斯多德学派的；亚里斯多德学派的人
arterial [ɑ:'tiəriəl] adj. 动脉的
artery ['ɑ:təri] n. 动脉；要道
arthritis [ɑ:'θraitis] n. 关节炎
articulation [ɑ:ˌtikju'leiʃən] n. 清晰度
artifact ['ɑ:tifækt] n. 人造物品

PART THREE ACADEMIC GLOSSARY

artificiality [ˌɑːtifiʃ'æliti] n. 人工；不自然之物；人造物
artisan [ˌɑːti'zæn] n. 工匠；技工
ascertain [ˌæsə'tein] vt. 确定；探知
ascribe [əs'krɑib] vt. 归因于；归咎于
asphalt ['æsfælt] n. 沥青
astonish [əs'tɔniʃ] vt. 使惊讶
asymmetry [æ'simətri] n. 不对称
atmosphere ['ætməsfiə] n. 大气；空气；气氛
atrium ['ɑːtriəm] n. (罗马建筑内部的)中庭；门廊
attentive [ə'tentiv] adj. 注意的；专心的；留意的
attenuate [ə'tenjueit] v. 削弱
auction ['ɔːkʃən] vt. 拍卖
audacity [ɔː'dæsiti] n. 大胆；胆识
augment [ɔːg'ment] v. 增大；增加
authoritarian [ɔːˌθɔri'tɛəriən] adj. 权力主义的；独裁主义的
authority [ɔː'θɔriti] n. 权威；权力；权势
autonomous [ɔː'tɔnəməs] adj. 自治的
auxiliary [ɔːg'ziliəri] adj. 辅助的；补助的
avail [ə'veil] v. 有益于；有帮助；有用，有利
avenue ['ævinjuː] n. 大街，途径；林荫路
axial ['æksiəl,-sjəl] adj. 轴的；轴向的
axis ['æksis] n. 轴
a new Usonian city "美国风"的住宅新体系。
absolute minimum 绝对极小值
account for 说明；占；解决；得分
actual conditions 实际情况
agricultural production 农业生产
AIA (abbr. = American Institute of Architects)美国建筑学会
air traffic 空中交通
albeit of 虽然
allow with 考虑到
along with 连同……一起
alternating net 交互网

alternative society 替换社会(其文化价值标准完全不同于现存社会秩序的一种社会集团)
an array of 一排；一群；一批
apartment block 公寓楼
argue on 辩论[争论]某事
Arnold Toynbee 英国经济历史学家阿诺德·汤因比
arrive at 得出
at large 未被捕；详尽；普遍
auction off 拍卖

B

balcony ['bælkəni] n. 阳台；包厢；(戏院)楼厅
Balzacian [bæl'zeiʃən] adj. (法国小说家)巴尔扎克的；巴尔扎克风格的
banal [bə'nɑːl] adj. 平凡的、陈腐的；老一套的
barbarian [bɑː'bɛəriən] adj. 野蛮(人)的；未开化的；不文明的
barbarous ['bɑːbərəs] adj. 野蛮的；残暴的；粗野的；(声音)刺耳的；沙哑的
barren ['bærən] adj. 不生育的；不孕的；贫瘠的
basement ['beismənt] n. 底；基层；地下室
basin ['beisn] n. 盆；盆地；水池
bedrock ['bed'rɔk] n. 基本事实[原理]；最低点[额]；最小量
besiege [bi'siːdʒ] vt. 围困；围攻；包围
bestowing [bi'stəuiŋ] n. 砖窑中砖堆上层已烧透的砖
bleak [bliːk] adj. 寒冷的；阴冷的；荒凉的；凄凉的；黯淡的
Bologna [bə'ləunjə] n. 博洛尼亚(意大利城市)
boulevard ['buːlivɑːd] n. <美>林荫大道
boundary ['baundəri] n. 边界；分界线
bounded ['baundid] adj. 有界限的；有限制的
breakage ['breikidʒ] n. 破坏；破损；破损量
buffer ['bʌfə] n. 缓冲器
bureaucracy [bjuə'rɔkrəsi] n. 官僚主义；官僚政治；官僚机构
busway ['bʌswei] n. [电]汇流条通道；配电通道；母线通道
Baron Haussmann 豪斯曼男爵(拿破仑三世时期的法国城市设计师)

baroque network model 巴洛克典型型制
bay window 凸窗
be accustomed to 习惯于
be compatible with 与……共存
be congenial to 志趣相投
be imbued with 充满
be incorporated into 加入
be indebted to 感谢
be instrumental to 对……有益
be struck by 被……打动
bear in mind 记住
beyond the limits 越出；超出（范围、限度）
blind acceptance 盲目接受
booking office 售票处
break down 毁掉；制服；压倒；停顿；倒塌；中止；垮掉；分解
bridge-point 渡口
broadacre city 广亩城市
brownish-yellow 黄褐色
building block （儿童游戏用的）积木
building envelope 建筑物外体
building lot 建筑房屋用地；建筑地基
building performance 建筑性能
building project 建设项目
built environment 城市环境
bus lane （街道上的）公共汽车专用车道
bus shelter 公共汽车候车站
business section 商业区

C

campanile [kæmpə′niːli] n. 钟楼；钟塔
canyon [′kænjən] n. 峡（谷）
cardinal [′kɑːdinəl] adj. 主要的；最重要的
carnival [′kɑːnivl] n. 狂欢节；饮宴狂欢

cartage ['kɑːtidʒ] n. 货车运输；货车运费
category ['kætigəri] n. 种类；别
cede [siːd] vt. 放弃
centerpiece ['sentəpiːs] n. 中心件；中心装饰品
centralization ['sentrəlɑi'zeiʃən] n. 集中；中央集权化
chaos ['keiɔs] n. 混乱；混沌
chaotic [kei'ɔtik] adj. 混乱的；无秩序的
characterize ['kærɪktərɑɪz] vt. 表现……的特色；刻画的……性格
chiller ['tʃilə] n. 使寒冷之人或事物；冷却器
Christian ['kristjən] n. adj. 基督徒；信徒；基督教的；信基督教的
circular ['səːkjulə] adj. 圆形的；循环的
circulation [ˌsəːkju'leiʃən] n. 循环；流通
circulatory [sɛːkjʊ'leɪtəri] adj. 循环的
circumference [sə'kʌmfərəns] n. 圆周；周围
circumstantial [ˌsəːkəm'stænʃəl] adj. 依照情况的
civic ['sivik] adj. 市的；市民的；公民的
clarification [ˌklærifi'keiʃən] n. 澄清；净化
claustrophobia [ˌklɔːstrə'fəubjə] n. 幽闭恐惧症
climatic [klɑi'mætik] adj. 气候上的
cluster ['klʌstə] n. 串；丛
clutch [klʌtʃ] n. 抓住；攫住
cognitive ['kɔgnitiv] adj. 认知的；认识的；有感知的
coherent [kəu'hiərənt] adj. 黏着的；有凝聚力的；互相密合的
collaborate [kə'læbəreit] vi. 合作；通敌
collaboration [kəˌlæbə'reiʃən] n. 协作；通敌
colloidal [kə'lɔidl] adj. 胶状的；胶质的
colonnade [ˌkɔlə'neid] n. 柱廊
colossal [kə'lɔsl] adj. 巨大的；庞大的
commanding [kə'mɑːndiŋ] adj. 指挥的；发号施令的
commensurate [kə'menʃərit] adj. 相称的；相当的
commiseration [kəˌmizə'reiʃən] n. 同情
commission [kə'miʃən] v. 委任；任命；委托；委托制作
commodity [kə'mɔditi] n. 日用品

communitarian [kə,mju:ni'tɛəriən] n. 共产主义社会的成员
commuter [kə'mju:tə] n. 通勤者；经常往返者
compact ['kɔmpækt] adj. 紧凑的；紧密的；简洁的
compartment [kəm'pɑ:tmənt] n. 间隔间；车厢
compass ['kʌmpəs] n. 罗盘；指南针；圆规
compatible [kəm'pætəbl] adj. 谐调的；一致的；兼容的
complement ['kɔmplimənt] n. vt. 补足物；补助；补足
complementary [kɔmplə'mentəri] adj. 补充的；补足的
complementation [,kɔmplimen'teiʃən] n. 互补
complexity [kəm'pleksiti] n. 复杂(性)；复杂的事物；复杂性
composition [kɔmpə'ziʃən] n. 写作；作文；成分；合成物
comprise [kəm'praiz] v. 包含；由……组成
concave ['kɔn'keiv] n. 凹；凹面
conceivable [kən'si:vəbl] adj. 可能的；想得到的；可想象的
conceive [kən'si:v] vt. 构思；以为；持有
conception [kən'sepʃən] n. 观念；想法；构思；构想
conceptual [kən'septʃuəl] adj. 概念上的
conceptualize [kən'septjuəlaiz] v. 使有概念
concretization [kɔn,kri:tai'zeiʃən;-ti'z-] n. 具体化
concretize [kɔn'kri:(:)taiz] vt. 使具体化；使有形化
confluence ['kɔnfluəns] n. 汇合
conform [kən'fɔ:m] v. 使一致；使遵守；使顺从；符合；相似；适应环境
conformity [kən'fɔ:miti] n. 相似；一致；遵从；顺从；整合
congenial [kən'dʒi:njəl] adj. 性格相似的；适意的
congestion [kən'dʒestʃən] n. 拥塞；拥挤
conglomerate [kɔn'glɔmərit] v. 聚结
conjuncture [kən'dʒʌŋktʃə] n. 事态；接合；危机
conscious ['kɔnʃəs] adj. 有意识的；有知觉的；故意的；羞怯的
consciousness ['kɔnʃəsnis] n. 意识；知觉；自觉
consecrate ['kɔnsikreit] vt. adj. 用作祭祀；献给；使神圣；被献给神的；神圣的
conserve [kən'sə:v] vt. 保存；保藏
conspicuous [kən'spikjuəs] adj. 显著的

conspicuously [kən'spikjuəsli] adv. 显著地；超群地
constancy ['kɔnstənsi] n. 不屈不挠；坚定不移
constitute ['kɔnstifju:t] vt. 制定(法律)；建立(政府)；组成；任命
constitution [ˌkɔnsti'tju:ʃən] n. 宪法；构造；体质
constraint [kən'streint] n. 约束；强制
consultation [ˌkɔnsəl'teiʃən] n. 请教；咨询；磋商
consumption [kən'sʌmpʃən] n. 消费；消费量
contemporaneous [kənˌtempə'reinjəs] adj. 同时期的；同时代的
content [kən'tent] n. 内容；容量
continuity [ˌkɔnti'nju(:)iti] n. 连续性；连贯性
continuously [kən'tɪnjʊəslɪ] adv. 不断地；连续地
contour ['kɔntuə] n. 轮廓；周线；等高线
contradict [kɔntrə'dikt] vt. 同……矛盾；同……抵触
conurbation [ˌkɔnə'beiʃən] n. 具有许多卫星城镇的大城市
conventional [kən'venʃnl] adj. 惯例的；常规的；习俗的；传统的
converge [kən'və:dʒ] v. 聚合；集中于一点
convergence [kən'və::dʒəns] n. 集中；收敛
convert [kən'və:t] vt. 使转变；转换……
coordination [kəuˌɔ:di'neiʃən] n. 同等；同位；对等；协调
corpse [kɔ:ps] n. 尸体
correspond [kɔris'pɔnd] vi. 符合；协调；通信；相当；相应
correspondence [ˌkɔris'pɔndəns] n. 相应；通信；信件
corridor ['kɔridɔ:] n. 走廊
corrode [kə'rəud] v. 使腐蚀；侵蚀
cosmic ['kɔzmik] adj. 宇宙的
cosmos ['kɔzmɔs] n. 宇宙
counterbalance [ˌkauntə'bæləns] v. 使平均；使平衡；弥补
counterpart ['kauntəpɑ:t] n. 副本；极相似的人或物；配对物
counterpoint ['kauntəpɔint] n. 对应物
counterpose ['kauntə'pəuz] vt. 使对立
courtyard ['kɔ:tjɑ:d] n. 庭院；院子；天井
craftsman ['krɑ:ftsmən] n. 手艺人；工匠；技工
cramped [kræmpt] adj. 狭窄的；局促的；难辨认的

crescent ['kresnt] n. 新月；月牙
crest [krest] n. 鸟冠；顶部；顶峰；浪头
crisscross ['kriskrɔs] v. 交错；交叉
critique [kri'ti:k] n. 批评；批判；评论；鉴定
crossing ['krɔsiŋ] n. 交叉点；十字路口；人行横道
cross-country [krɔs'kʌntri；(US)'krɔ:s-] adj. 越野的；横过田野的
cross-section ['krɔs'sekʃən] n. 横截[断]面；剖面图
crucial ['kru:ʃiəl, 'kru:ʃəl] adj. 至关紧要的
crystal ['kristl] n. 水晶；水晶饰品
crystalline ['kristəlain] adj. 水晶的
crystallize ['kristəlaiz] v. 明确
culminate ['kʌlmineit] v. 达到顶点
culmination [kʌlmi'neiʃ(ə)n] n. 巅峰；最高点
cult [kʌlt] n. 礼拜；祭仪；一群信徒；礼拜式
cultivate ['kʌltiveit] vt. 培养；耕作
curb [kə:b] n. 路边
curve [kə:v] vt. n. 弯；使弯曲；曲线；弯曲
cyclical ['sıklık(e)l] adj. 轮转的；循环的
cyclist ['saıklıst] n. 骑脚踏车的人
cabin fever (长期独处斗室引起的)幽闭烦躁症
call into question 怀疑，对……表示异议
call to mind 回想
call in 调用
capital accumulation [经]资本积累
capitalize on 利用
cardinal points 方位基点
carrying capacity 承载能力
child psychology of Piaget 皮亚杰儿童心理学
circulation area 流通面积
city dweller 城市居民
civic building 市政建筑
Civil Engineering 土木工程
clearing house 票据交换所

cognitive mapping 认知制图
coincide with 与……相符
collective spirit 集体精神
commanding point 操控点
community development 地区开发
complex system 复杂系统
comprehensive design 综合设计
computer console 计算机控制台；电脑控制台
concave profile （叶片）内弧形面
conceive as 被认为
concentric ring 同心环
conservation zone 保护区
consulting firm 咨询公司
consumer protection 消费者保护（法）
control department 控制部；管理部门
cosmic order 宇宙顺序
cost-effective 有成本效益的；划算的
cotton-wadded 用棉花填充的
cross section 交互区

D

de facto [dei'fæktəu] adj. 事实上的；实际的
debris ['debri:,'deib-] n. 碎片；残骸
decentralized [di:'sentrəlaizd] adj. 分散的
declaim [di'kleim] v. 巧辩；演讲；高声朗读
decongestion [,di:kən'dʒestʃən] n. （城市等）拥挤的消除（或缓解）
definitive [di'finitiv] adj. 最后的；确定的；权威性的
deliberate [di'libəreit] adj. 深思熟虑的；故意的；
deliberation [di,libə'reiʃən] n. 熟思；从容；商议；考虑
delineate [di'linieit] v. 描……的外形；画……的轮廓；勾画
demolition [,demə'liʃən] n. 破坏；毁坏；毁坏之遗迹
demoralization [di'mɔrəlaizifən] n. 道德败坏；纪律松弛；士气消沉
den [den] n. 兽穴，洞穴，（舒适的）私室（作学习或办公用）穴居居住或藏

在洞穴里

denigrate ['denigreit] v. 毁誉
denomination [di‚nɔmi'neiʃən] n. 命名；票面金额
denote [di'nəut] vt. 指示；表示
density ['densiti] n. 浓度；密度
departure [di'pɑ:tʃə] n. 启程；出发；离开
deplore [di'plɔ:] v. 表示悲痛
desegregation [‚di:segri'geiʃən] n. 废止种族歧视
designedly [di'zaınıdlı] adv. 故意地；特意地；有计划地
desolate ['desəlit] adj. 荒凉的；无人烟的
destructive [dis'trʌktiv] adj. 破坏(性)的
deteriorate [di'tiəriəreit] v. (使)恶化
determinant [di'tə:minənt] adj. 决定性的
dethrone [di'θrəun] v. 撵走；推翻权力地位
deviation [‚di:vi'eiʃn] n. 背离
diagram ['daiəgræm] n. 图表；图解；框图；立体图
dialectic [‚daiə'lektik] adj. 辩证的
dictatorship [dik'teitəʃip] n. 专政
diffuse [di'fju:z] v. 散播；传播；漫射
dimension [di'menʃən] n. 尺寸；尺度；维(数)；度(数)；元
dimensional [di'menʃənəl] adj. 空间的
diorama [‚daiə'rɑ:mə] n. 透视画；西洋景；立体模型
dirigisme [‚di:ri:'ʒi:sm] n. (政府对国民经济)干预或统制(主义)
discernible [di'sε:nəbl,-'zε:-] adj. 可辨别的
discontinuous ['diskən'tinjuəs] adj. 不连续的；间断的；中断的
disdainfully [dis'deinfuli] adv. 轻蔑地
dislocation [‚dislə'keiʃən] n. 混乱；断层；脱臼
dismember [dis'membə] v. 肢解
dispersal [di'pə:səl] n. 散布；分散；消散；驱散；疏散
displacement [dis'pleismənt] n. 移置；转移；取代；置换；位移
dispose [dis'pəuz] v. 处理；处置；部署
dispossessed [‚dispə'zest] adj. 无依无靠的；被逐出的
disruption [dis'rʌpʃən] n. 中断；分裂；瓦解；破坏

dissertation [ˌdisə(ː)'teiʃən] n. (学位)论文；专题；学术演讲
distinct [dis'tiŋkt] adj. 清楚的；明显的；截然不同的；独特的
distinction [dis'tiŋkʃən] n. 区别；差别
distinguish [dis'tiŋgwiʃ] v. 区别；辨别
distort [dis'tɔːt] vt. 弄歪(嘴脸等)；扭曲；歪曲(真理、事实等)；误报
distortion [dis'tɔːʃən] n. 扭曲；变形；曲解；失真
disturbance [dis'təːbəns] n. 骚动；动乱；打扰；干扰；骚乱；搅动
dominate ['dɔmineit] v. 支配；占优势
drainage ['dreinidʒ] n. 排水；排水装置
drastic ['dræstik] adj. 激烈的；猛烈的
dread [dred] n. v. 恐惧；恐怖；可怕的人(或物)；畏惧；惧怕；担心
dressing ['dresiŋ] n. 穿衣；装饰
ductwork ['dʌktwɛːk] n. 管道系统
duomo ['dwɔːmɔː] n. 大教堂；中央寺院
dweller ['dwelə(r)] n. 居住者；居民
dwelling ['dweliŋ] n. 住处
dynamic [dai'næmik] adj. 动力的；动力学的；动态的
dynapolis [dai'næpəlis] n. (交通干线附近的)新兴城市
demonstration project 示范项目
derive from 得自；由来；衍生
design discipline 设计原则；设计规程
direct interest 直接兴趣
division of labor 劳动力的分工
Dom-Ino house 多米诺住宅
Donella H. Meadows, Dennis L. Meadows, Jorgen Randers 美国麻省理工学院的经济学家梅多斯等人
dormitory town 卧城
Doxiadis 希腊学者、著名城市规划学家道萨迪亚斯
Dr. Erikson 加拿大建筑师亚瑟·埃里克森
draft stage 起草阶段(标准，专利用语)
drawing board 制图板
drug addict 吸毒成瘾者，药瘾者

drug pusher 毒品贩子

E

ecology [i(ː)'kɔlədʒi] n. 生态学
ecosystem [iːkə'sistəm] n. 生态系统
Ecumenopolis [ˌekjumi'nɔpəlis] n. 世界都市观（把世界看作是一个延伸的广大城市）
edifice ['edifis] n. 大厦；大建筑物
efficacy ['efikəsi] n. 功效；效验
egocentric [iːgəu'sentrik] adj. 自我中心的；利己主义的
elaborate [i'læbərət] adj. 精心制作的；详细阐述的；精细
elaboration [iˌlæbə'reiʃən] n. 苦心经营；苦心经营的结果；详尽的细节
elective [i'lektiv] adj. 选修课程
elector [i'lektə(r)] n. 选举者；有选举权的人
element ['elimənt] n. 要素；元素；成分；元件
elite [ei'liːt] n. 精英；精华；中坚
elude [i'ljuːd, i'luːd] v. 躲避
elusive [i'luːsiv] adj. 难懂的；难捉摸的，易忘的
embodied [im'bɔdid] vt. 使具体化；包含；收录
embody [im'bɔdi] vt. 具体表达；使具体化；包含；收录
empirical [em'pirikəl] adj. 完全根据经验的；经验主义的
emporia [em'pɔːriə] n. 商业中心；大百货店
empower [im'pauə] v. 授权与；使能够
enclosure [in'kləuʒə] n. 围住；围栏；围场
encompass [in'kʌmpəs] v. 包围；环绕；包含或包括某事物
endorse [in'dɔːs] v. 在（票据）背面签名；签注（文件）；认可；签署
endow [in'dau] v. 捐赠；赋予
engender [in'dʒendə] v. 造成
engross [in'grəus] v. 吸引；使全神贯注；独占
enshrine [in'ʃrain] v. 铭记
entail [in'teil] vt. 使必需；使蒙受；使承担
enthusiasm [in'θjuːziæzəm] n. 狂热；热心；积极性；激发热情的事物
entrant ['entrənt] n. 新会员；新成员；进入者

entrench [in'trentʃ] v. 使盘踞；固守；牢固树立；使处于有力地位
entresol ['ɔntrəsɔl] n. 夹层；阁楼；半楼[层]
entry ['entri] n. 登录；进入；入口
envisage [in'vizidʒ] v. 正视；面对（事实等）；想象；拟想；展望
envision [in'viʒən] v. 想象；预想
epistemological [ˌepisti(:)mə'lɔdʒikəl] adj. 认识论的
erect [i'rekt] vt. 盖；使竖立；使直立；树立；建立
erection [i'rekʃən] n. 直立；竖起；建筑物
erratic [i'rætik] adj. 不稳定的；奇怪的
eschew [is'tʃu:] vt. 避开；远避
esplanade [ˌesplə'neid] n. 平坦的空地；游憩场；散步路
essence ['esns] n. 基本；[哲] 本质
esthetic [i:s'θetik] adj. 感觉的
esthetics [i:s'θetiks] n. 美学；审美学
ethics ['eθiks] n. 道德规范
evaluate [i'væljueit] vt. 评价；估计；求……的值
eviction [i(:)'vikʃən] n. 逐出；赶出
evidently ['evidəntli] adv. 明显地；显然
excavation [ˌekskə'veiʃən] n. 挖掘；发掘；挖掘成的洞；出土文物
exhilarating [ig'ziləreitiŋ] adj. 令人喜欢的；爽快的；使人愉快的
existential [ˌegzis'tenʃəl] adj. 有关存在的
exotic [ig'zɔtik] adj. 异国情调的；外来的；奇异的
expanse [iks'pæns] n. 宽阔的区域；宽阔；苍天；膨胀扩张
experienced [ik'spiəriənst] adj. 富有经验的
explicit [iks'plisit] adj. 外在的，清楚的，直率的，（租金等）直接付款的
expressionless [ik'spreʃənlıs] adj. 无表情的
extension [iks'tenʃən] n. 延长；扩充；范围
extinction [ikstiŋkʃən] n. 消失；消灭；废止
extol [iks'tɔl] v. 赞美
exurban [eks'ɛ:bən] adj. 城市远郊的
eyesore ['aisɔ:(r)] n. 刺眼的东西
Ebenezer Howard 英国"田园城市"运动创始人埃比尼泽·霍华德（1850～1928）

economic geography 经济地理
economic reform 经济改革
egocentric stage 自我中心阶段
electrical conduit 电缆
elevated roadway 高架车道
encircling band 环形带
energy efficiency 能量效率
engage in 从事于；涉及
entrance hall 门廊
environmental degradation 环境退化
environmental design 环境设计
environmental totality 环境整体
Esprit nouveau《新精神》杂志
ethnic group 同种同文化之民族
exporting labor 劳务输出

F

facade [fə'sɑːd] n. 正面
facile ['fæsɑɪl;(US)'fæsl] adj. 易做到的，易得到的；不花力气的；敏捷的；流畅的；(性格)柔顺的；温和的；容易的
facilitate [fə'siliteit] vt. (不以人作主语的)使容易；使便利；推动，帮助，使容易；促进
facility [fə'siliti] n. 容易；简易；灵巧；熟练；便利，
failing ['feiliŋ] n. 缺点；过失；失败
Fascism ['fæʃizəm] n. 法西斯主义
favorable ['feivərəbl] adj. 赞成的；有利的；赞许的；良好的
fertile ['fəːtɑil;'fəːtil] adj. 肥沃的；富饶的；能繁殖的
fetal ['fiːtl] adj. 胎儿的；胎的
fibrous ['fɑibrəs] adj. 纤维状的；坚韧的
fiend [fiːnd] n. 魔鬼；邪；能手
fixation [fik'seiʃən] n. 定置；固定；定色
flora ['flɔːrə] n. 花神
Florence ['flɔːrəns] n. 佛罗伦萨(意大利都市名)

fluctuate ['flʌktjueit] vi. 变动；波动；涨落；上下；动摇
fluidity [flu(:)'iditi] n. 流动性；流质；变移性；流度
foci ['fəusɑi] n. 焦距；配光
foliage ['fəuliidʒ] n. 树叶；植物
foothold ['fuθəuld] n. 立足处
ford [fɔ:d] n. 浅滩
forgo [fɔ:'gəu] v. 摒绝；放弃
formalist ['fɔ:məlist] n. 形式主义者
format ['fɔ:mæt, -mɑ:t] n. 开本；版式；形式；格式
formidable ['fɔ:midəbl] adj. 强大的；令人敬畏的；可怕的；艰难的
formulate ['fɔ:mjuleit] vt. 用公式表示；明确地表达；作简洁陈述
formulation [ˌfɔ:mju'leiʃən] n. 有系统而确切的陈述或说明；设计；规化
forsake [fə'seik] v. 放弃；抛弃
forum ['fɔ:rəm] n. 古罗马城镇的广场(或市场)；论坛；法庭；讨论会
foster ['fɔstə] vt. 养育；抚育；培养；鼓励；抱(希望)
fountain ['fauntin] n. 泉水；喷泉
fragmentary ['frægməntəri] adj. 由碎片组成的；断断续续的
fragmentation [ə'næləgəs] n. 分裂；破碎
freestanding ['fri:stændiŋ] adj. 独立式的；不需依靠支撑物的
frightening ['fraitəniŋ] adj. 令人恐惧的；引起突然惊恐的
frigid ['fridʒid] adj. 寒冷的；冷淡的；(妇女)缺乏性感的
frontage ['frʌntidʒ] n. 房子的正面；前方；临街地
fugitive ['fju:dʒitiv] adj. 逃亡的；无常的；易变的
fulfillment [ful'filmənt] n. 履行；实行
full-grown ['ful'grəun] adj. 生长完全的；发育完全的
fundamental [ˌfʌndə'mentl] adj. 基础的；基本的
funnel ['fʌnəl] n. 漏斗；烟窗
furniture ['fə:nitʃə] n. 家具；设备；储藏物
fuzzy ['fʌzi] adj. 有绒毛的；模糊的；失真的
fast traffic 快速运输
ferrous metal [铁类]金属
figure-ground relationship 人物—背景关系
fitness facility 健身设施

flow diagram 流程图;作业图;生产过程图解
flush out of (从隐蔽处)驱逐出去
focal point 焦点
food processing 食品加工
foundation stone 基石;基础
four dimensions 四维空间
Frank Lloyd Wright 弗兰克·劳埃德·赖特(1869~1959),美国建筑师
from time to time 有时
frontage association 临街建筑
full range 全范围
future shock 未来冲击,未来震憾

G

gable ['geibl] n. 尖顶屋两端的山形墙
galleria [ˌgæləriə] n. 风雨商业街廊
gangsterism ['gæŋstərizəm] n. 犯罪;歹徒及其犯罪行为
gauge [gedʒ] n. 标准尺;规格;量规,量表
generality [ˌdʒenə'ræliti] n. 一般性;概论;概说
generation [ˌdʒenə'reiʃən] n. 产生;发生
genesis ['dʒenisis] n. 起源
geographic [ˌdʒiə'græfik] adj. 地理学的;地理的
geometrical [dʒiə'metrikəl] adj. 几何学的;几何的
geometry [dʒi'ɔmitri] n. 几何学
Gestalt [gə'ʃtɑːlt] n. [心]完全形态;完形
gigantic [dʒai'gæntik] adj. 巨人般的;巨大的
gigantism ['dʒaigæntizəm] n. [医]巨人症
globalization [ˌgləubəlai'zeiʃən] n. 全球化;全球性
gospel ['gɔspəl] n. 福音;主义;信条
gradient ['greidiənt] adj. 倾斜的
grandeur ['grændʒə] n. 伟大;高贵;庄严;富丽堂皇
graphic ['græfik] adj. 绘画似的;图解的
grappling ['græpliŋ] n. (打捞用的)抓机;爪钩
gratifying ['grætifaiiŋ] adj. 悦人的;令人满足的

greenery ['griːnəri] n. 温室；草木
grid [grid] n. 格子；栅格
grievance ['griːvəns] n. 委屈；冤情；不平
grove [grəuv] n. 小树林
guardian ['gɑːdjən] n. 护卫者；保护人；监护人
gypsum ['dʒipsəm] n. [矿]石膏；[农]石膏肥料
gyratory ['dʒaiərətəri] adj. 旋转的
garden city 花园城市；田园城市
general office 总办公处
genius loci 场所精神；一个地方的风气或特色
Georg Trakl 特拉克尔（人名）
Gestalt psychology 格式塔心理学
get about 走动；旅行
give life to 为……注入活力
give rise to 引起
glass tile 玻璃瓦
go beyond 超出
goods station 货运站；货运码头
grand view 宏观视角
green fields 绿色场；绿地
grid system 栅格系统
ground floor 第一层
ground plan 平面图
ground slope 地面坡度

H

habitat ['hæbitæt] n. （动植物的）生活环境；产地、栖息地；居留地；自生地；聚集处
habitation [ˌhæbi'teiʃən] n. 住所；住宅；聚居地
handicapped ['hændikæpt] n. adj. 残疾人；身体有缺陷的人；残废的
harmony ['hɑːməni] n. 协调；融洽
haven ['heivn] n. 港口；避难所
haystack ['heistæk] n. 干草堆

hazard ['hæzəd] n. 冒险；危险；冒险的事
hazardous ['hæzədəs] adj. 危险的；冒险的；碰运气的
Hegel ['heigl] n. 黑格尔
heighten ['haitn] v. 提高；升高
hierarchical [ˌhaiə'rɑːkikəl] adj. 分等级的
hierarchy ['haiərɑːki] n. 层次；层级
highrise ['hairaiz] adj. 高耸的
hinder ['hində] v. 阻碍；打扰
holding ['həuldiŋ] n. 把握；支持；持有；所有物；财产
holistic [həu'listik] adj. 整体的；全盘的
homogeneous [ˌhɔməu'dʒiːnjəs] adj. 同类的；相似的；均一的，均匀的
homogenization [ˌhəumədʒənai'zeiʃən] n. （均）匀化；均质化；同质化；纯一化
Honolulu [ˌhɔnə'luːluː] n. 火奴鲁鲁（即"檀香山"，美国夏威夷州的首府和港市）
husbandry ['hʌzbəndri] n. 管理；农事；饲养业
hybrid ['haibrid] n. 混合；融合
hygienic [hai'dʒiːnik] adj. 卫生的；保健的；清洁的
hypertrophy [hai'pəːtrəfi] n. [医]肥大；过度生长；过度增大
hypotheses [hai'pɔθisiːz] n. 假设；假说
Henry George 法国章牌设计师乔治·亨利
Herder 赫尔德（人名）
high density 高密度
hinge upon 决定（由……决定）
hot zone 断字区
house building 住宅建筑物
house heating 住房供热
housing development 住宅新区
housing estate 居民区；居住区
housing finance 住宅信贷
housing refugee 住房难民
human development 人类发展
human scale 人类尺度

I

icicle ['aisikl] n. 垂冰；冰柱
idee fixe [i:del'fi:ks] <法>固定观念；对一事的偏执
identification [ai,dentifi'keiʃən] n. 辨认；鉴定；证明
identity [ai'dentiti] n. 同一性；身份；一致
igloo ['iglu:] n. 圆顶建筑
illuminate [i'lju:mineit] vt. 照明；照亮；阐明；说明
illusion [i'lu:ʒən, i'lju:-] n. 幻想
imageable ['imidʒəbl] adj. 可成像的；能引起意象的
immediate [i'mi:djət] adj. 直接的；紧接的；紧靠的；立即的
immoral [i'mɔrəl] adj. 不道德的；邪恶的
immovable [i'mu:vəbl] adj. 固定的；不动的；不改变的
impart [im'pɑ:t] vt. 给予（尤指抽象事物）；传授；告知；透露
impasse [æm'pɑ:s, im-] n. 僵局
imperative [im'perətiv] adj. 绝对必要的；紧急的；迫切的；不可避免的
imperial [im'piəriəl] adj. 皇帝的
implement ['implimənt] vt. 贯彻；实现
implication [,impli'keiʃən] n. 牵连；含意；暗示
impose [im'pəuz] vt. 征税；强加；以……欺骗
inadequate [in'ædikwit] adj. 不充分的；不适当的
inaugurate [i'nɔ:gjureit] v. 举行开幕
incarnation [,inkɑ:'neiʃən] n. 赋予肉体；具人形；化身
incentive [in'sentiv] n. 动机
inclined [in'klaind] adj. 倾向……的
incompatibility ['inkəm,pætə'biliti] n. 不两立；不相容
incompatible [,inkəm'pætəbl] adj. 性质相反的；矛盾的；不调和的
indicator ['indikeitə] n. 指示器；[化]指示剂
indigenous [in'didʒənəs] adj. 本土的
individual [,indi'vidjuəl] adj. 个人的；个体的；单独的；独特的
ineffectual [,ini'fektʃuəl] adj. 无效的；不成功的
inertial [i'nə:ʃəl] adj. 不活泼的；惯性的
influx ['inflʌks] n. 流入（量）；注入（量）；汇集；涌进

informed [in'fɔ:md] adj. 见多识广的
infrastructure ['infrə'strʌktʃə] n. 下部构造；基础下部组织
ingather [in'gæðə] v. 收获；收入；收集
inhabitant [in'hæbitənt] n. 居民；居住者
inherent [in'hiərənt] adj. 固有的；内在的；与生俱来的
inhuman [in'hju:mən] adj. 野蛮的
initial [i'niʃəl] adj. 最初的；词首的；初始的
initiative [i'niʃiətiv] n. 主动
innovation [ˌinəu'veiʃən] n. 改革；创新
inseparable [əin'sepərəbl] adj. 不能分的
insignificant [ˌinsig'nifikənt] adj. 无关紧要的；可忽略的；无意义的
inspection [in'spekʃən] n. 检查；视察
inspiration [ˌinspə'reiʃən] n. 灵感
institution [ˌinsti'tju:ʃən] n. 公共机构；协会；制度
institutional [ˌinsti'tju:ʃənəl] adj. 制度上的
instrumental [ˌinstru'mentl] adj. 仪器的；器械的；乐器的
insulation [ˌinsju'leiʃn] n. 绝缘
insurmountable [ˌinsə'mauntəbl] adj. 不可克服的；难以逾越的
integral ['intigrəl] adj. 完整的；整体的
integrity [in'tegriti] n. 完整；完全；完整性
intemperate [in'tempərit] adj. 过度的；激烈的
intensifier [in'tensifaiə] n. 使更激烈之物；增强剂
interdependent [ˌintə(:)di'pendənt] adj. 相互依赖的；互助的
interdisciplinary [ˌintə(:)'disiplinəri] adj. 各学科间的
interfere [ˌintə'fiə] vi. 干涉；干预；妨碍；打扰
interior [in'tiəriə] adj. 内部的；内的
intermediate [ˌintə'mi:djət] adj. 中间的
intermingle [ˌintə(:)'miŋgəl] n. 混合
internal [in'tə:nl] adj. 内在的；国内的
internship ['intɛ:nʃip] n. 实习医师；实习期
interpret [in'tə:prit] v. 解释；说明
interpretation [inˌtə:pri'teiʃən] n. 解释；阐明
interpretive [in'tə:pritiv] adj. 作为说明的女子；解释的

interrelation ['intə(ː)ri'leiʃən] n. 相互关系
intersect [ˌintə'sekt] vi. (直线)相交；交叉
intersection [ˌintə(ː)'sekʃən] n. [数]交集；十字路口；交叉点
interstice [in'təːstis] n. 空隙；裂缝
interstitial [ˌintə(ː)'stiʃəl] adj. 空隙的；裂缝的
interval ['intəvəl] n. 间隔；距离；幕间休息
intervale ['intə(ː)veil] n. 丘陵间低地
intervention [ˌintə(ː)'venʃən] n. 干涉
intervisible [ˌintə'vizəbl] adj. 可通视的
intimate ['intimit] adj. 亲密的；隐私的
intractable [in'træktəbl] adj. 难驾御的；难管理的；难处理的；难加工的
intricate ['intrikit] adj. 复杂的；错综的；难以理解的
intuitive [in'tju(ː)itiv] adj. 直觉的
Invalides [in'vælidis] n. 巴黎荣军院；残老军人院
invariably [in'vɛəriəb(ə)li] adv. 不变地；总是
invariance [in'vɛəriəns] n. 不变性；恒定性
investigation [inˌvesti'geiʃən] n. 调查；研究
invisible [in'vizəbl] adj. 看不见的；无形的
invoke [in'vəuk] v. 调用
ironclad [ɑiən'klæd] adj. 装甲的；打不破的
irrationality [iˌræʃə'næləti] n. 不合理
irreversible [ˌiri'vəːsəblˌ-sib-] adj. 不能撤回的；不能取消的
isolate ['ɑisəleit] vt. 使隔离；使孤立
isotropic [ˌɑisəu'trɔpik] adj. 等方性的
Istanbul [ˌistæn'buːl] n. 伊斯坦布尔(土耳其西北部港市)
itch [itʃ] n. 发痒；渴望
Ice and Snow Festival 冰雪节
immediate environment 直接环境
impact analysis 冲击分析
in conformity with 与……一致
in regard to 关于
in relation to 关于；涉及；与…相比
in terms of 根据；按照；用……的话；在……方面

indulge in 沉湎于
industrial process 工业生产过程
industrial quarter 工业区
industrial structure 产业结构
initial animistic stage 万物有灵阶段
inner city 市中心区
institutional change 机构改革
interfere with 打扰
item by item 逐条；逐项

J

justification [ˌdʒʌstɪfɪˈkeɪʃ(ə)n] n. 认为有理；认为正当；理由；辩护；释罪
juxtaposition [ˌdʒʌkstəpəˈzɪʃən] n. 并置；并列；邻近；毗连
Jersey City 泽西市
Johnson Wax Company administration building 约翰逊制蜡公司总部办公楼

K

kinesthetic [ˌkinisˈθetik, ˌkai-] adj. 肌肉运动知觉的
kinetic [kaiˈnetik] adj. 动力(学)的；运动的
Kyoto [kiˈəutəu] n. 京都(曾是日本古都)
key industry 基础工业

L

lamenting [ləˈmentiŋ] adj. 悲伤的；悲哀的
landmark [ˈlændmɑːk] n. (航海)陆标；地界标；里程碑；划时代的事
landscape [ˈlændskeip] n. 风景；地形；前景
lantern [ˈlæntən] n. 灯笼；提灯；幻灯；信号；天窗
lapse [læps] n. 失误；下降；流逝；丧失；过失
latent [ˈleitənt] adj. 潜在的；潜伏的；隐藏的
lateral [ˈlætərəl] adj. 横(向)的；侧面的
lattice [ˈlætis] n. 格子
layout [ˈleiˌaut] n. 规划；设计；布局图

legislation [ˌledʒisˈleiʃən] n. 立法；法律的制定（或通过）
legitimate [liˈdʒitimit] adj. 合法的；合理的；正统的
lethal [ˈli:θəl] adj. 致命的
leverage [ˈli:vəridʒ] n. 杠杆作用
liaison [li(:)ˈeizɑ:n, -zən] n. 联络
libertarian [ˌlibəˈtɛəriən] adj. 自由意志论者的；鼓吹思想和行动自由的
limpid [ˈlimpid] adj. 清澈的；透明的
linkage [ˈliŋkidʒ] n. 联接
linoleum [liˈnəuljəm] n. 油布；油毯
loath [ləuθ] adj. 不情愿的；勉强的
locale [ləuˈkɑ:l] n. （事故等发生的）现场；地点；场所
locality [ləuˈkæliti] n. 位置；地点
location [ləuˈkeiʃən] n. 位置；场所；特定区域
locus [ˈləukəs] n. 地点；所在地
longevity [lɔnˈdʒeviti] n. 长命；寿命；供职期限，
loop [lu:p] n. 让车道；环道
lordly [ˈlɔ:dli] adj. 有威严的；贵族似的；高傲的
lucidly [ˈlu:sidli] adv. 清透地；透明地
luminous [ˈlju:minəs] adj. 发光的；明亮的
lush [lʌʃ] adj. 青葱的；味美的；豪华的；繁荣的
luxuriant [lʌgˈzjuəriənt] adj. 丰产的；丰富的；肥沃的；奢华的
La Chaux-de-Fonds 拉乔克斯·德·芳兹职业艺术学院
laissez faire 自由主义
landing platform 起降平台
landing stage 栈桥
Lantern Festival 花灯节
large-scale 大规模的；大比例尺的；大范围的
lateral boundary 边线
Le Corbusier 勒·柯布西耶（1887~1965）（20世纪最重要的建筑师之一）
left-over 剩余的
legal action 诉讼
less and less 越来越少的；更少的
Lewis Mumford 美国社会学家、城市规划师刘易斯·芒福德

light pattern 光图象；(录音)光带 轻型
living standard 生活水平
location theory 企业选地理论
Louis Sullivan 路易斯·沙利文(美国最有影响力的建筑师之一)

M

maintenance ['meintinəns] n. 维护；保持；生活费用
majestic [mə'dʒestik] adj. 宏伟的；庄严的
maneuverable [mə'nuːvərəbl] adj. 容易操作的；有机动性的
manicured ['mænikjuəd] adj. (花园、草坪)修剪整齐的
manifest ['mænifest] adj. 显然的；明白的
manifestation [ˌmænifes'teiʃən] n. 显示；表现；示威运动
manifold ['mænifəuld] adj. 多种形式的；多方面的
manipulate [mə'nipjuleit] vt. (熟练地)操作；巧妙地处理
manually ['mænjuəli] adv. 用手
marketplace ['mɑːkit'pleis] n. 市场
masonry ['meisnri] n. 石工术；石匠职业
matrix ['meitriks] n. 矩阵；发源地；策源地
maximization [ˌmæksəmɑi'zeiʃən] n. 最大值化；极大值化
maze [meiz] vt. 使迷惘；使混乱
meager ['miːgə(r)] n. 兆
mechanics [mi'kæniks] n. 结构；构成法；技巧
Medieval [ˌmedi'iːvəl] adj. 中古的；中世纪的
mediocrity [ˌmiːdi'ɔkriti] n. 普通；平凡；平凡的人[能力]
megacity ['megəˌsiti] n. (人口超过100万的)大城市
megalopolis [ˌmegə'lɔpəlis] n. 特大城市(由几个城市和郊区连成的)；特大城市的生活方式；以大城市为中心的人口稠密区
melancholy ['melənkəli] n. 忧郁
mellow ['meləu] v. 软化
mentality [men'tæliti] n. 智力；精神；心理
merit ['merit] v. 有益于
mesh [meʃ] vt. 啮合；编织
methodology [ˌmeθə'dɔlədʒi] n. 方法学；方法论

城市规划与管理专业英语

meticulous [mɪ'tɪkjʊləs] adj. 小心翼翼的
metropolis [mi'trɔpəlis] n. 首都；主要都市；都会；大主教教区；大城市
metropolitan [metrə'pɔlit(ə)n] adj. 首都的；主要都市的；大城市
mezzanine ['mezəniːn] n. （尤指介于一层与二层之间的）中层楼
microclimate ['maɪkrəʊklaɪmɪt] n. [气]小气候（指森林、城市、洞穴等局部地区的气候）
milieu ['miːljəː] n. 周围；环境
Minamata [ˌminə'maːtə] n. 水俣病（汞中毒引起的一种严重神经疾病）
minimization ['minimaɪˌzeiʃən] n. 小型化；化为最小值；最简化
mitigate ['mitigeit] v. 减轻
mob [mɔb] n. 暴民；暴徒；下层民众
mobilise ['məʊbɪlaɪz] v. (= mobilize)动员；赋予可动性
mobility [məʊ'biliti] n. 可动性；流动性；能动性
mobocracy [mɔ'bɔkrəsi] n. 暴徒统治；暴民政治
modification [ˌmɔdifi'keiʃən] n. 更改；修改；修正
modulation [ˌmɔdju'leiʃən] n. 调制
module ['mɔdjuːl] n. 模数；模块；登月舱；指令舱
monograph ['mɔnəʊɡrɑːf] n. 专论
monotonous [mə'nɔtənəs] adj. 单调的；无变化的
Montesquieu [ˌmɔntes'kjuː] n. 孟德斯鸠（Charles，1689~1755，男爵，法国政治哲学家、法学家、启蒙思想家）
moralistic [mɔrə'lɪstɪk; (US)mɔːr-] adj. 道学的；说教的；教训的
motif [məʊ'tiːf] n. 主题；主旨；动机；图形
multiply ['mʌltipli] v. 繁殖；乘；增加
municipal [mju(ː)'nisipəl] adj. 市政的；市的；自治区的，内政的
municipality [mjuːˌnisi'pæliti] n. 市政当局；自治市
M. Phil. (Master of Philosophy) 哲学硕士学位
M. Sc. (Master of Science) 理学硕士学位
main artery 主要干线
main line 干线；大静脉
maintenance area 养护面积
mark off 划分出
mass transit 公共交通；公共交通工具(总称)大量客运

mass-production 大量生产
master plan 总平面图,总体规划
material condition 实质条件
means of production 生产手段;生产工具;生产资料
minimum distance 最小距离
mobile organism 移动机制
more and more 越来越多
motive forces 动力
multiple-function 多功能的
multi-purpose 多用途的;多功能的
multi-speed 多极的;多(种)速(度)的
Museum of Modern Art 纽约现代艺术馆

N

negligible ['neglidʒəbl] adj. 可以忽略的,不予重视的
neon ['niːɔn] n. [化]氖
noncommittal ['nɔn'kɔmitəl] adj. 不明朗的;不承担义务的
Notre-Dame [ˌnəutrə'dɑːm] n. 〈法〉(巴黎)圣母院
novice ['nɔvis] n. 新手;初学者
nucleus ['njuːkliəs] n. [nuclear 的复数;见 nuclear]核子
nurture ['nəːtʃə] vt. 养育;给与营养物;教养
national census 人口普查
natural daylight 自然光

O

obscure [əb'skjuə] adj. 暗的;朦胧的;模糊的;晦涩的
obsession [əb'seʃən] n. 迷住;困扰
occupant ['ɔkjuːpənt] n. 占有者;居住者
offset ['ɔːfset] vt. 弥补;抵销;用平版印刷
omission [əu'miʃən] n. 省略
opaque [əu'peik] adj. 不透明的;不传热的;迟钝的
opportunism ['ɔpətjuːnizm] n. 机会主义;投机主义

城市规划与管理专业英语

optimize [ˈɔptimaiz] v. 表示乐观；优化
optimum [ˈɔptiməm] n. 最适宜（条件）；最适度
orchestration [ˌɔːkiˈstreiʃən, -ke-] n. 管弦乐编曲；管弦乐作曲法
ordeal [ɔːˈdiːl] n. 严峻的考验；痛苦的经验；折磨
organic [ɔːˈgænik] adj. 有组织的；有系统的
organism [ˈɔːgənizəm] n. 生物体；有机体
orientate [ˈɔːrienteit] v. 向东；朝向
orientation [ˌɔː(ː)rienˈteiʃən] n. 方向；方位；定位；倾向性；向东方
ornamental [ˌɔːnəˈmentl] adj. 装饰性的；装饰的；装饰用的
orthogonal [ɔːˈθɔgənl] adj. 直角的；直交的
ostensibly [ɔsˈtensəbli] adv. 外表地；表面上地
osteomalacia [ˌɔstiəuməˈleiʃiə] n. [医] 骨软化
outpour [autˈpɔː] v. (使) 泻出；(使) 流出
outskirts [ˈautskəːts] n. 边界；(尤指) 市郊
overflow [ˈəuvəˈfləu] v. (使) 泛滥；(使) 溢出；(使) 充溢
overlap [ˈəuvəˈlæp] v. (与……) 交迭
overlapping [ˈəuvəˈlæpiŋ] n. 重叠；搭接
overlay [ˌəuvəˈlei] n. 覆盖；覆盖图
ozone [ˈəuzəun, əuˈz-] n. 新鲜的空气；[化] 臭氧
office building 办公楼
oil heating 油热法
one-way 单行道的
open space 露天场所；空地（特指城市中没有建筑物的空地）
operate on 操作；运转；开动；起作用；动手术；开刀
operational problem 操作问题
optimum dimension 最佳尺寸
optimum distance 最佳距离
optimum synthesis 最优分析
oriented element 有向元
outer ring 外环
overall pattern 总体图

P

palatial [pəˈleiʃəl] adj. 富丽堂皇的；宏伟的；庄严的

panel ['pænl] n. vt. 面板；嵌板；嵌镶板
papal ['peipl] adj. 罗马教皇的
par [pɑ:] n. adj. 同等；(股票等)票面价值；票面的；平价的；平均的；标准的
parallax ['pærəlæks] n. 视差
parameter [pə'ræmitə] n. 参数；参量；<口>起限定作用的因素
parasite ['pærəsɑit] n. 寄生虫；食客
partaking [pɑ:'teikiŋ] n. 参与；分担；分享
participatory [pɑ:'tɪsɪpeɪtən,pə-] adj. 供人分享的
passivity [pæ'sivit] n. 被动；消极情绪[状态]；服从；忍受
pathological [pæθə'lɔdʒik(ə)l] adj. 病理学的；病理上的
patio ['pɑ:tiəu] n. 天井；院子
pedal ['pedl] v. 踩……的踏板
pedestrian [pe'destriən] adj. n. 徒步的；呆板的；通俗的；步行者
penetrate ['penitreit] vt. 穿透；渗透；看穿；洞察
penetration [peni'treiʃən] n. 穿过；渗透；突破
peninsular [pi'ninsjulə] adj. 半岛(状)的(居民)；形成半岛的
penthouse ['penthɑus] n. 小棚屋；雨篷
perception [pə'sepʃən] n. 理解；感知；感觉
perceptual [pə'septjuəl] adj. 知觉的；有知觉的
periphery [pə'rifəri] n. 外围
permeate ['pə:mieit] v. 弥漫；渗透；透过；充满
perspective [pə'spektiv] n. 透视(画，画法)；远景；景色
pertain [pə(:)'tein] v. 适合；属于
peruse [pə'ru:z] v. 细读
phenomena [fi'nɔminə] n. 现象
phenomenology [fi,nɔmi'nɔlədʒi] n. 现象学
physical ['fizikəl] adj. 身体的；物质的；自然的；物理的
piazza [pi'ætsə] n. 广场；走廊；露天市场
pilgrim ['pligrim] n. 圣地朝拜者；朝圣
pivotal ['pivətl] adj. 枢轴的；关键的
plateau ['plætəu,plæ'təu] n. 高地；高原；(上升后的)稳定水平(或时期、状态)

城市规划与管理专业英语

Plato ['pleitəu] n. (427~347BC，古希腊哲学家)柏拉图
playful ['pleiful] adj. 好玩的；嬉戏的；十分有趣的；顽皮的
plea [pli:] n. 恳求；请求；辩解；藉口
plurality [pluə'ræliti] n. 复数；较大数；多数；兼职
poetical [pəu'etikəl] adj. 诗的；理想化的
polemic [pɔ'lemik] n. 争[辩]论；论战；攻击；驳斥
polemical [pə'lemikəl] adj. 辩论法；辩论术；好辩的；挑起争端的
polemics [pɔ'lemiks] n. 辩论术；辩论法
polis ['pəulis] n. (古希腊的)城邦
porch [pɔ:tʃ] n. 门廊；走廊
portico ['pɔ:tikəu] n. [建](有圆柱的)门廊，柱廊
potent ['pəutənt] adj. 有力的；有效的
potential [pə'tenʃ(ə)l] adj. 潜在的；可能的
practical ['præktikəl] adj. 实际的；实践的；实用的
practitioner [præk'tiʃənə] n. 从业者；开业者
pragmatic [præg'mætik] adj. 实际的；注重实效的
Prague [prɑ:g] n. 布拉格
precedent [pri'si:dənt] n. 先例
precinct ['pri:siŋkt] n. 区域；围地；范围；界限；选区
preconceived ['pri:kən'si:vd] adj. 预想的
predecessor ['pri:disesə] n. 前任[辈]；祖先
prefect ['pri:fekt] n. (古罗马的)行政长官;高级文武官员;(法国的)省长
preferable ['prefərəbl] adj. 更可取的；更好的；更优越的
premise ['premis] n. 前提；立前提
prenatal ['pri:'neitl] adj. 出生前的；胎儿期的
preordain ['pri:ɔ:'dein] v. 命中注定；预先规定
preposition [ˌprepə'ziʃən] n. 介词
prerequisite ['pri:'rekwizit] n. 先决条件;必备条件
prescribe [pris'krɑib] v. 指示；规定；建议
prescription [pri'skripʃən] n. 指示；规定；命令；处方；药方
preservation [ˌprezə(:)'veiʃən] n. 保存；保藏;保护
presuppose [ˌpri:sə'pəuz] v. 预示
pretension [pri'tenʃən] n. 矫饰；虚饰；虚荣；做作

prevailing [pri'veiliŋ] adj. 占优势的；主要的；流行的
prevalence ['prevələns] n. 流行
primary ['praiməri] adj. 第一位的；主要的；初级的；根源的
priori(a priori) [eiprai'ɔːrai] adj.〈拉〉先验(的)
prism ['prizəm] n. 棱镜；棱柱
proactive [ˌprəu'æktiv] adj. [心理]前摄的
problematic [prɔblə'mætik] adj. 问题的；有疑问的；或然性的
proclamation [prɔklə'meiʃn] n. 宣布；宣言
promenade [ˌprɔmi'nɑːd] n. 散步的场所
promontory ['prɔməntəri] n. 岬；隆起；海角
promotional [prəu'məuʃənəl] adj. 增进的；奖励的
pronounced [prə'naunst] adj. 显著的；明确的
propagandize [ˌprɔpə'gændaiz] v. 宣传；传播；(对……)作宣传
propel [prə'pel] v. 推进；驱使
property ['prɔpəti] n. 财产；所有物；所有权；性质；特性
prophetic [prə'fetik] adj. 预言的；预示的；先知的
proprietor [prə'praiətə] n. 所有者；业主
protagonist [prəu'tægənist] n. (戏剧、故事、小说中的)主角；领导者；积极参加者
protective [prə'tektiv] adj. 给予保护的；保护的
prototype ['prəutətaip] n. 原型
province ['prɔvins] n. [pl.] 地区；乡间；(首都或大城市以外的)地方
proximity [prɔk'simiti] n. 接近；亲近
psychic ['saikik] adj. 精神的
psychological [ˌsaikə'lɔdʒikəl] adj. 心理(上)的
psychology [sai'kɔlədʒi] n. 心理学；心理状态
punctuate ['pʌŋktjueit] v. 加标点于；不时打断
Paris under Haussman 奥斯曼的巴黎改造计划
parking place 停车场
parliamentary government 代议政府；议会内阁制；议会政体
patterns of consumption 消费结构
pedestrian environment 步行交通
pedestrian mall 步行街；人行林荫路

physical aspects 物理性质
physical fabric 相关组构,机能组构
physical planning 实体规划;形体规划
physical structure 物理结构
Plan Voisin "伏瓦生规划"方案(柯布西耶为巴黎市中心区改建提出的规划方案
planning models 规划模型
point of departure 出发点
Pont Neuf 巴黎新桥(塞纳河上所有桥梁中最为古老、最长的桥)
post-and-beam 梁和柱
potential source 位源;势源;电源
Pratt Center 美国丹佛市的普拉特社区发展中心
primary node 主要节点
productive capacity 生产能力
protected zone 防护带;被保护区域
public building 公共建筑物;国家建筑物
public facilities 公共设施
public sector 公共部门
public transport fare 公共汽车费
public-private partnership 公司合营

Q

quadruple ['kwɔdrupl] v. 使成四倍
qualitative ['kwɔlitətiv] adj. 性质上的;定性的
quill [kwil] n. 羽茎;大翎毛;羽绒被
quota ['kwəutə] n. 配额;限额
quality and quantity 质与量

R

radiant ['reidjənt] adj. 发光的;辐射的;容光焕发的
radiator ['reidieitə] n. 散热器;水箱;冷却器;电暖炉;辐射体
railing ['reiliŋ] n. 栏杆;扶手

ramification [ˌræmifiˈkeiʃən] n. 分枝;分叉; 衍生物; 支流
ramp [ræmp] n. 坡道;斜坡
ranch [ræntʃ, rɑːntʃ] n. 大农场
range [reindʒ] n. 范围; 射程
rationality [ˌræʃəˈnæliti] n. 合理性; 唯理性
realm [relm] n. 王国;国土
rebar [riˈbɑː] n. 钢筋;螺纹钢筋
recast [ˈriːˈkɑːst] v. 重铸; 彻底改动; 重做; 重新铸造
recede [riˈsiːd] v. 退回; 后退; 向后倾斜
recession [riˈseʃən] n. 撤回; 退回; 退后; 工商业之衰退; 不景气
reciprocal [riˈsiprəkəl] adj. 互惠的; 相应的; 倒数的; 彼此相反的
recognizable [ˈrekəgnaizəbl] adj. 可认识的; 可辨认的
reconcile [ˈrekənsail] vt. 使和解; 使和谐; 使顺从
reconstruction [ˌriːkənˈstrʌkʃən] n. 重建;改造;翻修
recount [riˈkaunt] v. 叙述
rectangle [ˈrektæŋgl] n. 长方形; 矩形
rectangular [rekˈtæŋgjulə] adj. 矩形的; 成直角的
reflection [riˈflekʃən] n. 反射; 反省; 沉思
refuge [ˈrefjuːdʒ] n. 庇护; 避难; 避难所
refuse [riˈfjuːz] n. 废物;垃圾
regime [reiˈʒiːm] n. 政体; 政权; 政权制度
rejection [riˈdʒekʃən] n. 拒绝
relief [riˈliːf] n.(痛苦等的)减轻;(债务等的)免除;救济, 安慰;浮雕; 地貌
renovation [ˌrenəuˈveiʃən] n. 革新
repeal [riˈpiːl] v. 废止; 撤销;否定; 放弃; 废除
repose [riˈpəuz] n. 休息;睡眠;静止
repudiate [riˈpjuːdieit] v. 批判
repudiation [riˌpjuːdiˈeiʃən] n. 批判
reside [riˈzaid] vi. 居住
residual [riˈzidjuəl] adj. 剩余的; 残留的
resort [riˈzɔːt] n. 常去之地;胜地
respectability [rispektəˈbiləti] n. 可尊敬之人或物; 值得尊敬之性质或状态

restive ['restiv] adj. 难控制的
restrictive [ris'triktiv] adj. 限制性的
resurrect [ˌrezə'rekt] v. 使复活；复兴
retention [ri'tenʃən] n. 保持力
retreat [ri'triːt] v. 撤退；退却
retrofit ['retrəˌfit] n. 式样翻新；花样翻新
retrospective [ˌretrəu'spektiv] n. 回顾；回忆
reversibility [riˌvəːsə'biliti] n. 可逆性；可取消
revitalization [riːˌvaitəlaiˈzeiʃən,-lı'z-] n. 新生；复兴
revitalize ['riːˈvaitəlaiz] v. 新生
revival [ri'vaivəl] n. 苏醒；更[再]生,复活[兴]；再流行
rhythm ['riðəm,'riθəm] n. 节奏；韵律
ridge [ridʒ] n. 背脊；山脊；屋脊；山脉；犁垄
rind [raind] n. 外壳
rink [rink] n. 溜冰场；冰球场；室内溜冰场
Rio de Janeiro ['riː(ː)əudədʒəˈniərəu] n. 里约热内卢（巴西港市；州名）
rippling ['riplin] adj. 起涟漪的；潺潺流水般声音的
riverfront ['rivəfrʌnt] n. （城镇的）河边地区；河边陆地
robust [rə'bʌst] adj. 精力充沛的
Romanesque [ˌrəuməˈnesk] n. 罗马式
R. I. B. A. (Royal Institute of British Architects) 英国皇家建筑师学会
R. T. P. I. (Royal Town Planning Institute) 英国皇家城市规划学会
racial segregation 种族分离；种族隔离
renewable resources 可再生资源
residential block 住宅区
resolving power （光学仪器等）分辨能力
resource management 资源管理
rest with 取决于；在于
retail bank 小额银行业务
rue de Rivoli 巴黎的里沃黎街
run through 跑着穿过；刺；戳；贯穿；匆匆处理；划掉；挥霍

S

sacred ['seikrid] adj. 神的；宗教的；庄严的；神圣的

salvage ['sælvidʒ] vt. 海上救助；抢救；打捞；营救
sanitary ['sænitəri] adj. (有关)卫生的；(保持)清洁的
sanitation [ˌsæni'teiʃn] n. 卫生；卫生设施
Sanskrit ['sænskrit] adj. 梵语的；梵文的
Sapporo [sə'pɔːrəu] n. 札幌[日本北海道西部城市]
save [seiv] prep. 除……之外
savor ['seivə] vt. 加调味品于；使有风味；尝到或闻到；尽情享受
scarce [skɛəs] adj. 缺乏的；不足的；稀有的；不充足的
scarcity ['skɛəsiti] n. 缺乏；不足
scattered ['skætəd] adj. 离散的,分散的
schematic [ski'mætik] adj. 示意性的
sculpture ['skʌlptʃə] n. 雕刻；雕刻品；雕塑，雕塑品
seminar ['seminɑː] n. 研究班；专题讨论会
Semiramis [se'mirəmis] n. 塞米勒米斯(古代传说中的亚述女王)
sensibility [ˌsensi'biliti] n. 敏感性
sensitive ['sensitiv] adj. 敏感的；灵敏的；感光的
sensitivity ['ledʒis'leiʃən] n. 敏感；灵敏(度)；灵敏性
sensitize ['sensitaiz] vt. 使变得敏感；使具有感光性
sensuous ['sensjuəs] adj. 感觉上的；给人美感的
sequel ['siːkwəl] n. 继续；后ас；续集[篇]；下篇
sequential [si'kwinʃəl] adj. 连续的；有顺序的；结果的
serene [si'riːn] adj. 宁静的；没有风波的
setback ['setbæk] n. 顿挫；挫折；退步；逆流
settlement ['setlmənt] n. 居留地；新建区；住宅区
shell [ʃel] n. 薄片；房屋的框架
shelter ['ʃeltə] n. v. 掩蔽处；保护；庇护所掩蔽；躲避
silhouette [ˌsiluː'et] n. 侧面影象；轮廓
similarity [ˌsimi'læriti] n. 类似；类似处
simultaneously [siməl'teiniəsly;(US)saim-] adv. 同时地
singularity [ˌsingju'læriti] n. 单一；异常；奇异；奇妙；稀有
siting ['saitiŋ] n. 建筑工地选择(道路等)定线
skepticism ['skeptisizəm] n. 怀疑论
sketch [sketʃ] n. 略图；草图；概略

城市规划与管理专业英语

skyscraper ['skaiskreipə(r)] n. 摩天大楼
slaughter ['slɔːtə] v. 屠宰；残杀；屠杀
sled [sled] n. 雪橇；摘棉
slope [sləup] n. 斜坡；斜面；倾斜
sloping ['sləupiŋ] adj. 倾斜的；有坡度的
sociability [ˌsəuʃə'biliti] n. 交际活动
solemn ['sɔləm] adj. 庄严的；隆重的；严肃的
solstice ['sɔlstis] n. [天]至；至日；至点
sombre ['sɔmbə] adj. 昏暗的；阴沉的
soot [sut] n. 煤烟；烟灰
soothe [suːð] vt. 使(某人)平静；安慰；使(痛苦,疼痛)缓和或减轻
sophistication [səˌfisti'keiʃən] n. 强词夺理；诡辩；混合
sovereign ['sɔvrin] n. 统治者；主权者
sparing ['spɛəriŋ] adj. 节俭的；保守的
spatial ['speiʃəl] adj. 空间的
specify ['spesifai] vt. 指定；详细说明；列入清单
speculate ['spekjuˌleit] vi. 推测；思索；做投机买卖
speculative ['spekjulətiv,-leit-] adj. 投机的
sphere [sfiə] n. (活动)范围；(研究)领域
spontaneous [spɔn'teinjəs,-niəs] adj. 自发的；自然产生的
sprawl [sprɔːl] v. 四肢伸开地坐(或卧)；爬行；蔓生；蔓延
stability [stə'biliti] n. 稳定性
staggering ['stæɡəriŋ] adj. 蹒跚的；摇晃的；另人惊愕的
stagnate [stæɡ'neit] v. (使)淤塞；(使)停滞；(使)沉滞；(使)变萧条
stakeholder ['steikhəuldə(r)] n. 赌金保管者
stanza ['stænzə] n. 节；演出期；比赛中的盘
stark [staːk] adj. 刻板的；十足的；赤裸的；荒凉的
statism ['steitiz(ə)m] n. 中央集权下的经济统制
sterile ['sterail] adj. 贫瘠的；不育的；不结果的
stifle ['staifl] v. 使窒息；抑制；扼杀
stimulus ['stimjuləs] n. 刺激物；促进因素；刺激；刺激
stipulate ['stipjuleit] v. 规定；保证
straggling ['stræɡliŋ] adj. 脱离队伍的；落后的

straightjacket ['streɪtˌdʒækɪt] n. 紧身衣
strangle ['stræŋgl] v. 扼死
stride [straɪd] v. 大步走；跨过；大步行走
stringently ['strɪndʒəntli] adv. 严厉地；迫切地
stroll [strəul] v. 闲逛；漫步；跋涉于
structural ['strʌktʃərəl] adj. 结构的；建筑的
stucco ['stʌkəu] vt. 涂以灰泥；粉刷
studio ['stjuːdiəu] n. 工作室；演播室；电影制片厂
subject-matter ['sʌbdʒiktˌmætə] n. 主题；素材
sublime [sə'blaɪm] adj. 极度的；完全的；极端的；异常的
subregion ['sʌbˌriːdʒən] n. (动植物分布的)亚区
subsequent ['sʌbsikwənt] adj. 后来的；并发的
subsidy ['sʌbsidi] n. 补助金；津贴
substantial [səb'stænʃəl] adj. 坚固的；实质的；真实的
substantive ['sʌbstəntiv] adj. 独立存在的；真实的；有实质的；大量的，
subsumption [sʌb'sʌmpʃən] n. 包容；包含
subtle ['sʌtl] adj. 狡猾的；敏感的；微妙的；精细的；稀薄的
suburban [sə'bəːbən] adj. 郊外的；偏远的
sub-basement ['sʌbˌbeɪsmənt] n. 地下室以下的地下室(建筑物的最底层)
successive [sək'sesiv] adj. 继承的；连续的
suffice [sə'faɪs] vi. 足够；有能力
supplement ['sʌplimənt] v. 补充
survey [səː'vei] n. 测量；调查；俯瞰
survival [sə'vaɪvəl] n. 幸存；幸存者；残存物
sustain [səs'tein] vt. 支撑；撑住；维持；持续
symbolical [sim'bɔlikl] adj. 表示象征的；符号的
symbolization [ˌsɪmbəlaɪ'zeɪʃən;-lɪ'z-] n. 象征；符号表现
symbolize ['simbəlaɪz] vt. 象征；用符号表现
symmetry ['simitri] n. 对称；匀称
sympathy ['simpəθi] n. 同情；同情心
symposium [sim'pəuziəm] n. 专题讨论会；座谈会；学术报告会
syndicalist ['sindiklist] n. 工会组织主义者；工团主义者
synthesis ['sinθisis] n. 综合；合成

synthetic [sin′θetic] adj. 合成的；人造的；综合的
safety valve 安全阀
Salon d'Automne 法国巴黎秋季沙龙
sanitary arrangement 卫生设备
search committee 遴选委员会
set forth 阐明；宣布；提出；陈列；出发；把（会议等）提前动身
sharp line 尖锐谱线；清晰谱线
shopping node 购物节点
Sick Building Syndrome 病态建筑综合症（建筑内的人员出现急性部舒适症状,症状原因不明,离开建筑以后,症状很快就消失）
side effect 副作用
sine qua non 必要条件；要素
single out 挑选
sink down 沉落
skim over 掠过；滑过；浏览
social geography 社会地理学
social intercourse 社交
source of energy 能源
spontaneous movement 固有运动
Spring Festival 春节
stabilitas loci 稳定性
start-climax-finish form 开端—高潮—结尾形式
street line 街道线
street scene 街道
structural adjustment 结构调整
structural property 结构特征
subject matter 主题
suburban line 郊区线路
sum up 计算……的总数；概括，总结
land tenure 土地所有制
surface relief 地势
sustainable development 可持续发展

symbolic point 焦点
system of orientation 定位系统

T

tactile ['tæktɑil] n. [心]触觉型
tapping ['tæpiŋ] n. 出渣,出钢,出铁
tempo ['tempəu] n. (音乐)速度、拍子；发展速度
temporal ['tempərəl] adj. 时间的；当时的；暂时的,
temporary ['tempərəri] adj. 暂时的；临时的；临时性
tend [tend] v. 趋向；往往是；照管；护理
tenet ['ti:net,'tenit] n. 原则
tentacular [ten'tækjulə] adj. 有触手的
terminate ['tə:mineit] v. 停止；结束,终止
termini ['tə:minɑi] n. 目的地；界标
terrace ['terəs] n. 柱廊；平屋顶
terrain ['terein] n. 地域；地带；地势；地形
terrestrial [tə'restri:əl] adj. 陆地
testimony ['testiməni] n. 证词(尤指在法庭所作的),宣言；陈述
textile ['tekstɑil] n. 织物；纺织品；纺织原料
thematic [θi:'mætik] adj. 词干的；题目的；主题的；论题的
thesis ['θi:sis] n. 论题；论文
threshold ['θreʃhəuld] n. 开始；开端；极限
throughout [θru(:)'ɑut] prep. 遍及；贯穿
thwart [θwɔ:t] vt. 反对；阻碍；横过
tile [tɑil] n. 瓦片；瓷砖
tissue ['tisju:] n. 薄的纱织品；薄纸 [生]组织；连篇
tobogganing [tə'bɔgəniŋ] n. 乘橇作滑雪运动
tonic ['tɔnik] adj. 激励的；滋补的
topographical [,tɔpə'græfikəl] adj. 地形学的
top-heavy [tɔp'hevi] adj. 头重脚轻的
totalitarian [,təutæli'tɛəriən] adj. n. 极权主义的；极权主义者
totality [təu'tæliti] n. 全体；总数
townscape ['tɑunskeip] n. 城市风景画；城市风景

城市规划与管理专业英语

toxic ['tɔksik] adj. 有毒的；中毒的
track [træk] n. 轨道；车辙
transit ['trænsit] vt. 横越；通过；经过
transpose [træns'pəuz] vt. 调换；颠倒顺序；移项
transposition [ˌtrænspə'ziʃən] n. 调换；变换
traverse ['trævə(ː)s] v. 横过；穿过；经过；在……来回移动
trespasser ['trespəsə] n. 侵害者；违反者；侵入者
tribute ['tribjuːt] n. 表示尊敬或赞美的言辞或行为
triumphant [trai'ʌmfənt] adj. 胜利的；成功的；狂欢的
trivialize ['triviəlaiz] vt. 使平凡；使琐碎
truncate ['trʌŋkeit] v. 截去尖端；修剪（树等）；把……截短
tube ['tjuːb] n. 隧道；地下铁道
tumor ['tjuːmə(r)] n. 肿块；肿瘤
typology [tai'pɔlədʒi] n. 类型学；血型学；体型学；象征学
tyranny ['tirəni] n. 暴政；苛政；专治
take action 采取行动；提出诉讼
take on board 考虑；接受
take precedence over 优先于
take pride in 以……为傲
target group 目标群
technical information 技术情报
the course of the day 日夜更迭
The Edgar Kaufmann house 考夫曼别墅（流水别墅）
the Imperial Hotel 东京帝国饭店
the Kennedy School 哈佛大学肯尼迪学院
the last word 定论；最新成就；最新品种
the Machine Age 机器时代（介于一战与二战之间的工业文明时代）
the ownership of land 土地所有权
The Radiant City "光明城市" 理论
the Society for Industrial Enterprises 军工企业协会
the spirit of enterprise 进取精神
the University of California at Berkeley 加利福尼亚大学伯克利分校
the University of Pennsylvania 宾夕法尼亚大学

the Woodrow Wilson School of Public Affairs 普林斯顿最有名的专业学院——伍德罗·威尔逊公共和国际关系学院

three-dimensional geometry 三维几何学
time-honored 历史悠久的；老字号的
time series 时间数列［序列］
to the extent that 达到这种程度以至……
to the eye 从表面上看来；当面；公然
to the fore 在近处；在手头；在前面
top soil 表土
topological sense 拓扑结构
total administration 总体管理
Town and Country Planning Act 城市和乡村规划（苏格兰）法令
town hall 市政厅
town map 城镇图
town planning 城镇规划
trade agreement 贸易协定
trailer camp 活动房营地
transit line 运输线
transport facility 交通运输工具
transportation infrastructure 运输基本设施
tropical and temperate rainforests 热带和温带雨林

U

ubiquitous ［juː'bikwitəs］ adj. 无所不在的；普遍存在的
ultimately ［'ʌltımətlı］ adv. 最后；终于；根本
unattainable ［ˌʌnə'teinəbl］ adj. 难到达的；做不到的
unconscious ［ʌn'kɔnʃəs］ adj. 不省人事；未发觉的；无意识的
underachieve ［ˌʌndərə'tʃiːv］ v. 学习成绩不良未能发挥学习潜能
underlay ［ˌʌndə'lei］ v. 铺在……的下面；从下面支撑［垫起］
underlying ［ˌʌndə'laiiŋ］ adj. 在下面的；根本的；潜在的
underpass ［'ʌndəpɑːs］ n. 地下道；高架桥下通道
uninhabitable ［ˌʌnin'hæbitəbl］ adj. 不适于人居住的

unleash [ˈʌnˈliːʃ] v. 释放
unmitigated [ʌnˈmitigeitid] adj. 绝对的；纯粹的；彻头彻尾的
unobstructed [ˈʌnəbˈstrʌktid] adj. 无阻的；不受阻拦的
unparalleled [ʌnˈpærəleld] adj. 无比的；无双的；空前的
unreliable [ˈʌnriˈlaiəbl] adj. 不可靠的
untapped [ʌnˈtæpt] adj. 未使用的
upheaval [ʌpˈhiːvəl] n. 剧变
uproar [ˈʌprɔː] n. 喧嚣；骚动
upthrust [ˈʌpˌθrʌst] n. 向上推；向上冲；[地]上冲断层
urban [ˈəːbən] adj. 城市的；市内的
urbanism [ˈəːbəˌnizəm] n. 城市规划；都市建筑规划；都市生活方式
urbanity [əːˈbæniti] n. 有礼貌；文雅
urbanization [ˈəːbənaiˈzeiʃən] n. 使具有城市特点；城市化
utopia [juːˈtəupjə, -piə] n. 乌托邦；理想的完美境界
utopian [juːˈtəupjən] adj. 乌托邦的；理想化的
UNCHS (abbr. = United Nations Centre for Human Settlement) 联合国人类居住中心
university town 大学城
urban design 城市设计
urban fabric 城市建筑
urban system 城市体系
user-friendly [计] 用户界面友好的；用户容易掌握使用的

V

valid [ˈvælid] adj. [律] 有效的；有根据的；正当的
variation [ˌvɛəriˈeiʃən] n. 变更；变化；变异；变种
variegated [ˈvɛərigeitid] adj. 杂色的；斑驳的；多样化的
vaunted [ˈvɔːntid] adj. 自夸的；大肆吹嘘的；自负的
Vendome [ˈvendəm] n. 巴黎的凡登广场
Venetian [viˈniːʃən] adj. 威尼斯的
Veneto [ˈvenetɔː] n. 威尼托区 [意大利行政区名]
ventilation [ˌventiˈleiʃn] n. 通风；流通空气
veranda [vəˈrændə] n. 阳台；走廊

vernacular ['və'nækjulə] adj. 本国的
vertical ['və:tikəl] adj. 垂直的；直立的；顶点的
vesper ['vespə] n. 薄暮；晚祷
via ['vaiə, 'vi:ə] prep. 经；通过；经由
vicinity [vi'siniti] n. 邻近，附近，接近
vista ['vistə] n. 狭长的景色；街景
visualize ['vizjuəlaiz] v. 使看得见；使具体化；想象；显形
vitality [vai'tæliti] n. 活力；生命力；生动性
vitiated ['viʃieitid] adj. 损坏的；污浊的；失效的
vivify ['vivifai] vt. 给与生气；使复生；使生动；使活跃
volumetric [vɔliu'metrik] adj. 测定体积的
vulnerable ['vʌlnərəbl] adj. 易受攻击的；易受……的攻击
vantage point 优势地位
vernacular architecture 地方性建筑
vesper bell 晚祷钟
volatile organic compound 挥发性有机化合物

W

Waikiki ['waiki:ki:, ˌwaiki'ki:] n. 怀基基海滩[美国夏威夷州]
wanderer ['wɔndərə(r)] n. 流浪者；徘徊者
warehouse ['wɛəhaus] n. 仓库；货栈
waterfront ['wɔ:təfrʌnt] n. 水边地码头区；滨水地区
whilst [wailst] conj. 当……的时候；和……同时
wholesome ['həulsəm] adj. 卫生的；有益的；健康的；有益健康的
windbreak ['windbrek] n. 防风林；防风物；防风墙；防风设备
wondrous ['wʌndrəs] adj. 令人惊奇的；非常的
workable ['wə:kəbl] adj. 可经营的；可使用的
workshop ['wə:kʃɔp] n. 研讨会；专题研究组
wrought [rɔ:t] adj. 做成的；形成的；精炼的
wealth and income distribution 财富和收入分配
Winter Solstice 冬至
work of art 艺术作品
World Commission on the Environment and Development 世界环境与发展委员会

Z

zoning [ˈzəuniŋ] n. 分带;分区制
zero growth 零增长;不增长

REFERENCES

[1] HOWARD E. Garden cities of tomorrow[M]. Cambridge: The MIT Press, 1965.
[2] ASHIHARA Y. The aesthetic townscape[M]. Cambridge: The MIT Press, 1983.
[3] CORBUSIER LE. The city of tomorrow[M]. Cambridge: The MIT Press, 1971.
[4] DOXIADIS C A. Anthropopolis—city for human development[M]. New York: W. W. Norton & Company, Inc., 1975.
[5] LYNCH K. Good city form [M]. Cambridge: The MIT Press, 1985.
[6] LYNCH K. The image of the city[M]. Cambridge: The MIT Press, 1960.
[7] FISHMAN R. Urban utopias in the twentieth century: Ebenezer Howard, Frank Lloyd Wright, and Le Corbusier[M]. Cambridge: The MIT Press, 1977.
[8] SCHULZ N. Genius loci—towards a phenomenology of architecture [M]. New York: Rizzoli, 1976.
[9] ROSSI A. The architecture of the city[M]. Cambridge: The MIT Press, 1986.
[10] KERIER L. The size of a city [J]. Architectural Design, 1984, 54 (7/8): 103-105.
[11] SYMES M. Urban design education in Britain and America [J]. Education for Urban Design, 1981 (5): 60-70.
[12] KERIER L. Rational architecture [M]. New York: Wittenbom, 1978.
[13] SAARINEN E. The city: its growth, its decay, its future[M]. New York: Reinhold, 1943.

[14] JACOBS J. The death and life of great American cities [M]. New York: Random House, 1961.
[15] KRIER R. Urban space [M]. New York: Rizzloi International, 1979.
[16] RAPOPORT A. Human aspects of urban form [M]. New York: Pergamon, 1977.
[17] MCHARG I L. Design with nature [M]. New York: The Natural History Press, 1969.
[18] PARSONS K C. Collaborative genius: the regional planning association of America [J]. Journal of the American Planning Association, 1994, 60 (4): 462-482.
[19] RAMON J, VERDEJO J. Considerations concerning measurements relating to the urban design of the Spanish-American city [J]. Journal of Asian Architecture and Building Engineering, 2007, 6 (1): 9-16.
[20] CORBURN J. Reconnecting with our roots: American urban planning and public health in the twenty-first century [J]. Urban Affairs Review, 2007, 42 (5): 688-713.
[21] KRIER L. The city within the city [J]. Architectural Design, 1984, 54: 70-105.
[22] CLIFF E. The new urbanism: critiques and rebuttals [J]. Journal of Urban Design, 2002, 7 (3): 261-291.
[23] SYMES M, PAUWELS S. The diffusion of innovation in urban design: the case of sustainability in the Hulme development guide [J]. Journal of Urban Design, 1999, 4(1): 97-117.